PREFACE

The Bible is one of God's greatest gifts to mankind. Its revelation of truth concerning God and human redemption constitutes a priceless treasure. Its spiritual ministry to the race places it in a category of incomparable uniqueness and importance.

No small part of the unique importance of the Bible is the relevance of its spiritual message today. Yet it sprang out of a time and a culture far removed from our modern world. All of its contents is separated from today's scene by many centuries, some parts of it by more than three millennia.

Does this fact make the Bible incomprehensible to modern man? No. The great truths of the Bible are omnitemporal. They transcend the centuries and the cultures out of which they rose.

Yet much of the Bible suffers from neglect and misunderstanding because its historical, geographical, social, and political backgrounds are obscure. Further, the message of the Bible often is interpreted without the light of the manners and customs of peoples in ancient Bible lands.

This survey begins with introductory insights concerning facts about the Bible, principles of interpretation, and the teachings of the Bible as a whole. Background studies include an evaluation of extrabiblical writings and an historical-archaeological review of the biblical period. Then follows a careful book-by-book survey of each Bible book, with emphasis on the main themes and the difficulties of proper interpretation.

This volume is sent forth with an earnest prayer that it will be a useful tool in unfolding the eternal truths of God's Word.

—*Merrill F. Unger*

CONTENTS

Unger's
Survey of
the Bible

INTRODUCTORY INSIGHTS

What the Bible Is

The Bible is the revelation of God to fallen and sinful mankind. Preserved for us in written form, the Bible consists of 39 books of the Old Testament and 27 books of the New Testament. These 66 books together actually form one book, the Bible. This word is derived from the Latin word *biblia,* meaning "book" and stresses the unity of the theme and purpose of the Holy Scriptures.

Theme of the Bible

The Bible reveals the divine plan and purpose for the redemption of fallen man. Although it gives fleeting glimpses into eternity past, these matters are secondary. They serve mainly as background material to the central theme of the Bible — *the redemption of lost mankind.*

The Bible thus begins not with eternity but with time. The opening chapter of Genesis describes the renovation of a chaotic earth for the latecomer, man, God's last created order of beings. Sinless man's tragic response to the temptation of the Edenic serpent, the tool of Satan (Gen. 3:1-12), quickly sets the stage for the unfolding of the drama of human redemption.

The first pronouncement of the gospel in "the seed of the woman" (Gen. 3:15) anticipated the virgin-born Son of God (Isa. 7:14; Matt. 1:18-25; Luke 1:35; Gal. 4:4, 5). The Eternal Son, the Word, who was "with God and was God" (John 1:1), became incarnate in the Person of Jesus Christ (John 1:14). As God and man united in one

A devout Jew bows in prayer as an Israeli guard looks on at the Temple "Wailing Wall" recaptured from the Arabs. *(IGTO photo)*

Person, God became man to take away man's sin and to restore man to fellowship with himself (Heb. 1:1-3).

As the result of his sinless life, vicarious death, and bodily resurrection, Jesus Christ effected man's salvation from the curse of sin. The eventual result will be a sinless, blissful eternity enjoyed by unfallen angels and redeemed, glorified men (Heb. 12:22-24; Rev. 21:1-27). Satan, fallen angels, and Christ-rejecting men will be quarantined in eternal hell (Rev. 20:11-15), never to pollute God's sinless universe again.

Purpose of the Bible

The Bible was given 1) *to reveal God and his plan of salvation for fallen man,* so that man might trust Christ and be saved; 2) *to warn the unsaved of eternal hell,* the penalty of breaking God's moral law and rejecting Christ as the Redeemer (Gen. 2:17; Matt. 25:41; Rev. 20:11-15; and 3) *to reveal the total authority of the eternal moral law of God.* Both unsaved and saved mankind will be judged for their deeds, that is, the degree of response of each human being to the moral law.

The Bible thus reveals that there will be different degrees of punishment in hell (Rev. 20:11-15) as well as different degrees of reward in heaven.

Although the Bible has a message of salvation for all mankind and specific warnings for the unsaved, it is directed mainly to the saved, to inculcate in them Christian truths and principles of godly living and to reprove and correct in the case of error and sin, "that the man of God may be perfect (complete), throughly furnished unto all good works" (2 Tim. 3:17).

A portion of Isaiah from a ninth-century copy of the Septuagint translation (© *MPS*)

Importance of the Bible

In revealing God's saving grace in Christ to fallen mankind, and in warning the impenitent of the consequences of unbelief, the Bible is forever stamped as the most important and practical Book in the world. As God's inspired and authoritative revelation to man, the Bible stands in a category that is completely unique.

Other books are written by men; *God* is the Author of the Bible (2 Tim. 3:16). Other books contain man's wisdom; the Bible is a record of *God's* wisdom. Other books may *expound* God's revelation; the Bible *is* God's revelation. Viewing the Scriptures as the moral and spiritual guide of the human race, Abraham Lincoln aptly described the Bible as "the best gift that God has given to man."

Any book that tells a man how to know God and fellowship with him is a book of supreme importance. But the significance of the Bible goes beyond this. The Holy Scriptures open up man's destiny beyond the grave and set forth the status of each man in eternity (Rev. 20:11 – 22:21).

Languages of the Bible

Hebrew is the language of the Old Testament, except for a few small portions written in Aramaic (Dan. 2:4 – 7:28; Ezra 4:8 – 6:18; 7: 12-26; Jer. 10:11). Both Hebrew and Aramaic belong to the Semitic group of languages, spoken by the descendants of Noah's son Shem (Gen. 10:22).

Greek is the language of the New Testament – not the formal classical Greek of the intellectuals but the common or "koine" Greek, the universal speech that came into the Greco-Roman world following the conquests of Alexander the Great. This wonderfully expressive cosmopolitan tongue, widely spoken from 300 B.C. to A.D. 330, was the current speech of the common people and a providentially prepared vehicle for the New Testament revelation.

Christianity came with a message of hope for the poor, the uneducated, and the oppressed. The gospel of Christ was to be heralded to the masses. Thus God recorded the great revealed truths of human redemption in the simple language of the common people.

Origin of the Bible

The Bible came into existence as God revealed himself to human agents in such a manner that they recorded accurately and free from human error whatever was divinely disclosed to them (2 Tim. 3:15, 16; 2 Pet. 1:20, 21). This process, called *inspiration,* means that God breathed his Word into the minds of the human authors. They, in turn, under the Spirit's control wrote down for posterity what was given to them as a result of the divine inbreathing.

The result of inspiration is *a written revelation once for all given and thoroughly accredited.* Miracles, fulfilled prophecy, and redemptive power in human experience all attest the fact of the inspiration of Scripture. The written revelation, unique in its origin and preservation as inspired Scripture, constitutes the 39 books of the Old Testament and the 27 books of the New Testament. This divine library of 66 books is at the same time *one* book, with God as its one Author. Its one theme is Christ the Redeemer, and its one purpose is the record of human redemption.

The Old Testament came into being during the thousand-year period from 1400 B.C. (the time of Moses) to 400 B.C. (the time of Malachi). From the time of Malachi until the writing of the New Testament books, revelation and inspiration that produced canonical Scripture were in abeyance. The New Testament was produced during the last two-thirds of the first century, from about A.D. 33 to A.D. 100.

Thus the entire Bible was produced over a period of about a millennium and a half, from 1400 B.C. to A.D. 100. Each book had from its beginning the stamp of divine inspiration and authority, and each one was recognized by the faithful, even though their canonization in the familiar form we know today took centuries and is veiled in obscurity. (The canonicity of some Old Testament books, as Song of Solomon, Ecclesiastes, Esther, and Proverbs was questioned by some rabbis as late as the second century A.D.)

By A.D. 200 the New Testament books generally recognized as canonical were the same as we acknowledge today. However, not until around A.D. 400 in the West and A.D. 500 in the East were all questions of canonicity finally settled.

Inspiration and Authority of the Bible

A sound position on inspiration, which subscribes to the testimony of Scripture on this question, holds what is called the *plenary verbal* view. Such a view—that *"all* scripture" (that is, in the original copies or autographs) is "inspired by God" or "God-breathed" (2 Tim. 3:15) in its very words as well as its thoughts, and equally in all its parts—results in a *fully authoritative* Bible in and through which God himself speaks.

Authority accordingly resides in the divinely inspired Word itself interpreted by God's Spirit operating through Spirit-taught human agents. Orthodox Protestantism claims no authority other than canonical Scripture as the voice of the Holy Spirit. In contrast, the Church of Rome sets ecclesiastical tradition alongside the Holy Scriptures (including some extra-canonical Old Testament books) as the source of authority in matters of faith and morals.

Neo-orthodox and liberal segments of Protestantism deny final authority to Scripture as inerrant and infallible. Substituted is some other source of authority, such as conscience, experience, Christ speaking through the Holy Spirit, etc. The question of authority is of primary concern in today's religious world.

The Bible and Non-Christian Sacred Writings

Other religions also have their holy writings. Brahmanism, for example, is based on a collection of sacred writings known as the Veda, the holy Scriptures of the ancient Hindus. Taoism, one of the principal forms of Chinese religion, is founded on the writings of Lao-tse, a teacher of the sixth century B.C. Confucianism is a system of moral philosophy based on the writings of the Chinese teacher Confucius, of the fifth century B.C. The Koran is the holy book of Islam, claimed by millions of Muslims to contain the revelations of Allah (God) to Mohammed (died A.D. 632).

One question of supreme importance is the relation of the Christian Scriptures to the holy writings of non-Christian faiths. Is the Bible just another holy writing, or is it *uniquely the Word of God, divinely inspired and fully authoritative* in a sense different from all other literature (including the sacred literature of non-Christian religions), so that it is *the standard of truth by which all other faiths are to be measured and evaluated?* Negative, destructive, unbelieving "scholarship," employing many specious but unsound arguments, denies the Bible its unique inspiration and authority in the moral and spiritual realm and makes it merely one sacred book among several sacred books of the world.

This denial is a serious error because it undermines the foundations of revealed truth and opens the door to every heresy and false teaching instigated by demonic spirits (1 Tim. 4:1, 2; 1 John 4:1-3). It also fails to see the sublime superiority of divinely revealed truths over the treatment (if any) of these majestic themes in non-Christian holy writings. (The Hebrew Scriptures are regarded as an integral part of Christian Scripture, since they intrinsically form the foundation upon which the Christian revelation was given.)

This denial of the Bible's authority reduces Christianity to the status of "just another religion," robbing it of its uniqueness. For only the Bible shows lost humanity the one way of salvation through the vicarious death and glorious bodily resurrection of Jesus the Christ, the Savior of the world. Thus this denial nullifies the Christian gospel and the believer's hope of eternal life and glorification of the body through Christ's conquest of sin, death, and hell.

All of this means that by the denial of the full inspiration and authority of the Christian Scriptures, Christianity would become a religion originated and propagated by "spirits not of God" (1 John 4:1, 2) instead of by the Spirit of truth (John 16:12, 13), and would become, like non-Christian religions, a system of "doctrines of demons," that is, doctrines instigated by demon spirits (1 Tim. 4:1, 2).

Authenticity of the Bible Text

OLD TESTAMENT AUTHENTICITY

EXTERNAL EVIDENCE. The reception of the Hebrew Scriptures from the earliest times as the inspired Word of God and their early inclusion in the Sacred Canon are attestations of their authenticity. Added to this is the fact that the revelation of truth and the historical narrative they contain have been validated by Old Testament believers and by the unanimous witness of the Jewish nation.

The authenticity of the Old Testament has been further attested by the New Testament. The foundation of revelation established in the Old Testament supports the superstructure of truth revealed in the New Testament; likewise, the types and prophecies enumerated in the Old Testament are realized and fulfilled in the New Testament. The New Testament truly forms the capstone of the Old Testament revelation.

The Old Testament has been remarkably authenticated by the Jewish historian Flavius Josephus (A.D. 37-95) and by other extrabiblical writers, so that it may truly be said that secular history accredits the authenticity of the Old Testament.

Archeology, the handmaid of history, also adds its voice. Modern archeological research in Bible lands has had a truly phenomenal ministry not only in exploding the radical, negative, critical theories of destructive critics but in attesting, illustrating, and supplementing the biblical record and in verifying its accuracy in historical and general matters.

Archeology has in hundreds of cases shown the Old Testament to be correct, even in instances where the gravest critical doubts and denials had previously existed. Of course, this does not mean that archeology will necessarily solve every difficulty or remove every problem. In some cases it creates new problems instead of solving old ones. We must recognize that faith will always be a necessary prerequisite to *everyone* who approaches God's Word to drink of the water of salvation it offers. But it can truly be said that no archeological evidence, objectively and impartially interpreted, has ever proved the Scripture record to be in error. In the realm of authentic local color — in physical and geographical allusions, in social customs and religions, in political and linguistic affiliations — scientific research has demonstrated the accuracy of the Old Testament.

INTERNAL EVIDENCE. The theology of the Old Testament authenticates it as the Word of God. This is demonstrated in its *lofty doctrine of God,* who is presented as Creator and Redeemer, infinite in holiness, wisdom, and power; in its *realistic view of man,* showing him to be fallen, sinful, lost, separated from God, and under the sentence of death; in its *gospel of saving grace,* which offers redemption by the shed blood of the Lamb of God, the world's Savior to come; and in its *hope of life after death,* which looks forward to a redeemed humanity, a restored earth, and a regained paradise in a sin-cleansed eternal state. Its theology and theme are totally unique and incomparably superior to those of other pre-New Testament holy writings of the non-Christian religions of the world.

NEW TESTAMENT AUTHENTICITY

EXTERNAL EVIDENCE
Christian testimony. All during the first three centuries of Christianity, Christian writers residing in all parts of the civilized world testified to the life, death, resurrection, and ascension of Christ and the resulting gospel of grace.
Non-Christian testimony. The *Annals* of Tacitus, the *Biographies* of Seutonius, and the *Letters* of Pliny all attest the life and death of Jesus Christ under Pontius Pilate, the remarkable spread of the Christian gospel throughout the Roman world, and the vast numbers of converts who worshiped Christ as God and thereby suffered cruel persecution.
Archeological testimony. Evidence from the excavation of buried cities — coins, inscriptions, letters, papyri, etc. — all bear evidence of the truthfulness of the New Testament in general and of the historical narratives of Luke in the Book of Acts in particular. Allusions to such

varied places as Antioch in Syria, Antioch in Pisidia, Cyprus, Iconium, Thessalonica, Philippi, Athens, Corinth, and Rome are found to be thoroughly correct. References to such details as imperial and senatorial provinces, Roman procurators and proconsuls, Greek "politarchs" and Asiatic aediles, and natives of pagan districts such as Lycaonia and the island of Malta invariably prove authentic. Even where critics have alleged discrepancies, mounting evidence continues to support the New Testament. Difficulties that persist await solution by future discoveries. Meanwhile the New Testament merits trust in its integrity, based upon its past record of vindication by archeological discovery.

INTERNAL EVIDENCE. The theology of the New Testament builds upon and combines with the theology of the Old Testament to authenticate the whole Bible as the Word of God. No other sacred literature in the world presents the doctrine of God, man's lost condition, the gospel of redemptive grace, the position and glorious destiny of those redeemed by Christ, and the fate of the unregenerate as does the New Testament in harmony with the Old Testament. In this realm the Bible is absolutely unique. No other literature can compare with it. It is God's revelation to fallen men – the *one and only* true revelation that shows lost man how to be saved. The efficacy of the New Testament as a regenerative dynamic attests it as the Word of God – God's way of salvation for fallen man.

Integrity of the Bible Text

THE OLD TESTAMENT HEBREW TEXT

EARLIEST EXTANT HEBREW MANUSCRIPTS. Before the sensational discovery of the Dead Sea Scrolls in 1947, the oldest available Hebrew manuscripts did not date much before A.D. 900, if even this early. The Leningrad Codex of the Prophets is dated A.D. 916. An undated British Museum document of the Pentateuch is possibly somewhat earlier, as well as a manuscript in the Cambridge University Library. The earliest manuscript of the complete Hebrew Bible does not date earlier than the eleventh century.

THE MASORETIC TEXT OF THE HEBREW SCRIPTURES. These pre-Dead Sea Scroll manuscripts and fragments represent the traditionally transmitted Hebrew text of the Bible as it emerged from the Masoretic period (about A.D. 500-900). The Masoretes were learned rabbis who adhered rigidly to the traditional Hebrew text. They standardized and "froze" the text to give it the form it had had for many centuries. This same form has remained with us all through the era of early and modern printing. The task of the Masoretes or "traditionalists" was to determine the exact text transmitted to them from all available sources and to solidify it in an unalterable form, so that it might be passed on to future generations without change. One feature of this text is that it contains vowel signs and accentual marks intended to standardize pronunciation of the Old Testament Hebrew language.

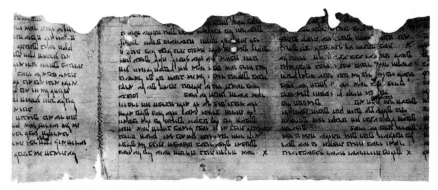

A portion of the famed Dead Sea Scrolls in an Israeli museum *(Russ Busby photo)*

THE DEAD SEA SCROLLS AND THE HEBREW TEXT. The discovery of these manuscripts revolutionized scholarly approach to the text of the Old Testament. These scrolls are handwritten manuscripts that date 800 years before the Masoretic apparatus and approximately a thousand years before the oldest previously available documents! Consequently they cast a dramatically different light on the critical allegation that all divergent texts had been suppressed about A.D. 100. But the greatest significance of the Dead Sea manuscripts is that they controvert the former critical contention that the original form of the ancient autographs was irretrievably lost. Instead, they provide remarkable confirmation of the reliability of the transmission of the currently accepted text. The Isaiah Scroll from Qumran, for example, contains scribal phenomena peculiar to an early period, but wording strikingly in accord with the much later standard Masoretic text, the text of modern Hebrew Bibles.

The new manuscript discoveries from Qumran vindicate the reverential attitude of the Jews toward their Holy Scriptures and their meticulous care in transmitting them accurately. As the ancient Jewish historian Josephus said, "We have given practical proof of our reverence for our Scriptures. For, although such long ages have now passed, no one has ventured either to add, or to remove, or to alter a syllable; and it is an instinct with every Jew, from the day of his birth, to regard them as the decrees of God, to abide by them, and, if need be, cheerfully to die for them" (*Against Apion I,* pp. 179-180, Loeb Edition.)

THE SAMARITAN PENTATEUCH. This valuable witness to the reliability of the text of the Old Testament dates from the fifth century B.C. and represents a form of the books of Genesis, Exodus, Leviticus, Numbers, and Deuteronomy that was transmitted by the separatist Samaritan religious sect at Mount Gerizim (near ancient Shechem) in complete independence from the Hebrew text of the Jews. When the first copy of the Samaritan Pentateuch came to the attention of modern scholars in 1616, great contributions to textual criticism were expected of it. Long and careful study by scholars, however, has resulted in one basic conclusion: this independent text strikingly attests the textual authenticity of the Pentateuch. The text does contain numerous variations in spelling and grammar, but these are apparently due to the preservation of North Israelite dialectal peculiarities and actually form a valuable witness to the substantial purity of the Hebrew text as preserved in the Masorete tradition.

THE GREEK SEPTUAGINT. Sometimes called "the Version of the Seventy," the Septuagint is a translation of the Hebrew Old Testament into Greek, the common language of the civilized world of the day. It was executed about 250 to 150 B.C. and represents, so far as we know, the oldest translation not only of the Scriptures but of any book into any other language. Despite variations between the Septuagint and the Hebrew text, especially in some of the prophetic books and the writings (Psalms, Proverbs, Job, Song of Solomon, Ruth, Lamentations, Ecclesiastes, Esther, Daniel, Ezra, Nehemiah, and Chronicles), there is substantial agreement overall, thereby attesting the careful and accurate transmission of the Hebrew text.

Important manuscripts of the Greek version of the Old Testament are written in large, separate capital letters called *uncials* (from the Latin *uncia,* "an inch," and *uncialis,* "large") in distinction to later *cursives* (from the Latin *curro,* "run, flow") written in small "flowing" script (and less valuable critically). About 170 uncial manuscripts have been discovered. The oldest and most important of these are *Codex*

Vaticanus (B), dating about A.D. 325 to 350, *Codex Alexandrinus* (A), dating about A.D. 450, *Codex Sinaiticus* (Aleph), belonging to the late fourth century, and *Codex Ephraemi Rescriptus* (C), from the fifth century.

THE TARGUMS. Like the Septuagint, the Targums were rendered from the original Hebrew texts. However, unlike the Septuagint, the Targums are not strict translations. They are free paraphrastic renderings of the Hebrew Bible into the Aramaic language (which from the time of Ezra began to supplant Hebrew as the common tongue of the people — see Neh. 8:8). The *Targum of Onkelos* (Aquila) is the oldest and best Targum of the Pentateuch and attests the reliability of the Hebrew text. The *Targum of Jonathan* on the Prophets is more paraphrastic and free. The *Targums on the Hagiographa* (the third section of the Hebrew Scriptures) are late and have less value than the Targums of Onkelos and Jonathan. There is one Targum of Psalms, Job, and Proverbs, another of the rolls (Song of Solomon, Ruth, Lamentations, Ecclesiastes, and Esther), another of Chronicles, and another of Esther. In elucidating the meaning of the language in the original Hebrew text, the Targums constitute a valuable witness to the authentic nature of the text.

THE NEW TESTAMENT GREEK TEXT

General evidence for the text of the New Testament comes from four sources: manuscripts, lectionaries, patristic quotations, and ancient versions.

MANUSCRIPTS. Manuscripts of all or part of the New Testament constitute the most important source for establishing the text of the New Testament. These are of such antiquity and quality that it can be said that no work handed down to us from classical writers has a better attested text than the Greek New Testament. Several manuscripts of the Roman poet Virgil (70 to 19 B.C.) claim an antiquity as high as the fourth or fifth century, but in general the available manuscripts of the secular classics date from the ninth to the fifteenth centuries.

As in the case of the Greek version of the Old Testament, the earliest manuscripts of the New Testament are uncials, written in large letters on fine vellum (the highly prepared skins of calves or kids). The uncials date earlier than the ninth century while the cursives date from the ninth century to the fifteenth century. After the fifteenth century, printing became the dominant method of transmitting Scripture.

Of uncial manuscripts of the New Testament, somewhat more than a hundred are known, while of cursives some 2,533 have now been cataloged. While generally less important than uncials, cursive manuscripts may possess high value if they happened to be copied from an early uncial manuscript. The mass of manuscript evidence available for the New Testament is truly overwhelming. This becomes all the more striking when we remember that ten or twelve manuscripts, usually modern, are all that exist for determining the text of most classical authors!

Of the 241 uncials that appear in the latest official lists, the following are the most important: 1) *Codex Sinaiticus* (Aleph), fourth century; discovered by Count Tischendorf in 1859 at Saint Catherine's Convent on Mount Sinai. The New Testament is complete, the Old Testament incomplete; 2) *Codex Alexandrinus* (A), fifth century; donated to Charles I in 1627 and now in the British Museum. Neither the Old Testament nor the New Testament is complete. Of the latter are missing Matthew 1:1-25; 6:1-34; John 6:50−8:52; 2 Corinthians 4:13−12:6; 3) *Codex Vaticanus* (B) fourth century; lacks 1 and 2 Timothy, Titus, and Philemon. Hebrews 9:14 to the end of Revelation have been supplied by a much later hand (fifteenth century). In the Old Testament it offers on the whole the best text of the Septuagint; 4) *Codex Ephraemi Rescriptus* (C), fifth century; in addition to fragments of the Septuagint it contains about three-fifths of the New Testament. It is a palimpsest; the original writing was erased in the twelfth century and Greek translations of Ephraem Syrus' works were written over it; 5) *Codex Bezae* (D), sixth century; discovered by Theodore Beza (1519-1605), the French theologian and textual scholar, in the Monastery of Saint Irenaeus at Lyons in 1562, and presented by him to the University of Cambridge. For the text of the Gospels and the Acts this manuscript in both Greek and Latin is of fundamental significance; 6) *Codex Claromontanus* (D^p), sixth century; contains all the Pauline Epistles in Greek and Latin and is in the Paris Library; 7) *Codex Laudianus,* (E^a), sixth century; contains the Acts in Greek and Latin; finally fell into the hands of Archbishop Lau, who presented it to the Bodleian Library, Oxford, in 1636; 8) *Codex Coislinianus* (H^p), sixth century; consists of 43 leaves of Paul's Epistles, scattered among a number of libraries in France, Russia, Italy, etc.; 9) *Codex Cyprius* (K), ninth century; one of the most important of late uncials. It contains the Gospels (except Matt. 4:22−5:14; 28:17-20; Mark 10:16-20;

John 21:15-25). It agrees remarkably with the quotations found in Origen and with Codex Vaticanus.

LECTIONARIES. The lectionaries are the service books that contain the lessons to be read on every day of the calendar year and of the church year. Selections were made from the Gospels and from the Epistles. The number of lectionaries that are now included in the official catalog of manuscripts is 1,838. They date from the fourth to the seventeenth century. Recent scholarship has established the value of the lectionaries in the study of the history of the transmission of the text, and these sources will in the future play an ever-increasing role of importance in textual research of the New Testament.

PATRISTIC QUOTATIONS. Quotations of the New Testament by the Church Fathers are important for the study of the text because the time and place of their writing can be definitely established. The *Index Patristicus* compiled by J. W. Burgon and housed in the British Museum contains 86,489 quotations. But even this is incomplete. Moreover, the problem of loose or paraphrastic quotation complicates the usefulness of this source of information. Quotations are of value only from a critical edition and when supported by other good evidence.

Ancient Versions of the Bible

The most significant versions for the study of the text of the New Testament are those which were executed before the year 1000 and which are *direct* translations from the Greek. The most important of these are in a) *Latin* (Old Latin and the Vulgate), b) *Syriac* (Old Syriac, Peshitta, Philoxenian, and Palestinian), c) *Coptic* (Sahidic and Bohairic), d) *Armenian*, e) *Old Georgian*, f) *Old Slavic*, and g) *Gothic*.

OLD TESTAMENT VERSIONS

THE SEPTUAGINT. The Greek term *septuaginta,* meaning "seventy," refers to the seventy elders who are said to have translated the Torah (the Pentateuch) into Greek. Later the name was applied to the whole Old Testament as it was gradually translated into Greek (about 250-150 B.C.). The Septuagint is also known as the *Alexandrian Version* because it was made at Alexandria, Egypt, for use by the large Jewish population there. The Septuagint is the oldest and most important translation of the Hebrew Old Testament. The Pentateuch, which was translated first, is carefully and literally executed; the Prophets are somewhat less literally translated, and the Writings are the least literal of all.

In the course of centuries the Septuagint became corrupt through repeated copyings and required revision. A notable revision was undertaken by Origen in the third century A.D. The earliest Septuagint documents (Codex Sinaiticus, Codex Alexandrinus, Codex Vaticanus, and Codex Ephraemi Rescriptus) antedate the pre-Dead Sea Scroll Hebrew manuscripts (early tenth century A.D.) by more than a half-century. Despite the exciting biblical manuscript discoveries made since 1947, the Septuagint still remains the earliest available witness to the original Old Testament text (except for the Samaritan text of the Pentateuch). However, for a number of reasons the Septuagint's critical value in determining the pure Hebrew text is somewhat limited.

AQUILA'S VERSION. Made about A.D. 130, this was a slavishly literal Greek translation intended to substitute for the Septuagint for Greek-speaking Jews. Although making the text almost incomprehensible, the extreme literalness of the version does give it value for textual criticism. Aquila had become a Jewish proselyte and had received a thorough training under the noted Rabbi Akiba, thus enabling him to accomplish the translation.

THEODOTIAN'S VERSION. Early in the second century, at about the time Aquila made his version, Theodotian, an Ebionite or Judaizing Christian, revised the Septuagint to bring it into harmony with the Hebrew text. He was not a disciple of Rabbi Akiba nor a slavish literalist. His version became popular among Christians and his rendering of Daniel prevailed over the weak Septuagint version.

SYMMACHUS' VERSION. This was a revision of Aquila's version in reaction against the frequent incomprehensibly literal renderings of that translation. It was executed with the aid of the Septuagint and Theodotian and was aimed at the sense rather than the letter.

ORIGEN'S VERSION. Origen (A.D. 185-254) undertook to purify the text of the Septuagint, which had become woefully corrupt in his day. He accomplished this in a six-column textual apparatus called the *Hexapla* ("sixfold"). The first column was Hebrew. The other five columns were Greek, as follows: Hebrew rendered in Greek letters, Aquila's Version, Symmachus' Version, revised Septuagint, and Theodotian's Version. The important fifth column (Origen's revised Septuagint) was recopied repeatedly, but when it became separated from the footnotes and textual apparatus it lost its critical value. However, a valuable Syriac translation of part of the fifth column with critical notes, called the Syro-Hexaplaric Version, has survived in fragments.

VERSIONS OF THE WHOLE BIBLE

THE SYRIAC VERSION. Evidently produced in the second century, this version enjoyed wide circulation, becoming known by the ninth century as the *Peshitta*, that is, the "simple" or "plain" version. The translators were well acquainted with Hebrew, a sister Semitic tongue of Syriac. Despite the influence of the Septuagint, the books of the Old and New Testament are rendered with precision. At the beginning of the seventh century the Syriac New Testament was revised by Thomas of Harkel. The resulting *Harcleian Syriac*, like Aquila's Greek Version, is marked by extreme literality.

THE PALESTINIAN SYRIAC. This was another Syriac version apparently made for "Hebrew" Christians in distinction to Hellenists (Greek-speaking Jews — Acts 6:1). It survives only in fragments in a tongue resembling Aramaic.

THE OLD LATIN VERSIONS. Apparently several of these existed to accommodate Latin-speaking Christians, especially in North Africa, where the Church was Latin-speaking from the outset. Another Old Latin Version appeared in Europe and was superseded by a revised text known as the *Italian*. In the Old Testament these versions were made from the then-current unrevised Septuagint text.

THE LATIN VULGATE. The Old Latin (Italian) version was succeeded by the Vulgate. This important version was executed by Eusebius Hieronymus, better known as Jerome, who mastered both Hebrew and Greek in order to translate the Bible into the language of the day. Jerome's Latin Bible in its completed form was a composite work. It consisted of the following: the Old Testament, except the Psalms, from the *original* Hebrew; the Psalms in the Old Latin revised with the aid of Origen's Hexaplaric text of the Septuagint; the Gospels, consisting of the Old Latin revised from the original Greek; and finally, the rest of the New Testament more superficially revised. The Apocrypha were added, but they were not considered a part of the Canon.

A path of Paul, the Appian Way, into Rome *(Russ Busby photo)*

The Latin Vulgate was executed between A.D. 383 and 405. From A.D. 500 to 1500, when Latin held sway as the *lingua franca* of Western Europe, Jerome's translation was *the* Bible of the Western World. In the thirteenth century it became known as "the Vulgate," i.e. "the Common Version" of the people. In 1228 it was divided into chapters, and in 1455, after the printing press was invented, it was the *first* book ever printed in movable type. It was revised during 1590 to 1592 for use as the standard text of the Roman Catholic Church. In 1907 work on a modern critical edition was begun, with various books appearing since 1926.

OTHER VERSIONS. Besides the Syriac and the Latin, many other versions were made at different times and in various lands. These include the Gothic, the Armenian, the Arabic, the Ethiopic, and the Coptic (Egyptian). These are for the most part independent testimonies and not mere copies of some one common original, as their verbal differences demonstrate. However, their complete agreement in all essential points attests the care with which the Sacred Scriptures have been prepared and transmitted. More important, these ancient versions establish the integrity of the Bible more satisfactorily than that of any other ancient book.

Modern Translations of the Bible

ANGLO-SAXON VERSIONS

Aldhelm, Bishop of Sherborne (eighth century), is said to have translated the Psalter into Anglo-Saxon verse. In the tenth century Alfred the Great reputedly did the same. The famous Vespasian Psalter appeared about A.D. 900. Aelfric at the end of the tenth century produced a version of the Pentateuch and Joshua in West Saxon, and the West Saxon version of the Gospels appeared A.D. 1000. Anglo-Saxon Homilies give evidence of a native version of the Scriptures prior to the Norman Conquest.

ENGLISH VERSIONS

Wycliffe's Bible, a translation into English from the Latin Vulgate, appeared in 1382.

The style, tone, and to a large extent the wording of the English Bible were settled permanently by William Tyndale. *Tyndale's New*

Testament appeared in 1525 and Tyndale's Pentateuch in 1530. His last revision (the true primary version of the English New Testament) appeared during 1534 to 1535.

The first printed version of the entire English Bible was the *Coverdale Bible* (1535), translated by Miles Coverdale from Luther's Bible and the Vulgate.

Next in order of importance after Tyndale's publication was *Matthew's Bible* (1537), giving the results of Tyndale's latest work. It consisted of Tyndale's translation to the end of 2 Chronicles and Tyndale's New Testament of 1534 and 1535. All the rest was taken from Coverdale's Bible of 1535 and was actually the first "Authorized Version," being published by Grafton and Whitchurch of London with the king's license.

The Great Bible (1539) was a revision of the Coverdale Bible of 1535.

The Whittingham New Testament (1557) was the first English testament divided into verses.

The Geneva Bible (1560) was printed in Geneva, Switzerland, and was the first complete Bible divided into verses.

The Bishop's Bible (1568) was a revision of the Great Bible of 1539, named after the nine bishops and scholars who produced it at the suggestion of Archbishop Parker. Its text as printed in the 1602 edition was taken as the basis of the Authorized Version of 1611.

The Rheims Version of the New Testament (1582), an accurate and literal translation of the Vulgate made at Rheims, exerted a very powerful influence on the King James Version of 1611.

The King James Version (1611), commonly called the *Authorized Version* and which became *the* English Bible for the past three-and-one-half centuries, was never actually officially authorized by either King James or the church. It was simply appointed to be read in the churches in the place of the Bishop's Bible.

The Revised Version (1881-85) was a revision of the Authorized Version of 1611 based on a literal translation of the Hebrew and Greek texts by 65 English scholars. It did not capture public fancy.

The American Standard Version (1901) was issued by a group of American scholars as a revision of the Revised Version of 1885, including preferred readings and format changes. It never supplanted the Authorized Version for popular use, but it was used fairly widely in scholarly circles.

The New Testament in Modern Speech (1903), by Richard F. Weymouth, was one of the first translations rendered in truly modern

English. The work enjoyed a fair measure of popularity for several years. It has been revised by others since its original publication.

The New Testament: A Translation in the language of the People (1937), by Charles B. Williams, is generally well regarded by scholars but has achieved only moderate acceptance with the reading public.

The Revised Standard Version (1952; New Testament only, 1946) was a revision of the *American Standard Version* by mostly liberal scholars. This work was intended to become the standard text for public and personal use. Despite certain excellencies of translation it never achieved this goal, though it has been fairly popular among certain ecclesiastical groups.

The New Testament in Modern English (1958), by J. B. Phillips, was actually a loose translation or paraphrase, and had great appeal to the reading public.

The Holy Bible: The Berkeley Version in Modern English (1959) has been revised and renamed *The Modern Language Bible*. Originally the work of Gerrit Verkuyl in the New Testament and twenty conservative American scholars in the Old Testament, the work has been revised carefully to provide uniformity of style. It is now generally regarded as fairly readable without being excessively paraphrastic and reasonably accurate without being overly literal.

The New Testament—An Expanded Translation (1961), by Kenneth S. Wuest, was designed as a precise translation of the Greek. The work uses as many English words as the translator deemed necessary to convey the meaning of the original. Though rather wordy for this reason, the translation has become moderately popular with serious Bible students.

The Amplified Bible (1965; New Testament only, 1958) was undertaken by a group of unspecified translators headed by Frances Siewert. This version seeks to clarify the meaning of the original languages by including explanatory words and phrases in the immediate text of the translation. The translation has enjoyed widespread popularity.

Good News for Modern Man: The New Testament in Today's English Version (1966) is a semi-paraphrase translated by Robert G. Bratcher and sponsored by the American Bible Society. It has been one of the most widely distributed of all modern versions of the New Testament.

The New English Bible (1970; New Testament only, 1961) was prepared as a totally new translation by a group of British scholars under the direction of C. H. Dodd. This translation, like the earlier

Revised Standard Version, was intended to dominate public and private use of the Bible. While it did not reach this goal, it is enjoying a steadily widening distribution.

The New American Standard Bible (1971; New Testament only, 1960-63) is a careful revision of the American Standard Version (1901) by a group of 58 unnamed conservative scholars. It is a fairly literal translation, with up-to-date diction, and is becoming recognized as a valuable study version.

The Living Bible (1971; portions published earlier) is a thoroughly evangelical paraphrase produced by Kenneth N. Taylor and reviewed by various scholars. It has become established as one of the most popular versions of recent times.

Principles of Interpreting the Bible

The Bible is to be interpreted as the divine-human book it is. As a *divine* book it is to be recognized as a God-given revelation, inspired in its thoughts and in its words by God's Spirit, imbued with intrinsic authority as God's voice, and understood only by complete dependence of the regenerated expositor upon the tuition of the Holy Spirit himself (John 16:12, 13). As a *human* book the Bible is to be interpreted like any other piece of literature, using the rules of grammar, the facts of history, and the principles of sound logic.

The Bible is to be interpreted as a coherent and coordinated body of revealed truth. Although it consists of 66 books, these must be seen not as disconnected entities but as *one* book comprising *a unified whole with a definite theme and consummation,* just like any other orderly and well-written narrative. The theme of Scripture is *human redemption.* The principal character is *the world's Redeemer,* Jesus Christ, God incarnate. Everything in the Old Testament that precedes his incarnation points to this grand event and its outworking in human redemption. The culmination of the Bible's story of redemption is *a sinless universe* peopled with unfallen angels and redeemed and glorified humanity. The only isolation ward is Gehenna, the lake of fire (Rev. 20:11-15), reserved for fallen angels, demons, and unregenerate men (Matt. 25:41). Thus the Bible has a *definite plan* and a *clear purpose,* which must be ascertained for correct interpretation.

The Bible is to be interpreted in the light of its overall plan and purpose. The Bible's plan and purpose must be determined by inductive logic (reasoning from the particulars to the generalizations) and not by *deductive* logic (reasoning from generalizations to the particulars). Thus it is the business of the interpreter to allow the Spirit of God to say freely through the human author exactly what he intends to convey rather than what the interpreter thinks he ought to say. This is another way of saying that *every biblical text must be interpreted in its context*—both in its immediate connection with the chapter and book in which it occurs and also in its general connection with the overall plan and purpose of the Bible.

The Bible is to be interpreted literally as the inspired Word of God. The literal method seeks to arrive at the precise meaning of the language of each of the Bible writers as is required by the laws of grammar, the facts of history, and the common-sense logic used in communication between rational creatures. This means of arriving at the normal, original meaning of each Bible text does not entail a wooden literalism that disregards figurative language or symbology, nor does it preclude spiritual applications of the literal interpretation of the passage.

The literal interpreter takes the Scriptures at face value. He honors the Word by treating it honestly, as one would treat any piece of literature. He realizes that Scripture is its own best illustrator, and so constantly compares Scripture with Scripture, seeking the *one* true interpretation of each passage, following the rule of thumb that the simplest interpretation is to be preferred when there is a choice.

The Bible is to be expounded under one consistent method of interpretation. The literal method must be applied to the *entire* Bible—to the prophetic as well as to the nonprophetic portions. Premillennial interpretation is consistent in applying inductive logic in the literal interpretation of all Scripture. It allows the details to dictate the generalizations.

Time-Periods of the Bible

NECESSITY OF TIME DISTINCTIONS

The biblical story of human redemption, like any other story of quality, has plot, plan, and purpose, and hence has necessary time distinctions to suit these. A simple illustration will demonstrate this. Suppose a biography is written about a particular person, depicting his life as a boy, as a married man with a family, and then as a widower, deprived of his wife and children by their sudden and tragic death. In quoting and interpreting what this man said and did, his words and deeds must obviously be placed in *the time-period* to which they belong. To ignore such time-periods and to quote his words and deeds without relationship to the time context and circumstances under which they were uttered would violate common-sense principles of correct interpretation and would result in biographical havoc.

May not the story of human redemption be expected to have time periods similar to any other logically written story? Can it be correctly interpreted apart from the time context of its texts? Can its various eras be denied or ignored without violating its message, distorting its meaning, and dissipating its deserved respect? Yet this is exactly how the story of redemption is treated by many who attempt to interpret the Bible!

THE COVENANTS AND ADMINISTRATIONS OF SCRIPTURE

A time-period in the story of human redemption is called an *era, economy, dispensation,* or *administration.* During each such period man is given a specific revelation of God's will for him in a relationship of responsibility called a *covenant.* God monitors man's response to his divinely-revealed covenant for the duration of each such time-period. God has seen fit to make several important covenants with man, each of which relates to man's moral and spiritual history on the earth. Each covenant introduces a new administration having a time element and expiring at a certain period. The administrations which correspond to nine important covenants of Scripture can be arranged as follows.

THE EDENIC COVENANT AND THE ADMINISTRATION OF INNOCENCE. This covenant was given to Adam and Eve in Eden, before the fall of man, and inaugurated the Administration of Innocence (Gen. 1:28-30; 2:15-17). The conditions of this covenant were 1) *to populate the earth* with an unfallen race; 2) *to subdue the earth to man's needs* by learning to control the forces of nature; 3) *to have dominion over the animals* (Psa. 8:3-9); 4) *to live on a vegetable diet;* 5) *to till the Garden* (seen as delightful light work); 6) *to abstain from eating of the tree of the knowledge of good and evil.* Man was innocent, not knowing what sin was. Had he obeyed God, he would have remained forever free of sin. Instead, he disobeyed, broke the Covenant, and learned what sin was; 7) *to avoid death.* The punishment of disobedience and loss of innocence was *threefold death* (Gen. 2:17): *immediate spiritual death* (estrangement from God and loss of fellowship with

25

God); *gradual physical death* (note that Adam lingered on for 930 years); and *eventual eternal death* in everlasting separation from God in Gehenna. Adam was delivered from eternal death by God's grace in view of Christ's redemptive work (Gen. 3:21).

Had God not intervened and instituted a new covenant, Adam and Eve would have met with instant physical death as well as irrevocable spiritual and eternal death as the penalty of their disobedience. Thus the Edenic Covenant was abrogated completely and the Administration of Innocence ended.

THE ADAMIC COVENANT AND THE ADMINISTRATION OF CONSCIENCE AND MORAL RESPONSIBILITY. This covenant was given to Adam and Eve in their fallen state, and included the whole fallen race descended from them (Gen. 3:14-19). It introduced the Administration of Conscience and Moral Responsibility. Although man had lost his innocence and had become a sinner, God remained unchangeably holy and thus required his creatures, though fallen, to honor their Creator by keeping his moral law written in man's heart and conscience. Man, in token of his inability to do this in the degree necessary to satisfy God's holiness, was required to approach God by animal sacrifice, showing that he appealed to God's grace (eventually to be manifested in Christ's atoning death — see Genesis 3:21; 4:4, 5). Hence, the Adamic Covenant governs the fallen race and is operative upon all unglorified men, whether redeemed or unredeemed, as long as they are on the earth. Thus the Administration of Conscience and Moral Responsibility *overlaps and spans all succeeding administrations.* As a specific period of testing, it ended in the Noahic flood, God's divine judgment on man's thorough immorality.

The Adamic Covenant embodied a fourfold "curse," involving the serpent, the woman, the man, and the earth, and operative throughout the entire Administration of Conscience and Moral Responsibility.

The Serpent. Satan's agent in the temptation was changed from a beautiful, upright, intelligent creature to a loathsome, crawling reptile. *The Woman.* Her state was altered in three particulars: *multiplied conception* would occasion a population explosion, as the young race became very productive to "fill" the earth; *sorrowful motherhood* would occasion the peril, pain, and anguish of childbirth; *the headship of man* would entail the loss of equality which woman had by creation, because she caused man's fall (see 1 Tim. 2:12-15). *The Man.* The earth was cursed because of his disobedience. In contrast to the delight it had been to cultivate the Garden, now man must wrest a living from the soil by sweat and toil, which would exhaust him and finally eventuate in his physical death.

The Earth. From the moment man disobeyed God and became a sinner, the ground was cursed with "thorns" and "thistles." Weeds, blight, drought, and everything that would make food-getting and livelihood difficult would appear in an earth under the curse of man's sin.

The Promise. The Adamic Covenant was without conditions, and embodied a *promise* to offset the *curse.* This promise was the glorious prediction that "the seed of the woman" (the virgin-born Christ) would bruise "the serpent's head" (Satan) and redeem fallen mankind from Satan's power and from sin, death, and hell (Gen. 3:15).

THE NOAHIC COVENANT AND THE ADMINISTRATION OF HUMAN GOVERNMENT. This Covenant was enacted with Noah. As the Adamic Covenant extends to the entire fallen race in Adam, so the Noahic Covenant extends to the entire race descended from Noah (Gen. 8:20 – 9:17). The Administration of Human Government which it initiated governs antediluvian man, and, like the Administration of Conscience and Moral Responsibility which it overlaps, is operative so long as fallen, unglorified mankind exists on the earth. Hence it too spans *all* succeeding ages in time, till the creation of the new heaven and new earth (2 Pet. 3:7-13; Rev. 21:1 – 22:5). However, as a *specific period of testing*, this administration ended in the judgment upon sinful man's first attempt to establish a world state in opposition to the divine rule. This judgment took the form of the confusion of languages at Babel (Gen. 11:1-9) and God's abandonment of mankind at large, "giving them up" to universal idolatry (Rom. 1:24, 26, 28).

The fact that the Noahic Covenant is coterminous with the Adamic Covenant shows that the administrations, although successive, are *not* necessarily mutually exclusive. Rather, they overlap other administrations in a number of cases. This is true because the particular covenant which governs a certain administration still continues in force despite the fact that another covenant, introducing a new administration, may be instituted. Failure to see this has produced much of the present hostility against scriptural time-distinctions.

The Noahic Covenant, in force till the establishment of the new heaven and new earth, contains the following provisions. 1) *Protection of the earth from another universal catastrophe* such as the flood (Gen. 8:21; 9:11). This will be operative until the renovation of the earth by fire (2 Pet. 3:10-13) in preparation for eternity (Rev. 21:1). The sign of the covenant is the rainbow (Gen. 9:12-16), the symbol of the orderly ongoing of nature (Gen. 8:22). This sign intimates that the deluge was a *supernatural* catastrophe, never to be repeated in time (Gen. 8:22). 2) *Institution of human government.* Since the threat of divine judgment in the form of another flood had been removed, the Noahic Covenant instituted the principle of human government to check the rise of lawlessness. Man was made responsible to protect the sanctity of human life, even to the extent of administering capital punishment (Gen. 9:5, 6; cf. Rom. 13:1-7). 3) *Reaffirmation of the conditions of life of fallen man as contained in the Adamic Covenant.* This is to be expected, since the two covenants overlap each other and are coterminous. Noah and his descendants were to multiply and fill the earth (Gen. 9:1) and to dominate the animal creation (Gen. 9:2). Animal food, however, was added to man's diet in the Noahic Covenant (Gen. 9:3, 4). Apparently this had been restricted from man's previous vegetable diet.

THE ABRAHAMIC COVENANT AND THE ADMINISTRATION OF PROMISE. This covenant was originally made with Abraham (Gen. 12:1-3) and was confirmed to Isaac (Gen. 26:1-5) and Jacob (Gen. 28:10-15). Until the call of Abraham, the race had been a unit. There was neither Jew nor Gentile. By Abraham's time, however (about 2000 B.C.), the race had become wholly idolatrous. To purge off a pure remnant to be a witness to the worship of the one true God, God called a descendant of Shem to form a separated people. Israel was to become a witness to all other nations of the blessing of serving the one true God and looking for his promised Redeemer.

The Abrahamic Covenant introduced the Administration of Promise. The promise of the Redeemer, given to the entire race in Adam (Gen. 3:15) but utterly lost sight of through idolatry, was now revived. Abraham and his descendants became heirs of the promise of redemption. *As a specific period of testing* the Administration of Promise ended with the Israelites' acceptance of the Law and Mosaic Covenant at Sinai (Exod. 19:8). However, the conditions of this covenant span all succeeding ages, like those of the previous Administrations of Moral Responsibility and Human Government. Although the covenant centers in the nation of Israel, its blessings reach out to all mankind.

The Abrahamic Covenant, in force till the new heaven and earth, contains the following promises, all of which are *unconditional.* 1) *Blessings through Abraham's posterity. The nation Israel* is privileged to provide the Messiah-Redeemer and to inherit a specific territory forever (Gen. 12:2; 15:18-21; 17:7, 8). *The Church* becomes the heir of salvation, promised to all who believe (Gal. 3:16, 28, 29). *The Gentile nations* will be recipients of Christ's salvation in the coming age when Israel accepts the Messiah at the second advent (Gen. 12:3; Deut. 28: 8-14; Isa. 60:3-5). 2) *Blessing to those who bless Abraham's descendants and a curse upon those who curse them* (Gen. 12:3; Matt. 25:31-46). This promise coupled with warning was particularly evident during the specific period of testing of the Administration of Promise. It is seen working on individuals (Gen. 12:17; 20:3, 17) and nations (especially Egypt — see Gen. 47 — 50, Exod. 1 — 15), but appears throughout the entire span of this administration. The sign of this covenant was circumcision (Gen. 17:9-14).

THE MOSAIC COVENANT AND THE ADMINISTRATION OF LAW. This covenant was made with the nation Israel through Moses. It was never made with Gentiles. The legal economy which it introduced consequently comprehended only the nation Israel. During this era Israel as an *elect* people through Abraham and as a people redeemed out of Egypt (Exod. 15:13) were placed on exhibition before all the nations of the world. They were to be witnesses to the fact that a) the infinitely holy God could save fallen mankind only by the atoning death of the Savior to come (prefigured by Israel's sacrificial system and priesthood), and that b) a redeemed people can glorify God only by keeping his eternal moral law, summarized in the Decalogue from Sinai.

The Mosaic Covenant was in force from Sinai to Calvary (Matt. 27:50, 51). It was conditioned on a) faith in God's grace to save sinners by blood sacrifice and b) obedience to the moral law of God as a means of exemplifying the efficacy of God's redeeming power. Hence it consists of three parts: 1) *the moral law* (Exod. 20:1-17), summarizing the requirements of the infinitely holy God of his redeemed people; 2) *the civil law,* conditioning the social life of Israel (Exod. 21:1 — 24:11). 3) *The ceremonial law,* governing the religious life of Israel (Exod. 24:12 — 31:18). The ceremonial law was abolished when Christ died and fulfilled its prescriptions, which pointed to him.

The moral law of God was adapted to the Mosaic Covenant at Sinai. As a reflection of the eternal character of God it was binding upon *all* men from the beginning. It condemned fallen man and showed him his lost condition and his need of God's redemptive grace. It disclosed to redeemed man how he ought to live in order to glorify his Creator-Redeemer. The moral law of God, accordingly, far transcends its form in the Ten Commandments. It extends to *all* administrations and underlies *all* the covenants. *All* men, both saved and unsaved, of every era will be judged by their response to it. This means that there will be degrees of punishment in Gehenna for the lost (Rev. 20:11-15) as well as degrees of reward in the future sin-cleansed universe for the saved (2 Cor. 5:10).

The Sabbath was the *sign* of the Mosaic Covenant. The fourth commandment (Exod. 20:8-11) constituted the one unique feature of the Moral Law *in its Mosaic dress.* The Sabbath as such was never imposed upon *fallen* man, but only upon unfallen man (Gen. 2:2, 3). When man fell, *God's Sabbath rest in creation was broken.* God then began *working* in redemption (John 5:17; Gen. 3:15, 21). Later God imposed the Sabbath upon *the redeemed nation Israel* (Exod. 20:8-11; 31:12-17). This was in token that his creation rest would one day be restored by that nation. Restoration will transpire when Christ redeems Israel at the second advent and through Israel mediates this redemption to all the nations of the earth during the kingdom age (Isa. 11:1-16; 60:1-22).

For this reason Sabbath-keeping is not Christian but Mosaic. It is legalistic, the badge of the Mosaic Covenant. The commandment of Sabbath-keeping represents the moral law of God only as it was adapted to the requirements of the Mosaic Covenant and the elect nation Israel. It has no direct relevance to the Church or Christianity.

THE NEW COVENANT AND THE ADMINISTRATION OF THE CHURCH. The New Covenant was secured by Christ's blood (Luke 22:20), which purchased the Church of God (Acts 20:28), the Body of Christ (1 Cor. 12:12, 13). The Apostle calls the Church "the mystery . . . which in other ages was not made known" (Eph. 3:3-6), being "hid in God" from "the beginning of the world" (Eph. 3:9). The Administration of the Church comes between Israel's rejection because of unbelief and the nation's restoration at the second advent. During the interval God is visiting the Gentiles to take out of them "a people for his name" (Acts 15:14). During this era the divine purpose comprehends a wholly new entity, the Church, composed of regenerated Gentiles and Jews baptized by the Holy Spirit into vital union with each other in Christ. This is the mystery which welds together believing Jews and Gentiles in a completely new entity, the Church, through the blood of the New Covenant shed at Calvary.

This age is often called "the Dispensation of the Holy Spirit" because the Spirit has been especially manifested by his formation and indwelling of the Church (John 16:7, 8, 13). The age will be consummated by his completion and glorification of the Church (2 Thess. 1:7,

10). This age is also often called "the Dispensation of Grace." Although God's grace operates in every dispensation, the present period is nevertheless a special era of grace. This appears in the vast multitude of Gentile sinners saved in it. God's purpose is that "in the ages to come he might show the exceeding riches of his grace in his kindness toward *us* through Christ Jesus" (Eph. 2:7). In this age God's grace is on display *now* as well as for the ages to come.

THE DAVIDIC COVENANT AND THE ADMINISTRATION OF THE KINGDOM. This covenant was made with King David (2 Sam. 7:4-17). It spans from David's time through the era of the Church, but finds its special fulfillment in Christ (Luke 1:30-33) and the coming kingdom over Israel. It secures three paramount advantages to Israel through the Davidic house. 1) *An everlasting throne.* David's kingdom is in abeyance now, but will be restored someday. Since the Babylonian exile, only one king of the Davidic family has been crowned — and he with thorns (Matt. 27:29). But the Davidic Covenant provides that this thorn-crowned one shall receive the kingdom when the time comes to restore it to David's Son and Lord (Psa. 2:1-12; 110:1; Luke 1:30-33). 2) *An everlasting kingdom.* David's Son and Lord is guaranteed an earthly sphere of rule that will extend over the entire millennial earth. He will have dominion "from sea to sea, and from the river to the ends of the earth" (Psa. 72:1-20). 3) *An everlasting King.* This will be realized in the second advent of Christ as King par excellence and Lord par excellence (Rev. 19:16).

THE PALESTINIAN COVENANT AND THE MESSIANIC ADMINISTRATION. This covenant discloses what the Lord will yet do in regathering, restoring, and blessing Israel to and in her own land (Deut. 30:1-10). It takes the place of the Mosaic Covenant, which came to an end with the crucifixion of Christ, the destruction of Jerusalem, and the dispersion of the Jewish nation in A.D. 70. This covenant ushers in the millennial age and, like the Davidic Covenant, finds its fulfillment in kingdom blessing.

THE NEW COVENANT AND THE ADMINISTRATION OF THE FULLNESS OF TIMES. The New Covenant, based on the redemptive work of Christ, has application not only to the Church in this age but also to the restored nation Israel in the age to come (Jer. 31:31-34; Heb. 8:6-13). In its application to the Church the covenant is "new" in the sense that it is the basis for the outcalling of the new people of God, the Church. In Israel's case it is "new" in that it supersedes the Mosaic Covenant, which Israel broke. On the other hand, it does not alter or conflict with the Palestinian, the Abrahamic, or the Davidic Covenants. Its blessings, yet future, and assured by God's faithfulness, include spiritual regeneration and fellowship with God as a result of *forgiveness,* that is, the complete removal of sin (Jer. 31:33, 34). Guaranteeing eternal salvation, this covenant will cover the kingdom age and the perfect age of the new heaven and new earth that follows, in which righteousness shall dwell and all sin will be removed (Rev. 21:1 – 22:5). It is called "the dispensation of the fullness of times" (Eph. 1:10). This perfect age is the prelude to eternity, when Christ will surrender his perfect kingdom to the Father, "that God may be all in all" (1 Cor. 15:28).

The ancient Scriptures still live in modern Jerusalem. *(Russ Busby photo)*

Major Themes of the Bible

Side by side with its presentation of the grand theme of human redemption, the Bible sets forth numerous other vital teachings that are essential to the exposition of its main subject of salvation. Chief among these are the following corollary themes.

THE BIBLE AS THE WORD OF GOD

Internal and external evidence, as well as the witness of the Holy Spirit, combine to authenticate the Bible as the fully inspired and authoritative Word of God. The Bible throughout assumes this fact in hundreds of passages (e.g. Psa. 12:6; Isa. 55:10, 11; Rom. 10:17) and directly declares it in Second Timothy 3:15, 16. Externally, the nature of the Bible, its subject matter, and its regenerative ministry among men support this truth.

THE UNITY AND TRINITY OF THE GODHEAD

The Old Testament emphasizes the unity of God (Deut. 6:4; Exod. 20:3) but also intimates a triune relationship (Gen. 1:26; 3:22; 11:7; Isa. 9:6; Psa. 2:7). The New Testament emphasizes the trinity (Matt. 28:19; John 14:16) and intimates the unity (John 10:30; 14:9; Col. 1:15). The primary Old Testament names of God (Elohim, Jehovah, Adonai) suggest unity in trinity, as do the various attributes of God.

GOD THE FATHER

THE FATHER OF CHRIST THE SON. The Father begot the Son (Psa. 2:7; John 1:14, 18; 3:16; John 9:35). This was acknowledged by the Son (Matt. 11:27; 26:63, 64; John 17:1; 8:29) and by men (Matt. 16:16; John 1:34). Even the demons recognized this relationship between the Father and the Son (Matt. 8:29).

THE FATHER OF THOSE WHO BELIEVE ON CHRIST THE SON. This truth is taught in Matthew 5:44, 45; John 1:12; Romans 8:14-17; Second Corinthians 6:16-18; and Galatians 4:4-7. The unregenerate are children of the Wicked One (Matt. 13:38; John 8:44; Eph. 2:2, 3).

GOD THE SON

His preexistence is taught in Isaiah 9:6, 7; Micah 5:2; John 8:58 and 17:5; and Hebrews 1:2, 3 and 13:8.

His incarnation is described in John 1:14, 18; Philippians 2:6-8; and First Timothy 3:16.

His substitutionary death is seen in Isaiah 53:4-6; Romans 3:24, 25; John 1:29; Second Corinthians 5:21; and many other passages.

His resurrection is intimated in Genesis 22:1-18; Psalm 16:10; Isaiah 26:19 and 53:10-12; it is clearly expounded in First Corinthians 15:3-8, 12-20; First Timothy 6:14-16; and Second Timothy 1:10.

His ascension is intimated in Leviticus 16:1-34 and taught in Hebrews 9:24, 25; John 20:17; Acts 1:9-11; and First Timothy 3:16.

His priestly ministry is explained in First John 1:9 and 2:1; Hebrews 7:22-27; 8:1, 2; 9:11, 12, 24; and Romans 8:34.

His second advent is referred to in dozens of Scripture passages. First he comes *for* his own, as shown in Philippians 3:20, 21; First Thessalonians 4:13-18; and First John 3:1, 2. Later he comes *with* his own to establish his everlasting kingdom, as seen in Colossians 3:4; First Thessalonians 3:13; and Jude 1:14, 15.

GOD THE HOLY SPIRIT

HIS PERSONALITY. John 14:16, 17 and 16:7-15 show that the Holy Spirit is an actual personage and not merely an "influence for good."

HIS ADVENT. He was present in the world before his advent at Pentecost (Gen. 1:2; 41:38; Exod. 31:3; Psa. 139:7; Zech. 4:6), though it was at Pentecost that he took up residence in the Church (John 14: 16, 17; 16:7; Eph. 2:18-22).

HIS DEPARTURE. He will leave the earth when the Church is completed (2 Thess. 2:7) in the special sense in which he came to institute the Church's formation at Pentecost (Acts 1:5; 11:15, 16). He will then resume his pre-Pentecost ministry in the tribulation period and will inaugurate a special ministry during the kingdom age (Isa. 11:1-3; Joel 2:28, 29).

HIS MINISTRY. He restrains lawlessness and sin (2 Thess. 2:7). He convicts sinners of 1) the sin of disbelief in the Savior, of 2) God's justifying righteousness provided in Christ, and of 3) divine judgment to come upon all who reject Christ's atonement (John 16:7-11). He regenerates the believing sinner (John 3:5), baptizing him into vital union with Christ and with all other believers (1 Cor. 12:13; Rom. 6:3, 4; Gal. 3:27). The Holy Spirit also indwells him (1 Cor. 6:19), anoints him (2 Cor. 1:22; Eph. 1:13; 4:30), and fills him for power and service (Acts 2:4; 4:8; Eph. 5:18).

THE ANGELS

As a special order of creation, angels are incorporeal persons or spirits, having a heavenly position above the earthly sphere of man but infinitely below that of God (Psa. 8:5; Heb. 2:7). They consist of two categories: unfallen and fallen. The unfallen angels are ministering spirits for believers (Heb. 1:14) and are called "holy" (Matt. 25:31). The fallen angels (Satan and the demons) primevally rebelled against God (Isa. 14:12-14; Ezek. 28:11-19). Some of the demons are free and are at work in the world today (1 Tim. 4:1; 1 John 4:1, 2; cf. Mark 5:6-13; Luke 8:30). Others are bound in the abyss (Rev. 9:1-12; 2 Pet. 2:4).

SATAN

Satan is an angelic personality originally created holy and sinless who fell through pride and introduced sin into an originally sinless universe (Ezek. 28:11-19; Isa. 14:12-17). He reigns as king over the realm of darkness comprising the fallen angels and demons (Matt. 12:26). Satan works through man's fallen nature and the evil world system to keep men from Christ's salvation and from obedience to and fellowship with God (Eph. 2:2; 6:10-20; 2 Cor. 4:3, 4; 1 Pet. 5:8; 1 John 5:19; 1 Tim. 4:1). His destiny is Gehenna (Rev. 20:10), the lake of fire prepared for him and his angels (Matt. 25:41).

MAN

Man is a special order of God's creation, lower than the angels but higher than the animals. God created man, permitted his temptation and fall, and planned his redemption through the sacrificial death of the incarnate Word. The result will be not only man's glorification but earth's deliverance from the curse of sin (Eph. 1:13, 14; Rev. 21:1, 2; Rom. 8:20-23). Unbelieving mankind will suffer the fate of Satan and the fallen angels in Gehenna (Matt. 25:41). Eternity will realize a sin-cleansed universe.

SIN

Sin is a terrible reality and "exceedingly sinful" (Rom. 7:13). Going far deeper than human speculation, Scripture presents sin as any lack of conformity to the infinitely holy character of God (Isa. 6:1-5). Fallen man is found to be totally unacceptable to God in the face of the infinite purity of Deity. Man is helplessly cast upon the divine grace revealed in Christ's redemption (Rom. 3:9-31).

IMPUTED SIN. Adam's sin is imputed (reckoned or attributed) to the fallen race. This forms the basis of the doctrine of original sin (Rom. 5:12-18). Man's sin is in turn imputed to Christ, forming the basis of the doctrine of salvation. God's righteousness is imputed to those who believe in Christ, forming the basis of the doctrine of justification.

SIN NATURE. Every descendant of Adam is born with a fallen nature constantly prone to sin. Though this evil disposition was judged by Christ on the cross (Rom. 6:10), it is never said to be removed in this life. But for the believer, overcoming power is provided through the indwelling Spirit (Rom. 8:4; Gal. 5:16, 22-25).

THE SINFUL AND LOST STATE OF THE RACE. Fallen humanity is regarded by God as "under sin" (Rom. 3:9; Gal. 3:22; Rom. 11:32). God looks upon all mankind as totally lacking in merit which might contribute to salvation, so that every sinner is totally confined to God's grace in Christ (Eph. 2:8, 9).

PERSONAL SIN. Everything in the daily life of the individual that fails to conform to God's character is included under this category.

GOD'S REMEDY FOR SIN. The cross of Christ, whether in prospect (Lev. 1:4; Acts 17:30; Rom. 3:25) or retrospect (John 3:16; 1 Pet. 2:24) is the divine remedy for sin. Only faith in Christ's atoning death removes the penalty of sin, eternal death. The unsaved will answer for their sin by punishment both here and eternally in Gehenna. The saved will also answer by loss of blessing now and forfeiture of reward in heaven (1 Cor. 3:9-15; 2 Cor. 5:10).

SALVATION

This term represents the whole work of God, in which he rescues man from the ruin of sin, bestows on him eternal life now, and grants him eternal glory hereafter in accordance with the riches of his grace. Salvation is in every respect an undertaking of God in behalf of man (Jonah 2:9). In no sense is it an activity of man in behalf of God.

THE THREE TENSES OF SALVATION. In the *past tense* the believer became saved when he believed on Christ (Luke 7:50; 1 Cor. 1:18; 2 Cor. 2:15; Eph. 2:5-8). In the *present tense* the believer *is being delivered* from the power of sin by counting on what he is in union with Christ (Rom. 6:11; Gal. 2:19, 20; 2 Cor. 3:18). In the *future tense* the believer *will yet be saved* into full conformity to Christ (Rom. 8:29; 13:11; 1 Pet. 3:2; 1 John 3:2).

THE TWO ASPECTS OF SALVATION. *The final work of Christ* must be distinguished from *the saving work of God.* The first has been completed to infinite perfection for *all* mankind (John 3:16; 19:30; Heb. 10:14) and provides the ground on which God in his infinite holiness can save guilty sinners, including the worst of them. The second of these — the saving work of God — is accomplished the moment the sinner believes; it includes redemption, reconciliation, propitiation, forgiveness, regeneration, justification, sanctification, and glorification (1 Cor. 1:30; 2 Cor. 5:21; John 1:12; 2 Cor. 5:17; Col. 2:10; Rom. 8:29).

THE ONE CONDITION OF SALVATION. Actual personal faith in the finished work of Christ on the cross is the one and only requisite for salvation (Acts 16:31; Eph. 2:8-10; John 3:16, 36; 5:24; Rom. 1: 16; 5:1). Confessing Christ, confessing sin, praying, making restitution, etc. ought to and do *accompany* genuine salvation experience, but are not *conditions* of salvation.

SANCTIFICATION

Sanctification is an integral part of salvation. It is the setting apart of the saved person for God's worship and service. As presented in Scripture, sanctification is in three aspects: past, present, and future.

PAST ASPECT. This is the position which *all* believers have from the moment they exercise saving faith in Christ the Redeemer (1 Cor. 1:2, 30). It represents the sphere in which God sees them "in Christ." It is static and unalterable, resting securely on the finished work of Christ.

PRESENT ASPECT. This represents the experience which all believers enjoy as they depend upon what they are in Christ (Rom. 6:11). It is progressive and changeable, depending upon the believer's yieldedness to God's Word (Rom. 6:13) and conformity to God's will (Rom. 12:2).

FUTURE ASPECT. This represents the final phase of sanctification, when we see the Lord and are made like him (1 Cor. 15:54; 1 John 3: 2). It is eternal, and will be our destiny in glory (Phil. 3:21; Rom. 8:29; 1 Cor. 15:49).

SECURITY

Scripture reveals that those whom Christ saves he saves eternally. The positive doctrine of security rests upon no less than twelve unchangeable facts about God's grace and its accomplishments in behalf of the believer.

GOD'S ETERNAL PURPOSE. This is realized and assured through sovereign grace, totally apart from human merit or work (Rom. 8:29, 30; John 5:24; 6:37; 10:38), through the new covenant of redemption (Heb. 8:6-13).

GOD'S POWER. The Bible declares that God, being free from every barrier to forgive sin, is able to preserve all who are redeemed by Christ (John 10:29; Rom. 4:21; 8:31, 38, 39; Jude 1:24).

GOD'S LOVE. His love for his own can never fail. If he loved men enough to give his Son to die for them when they were sinners and enemies, he will love them much more "now that they are reconciled to him" (John 3:16; Rom. 5:8-11).

CHRIST'S PRAYER. While on earth Christ prayed that those whom the Father had given him should be kept (John 17:9-12, 15, 20, 21). This prayer, which commenced on earth, is continued in heaven (Rom. 8:34; Heb. 7:25).

CHRIST'S DEATH. The efficacious, substitutionary death of Christ is the sufficient remedy for the condemning power of sin (Rom. 8:34). Christ bore *all* the sins of the believer — past, present, and future — so that salvation and safekeeping depend only on the sacrifice and merit of Christ. Thus all condemnation is removed forever (John 3:18; 5:24).

CHRIST'S RESURRECTION. Christ's resurrection makes possible God's gift of eternal life (John 3:16; 10:28). Since this life is the life of the resurrected Christ (Col. 2:12; 3:1-4), it is as eternal as he is eternal, as incapable of dissolution as is the risen Christ. Moreover, by union with the resurrected Christ, by baptism with the Spirit, and by impartation of eternal life, the believer is made a part of the new creation (2 Cor. 5:17; Gal. 6:15). Taken out of his place under the federal headship of the first Adam, he is placed "in Christ" under the federal headship of the Last Adam (1 Cor. 15:20-22, 45-48). Since the Last Adam (the risen Christ) cannot fall, it is impossible for the weakest saint united to him to fall. The infinitely Holy God regards *every* saint as "in Christ" now and forever.

CHRIST'S INTERCESSION. In this present ministry in glory Christ prays for his own who are in the world, having in view their weakness, ignorance, and immaturity (Luke 22:31, 32; John 17:9, 15, 20; Rom. 8:34). His heavenly intercession guarantees that they will be kept saved forever (John 14:19; Rom. 5:10; Heb. 7:25).

CHRIST'S ADVOCACY. Christ's present ministry as Advocate concerns the believer's sin. Since God is infinitely holy, the believer's sin in every case merits eternal condemnation. Moreover, that judgment would of necessity be executed if Christ as Advocate did not continually plead the saving efficacy of his own blood before the throne of God (1 John 2:1, 2; Rom. 8:34; Heb. 9:24).

THE SPIRIT'S REGENERATING WORK. The Spirit regenerates the child of God (John 1:13; 3:3-6; Tit. 3:4-6; 1 Pet. 1:23). By this operation the believer is constituted a son and joint-heir of God with Christ (Rom. 8:16, 17). Being born of God, he partakes of the divine nature, which is never removed or annulled.

THE SPIRIT'S BAPTIZING WORK. The moment the sinner believes, the Spirit baptizes him into the Body of Christ, the Church (1 Cor. 12:13) and into Christ, the Head of the Body (1 Cor. 12:12; Rom. 6:3, 4; Gal. 3:27). The believer is then in union with Christ and with all other believers. His new position "in Christ" is a vital and permanent one because God himself has personally placed him there. The believer is "accepted in the beloved" forever (Eph. 1:6).

THE SPIRIT'S INDWELLING. The Spirit now indwells *every* believer (John 7:37-39; Rom. 5:5; 8:9; 1 Cor. 2:12; 6:19; 1 John 3:24). He never leaves the believer (John 14:16). The Spirit may be *grieved* by unconfessed sin (Eph. 4:30) or *quenched* (suppressed) (1 Thess. 5:19), but as the divine Presence in the heart he is never removed. God's own remain his forever.

THE SPIRIT'S SEALING. All believers are sealed with the Spirit unto the day of full redemption or glorification (Eph. 4:30; 2 Cor. 1:22; Eph. 1:13). The Holy Spirit himself is the seal. He is God's stamp of the security of *all* who are saved.

ASSURANCE

Assurance is personal confidence in a present salvation. It rests upon two lines of evidence: a) an experience of genuine salvation through Christ and b) the truth of God's revealed Word.

CHRISTIAN EXPERIENCE. The impartation of new life from God is sure to be manifested in the believer. This new life is Christ himself indwelling the believer (Col. 1:27; 1 John 5:11, 12). On the basis of this fact the believer is to judge himself as to whether he is in the faith (2 Cor. 13:5). Normal manifestations of the indwelling Christ include the knowledge of God as Father (Matt. 11:27; John 17:3; 1 John 1:3), new ability to understand God's Word (John 16:12-15; 1 John 2:27), a new sense of the sinfulness of sin (Rom. 7:18), a new love for both the unsaved (2 Cor. 5:14; Rom. 9:1-3; 10:1) and the saved (John 13:34, 35; 1 John 3:14), a new concept of prayer (Rom. 8:26, 27; 1 Tim. 2:1, 2; Eph. 6:18, 19), a manifestation of Christ-likeness (John 13:34, 35; 15: 11, 12; 2 Cor. 3:18; Gal. 5:22, 23), and a consciousness of salvation through faith in Christ (Rom. 8:16; 2 Tim. 1:12).

THE VERACITY OF GOD'S WORD. Above and beyond Christian experience, which is at best tarnished by carnality, lies the sure foundation of the Word of God, upon which all experience is to be based and evaluated. Assurance springs from believing the Word (1 John 5: 13). The promises of Scripture are a title deed upon which faith can rest in confident assurance (John 6:37; 5:24; Rom. 1:16; 3:22, 24; 10:13).

THE CHURCH

THE LOCAL CHURCH. As employed in the New Testament, the word "church" denotes any called-out or assembled company of people. In its theological usage it refers to a local gathering of professing Christians who meet together for group worship and service.

THE MYSTICAL CHURCH. In its primary theological usage in the New Testament the word "church" denotes a company of people called out of the old creation into the new (1 Cor. 12:12, 13; Rom. 6:3, 4; Eph. 1:20-23). The Church (often capitalized to distinguish this mystical church from the local assembly) is composed of the total number of redeemed persons from Pentecost (Acts 1:5; 2:4; 11:14-16) to Christ's return to receive his own (1 Thess. 4:13-18; 1 Cor. 15:52). All members of the Church are united to Christ and to one another by the baptism with the Holy Spirit (Gal. 3:27; 1 Cor. 12:12, 13). Believing Jews and Gentiles in this manner become united in "the Church of God" (1 Cor. 10:32). The Church thus represents *all* the saved people of this age. God's purpose in this age is to call out his elect body principally from the Gentiles, but also from the Jews (Acts 15:14).

The mission of the Church is to represent Christ to an unsaved world as "ambassadors for Christ," beseeching men to be "reconciled to God" (2 Cor. 5:20) by believing the gospel of salvation (1 Cor. 15:2-4).

THE SABBATH

THE INSTITUTION OF THE SABBATH. God instituted the Sabbath to memorialize the finished work of the old creation (Gen. 2: 2, 3). It commemorated God's rest from the work of refashioning the earth for the latecomer man (Gen. 1:1-31). God could rest because everything he had made, including man, was "very good" (Gen. 1:31). It was upon *unfallen* man that God imposed the Sabbath — *not* upon fallen man. When man fell, God's creation rest was broken by man's sin. It was then that God began working in redemption (John 5:17). No longer could he rest in a "very good" creation, for creation had now been made "very bad" by sin.

THE SABBATH AND SINAI. Mankind from Adam to Moses was thus no longer under the law of Sabbath observance (despite the fact that the fallen race during this interval attempted to perpetuate the practice, as archeology shows). This fact explains the silence of Scripture about the Sabbath during this period. But with startling suddenness the Sabbath was revived in the fourth commandment of the Decalogue (Exod. 20:8-11). It was not merely one small part of the Mosaic Covenant but was one of its unique and dominant features (Exod. 31: 12-18). The severest penalty possible — death — was attached to its infraction (Num. 15:32-36). This was a warning to every Israelite that they were *God's* people, elect to be an example to all other peoples. God intended to show them that his plan to restore through Christ his creation rest in man and the earth centered in *them* as his chosen nation. The Sabbath was the sign that this was Israel's messianic calling.

THE SABBATH AND THE CHURCH. The Sabbath as the sign of the Mosaic Covenant was the peculiar stamp of the Jew. It was never imposed upon the Church, nor upon any other segment of the fallen race beside the nation Israel. Christians, who observe the first day of the week in honor of Christ's resurrection, are not only free from the obligation of the Sabbath but are actually *warned against* Sabbath-keeping as a form of grace-denying legalism (Col. 2:16, 17; Gal. 4:9, 10). While Christians are not under the Law of Moses, *they are under the eternal moral law of God as reflected in the Ten Commandments.* The fourth commandment enjoining Sabbath-keeping is the *one* and only exception. While all the other commandments are binding upon all ages and all peoples in all times, the Sabbath is strictly Jewish. It is the sign to all mankind that through his elect messianic nation, Israel, God will restore his creation rest destroyed by the fall and man's sin. The new heavens and the new earth will usher in an eternal Sabbath of rest (Rev. 21:1–22:6).

THE LORD'S DAY

THE OBSERVANCE OF THE LORD'S DAY. While the Sabbath (seventh day) is nowhere imposed upon the Church, abundant reasons support the observance of the *first* day of the week.

A new day was predicted and appointed under grace. The crucified Christ was the Stone rejected by Israel. Through his resurrection, however, he has been made the Headstone of the Corner (Psa. 118:22-24; Acts 4:10, 11). This marvelous event was God's doing, and the time of its accomplishment was divinely appointed as a day of rejoicing. Hence Christ's salutation to his own on the morning of his resurrection was "All hail!" or, literally, "O Joy!" (Matt. 28:9). It was indeed "the day which the Lord had made" and was thus aptly designated "the Lord's Day" (Rev. 1:10).

The New Testament supports the observance of the Lord's Day. This is true despite the fact that no command is given to keep the day, nor is any manner of its observance prescribed. This liberty is in accordance with the grace of God manifested in the finished redemption which it commemorates. It is to be observed willingly and from the heart. It preserves the concept that one-seventh of our time is to be devoted to God as a token that *all* of our time actually belongs to him. A day of rest under the Mosaic Law belonged to a people related to God by works which were to be accomplished. In the Church a day of ceaseless worship and service is the portion of a people who are related to God through the finished work of Christ.

Observance of the First Day is indicated by various events. On that day Christ arose (Matt. 28:1), he first met with his disciples (John 20:19), instructed them (Luke 24:13-45), and ascended to heaven as "the firstfruits" (John 20:17). It was on the *first* day of the week that the Spirit came at Pentecost (Acts 2:1-4) and that believers assembled for communion (Acts 20:7) and brought their offerings (1 Cor. 16:2).

THE LORD'S DAY AND THE NEW CREATION. As the Sabbath celebrated the old creation (Exod. 20:10, 11), so the Lord's Day celebrates the new creation. The latter began with the resurrection of Christ and consists of the called-out company of the redeemed (Acts 15:13-18) from Pentecost to the glorification of the Church. These are baptized by the Spirit into union with the risen and glorified Christ in heaven (Rom. 6:3, 4; Col. 2:12, 13; 3:1-4). The Body of Christ, the Church united to Christ its Head (Eph. 1:22; 4:15; Col. 1:18), forms the new creation (2 Cor. 5:17).

THE LOVE OF GOD

GOD'S ESSENTIAL NATURE. "God is love" (1 John 4:8). He is not only the *source* of love but he *is* love. Love is at the essence of his being. He is what he is in large measure because of his love. His love is everlasting and changeless (Jer. 31:3; John 13:1; 15:9) because it is a vital and inseparable part of his being. It is ceaseless in its activity (Rom. 5:8; 1 John 3:16). It is infinite in its purity (1 Pet. 1:22). It is inexhaustible in its benevolence (John 15:13; Tit. 3:4, 5). It is limitless in its intensity (Rom. 5:8-10; 8:35-39).

THE MANIFESTATION OF THE NEW NATURE. God's love is manifested not only *to* his own but *through* them. The impartation of the divine nature (2 Pet. 1:4) enables redeemed men to love as Christ loved (John 13:34, 35). This is the badge of regeneration (1 John 3:14) and one of the prime manifestations of the Spirit (Gal. 5:22). The supernatural character of God's love operating through the believer is described in First Corinthians 13:1-8.

PRAYER TO GOD

Prayer, whether petition, praise, or thanksgiving, assumes an important place in Scripture. It is the direct communion of man with God, and appears in various aspects.

PRAYER IN THE OLD TESTAMENT. Unfallen man had free and full communion with the Lord God (Gen. 3:8). Fallen man, however, could approach the infinite holiness only through the covering of sacrificial blood, which pointed to the coming Redeemer (Gen. 3:21; 4:3-5; 8:20). The basis of prayer consisted in pleading the covenants of the Lord (1 Kings 8:22-26; Dan. 9:4; Neh. 9:32), the holy character of God (Gen. 18:25; Exod. 32:11-14), and the shedding of sacrificial blood (Heb. 9:7).

PRAYER FOR THE KINGDOM. Both John the forerunner and Christ the Messiah at the outset of their ministries preached the messianic kingdom which had been promised to Israel in the Old Testament (Matt. 3:3; 4:17; cf. Dan. 2:44; 4:25, 32). During the early days of his preaching, before the kingdom was rejected, Christ taught his disciples to pray for this kingdom (Matt. 6:9-13). The prayer he gave them is adapted particularly to kingdom expectations, as are the prayer instructions found in Matthew 7:7-11 and Luke 11:2-13.

PRAYER IN THE CHURCH. Anticipating his death and resurrection, as well as the giving of the Spirit and the founding of the Church, Christ in the upper room discourse revealed the new dimensions which prayer would have in the economy soon to be inaugurated (John 14:12-14; 15:7; 16:23, 24). In the new age the believers, having been baptized by the Spirit into vital union with Christ and being indwelt continually by the Spirit (John 14:16, 17), would enjoy unique new privileges and blessings in prayer.

As a result of union with Christ, prayer was to become *a partnership of the believer with his Lord.* It is because his own would soon become a living part of him (Eph. 5:30) and share both his service and his glory that Jesus said, "Greater works than these shall he (the believer) do" (John 14:12). The believer would do these "greater works" through prayer. "And whatsoever ye ask in my name, that will I do, that the Father may be glorified in the Son. If ye shall ask anything in my name, I will do it" (John 14:13, 14). True prayer "in Christ's name" can be offered only by believers linked with Christ in a partnership of life and destiny.

As a result of union with Christ, *prayer was to become unlimited in its potential* within the will of God. "If ye abide in me" (depend upon your union with me) "and my words abide in you" (submit to my word and my will), "ye shall ask what ye will, and it shall be done unto you" (John 15:7).

As a result of union with Christ, *prayer was to be offered in his name.* Conversely, union with Christ would be the *prerequisite* for prayer in his name. Praying "in his name" is praying a prayer that Christ might pray; hence it is sure of an answer. This is what Jesus meant when he declared, "Whatever ye shall ask the Father in my name, he will give it you. Hitherto have ye asked nothing in my name" (John 16:23, 24). They had not yet prayed "in his name" because he had not yet died, risen, and given the Holy Spirit to baptize them into vital union with himself.

As a result of union with Christ *prayer was to be directed to the Father.* This is stated in Jesus' words, "In that day ye shall ask me nothing. Verily, verily, I say unto you, whatsoever ye shall ask the Father in my name, he will give it you" (John 16:23). At Pentecost the Holy Spirit baptized believers into union with Christ, so that they could pray in his name *to the Father.* The order of prayer, then, is *to the Father, in the name of Christ, by the power of the Holy Spirit* (Jude 1:20).

SERVICE

Service is any work performed for the benefit of another. In the case of God's people, service is to be first rendered to God and then to one's fellow man. If we love our Creator-Redeemer we will necessarily love his creatures as well (Exod. 20:1-17; Matt. 22:34-40).

SERVICE FOR GOD. *Service for God is a ministry of sacrifice.* It is the act of presenting our redeemed bodies "a living sacrifice to God" (Rom. 12:1). In the New Testament such priestly service in sacrifice toward God includes the dedication of self (Rom. 12:1), the sacrifice of the life in ceaseless praise (Heb. 13:15), and the sacrifice of material possessions in giving to God (Heb. 13:16).

The priest of the Old Testament typifies the believer's service of sacrifice. As he was born into the priestly family, likewise the believer is set apart by being born into God's family. As he was ceremonially cleansed by a once-for-all bathing at the beginning of his ministry (Exod. 29:4), so the believer is cleansed wholly and once-for-all at the moment he is saved (Tit. 3:5; 1 Cor. 6:11). This once-for-all bathing was followed, however, by a *partial* bathing at the bronze laver before any priestly service was undertaken. The New Testament believer, too, though wholly cleansed and forgiven when he becomes saved, is at all times to confess any known sin in order to be qualified for spiritual service and fellowship with God.

Service for God is a ministry of worship. Worship is basic to service in all ages. Acceptable service can only spring out of spiritual worship. Old Testament priests were governed in their worship by two prohibitions. No "strange" (unauthorized) incense was to be burned (speaking symbolically of man-devised religion and mere formality in worship—Exod. 30:9). Also, no "strange" fire was to be kindled (symbolizing the substitution of fleshly emotion for true spiritual zeal—Lev. 10:1; Col. 2:23).

Service for God is a ministry of intercession. The New Testament priest-believer has unhindered access to God on the basis of the blood of Christ continually presented in intercession before God (Rom. 8:26,

27; Heb. 10:19). Although the Mosaic priests represented the people before God, only the high priest himself could enter the Holiest Place, and this only once a year, and always with sacrificial blood. This prefigures Christ, who opened the way for all believers to draw near to God in intercession for others.

SERVICE FOR MAN. *Service for man is the inevitable result of service for God.* Dedication to God's will brings consecration, and with consecration spiritual anointing to serve man (Rom. 12:1, 2).

Service for man entails the exercise of spiritual gifts (Rom. 12:3-8). A gift is administered by the indwelling Spirit. The Spirit himself performs the service, employing the Christian as an instrument (1 Cor. 12:7-11). Normally the Spirit-filled life is active in service. Occasionally, however, it is God's will for all activity to cease and for the believer to "come apart . . . and rest awhile" (Mark 6:31).

STEWARDSHIP

A steward is someone who is entrusted with the management of the property of another. Christians are stewards because all that they are or have is given as a trust from God and is to be used for his glory. Stewardship is the use we make of all that God entrusts to us in the form of life, health, talents, and material possessions.

THE STEWARDSHIP OF LIFE. The believer belongs to God by creation and re-creation; hence he is to give *his whole being* to God *first*—before he attempts to give anything else (2 Cor. 8:5). This giving of oneself is concretely performed by presenting one's body to the Lord (Rom. 12:1), since in reality it already belongs to him anyway (1 Cor. 6:19, 20). This means one's time and energy are to be given to God.

THE STEWARDSHIP OF TALENT. Both natural endowments and spiritual gifts are to be freely and wholly given over to God to glorify him in service to man (Rom. 12:1-3).

THE STEWARDSHIP OF POSSESSIONS. This includes acquiring, possessing, and distributing material possessions for God's glory and man's benefit. For a Christian, *acquiring* money is to be actuated by the principle of doing everything "to the glory of God" (1 Cor. 10:31). *Possessing money* is to be guided by the principle that all a believer possesses, whether little or much, is a trust from God, held only as he directs, and always subject to his control. *Distributing money* is to be guided by Christ's example (2 Cor. 8:9), by yieldedness to God's will

(2 Cor. 8:2), by the principle of cheerful liberality (2 Cor. 9:7), and by the giving of oneself (2 Cor. 8:5). It is to be done in a systematic manner (1 Cor. 16:2), relying on God to graciously sustain the giver (2 Cor. 9:8-10). The believer realizes that true wealth is spiritual rather than material (Mark 8:36, 37).

OLD TESTAMENT PROPHECY

The pre-announcement by God of a certain thing he intends to do is called *prophecy*. Thus prophecy is actually history foretold. It forms a large part of divine revelation: nearly one-fourth of Holy Scripture was predictive when it was penned. The large number of biblical predictions that have now been literally and precisely fulfilled furnish a solid basis for deducing that all remaining prophecies will be as literally realized. Major themes of Old Testament prophecy include the following.

PROPHECY OF MESSIAH'S ADVENT. So completely was the present age of the outcalling of the Church hidden in the counsels of God that the Old Testament prophets saw the two advents as one. They were unable to determine how the two lines of prediction, one centering in his first advent and the other in his second advent, could be fulfilled *time*-wise (cf. 1 Pet. 1:10, 11). Jesus' quotation of Isaiah 61:1, 2 illustrates this. He ceased abruptly when he had finished reading about the features predicted for the first advent (Luke 4:16-21), making no mention of the remaining features to be fulfilled at his second advent. The angel Gabriel, too, when announcing the ministry of Christ, combined the undertakings which belong to both advents (Luke 1:31-33). Old Testament seers envisioned the Coming One as both an unresisting sacrificial Lamb (Isa. 52:13 – 53:12) and a glorious, conquering Lion (Jer. 23:5, 6).

Prophecy stipulated that the Messiah would be of the tribe of Judah (Gen. 49:10) and of the house of David (Isa. 11:1, 2; Jer. 33:20, 21); that he would be virgin-born (Gen. 3:15; Isa. 7:14) in Bethlehem of Judea (Mic. 5:2); that he would die an atoning death (Isa. 53:1-12) by crucifixion (Psa. 22:1-21; Zech. 12:10); that he would rise from the dead (Heb. 11:17-19; Psa. 16:8-11; Isa. 53:10-12); and that he would return to earth a second time (Deut. 30:3) in glory and power (Dan. 7:13, 14).

PROPHECY OF THE MESSIANIC KINGDOM. This is a very extensive forecast of Israel's restoration from worldwide dispersion to her own land, conversion at the second advent, and marvelous blessing as head of the nations (Deut. 28:13) in the kingdom age to come (Deut. 30:3-10; Isa. 11:1-16; 12:1-6; 35:1-10; 54:1−55:13; Jer. 23:3-8; Ezek. 36:32-38).

PROPHECY CONCERNING THE DAY OF THE LORD. The day of the Lord encompasses the prolonged period extending from the second advent and its accompanying earth judgments to the end of the kingdom age (Isa. 2:10-22; Zech. 12:1−14:21). Because the day of the Lord is closely associated with the second advent and the kingdom, Scripture prophecies regarding this "day" are very extensive.

PROPHECY CONCERNING THE TRIBULATION. The Tribulation is the time of unprecedented trouble in the earth preceding Christ's second advent (Deut. 4:29, 30; Psa. 2:5; Isa. 24:16-20; Jer. 30: 4-7; Dan. 12:1). It centers in Israel's end-time woes previous to her restoration and is distinctively "the time of Jacob's trouble" (Jer. 30:4-7), the period of chastisement for Israel's national sins.

PROPHECY CONCERNING THE NATIONS. Predictions about the nations begin with the descendants of Noah (Gen. 9:25-27). The various nations contiguous to Israel, such as Egypt, Babylon, Assyria, Chaldea, Moab, Ammon, Philistia, etc. form the subject of a large body of predictions. Daniel had visions of monarchies that would rule the world from his own time (about 600 B.C.) until the second advent of Christ (Dan. 2:37-45; 7:1-14). This entire period is called "the times of the Gentiles" (Luke 21:24) and encompasses the years during which Israel will be in servitude to foreign powers or in dispersion among the nations. The judgment of the nations (Joel 3:2-16; Zeph. 3: 8) and the eventual blessing of the Gentiles in the kingdom age are also subjects of prediction (Isa. 11:10; 42:1, 6; 49:6, 22; 60:3; 62:2).

PROPHECY CONCERNING ISRAEL. All Scripture from the Abrahamic Covenant (Gen. 12:1-3) to the end of Malachi relates directly or indirectly to God's elect people, Israel. To them has been granted a national entity (Jer. 31:36), a land (Gen. 13:15), a king (Jer. 33:21), a kingdom (Dan. 7:14), and a throne (2 Sam. 7:16; Psa. 89:36). These blessings may be interrupted by sin and divine chastisement, but they can never be abrogated; their fulfillment is certain.

PROPHECY OF ISRAEL'S DISPERSION AND RESTORATION. God prophesied that his people would be scattered because of sin (Lev. 26:14-39; Deut. 28:15-68; Jer. 18:15-17), but that they would also be regathered, converted, and blessed with every covenant promise made to them (Deut. 30:1-10; Jer. 23:3-8; Ezek. 37:21-28).

Worshipers and tourists mass at the Western (Wailing) Wall near Herod's ancient Temple site. *(IGTO photo)*

NEW TESTAMENT PROPHECY

The New Testament records the fulfillment of prophecies concerning the first advent of Christ and advances and broadens the message of prophecy contained in the Old Testament. This is particularly true in respect to Israel's sin and present worldwide dispersion, her regathering and suffering during the great tribulation (Matt. 24:4-51; Rev. 6:1 – 18:24), and her establishment in kingdom blessing (Rom.

11:25-36; Rev. 20:1-9). However, the new age and the new divine purpose, together with the judgment of believers and unbelievers and the eternal state of the saved and lost, constitute lines of truth which are confined solely to the New Testament.

THE NEW AGE. This period between the first and second advents is unrevealed in the Old Testament but constitutes a major New Testament prediction (Matt. 13:1-50; John 14:1 – 16:33; Rom. 9:1 – 11:36; 2 Tim. 3:1-9; Rev. 2:1 – 3:22).

THE NEW DIVINE PURPOSE. The Church, composed of saved Jews and Gentiles (1 Cor. 10:32) comprehends the new people of God (Acts 15:14-18). Its position is outlined and its earthly career and heavenly destiny are foreseen in Matthew 16:18; John 14:1-3, Philippians 3:20, 21; and First Thessalonians 4:13-17.

JUDGMENT OF THE BELIEVER'S WORKS

In dealing with judgment as it affects the believer, the doctrine of salvation must be clearly distinguished from the doctrine of rewards. The judgment of the believer's works *in no case* involves the issue of salvation, but simply that of rewards. Rewards depend on the quality of life and service *after* salvation.

THE DOCTRINE OF SALVATION. The judgment of the believer's sins at the cross (John 12:31) resulted in the death of Christ and the justification of the believer, who can now never again be faced with the penalty of sin, eternity in Gehenna (John 3:18; 5:24; Rom. 5: 1; 8:1; 1 Cor. 11:32). Salvation is by faith and is a gift, totally separate from works (Eph. 2:8, 9), and must never be confused with the issue of service.

THE DOCTRINE OF REWARDS. Although all the believer's sins have been atoned for and the penalty fully remitted (Heb. 10:17), every work must nevertheless come into judgment (2 Cor. 5:10; Rom. 14:10; Eph. 6:8; Col. 3:24, 25). The result is either bestowal or forfeiture of rewards (1 Cor. 3:11-15). This judgment occurs immediately following the coming of Christ to receive his glorified Church (1 Cor. 4:5; 2 Tim. 4:8; Rev. 22:12). Sinning saints who are unproductive in spiritual service will not only forfeit future rewards in eternity but will also be chastised in this life so that they may not be condemned with the unsaved (1 Cor. 11:32).

JUDGMENT OF THE WICKED

THE BASIS OF JUDGMENT. *All* of God's intelligent creatures, angels as well as men, will face judgment for their works. This includes redeemed man, as noted in the preceding section, as well as unredeemed man. Although Gehenna, also called "the lake of fire," was prepared for the Devil and his fallen angels rather than for human beings (Matt. 25:41; Rev. 20:10), unbelieving men must go there (Rev. 20:15). This fact is true not because the unsaved have been good or bad by human standards, but because they have rejected the knowledge of God through his creation and the conviction of sin through the Holy Spirit (Rom. 1:18-20; 2:14, 15). Men go to hell, therefore, because they fail to seek forgiveness and cleansing from the infinitely holy God on the basis of the righteousness of Christ (Rom. 3:23-26). Thus many "very good" or "highly moral" people (judged by human standards) will go to hell.

DEGREES OF PUNISHMENT. Just as there will be bestowal or forfeiture of rewards for the saved in an eventual sin-cleansed universe, so there will be degrees of punishment in the one isolation ward of eternity for sin and all sinners. This place is called Gehenna or "the lake of fire" (Rev. 20:11-15). This is the inescapable meaning of judgment according to works. No human being can keep the moral law of God to God's satisfaction. This is why God provided salvation through faith in Christ. Nevertheless, men are held accountable to keep the moral law of God *in degree.* This will not admit them to heaven, however, because sinful man can never meet the standard of infinite, divine holiness. But to the extent that men keep the moral laws of God their punishment in hell will be lessened. An unsaved man may not be able to refrain from hating his neighbor, but he can avoid killing him (Exod. 20:13). He may not be able to curb his petty stealing, but he had better not commit grand larceny (Exod. 20:15)!

THE RESURRECTIONS. There are two resurrections. The first embraces the redeemed (1 Cor. 15:22, 23; 1 Thess. 4:14-17). It is in stages and is *almost* entirely before the thousand years of the kingdom age. However, the end of it is coterminous with the second resurrection of the unredeemed at the end of the kingdom age (Rev. 20:5) since millennial saints will die and must of necessity be judged with the wicked. This is why "the book of life" is opened with "the books" in which the works of the unsaved are recorded (Rev. 20:12, 15). The white throne judgment, however, is predominantly a judgment of condemnation because it comprises the vast multitudes of the lost and the wicked from Adam to the end of time.

ETERNAL STATE OF THE REDEEMED

A SIN-CLEANSED UNIVERSE. God is working through Christ to effect a sin-cleansed universe. This will be accomplished by the resurrection and glorification of all the redeemed of all ages and the creation of new heavens and a new earth, "in which dwelleth righteousness" (2 Pet. 3:13; Rev. 21:1 – 22:5). All evil and evildoers will be rigidly isolated in Gehenna, the one quarantine ward in a sinless universe (Rev. 20:14, 15). This is the culmination toward which God's redemptive program for man is moving.

Heaven as the abode of God is only part of this sin-cleansed universe. To be sure, the unfallen angels and redeemed saints will have access to heaven, when "God shall be all in all" (1 Cor. 15:28). But the new heavens and the new earth will also be the habitation of the redeemed.

THE NEW JERUSALEM. This city is not heaven per se, since it descends "from God out of heaven" (Rev. 21:2). Yet together with heaven it is the eternal abode and destiny of the redeemed of all the ages. The inhabitants of the city will be God the Father, glorified Old Testament saints (Heb. 11:40), New Testament saints, myriads of holy angels, and our blessed Redeemer himself (Heb. 12:22, 23; Rev. 21:11-21). Both Israel and the Church appear prominently in the city (Rev. 21:12, 14). The great, high wall of the city denotes the security of its inhabitants, bathed in God's radiant and unveiled glory (1 Cor. 15:28).

BACKGROUND STUDIES

Extrabiblical Writings

Diana, the love goddess, bewitched the Ephesians. *(Russ Busby photo)*

THE APOCRYPHA

Introduction

DEFINITION. The Old Testament Apocrypha consist of fourteen books which came into existence largely between 200 B.C. and A.D. 200.

THE OLD TESTAMENT APOCRYPHA

Order in English Versions	Classification	Subject
1. First Esdras	Historical (621-539 B.C.)	Parallel to Chronicles, Ezra-Nehemiah
2. Second Esdras	Apocalyptic	Apocalyptic visions
3. Tobit	Didactic; fictional romance	Trials of a godly man and his vindication
4. Judith	Didactic; fictional romance	Exploits of a godly woman
5. Additions to Esther	Legendary additions to Esther	Hand of God in Esther
6. The Wisdom of Solomon	Wisdom literature	Antidote against idolatry
7. Ecclesiasticus	Wisdom literature	Everyday morality
8. Baruch (with Jeremiah's Letter)	Prophetic additions to Jeremiah	Confessions, promises, warning against idolatry
9. Azariah's Prayer and the Song of the Three	Legendary additions to the Book of Daniel	Prayer and praise for deliverance
10. Susanna		Defense of virtue
11. Bel and the Dragon		Exposé of idolatry
12. The Prayer of Manasseh	Legendary addition to 2 Chronicles	Manasseh's repentance in exile
13. First Maccabees	Historical (175-135 B.C.)	Struggle of Judaism against Hellenism
14. Second Maccabees	Historical (175-160 B.C.)	Panegyric of the Maccabean revolt

CONNECTION WITH THE OLD TESTAMENT. The Apocrypha formed part of the sacred literaure of the Jews in Alexandria, Egypt. With the exception of Second Esdras, these writings are found interspersed among the canonical Old Testament books in the ancient copies of the Septuagint (the first Greek version of the Old Testament). From the Septuagint they passed into the Latin Vulgate (translated about A.D. 400) and into early English translations. However, since 1629 they have been omitted in some editions. Since 1827 they have been omitted from practically all Protestant editions of the Bible.

QUESTION OF CANONICAL AUTHORITY. In its early years the Christian Church used as its Old Testament the Septuagint with the Apocrypha rather than the Hebrew Old Testament. For this reason both the Eastern and Western Church began to accept the Apocrypha as canonical, despite strong scholarly warning to the contrary. (It is important to note that the Hebrew Old Testament never contained any of the apocryphal books.) The Roman Church recognized eleven of the fourteen apocryphal books as canonical, rejecting only First and Second Esdras and the Prayer of Manasseh. (These were placed in an appendix at the end of the New Testament.)

At the advent of the Reformation, Protestant scholars renewed their commitment to the sole authority of God-inspired Scripture and in consequence rejected the Apocrypha, accepting instead only the books of the ancient Hebrew Canon.

The First Book of Esdras

First Esdras consists of an independent and somewhat free version of portions of Second Chronicles and Ezra-Nehemiah. The account extends from Josiah's Passover (2 Chron. 35, 621 B.C.) to Cyrus' Decree after the Exile (Ezra 1:1-3) in 539 B.C. The interesting thing about First Esdras is that it contains a section (3:1 – 5:6) that has no parallel in the Hebrew Bible. This is the account of a competition between three Jewish pages at Darius' court intended to determine the meaning of true wisdom. Zerubbabel, who was to become the governor of the restored community, won the contest. The prize was permission of the Jews to return to Palestine. The work ends with the reading of the Law by Ezra (9:36-55), as in Nehemiah 7:38 – 8:12.

The purpose of the unknown author of First Esdras was to emphasize the contributions of Josiah, Zerubbabel, and Ezra in reforming Israelite worship. The book is commonly dated toward the end of the second century B.C.

The Second Book of Esdras

Second Esdras differs from the other books of the Apocrypha in being an apocalypse, that is, an "unveiling" of the future. Like the book of Daniel and the Revelation, which are also apocalypses, Second Esdras contains numerous symbols involving mysterious numbers, strange beasts, and the disclosure of hidden truths through angelic visitants. The original and main part of the book (Chapters 3 – 14) was written by an unknown Jew toward the end of the first century A.D. It consists of a series of seven revelations – 3:1 – 5:20; 5:21 – 6:34; 6:35 – 9:25; 9:38 – 10:59; 11:1 – 12:51; 13:1-58; and 14:1-48. In these disclosures the seer is instructed by the angel Uriel. Second Esdras wrestles with the problem of theodicy, that is, the reconciliation of

God's justice, goodness, and power with the many evils that beset mankind. Chapters 1 and 2 and chapters 15 and 16 are later Christian additions to the original Jewish apocalypse.

Tobit

This religious fictionalized romance concerns Tobit, a devout Jew of Thisbe in Naphtali of Galilee. With his wife, Hannah, and their son Tobias, Tobit was carried away captive to Nineveh in the reign of the Assyrian emperor Shalmaneser IV (782-772 B.C.). In Nineveh he continued his good deeds, especially the giving of alms and the providing of proper burial to those of his own race cruelly slain by Sennacherib (705-681 B.C.). When the Emperor heard of this practice, Tobit was forced to flee Nineveh. But when Sennacherib's son, Esarhaddon (681-669 B.C.), came to the throne, Tobit was enabled to return to the capital through the influence of his nephew, Ahikar, who became the chief minister of the new king.

Improved fortune, however, was not unmixed with tragedy. Tobit was required to sleep outdoors in the courtyard because his continued practice of providing decent burial for his murdered countrymen rendered him ceremonially "unclean." One night as he slept, the droppings of sparrows fell into his eyes and cost him his sight. After four years of incurable blindness, he called upon God in utter despair.

At this very moment in Ecbatana, the capital of Media (in Persia), one Sarah was uttering a prayer for deliverance from her own plight. Sarah's condition was as tragic as Tobit's. Her seven husbands had been slain one by one in the bridal chamber by the jealous demon Asmodaeus. But now the prayers of both Tobit and Sarah were being heard. God was sending the angel Raphael ("God heals"), disguised as a man, to help them.

Tobit, believing that the time of his death was drawing near, made plans to send Tobias to Rages in Media, not far from Ecbatana, to recover from a kinsman, Gabael, a sum of money (ten talents of silver, about $20,000) which had been deposited for safekeeping with him years before. Raphael, posing as a dependable kinsman who knew the way, was engaged to conduct Tobias on the trip. In bidding them goodby, Tobit unwittingly implored God that his angel attend them.

As the travelers camped at the Tigris River, a large fish literally leaped at Tobias from the water, furnishing them a good meal. At Raphael's suggestion the heart, liver, and gall of the fish were saved for future use.

Before they arrived at Ecbatana, Raphael proceeded to tell young Tobias about Sarah, the attractive daughter of Raguel. He pointed out that by reason of kinship Tobias was the only eligible husband left for her. Before he was through with the matter, Raphael had persuaded Tobias to marry Sarah, instructing him to exorcize the husband-killing demon, Asmodaeus, by burning the heart and liver of the fish on the incense fire in the bridal chamber.

After the arrival, exchange of greetings, and consummation of the marriage, Tobias carried out Raphael's instruction, and the smoke and smell of the burned heart and liver of the fish drove Asmodaeus away into upper Egypt, the traditional home of magic and witchcraft (cf. Exod. 7:11), where Raphael quickly followed and fettered him. In the meantime, fearing the worst, Sarah's father had had a grave dug during the night. The next morning, however, he was overjoyed to find his new son-in-law alive. At Raguel's insistence a fourteen-day wedding celebration was carried on. During this time Raphael went on alone to Rages and obtained the money from Gabael.

Back in Nineveh, Tobit and Hannah were in despair at their son's long absence. What a rejoicing took place when Tobias returned with his new wife and Raphael! Then Tobias took the gall of the fish, whose heart and liver had already brought such wonderful deliverance, and with it anointed his father's eyes, according to Raphael's directions. Immediately Tobit's sight was restored.

Gratitude overwhelmed the family, and they offered Raphael half the fortune. But at this point the angel revealed his true identity. He bade them thank God for his mercies and vanished. Tobit thereupon uttered a beautiful prayer of thanksgiving (chap. 13). The book ends happily with instructions of Tobit to Tobias and with predictions of mercy and blessing for God's people (chap. 14).

Judith

Judith, like Tobit, belongs to the category of religious fiction. It has both a patriotic and a didactic purpose. It relates the exciting story of how a small Jewish town, inspired by the example of a devout woman, withstood the overwhelming power of a pagan army. The first part of the book (chapters 1−7) describes in somewhat tedious detail how Nebuchadnezzar's general, Holofernes, invaded the west and at length laid siege to the Jewish town of Bethulia. Situated strategically in relation to the plain of Esdraelon and the central mountain ridge of

Palestine, this fortress city barred access to the road leading to Jerusalem.

Amazed that the Jews should offer such audacious resistance, Holofernes called the chieftains of the Ammonites and Moabites to inquire about this strange people. Achior the Ammonite gave Holofernes a full account of the history of the Jews, declaring that the secret of their success was their faith in God. Since they were invincible as long as they did not sin against their God, Achior urged Holofernes to find out if there were any defection among them regarding the Lord. He advised the proud pagan general to refrain from attacking them if no unfaithfulness were found (1:1–5:19).

Holofernes replied to Achior, "Who is God except Nebuchadnezzar?" and ordered Achior bound and delivered to the foot of the steep hill on which Bethulia stood, to share the fate of the doomed city. The Jews, finding him, took him into the city. Meanwhile an immense army of 182,000 troops besieged the city for thirty-four days, making every effort to force its capitulation by hunger and thirst. When the cisterns of the city became empty, Ozias, the mayor of Bethulia, and his chief advisers decided to capitulate should no relief arrive within five days (5:20–7:32).

Judith, a beautiful and pious widow, is introduced in chapter 8. She was grieved by the decision to surrender. Such a course of action would open the road to Jerusalem and mean the destruction of the Temple and the nation. So Judith announced a bold plan. She declared that she would leave the city with her maid, hinting that God through her would accomplish Bethulia's deliverance. After first humbling herself before God in sackcloth and ashes, she put on her finest attire and proceeded from her beleaguered city to the camp of the pagan armies with her maid, who carried a bag of ceremonially clean food in her hand (8:1–10:5).

The Assyrian guards, smitten by Judith's beauty, conducted her at her request to Holofernes. She assured the general that Achior had told him the truth, that no harm could come to the Jews unless they would sin against their God. But the general need not despair, she assured him, since sin had already overtaken them in their plans to eat consecrated food to relieve their hunger. They would capitulate, she said, because their God-given resistance would vanish.

Delighted, Holofernes invited Judith to be his guest for three days. She accepted on the condition that she be allowed to eat only the clean food she had brought with her, and that she be allowed to go each night to the fountain of Bethulia to perform her ceremonial washings. On the fourth night Holofernes invited Judith to a banquet in his tent. Her beauty, wit, and finery made her the center of attention. After the subaltern officers left and Holofernes was alone with Judith, he fell asleep, overcome by the many toasts he had drunk to Judith's beauty.

Fortified by prayer, Judith quickly seized Holofernes' scimitar. With two quick blows she severed the general's head and handed it to her maid, who deposited it in her food bag. Both women left the camp without suspicion. However, this time Judith bypassed the spring and returned to Bethulia with her trophy.

The citizens of Bethulia were electrified with joy and courage. At daybreak they fell on the sleeping and leaderless army, which became easy prey to them. The huge host was cut to pieces in the ensuing confusion and the survivors were pursued in flight beyond Damascus. A great thanksgiving took place and Judith sang a psalm of praise to the Lord (10:6 – 16:25).

Written in Hebrew in the latter part of the second century B.C., the story has been transmitted to us today in three Greek and two Latin versions, as well as in a Syriac Version and later Hebrew recensions. It has inspired numerous works of painting, sculpture, and literature.

Additions to Esther

Apocryphal Esther consists of six passages (105 verses) which are not found in the Hebrew text of the canonical book. These additions were interspersed throughout the Greek translation in the Septuagint. They were apparently penned about 100 B.C. by an Alexandrian Jew who was eager to inject a more pronounced religious note into the canonical story and heighten its anti-Gentile character. The additions frequently refer to God, emphasize his choice of Israel, and highlight prayer. Jerome, when making the Latin Vulgate in the fourth century A.D., removed all the additions and put them in an appendix at the end of Esther, leaving only the original Hebrew as the text.

Some of the additions had evidently been introduced by Lysimachus, an Alexandrian Jew who resided at Jerusalem and translated the canonical book about 100 B.C. Other additions appear to have been inserted some years later.

The Wisdom of Solomon

This important apocryphal book of nineteen chapters belongs to the category of wisdom literature. As in the case of its sister apocry-

Underground "Solomon's stables," built by Crusaders over earlier stalls (*Russ Busby photo*)

phal book of Ecclesiasticus and the canonical book of Ecclesiastes, the Wisdom of Solomon (second century B.C.) expounds practical righteous living through fellowship with God and obedience to the moral law of God. The author, unknown but probably Jewish, personifies wisdom as a divine attribute of God (7:25-27). This contrasts with the canonical book of Proverbs (Prov. 8:22-36), where wisdom is more than the personification of an attribute of God or of the will of God, and is instead a distinct foreshadowing of the coming Messiah. Certain peculiar conceptions of the Logos and the Holy Spirit are also prominent features of the book (cf. John 1:1 and Heb. 1:1, 2 with Wisdom 7:26). Wisdom 9:17 combines God, wisdom, and the Holy Spirit in a manner that suggests the Christian doctrine of the Trinity.

The book falls into three sections. The first section (chaps. 1 – 5) is eschatological, portraying in vivid contrast the fate of the righteous and the ungodly. The second section (chaps. 6 – 10) is a noble poem extolling goodness and praising wisdom (which gives its names to the book). The third section (chaps. 11 – 19) is a theological interpretation of history, broken by a dissertation on the origin and evils of idolatry (chaps. 13 – 15). Chapters 11, 12, 16, 17, 18, and 19 contrast the lot of Israel in the wilderness with that of the Egyptians during the plagues. The writer seeks to prove two propositions: first, that "by what things a man sins, by these he is punished" (11:16); second, that by what things Israel's foes were punished, by these the Lord's people "in their need were benefited" (11:5).

Ecclesiasticus

Like the Wisdom of Solomon of the apocryphal books and like Job, certain Psalms, Proverbs, and Ecclesiastes of the canonical books, Ecclesiasticus belongs to the wisdom literature of the Hebrews. Called also "The Wisdom of Jesus, Son of Sirach," Ecclesiasticus (Latin "The Church Book") is a long and valuable ethical treatise (51 chapters) and contains a wide range of instructions in general morality and practical godliness. It is patterned after the model of Proverbs, Ecclesiastes, and Job, and has been popular in the Roman Catholic Church, where it is accorded canonical status.

Ecclesiasticus was composed originally in Hebrew by Ben Sira at about 180 B.C. and was later translated into Greek, in 132 B.C. Jerome knew the Hebrew text. In 1896 fragments of it turned up in the Cairo Geniza and also in the caves at Qumran. About two-thirds of the Hebrew text has been found.

Baruch

This book of five chapters purports to be the work of Jeremiah's secretary, Baruch (Jer. 32:12; 36:4), written during the exile in Babylon and sent to Jerusalem to be read on festal occasions as a confession of sins (1:14). Part one, in prose, consists of an introduction (1:1-14) and a confession of Israel's guilt (1:15 – 3:8). Part two is composed of two poems. One extols wisdom as the Lord's special gift to Israel (3:9 – 4:4). The other is occupied with the subject of comfort and restoration (4:5 – 5:9).

The book was originally written in Hebrew but exists today only in Greek, from which a number of ancient versions had been made. The date when the several component parts of the book were brought together is commonly placed between 150 and 60 B.C.

The Letter of Jeremiah

The so-called Letter of Jeremiah purports to be the copy of an epistle dispatched by Jeremiah to the Jews who were about to be deported to Babylon in 597 B.C. The letter warns against the peril of idolatry, so rampant in the country to which they were being taken. The author elaborates on Jeremiah 10:11: "Thus shall ye say to them: The gods who did not make the heavens and the earth shall perish from the earth and from under the heavens." The author also draws upon Jeremiah 10:3-9, Jeremiah 14, and Psalm 115:4-8 and echoes the anti-idol sentiment of Isaiah 40:18-20 and 41:6, 7. The refrain "this shows that there are no gods" runs through the discourse (verses 16, 23, 40, 44, 52, 56, 65, and 69).

The letter is commonly dated in the second century B.C. The oldest manuscript remains of the book are a tiny fragment of Greek papyrus containing a part of verses 43 and 44. These were discovered in Cave Seven at Qumran and date from about 100 B.C. Though the book has usually been attached to Baruch, the Revised Standard Version prints it as a separate book, since it actually has nothing to do with Baruch.

Azariah's Prayer and the Song of the Three

This is one of three important apocryphal additions to the canonical book of Daniel. The other two are Susanna and Bel and the Dragon. At chapter 3, verse 23 The Prayer and Song follow the account of the fiery furnace into which three Jewish captives were thrown for refusing to worship the golden image which Nebuchadnezzar had set up. The interpolation is in three parts: 1) Azariah's prayer (vv. 1-22) (Azariah being the Hebrew name for Abednego, his pagan name—Dan. 1:7); 2) description of the fiery furnace (vv. 23-27); and 3) The Song of the Three (vv. 28-68).

The refrains "Blessed art thou, O Lord . . . Blessed art thou . . . Bless the Lord" run through the entire song (vv. 26-28), endowing it with a deep solemnity and majestic rhythm. The unknown poet in the second or first century B.C. derived much of his inspiration from the antiphonal liturgies which appear in Psalms 136 and 148.

The History of Susanna

Of the three additions to Daniel, this tale of the triumph of virtue over villainy constitutes one of the finest short stories in world literature. The tale runs as follows.

Susanna, the lovely and virtuous wife of Joakim, a wealthy and honorable Jew of Babylon, becomes the object of the lust of two unscrupulous elders who had been made judges in the Jewish community. One morning they discovered each other near Joakim's garden, where Susanna walked, and acknowledged their mutual passion for the woman. They agreed to accost Susanna, but were repulsed with scorn. To protect themselves they accuse their victim. They betake themselves to the city and issue a summons to Susanna. Appearing with her household, she is ordered to be unveiled, while the elders appear as witnesses against her before the assembled people. They declare that they saw her commit adultery in her husband's garden with a youth who had escaped. The testimony of the elders leads the whole synagogue to condemn Susanna.

As Susanna is on the way to be executed in accordance with Mosaic Law, a youth (Daniel) questions the verdict and reopens the trial. He cross-examines the two witnesses. The one asserts the crime was enacted under "a mastic tree," the other under "an evergreen oak" (RSV). The discrepancy condemns both as false witnesses. Susanna ("lily") is exonerated, Daniel ("God is my Judge") is lauded, and the two elders are gagged, cast in a ravine, and devoured by fire from heaven (Deut. 19:16-21).

The position of this addition to canonical Daniel varies. In the Septuagint and the Latin Vulgate it follows chapter 12, being numbered chapter 13. In other ancient versions, such as Theodotian, Old Latin, Coptic, and Arabic it is prefixed to chapter 1 (cf. Susanna 1:45). The date of *all* the additions to Daniel is evidently the second or first century B.C. Hebrew (or Aramaic) was apparently the original language in which they were written.

Bel and the Dragon

This addition to the book of Daniel consists of two popular tales, both designed to satirize the folly of idolatry and expose the snare of pagan priestcraft. The first story concerns Bel or Marduk, the patron deity of Babylon. Bel's idol is represented as devouring huge quantities of food and drink every night. By this means the image was thought to prove itself a living god. But Daniel ridiculed the king's credulousness. In anger Cyrus, who became king in 538 B.C., challenged the seventy priests of Baal to tell him who was eating these provisions or die. If Bel were really eating them, then Daniel would die.

Playing the role of a clever detective, Daniel had a light coating of ash dust scattered on the floor after the king had personally placed the provisions in the temple and sealed all the doors with his own signet. Next morning as he and the king went to see what had transpired, they found the food gone and the seals unbroken. Gleefully Daniel interrupted the king's praise of Bel by pointing out to the king the footprints of the seventy priests with their wives and families on the ash-strewn floor. Then the king was enraged. He seized the priests and their wives and children. When they showed him the secret doors through which they were accustomed to enter and devour what was on the table, he "put them to death and gave Bel over to Daniel, who destroyed it and its temple" (1:22).

The dragon story concerns a serpent worshiped as a deity (cf. Num. 21:8, 9; 2 Kings 18:4). Daniel refuses to prostrate himself before the serpent. Instead he challenges the king. If permission is granted him, he will destroy the creature alleged to be a god. Granted his request, Daniel prepares a mixture of pitch, fat, and hair in cake form. When fed to the dragon, the concoction causes the dragon to burst open. Infuriated, the Babylonians accuse the king of destroying their gods and becoming a Jew. They thereupon demand that Daniel be handed over to them.

Hard-pressed to save his own life, the king releases Daniel to them. They promptly throw him to the hungry lions (making a second time that Daniel was put into the lions' den—see Daniel 6:16-24). On the sixth day, while Habakkuk in Judea is carrying lunch to the reapers, the angel of the Lord appears to him and directs him to take the food to Daniel in the lions' den in Babylon. When the prophet pleads his inability to comply, the angel takes him by the hair and sets him down in Babylon "right over the den" (v. 36).

Daniel gets up and eats the lunch and the angel of the Lord returns Habakkuk to Judea. On the seventh day, when the king comes to mourn Daniel, he finds him hale and hearty among the lions. Glorifying Daniel's God, he pulls Daniel out and throws Daniel's enemies in. They are devoured immediately before Daniel's eyes (v. 42).

In the Septuagint, Bel and the Dragon is appended to chapter 12 of Daniel. In the Latin Vulgate it appears as chapter 14, Susanna constituting chapter 13. Along with the other Danielic additions, it belongs to the second or first century B.C..

The Prayer of Manasseh

This classic of penitential devotion is attributed to Manasseh ("Manasses" in Greek), the idolatrous king of Judah. It is thought to follow Second Chronicles 33:18, 19, which outlines the king's wicked reign and his repentance when carried away prisoner by the Assyrians. It is known from archeology that Esarhaddon (681-669 B.C.) rebuilt Babylon and that he summoned Manasseh to Nineveh to see his new palace. The prayer is divided into fifteen verses. This division is generally followed and appears in the Revised Standard Version of the Apocrypha.

The prayer itself is constructed in accord with the best liturgical forms and breathes throughout a deep note of genuine contrition and profound religious feeling. The date of composition is hard to determine with precision. Most scholars date it sometime in the last two centuries B.C. It is not known whether it was composed originally in Hebrew, Aramaic, or Greek. It has survived in Greek, Latin, Syriac, Armenian, and Ethiopic.

The First Book of Maccabees

This is a first-class historical work, consisting of sixteen chapters. It narrates the heroic struggle of the Jews for religious liberty and political independence during the years 175 to 135 B.C., featuring in particular the exploits of Judas Maccabeus, who is regarded as the central figure in Jewish resistance against encroaching Hellenism.

The book sketches the conquests of Alexander the Great and the division of his empire, giving the background of the origin of Greek rule in the East (1:1-9). Then the author outlines briefly the causes of the Maccabean revolt against the Seleucid king Antiochus Epiphanes (1:10-64). The beginning of the struggle under Mattathias, the aged priest of Modin, is highlighted (2:1-70). Then are portrayed at length the political and military careers of Mattathias' heroic sons Judas (3:1–9:22), Jonathan (9:23–12:53), and Simon (13:1–16:17). The book ends with a short notice of the rule of Simon's son, John Hyrcanus (134-104 B.C.).

The book presents the continual providence of God over his people during the Greek era and may be dated about 110 B.C. It was most certainly written in Hebrew, as Jerome distinctly avers. Though the original Hebrew was lost at an early period, the work has been preserved in Greek and Latin as well as in several versions based on the Greek.

The Second Book of Maccabees

This historical work of fifteen chapters claims to be a condensation of a five-volume history (now lost) authored by a Hellenistic Jew, Jason of Cyrene (2:23). Second Maccabees itself is anonymous. It covers part of the same period as First Maccabees (175-160 B.C.) and is primarily concerned with the history of Judas Maccabeus. The book opens with two letters from the Jews of Judea to their colleagues in Egypt (1:1-9; 1:10—2:18). Both epistles are concerned with the observance of the Feast of Dedication, which celebrated the reconsecration of the sanctuary after it had been profaned by Antiochus Epiphanes. After a prologue describing the nature of the book as a condensation of the history of the period written by Jason of Cyrene (2:19-32), the epitome proper follows 3:1—15:36); the book ends with a brief epilogue (15:37-39).

The epitome is a theological interpretation of the patriotic revolt against the paganistic encroachments led by Judas. The following main headings constitute a general summary: 1) Divine blessing upon Jerusalem in the protection of the Temple from desecration by Heliodorus during the devout administration of the high priest Onias under Seleucus IV, 187-175 B.C. (chapter 3); 2) Divine punishment of Jerusalem under Antiochus IV Epiphanes (175-163 B.C.), with profanation of the Temple and proscription of Judaism (chapters 4—7); 3) Divine deliverance and reconsecration of the Temple as a result of the heroism of Judas and his men (8:1—10:9); and 4) Divine help for Judas and his men in their victories during the reign of Demetrius I, 162-150 B.C. (14:1—15:36).

THE PSEUDEPIGRAPHA

The Pseudepigrapha constitute another body of religious literature beside the Apocrypha that came into being in the general period of 200 B.C. to A.D. 200. Although these books have many affinities with the Apocrypha, they never vied for canonical status or were considered canonical in any sense by either Jews or Christians. They are commonly called Pseudepigrapha ("false writings") because, though attributed to worthies of a much earlier age, such as Adam, Enoch, Noah, Moses, Elijah, Isaiah, etc., they were actually penned by men in the first two centuries B.C. and A.D. These works are largely apocalyptic, legendary, and didactic, frequently using history to propagate the issue of Judaism versus Hellenism. Some of the more important pseud-epigraphical works are described below.

The Book of Jubilees

This is one of the longest and most important books of the pseud-epigraphical literature. It is a revised version of the book of Genesis and the first twelve chapters of Exodus, rewritten from the point of view of later Judaism. The utmost importance is placed on the Mosaic Law, and the writer of Jubilees traces the origin of its various enactments to the patriarchal age. Strict separation between Jew and Gentile is taught, so much so that intermarriage is prohibited under penalty of death. Circumcision and the Sabbath are emphasized as distinctive marks of Judaism. The book takes its name from the author's chronology. He divides history into jubilees or fifty-year periods (Lev. 25:8-12). The treatise was written in the period 135 to 115 B.C., evidently by a Pharisaic Jew who sympathized with the Maccabean movement and favored strict separation from the demoralizing influences of Greek customs.

The Book of Enoch

This apocalypse is not a single book but is rather a library of at least five volumes penned by various authors at different periods in the last two centuries of the pre-Christian era. The following table describes the contents of the book.

The Book of Enoch has undoubtedly had a large influence on New Testament theology, particularly in its messianic conceptions. It is in the Book of Enoch that the term "Christ" first appears in Jewish literature as the designation of the coming messianic king. "The Son of Man" (cf. Dan. 7), "the Righteous One," and "the Elect One" (Acts 3:14; 7:52) are other messianic designations in Enoch that are prominent in the New Testament, as well as the concept of Messiah as Judge (cf. John 5:22). Messiah is also depicted as "preexisting" and as "sitting on the throne of his glory" (cf. John 1:1, 18; Matt. 25:31).

67

THE BOOK OF ENOCH	
Book and Date	*Contents*
Book 1 (Chaps. 1—36) Before 170 B.C.	Deals with problem of evil. Origin of evil is placed not in Adam's fall but in fallen angels of Gen. 6:1-8. Demons are the result of angelic cohabitation with women. Millennium is a time of sensuous enjoyment.
Book 2 (Chaps. 37—70) 94-79 B.C.	"The Similitudes." Denounces later Maccabean princes and their allies, the Sadducees. Solution of problem of evil is given as the advent of Messiah.
Book 3 (Chaps. 71—82)	"Book of Celestial Physics." Attempts to establish a Hebrew calendar to offset pagan calendars then in vogue.
Book 4 (Chaps. 83—90) 166-161 B.C.	Evil laid to failure of 70 shepherds (angels) to whom God entrusted Israel. Israel will be restored through a righteous family (Judas Maccabeus).
Book 5 (Chaps. 91—104) 134-95 B.C.	Author a Pharisee. He finds the solution to the problem of evil in neither an earthly messianic kingdom nor the advent of a great deliverer, but instead in the future life. Righteous will be raised as spirits. Wicked doomed to eternal punishment in hell.

The Ascension of Isaiah

This apocalypse is in three parts.

The Martyrdom (1:1-3; 5:2-14; first century B.C.) recounts Isaiah's death by being "sawn asunder with a wooden saw" under wicked King Manasseh. It is a Jewish sacred legend.

The Testament of Hezekiah (3:13b—4:18) is a Christian apocalypse showing how Isaiah's prophecy of Christ's second advent will be fulfilled.

The Vision of Isaiah (chaps. 6—11) is also Christian rather than Jewish, dating from the second century A.D. It depicts Isaiah's journey through the seven heavens to God's throne. There the voice of the Most High is heard speaking to his Son ("The Beloved"), bidding him to descend through the heavens to the world. The Son ("The Beloved") does this by means of the incarnation and the virgin birth. The Beloved's life, death, resurrection, and ascension are described, as well as his return to the seventh heaven and his placement at the right hand of the "Great Glory." (Note that these concepts were obviously taken from the New Testament Scriptures.)

The Testaments of the Twelve Patriarchs

Consisting of twelve small pamphlets, this work purports to contain the last utterances of Jacob's twelve sons. Each of these men is represented as calling his children around him on his deathbed and giving them words of counsel with regard to life, after the manner of Genesis 49. The work is apparently Jewish in origin (109-107 B.C.), with later Jewish and Christian interpolations. The Jewish origin of the original is suggested by the recovery of Aramaic fragments of the Testament of Levi from the Cairo Genizah and at Qumran.

Scholars maintain that there is no Jewish document that has had a greater influence on the New Testament, particularly upon the thinking of Paul. The work also represents a high-water mark in the ethical teaching of Judaism, especially upon the subject of forgiveness. Another important feature of the book is its exceptionally broad outlook, broader than any other document of the period. The book teaches, for example, that the Law was given "to illuminate every man" (not merely the Jew) and envisions worldwide salvation for Gentiles.

The Sibylline Oracles

Between the second century B.C. and the fifth century A.D. both Jews and Christians composed verses which they published under the name and authority of the ancient Sibyls (pagan seeresses). Of the fifteen ancient Jewish and Christian Oracles three books (numbers 9, 10, and 15) are lost, and some of the others exist only in fragments. The Jewish books (numbers 3, 4, and 5) are apocalyptic and predict the destruction of pagan kingdoms and the ultimate triumph of the Jew in the messianic kingdom (3:702-704; 5:418-427). The Sibylline Oracles share with other apocalyptic writings a deep dissatisfaction with present conditions, as well as an assurance that divine intervention in history will right human wrongs and vindicate the faith of God's elect.

The Books of Adam and Eve

Written in Aramaic during the first century A.D. by a Jew, this is a legendary amplification of the Genesis story of Adam and Eve which has survived in Latin and Greek manuscripts. Christian interpolations have been added to the original Jewish work. Legends are interwoven around the expulsion from paradise, Cain's murder of Abel, and Seth's birth. On his deathbed Adam is portrayed blessing his sixty-three children. In answer to the prayers of angels, Adam is pardoned and his soul consigned to the angels, who bury his body near the earthly paradise but carry his soul to the heavenly paradise to await the resurrection.

The author envisions a period of lawlessness and wickedness before the golden age of divinely manifested power on earth. Future judgment is emphasized. In contrast to the judgment of water at the flood, the final judgment is seen to be by fire. The "body" of Adam is said to be placed in "paradise in the third heaven," suggesting a heavenly counterpart to the physical body buried on earth.

The Psalms of Solomon

These are eighteen Psalms apparently written as a result of the destruction of Jerusalem by the Roman general Pompey in 63 B.C., called "the sinner," "the lawless one," and "the adversary." The invader breaks down Jerusalem's wall, enters the Temple, pollutes the altar, massacres many, and sends many others into exile. Retribution, however, overtakes the conqueror for his profanity. He is assassinated in Egypt and his unclaimed body tossed on the waves of the sea.

The psalms were written by several Pharisees. They stress the chief tenets of Pharisaism as a corrective to the erroneous teachings of Sadduceeism. They particularly emphasize 1) *the belief in theocracy.* In the face of Roman domination their slogan was "The Lord is King"; 2) *the belief in the Mosaic Law.* This was the divine ideal. True righteousness consists of meticulously observing its ordinances and avoiding any violation of ceremonial purity. But the Pharisaism reflected here is on a much higher plane than that which Jesus encountered almost a century later. Much more stress is laid on the inner spiritual life of repentance, faith, and prayer; 3) *the belief in the future life.* The righteous will rise to life eternal, the wicked to eternal death. However, physical resurrection, a common tenet of Pharisaism, does not appear clearly in these Psalms, although the idea is not excluded.

The most noteworthy feature of the Psalms is the messianic prediction of Psalm 17:17-51. The prophesied Messiah, raised up by God to deliver the people from the Roman yoke, is purely human, in striking contrast to inspired Scripture's prophecy of him.

The Third Book of Maccabees

This work is historical fiction, the scene of which is laid in the reign of Ptolemy IV (222-204 B.C.). The book has no connection with

First and Second Maccabees, nor with the Maccabean age. It does, however, recount the story of God's faithfulness and the fidelity of the Jewish people in times of persecution. This is apparently the only point it has in common with the other books of Maccabees. It stresses the value of prayer and the working of "the unconquerable Providence." This is seen in the sudden paralysis which Ptolemy IV experienced when he attempted to enter the Temple at Jerusalem. It is seen, too, in the futility of his attempt to slaughter the Jews of Alexandria by having them trampled to death in the hippodrome by intoxicated elephants. In both instances the prayers of the godly priest brought about providential deliverance.

The Fourth Book of Maccabees

This is a hortatory address of fourteen chapters urging a life of faithfulness to God and self-control toward men. Dated probably between 50 B.C. and A.D. 50, this work portrays heroic events of the Maccabean age as illustrations of its religious and philosophical principles. Hence, unlike Third Maccabees, it *does* have a valid reason for its title. The writer's thesis and method of proof may be summarized in his own words. "I might prove to you from many other considerations that pious reason is the sole master of the passions, but I shall prove it most effectually from the fortitude of Eleazar, and of the seven brothers and their mother; for all these proved by their contempt of torture and death that reason has command over the passions" (1:7-9). But the author stipulates a limitation. Although reason is master over the passions, it is not master of its own affections, and so cannot control thoughts and motives.

Fourth Maccabees is of great value for the student of the New Testament, particularly in studies of the life of Paul. The stoic Pharisaism of the writer was essentially that of the Apostle before his conversion. It was only when Paul realized that the Law did not enable him to keep the commandment "Thou shalt not covet," and that it gave no power to rule the inner realm of the spirit, that the crisis came which proved to be the turning-point in the Apostle's spiritual life. This limitation, which the writer of Fourth Maccabees recognizes so acutely, gave Paul no peace till he found it in the gospel of Christ.

Important also to New Testament study is the prominence given to the concept of "propitiation" in the book. The idea presented is that the blood of the martyrs atones for the sins of the people (2 Mac. 17: 22). Paul, of course, also features propitiation. But in his inspired teaching it is the blood of Christ alone that atones for sin! (See Romans 3:25).

The Testament of Job

A legendary expansion of the canonical book of Job, this Aramaic Midrash stems from the first century B.C. Its fanciful tales were intended to comfort the godly in separatist Judaism in times of bitter persecution by inspiring them in the hope of the resurrection. It was also slanted to shield the faithful against the encroachments of Hellenism.

The unknown author weaves his legends around Job's wife, who is named Sitidos. She is pictured as supporting her husband when he is reduced to direst sickness and poverty. She lived to see her husband vindicated, but died before his fortunes were restored. On the day of her death, however, Job showed her that her children killed in the ruins of their house were safe in heaven. Bidding her and Job's three friends (who had given Job's wife no comfort in her children's safety) to turn their eyes toward the East, they saw the children wearing celestial crowns. Comforted in the truth of the resurrection and bliss in heaven, Sitidos died.

The Letter of Aristeas

Apparently written at Alexandria around 100 B.C., this pseudepigraphical Epistle of 322 verses claims to have been penned by an officer in the court of Ptolemy II Philadelphus (285-245 B.C.) to his brother Philocrates. It alleges to be an account of the translation of the Hebrew Pentateuch into Greek. Demetrius the librarian at Alexandria is represented as urging the king to send to Jerusalem to ask the high priest Eleazer to send six scholars from each of the twelve tribes. The request was complied with. The Jewish scholar worked for seventy-two days on the island of Pharos to produce the Greek Pentateuch, called the Septuagint ("the Seventy"), in memory of the seventy-two translators.

Scholars are hesitant to accept the historical reliability of the Letter. Perhaps it does preserve the germinal truth of the Septuagint's origin and does illustrate how Hellenistic Jews sought to bridge the gap between Hebrew and Greek thought.

The Lives of the Prophets

This work, written in Hebrew during the first century A.D., consists of a collection of extrabiblical traditions concerning the prophets.

The text deals with the four major prophets (Isaiah, Jeremiah, Ezekiel, and Daniel), the minor prophets, and, in addition, Nathan, Ahijah, Joed (Neh. 11:7; 2 Chron. 9:24), Azariah (2 Chron. 15:1-15), Zechariah (2 Chron. 24:20-22), Elijah, and Elisha.

Qumran—these desolate caves yielded the Dead Sea Scrolls, the oldest copies of the Hebrew Scriptures ever discovered. (© *MPS*)

THE DEAD SEA SCROLLS

In 1947 the ancient library of a monastic Jewish community with headquarters in the Wadi Qumran, northwest of the Dead Sea, was accidentally discovered. Eleven caves in the area yielded manuscripts of practically all of the Old Testament books as well as the apocryphal and pseudepigraphical works of Tobit, Ecclesiasticus, Enoch, Jubilees, and the Testament of Levi. The Qumran library also contained an important body of sectarian literature describing the life and distinctive doctrines of the religious community located not far from the caves where the manuscripts were discovered. The community flourished from its apparent founding at about 110 B.C. until the great earthquake of 31 B.C. It was rebuilt after Herod the Great's death in 4 B.C. and again flourished until destroyed by the Romans in A.D. 68. But the valuable library escaped destruction by the Romans because it had been removed to the nearby caves.

The Manual of Discipline

This document, dating about 70 B.C., presents the rules and liturgy of the community (1:1 — 3:12), its doctrines (3:13 — 4:26), its regulations concerning admission and punishment of crimes, and its description of the holy life to be cultivated in an evil world (5:1 — 9:26). The Manual supplies valuable insight into ceremonial Jewish legalism as practiced by an Essene sect during the time of Christ. Ritual washings were performed to remove uncleanness when transgressions of the code defiled the community. By contrast, Jesus' teachings plainly demonstrated that righteousness is a condition of the heart rather than a matter of external conformity to legal minutiae (Matt. 16:10, 11). The teaching of the Manual concerning two contrasts — light and darkness, truth and error — finds parallels in the New Testament (John 3:19; Rom. 13:12; 2 Cor. 6:14; 1 John 1:5). The Qumranian, like the Christian, was taught to turn from darkness to walk in the light.

The communal life at Qumran is also paralleled by the practice of the early Christian Church (Acts 4:32). The appendix of the Manual refers to a sacred meal which served as a foretaste of the future messianic banquet. Like the Christian communion supper, this meal was founded on the Jewish ceremonial custom of breaking bread and drinking wine at the beginning of each meal. Jesus took this traditional Jewish blessing and interpreted it in the light of his impending death, which would open the way for fellowship with his disciples at a future banquet in the kingdom of God (Mark 14:25).

The Damascus Document

This document represents the convictions of a Jewish sectarian group that fled to the desert northwest of the Dead Sea to escape persecution and to await deliverance from their foes and vindication of the principles for which they suffered. The full title of the work is "The Document of the New Covenant in the Land of Damascus." Whether the term "Damascus" is a prophetic name for the Qumran area or is a literal designation of the ancient city in the Anti-Lebanon district where the sect may have sojourned during the period that Qumran was abandoned (31-4 B.C.) is not known.

The Damascus Document consists of 1) an introductory exhortation and 2) a collection of ordinances. Rigid conformity to the ordinances based on the Mosaic Law was enjoined upon this sect of Judaism, which held the Hebrew Scriptures in high regard. The teachings of the Document have much in common with the tenets of the Pharisees. It inculcates the doctrine of the future life and affirms the existence of angels and spirits. It directs hope to the advent of a messianic deliverer. The Lord's people are exhorted to prepare themselves for his coming.

The people of the Damascus Document identified themselves with the priest Zadok (1 Chron. 24:3). The first fragments of the Damascus Document discovered in 1896-97 in a manuscript storeroom (*genizah*) in Old Cairo were entitled *Fragments of a Zadokite Work*. Because they placed proper emphasis on Old Testament prophecy, the Zadokites were naturally predisposed to accept Christ and doubtless formed part at least of the "great company of the priests" that became "obedient to the faith" (Acts 6:7).

The Thanksgiving Scroll

The Thanksgiving Scroll (*Hodayot*) is the hymn and praise book of the Qumran Community. The present copy, recovered from Caves One and Four, contains some gaps. These songs reflect fierce persecution and conflict (4:8, 9). Although couched in personal terms, the songs reflect the group experiences of the Qumran Community. The formula "I will praise thee, my Lord" occurs in many of the hymns, and faith in God's delivering and preserving power is emphasized. Messianic expectation imbues the poet. However, he envisions a severe trial that will first try men (3:26-36) as the prelude to God's intervention. Yet even in the present state of sin and persecution the pious community is considered a segment of "paradise" (8:5-7).

The Genesis Apocryphon

Made of four leather sheets sewed together, this is a document of 22 columns of Aramaic text. This scroll, unlike other Cave One documents from Qumran, was not stored in a jar. As a result it was severely damaged, and was published in 1956 only as the result of the most painstaking ingenuity.

The Apocryphon is a paraphrase of the book of Genesis, freely embellished with fictional details. The embellished text is sectioned into four parts: 1) The Story of Lamech (1 – 5); 2) The Story of Noah (6 – 15); 3) The Table of Nations (16, 17); and 4) The Story of Abraham (18 – 22). The Apocryphon was intended to encourage the persecuted numbers of the Community to remain true to their faith in view of the coming messianic age.

The War Scroll

More fully entitled "War of the Sons of Light with the Sons of Darkness," this document was recovered from Cave One at Qumran in 1947. It consists of 18½ columns of text, with from 16 to 18 lines on each column. It was written anonymously sometime after 63 B.C. Columns 1 through 9 deal with the rules for equipment and the tactics of battle. Columns 10 through 19 set forth exhortations and prayers. The sons of light (true Israel) are encouraged to fight in the light of God's promises and faithfulness to Israel in the past. Israel's enemies (the Kittim) are doomed to eventual defeat.

Although the Scroll deals with an eschatological war (reminiscent of biblical Armageddon – Rev. 16:12-16), the contest suggests a perennial spiritual struggle between light and darkness, as in John's Gospel and First Epistle. The Scroll also gives a realistic description of military operations of the first century B.C. as seen through Jewish eyes.

The Habakkuk Commentary

This commentary from Cave One expounds chapters 1 and 2 of Habakkuk in the light of the history of the Qumran community. It mentions the "Teacher of Righteousness," who broke with the Jerusalem priesthood and led a number of priests and laymen to Qumran to establish a settlement of the true Israel. It also deals with the foe of the Teacher of Righteousness, known as the "Wicked Priest." The commentator interprets the Chaldeans (Hab. 1:6) as the "Kittim" (Romans), who will devastate the nation and bring judgment upon the wicked priests at Jerusalem.

The precise date of the Habakkuk Commentary is not known and the identification of the Teacher of Righteousness and his wicked antagonist is uncertain. Fragments of other commentaries on Micah, Zephaniah, and the Psalms were found in Cave One. Cave Four yielded four commentaries on Hosea, two on the Psalms, and one on Nahum (all in fragmentary form). The Nahum Commentary clearly connects with the despotic rule of Alexander Jannaeus (103-76 B.C.).

This bas-relief sculpture found at Capernaum represents the Ark of the Covenant. (© *MPS*)

Historical-Archeological Backgrounds

The Bible as the revelation of God's plan of redemption for the lost human race is not history in the commonly accepted use of the term (the systematic record of events of the past). Even those parts of Scripture that are more closely associated with history, such as the books of Joshua, Judges, Kings, Chronicles, Ezra, and Nehemiah in the Old Testament, and the book of the Acts in the New Testament, are history only in a very specialized sense—the sense that they portray the story of human redemption.

In the strictest sense these books constitute a *philosophy* of history, for they interpret only highly selected events in the story of redemption. In the Old Testament these events focus first on the promised line through which the world's Redeemer was to come, then on the nation Israel and her relation to the Lord, and finally on God's redemptive program for the entire world. In the New Testament, after the nation Israel rejects the Messiah, God's new people, the Church, enter the stage of history.

THE BIBLE AND HISTORY

THE NATURE OF BIBLICAL HISTORY. Besides being a highly specialized and interpretive account of significant events in the story of human redemption, biblical history is always grounded in God-ordained morality. It realistically catalogs the evil as well as the good. Yet it never condones evil. Instead it warns against sin, presenting it as a dishonor to God, a violation of God's eternal moral laws, and the legitimate object of God's divine punishment. Biblical history is, therefore, eminently instructive. It teaches lessons in right living and admonishes against wrong conduct by both precept and example. The moral and spiritual tone of Old Testament history gives it timeless relevance and universal usefulness. This is why the books of Joshua, Judges, Samuel, and Kings (listed among the historical books in the English order) constitute the former *prophets* in the Hebrew Bible.

But the "historical" portions of the Old Testament are more than a specialized history of redemption or a philosophy of that history which emphasizes ethical and spiritual values. Redemptive history contains the *predictive* element in addition to the moral and ethical emphasis. Prediction of the Messiah by promise, type, and symbol is so thoroughly woven into the fabric of Old Testament redemptive history that it cannot be separated from it. The Old Testament must be seen as Messiah-centered history wedded to Messiah-centered prophecy in preparation for the advent of the Redeemer.

In the New Testament the book of the Acts as the account of the formation of the Church and the spread of Christianity is more like conventional history. However, the four Gospels are neither histories nor biographies of the life of Christ. Instead, they are *portraits* of Christ, presenting four different poses of the *one* unique personality. Yet each Gospel writer, while turning the spotlight on one feature of his Person, maintains his full-orbed character. Together they present four pictures that portray in wonderful fullness and clarity the one and same unique Person, the King of Israel, the Servant of the Lord, the God-Man, the Redeemer of humanity.

THE GOAL OF BIBLICAL HISTORY. While the Bible is accurate when it touches secular history, it is in no sense a secular account of events or of the lives of people. Its aim is strictly religious and redemptive. Hence, it begins with the earth when it was recreated for the latecomer man (Gen. 1:1-31), and not with the original creation of the universe. It traces man's creation upon the earth, his innocence, his fall, and the story of his redemption.

The goal of biblical history is to portray God's plan and purpose for the ages. It looks forward to a sin-cleansed universe in eternity, including a new heaven and a new earth (Rev. 20, 21). It envisions only one isolation ward for all sinners, angelic and human. As it moves through the arena of human history it includes only those things that relate to the unfolding of the divine plan for man's salvation.

THE BIBLE AND ARCHEOLOGY

THE SCIENCE OF BIBLICAL ARCHEOLOGY. Biblical archeology is concerned with the excavation, decipherment, and critical evaluation of those ancient records of the past that touch directly or indirectly on the Bible. Modern archeology had its beginnings in the early nineteenth century, when the antiquities of Egypt were opened up to scientific study by Napoleon's expedition. The treasuries of Assyria-Babylonia came to light toward the middle and latter part of the same century. Interest in Palestinian antiquities was given great impetus as a result of the discovery of the Moabite Stone in 1868.

However, the greatest discoveries of biblical archeology have been made in the twentieth century. During this period biblical archeology has become an exact science and has made remarkable contributions to the understanding of biblical history.

ARCHEOLOGY AND BIBLICAL HISTORY. Archeology has been called "the handmaid of history." As such it expands and clarifies historical backgrounds. In no sphere is this ministry more clearly illustrated than in the case of the Bible, particularly the Old Testament. Before the advent of the science of biblical archeology very little was known about the historical backgrounds of the Old Testament. As the result of archeological research in Bible lands, the Old Testament has now been authenticated in innumerable instances on the historical plane. In addition, its vastly broadened historical background has furnished a very effective setting for illustrating its manners, customs, and general narrative. Archeology has literally caused the Old Testament to come alive historically.

As far as the New Testament is concerned, the contributions of biblical archeology have not been nearly so dramatic as in the case of the Old Testament. Greek and Roman historians had supplied a great mass of background material. However, archeology has had a notable career in clearing up many historical difficulties, particularly validating Luke's accuracy as a historian in his Gospel and the Acts.

ARCHEOLOGICAL SURVEY OF OLD TESTAMENT HISTORY

THE PRIMEVAL PERIOD (10,000 to 2000 B.C.) The original earth, created in the dateless past, experienced various geologic ages and prehistoric stone ages before undergoing a gigantic catastrophe somewhere in the undated past. Much later it was refashioned for the latecomer man (somewhere between 6000 and 10,000 B.C., or possibly somewhat earlier).

The Creation Account in Archeology (Genesis 1 & 2). Polytheistic accounts of creation are found in *Enuma Elish,* the Babylonian flood story written in cuneiform script on seven clay tablets. Although the bulk of the creation epic was recovered from Ashurbanipal's library at Nineveh (late seventh century B.C.), it was composed much earlier, in the time of Hammurabi the Great (1728-1686 B.C.). However, the story goes back several millennia to the Sumerians, who entered the plain of Shinar in lower Babylonia as early as 4000 B.C. Their account comes down from the original event, preserved in the memory of the human race, and reflects the actual event described by inspiration in Genesis 1.

The Location of Eden (Genesis 2 & 3). Archeology has established the lower Tigris-Euphrates Valley as the general location of Eden and the earliest human civilization. The Hiddekel was the Tigris River.

The Fall (Genesis 3). The Myth of Adapa is not actually a parallel to the fall of Genesis 3, but it does deal with the perplexing problem of why mankind must suffer and die. However, elements in the legend correspond to Genesis. The "food of life" corresponds to "the fruit" of "the tree of life" (Gen. 3:3, 22).

Earliest Civilization (Genesis 4). Man's civilization began in farming and cattle raising, the occupations of Cain and Abel. The rise of urban life and the beginning of arts, crafts, and music (Gen. 4:16-24) are illustrated in the lowest levels of excavated cities in Mesopotamia, such as Nineveh, Tell Obeid, and Tepe Gawra. Tell Obeid, northwest of Ur, reveals the earliest clearly defined culture in lower Babylonia, showing that around 4000 B.C. the marshlands of that area were drained and occupied.

Long Life before the Flood (Genesis 5). Genesis 5 indicates that the pre-flood span of human life was as much as 969 years (Methuselah). Archeology has recovered a very ancient Sumerian king list that enumerates eight pre-flood rulers who reigned in Lower Mesopotamia for a total of 241,200 years, with the shortest reign set at 18,600 years. Such a parallel at least puts the comparatively modest figures of Gene-

Babylonian ruins — once the pride of King Nebuchadnezzar, now a monument to idolatry and divine judgment (© *MPS*)

sis in a different light and corroborates the biblical description of longevity before the flood.

The Noahic Flood (Genesis 6-9). The historicity of this event as a worldwide cataclysm (Gen. 6:19-24; cf. 2 Pet. 3:6) has been hotly debated. But attempts to make it local and connect it with C. L. Woolley's flood stratum at Ur or S. Langdon's at Kish are futile. Those who deny the historicity of the event as a worldwide catastrophe face the evidence of archeology. The flood tablets (both Sumerian and later Babylonian) unearthed at Nineveh (1853) furnish the most amazing and detailed extrabiblical parallel to any biblical event. If such a world-engulfing deluge never took place, how did the extrabiblical traditions and the biblical account arise?

The Ethnic Complexion of the Post-Flood World (Genesis 9:24 – 10:32). Genesis 9:24-27 presents a remarkable forecast of the moral and spiritual history of the nations after they descended from Noah's three sons. The purpose of this prophecy is to show the origin of the Canaanites and the source of their moral pollution, which centuries later was to lead to the loss of their land to Israel. Shem's blessing was religious.

All divine revelation was to be given through the Semitic line, from which Christ, humanly speaking, was born. From Japheth would rise the enlarged nations that would "dwell in the tents of Shem," that is, eventually share in the blessings of Shem's spiritual heritage.

Noah's prediction of the moral and spiritual history of the nations (Gen. 9:24-27) constitutes an indispensable introduction to the great prophecy of the ethnographical constitution of the postdiluvial world contained in Genesis 10. This so-called "Table of the Nations" displays a remarkable perception of the ethnic and linguistic complexion of the descendants of Noah. What is most amazing is that archeological research in the last century and a half has substantiated the accuracy of this remarkable document and illuminated virtually all of the names and places it contains.

The Tower of Babel (Genesis 11:1-9). The scene here depicted evidently belongs to a period not more than a century and a half after the flood (about 4800 B.C.). The tower was apparently the first tower attempted, and represented the symbol of man's revolt against God and his determination to promote and glorify himself. The polytheistic temple towers ("ziggurats") of later centuries were doubtless copied after it. More than two dozen such ziggurats are now known in Mesopotamia. They were gigantic artificial mountains of sun-dried bricks painted various colors. The oldest existing ziggurat is that at Uruk (biblical Erech; Gen. 10:10), dating from the fourth millennium B.C. Ruins of other famous ziggurats are found at Ur, Babylon, and Borsippa.

The Confusion of Languages (Genesis 11:1-9). This judgment took place about 4800 B.C. in connection with the pride of the Babel builders. The race was scattered over the ancient biblical world as a result. City-states arose in Babylonia. Archeology traces Halafian culture (about 4500 B.C.) at Tell Halaf, east of Carchemish. Obeidan culture (about 3600 B.C.) can be traced at Tell Obeid, near Ur. Warka (Erech, Uruk) flourished at about 3200 B.C., giving birth to the earliest writing and the first cylinder seals. Jemdet Nasr culture, near Babylon, developed about 3000 B.C. Various languages were spoken by different peoples.

Civilization developed early on the Nile River. The union of Lower and Upper Egypt took place at about 2900 B.C., with the first and second dynasties extending from 2900 to 2700 B.C. The Old Kingdom with its pyramids flourished between 2700 and 2200 B.C. Contemporaneous was the Sumerian period in Babylonia. The empire of Sargon I spread over much of the ancient Near East in the period from 2360 to 2180 B.C.

THE PATRIARCHAL PERIOD (2000 TO 1871 B.C.)

Terah's Home and Religion (Genesis 11:25-32). Abraham's father, Terah, was a native of Ur (modern Tell el-Muqayyar in lower Babylonia). C. L. Woolley has traced the history of this site from the Tell Obeid period (about 3600 B.C.) until it was abandoned about 300 B.C. The principal deity worshiped was Nannar, the moon god, whom Terah evidently adored (cf. Josh. 24:2). The famous temple tower or ziggurat built by Ur-Nammu, the founder of the prosperous third Dynasty at Ur (about 2150-2050 B.C.) dominated the city of the moon god. On its uppermost stage was the shrine of Nannar. In front of the temple tower were twin temples of the moon god and his consort, Nin-gal.

Ur of the Chaldees — this was a flourishing city when God called Abram away to the Promised Land in Canaan. (© *MPS*)

Abraham and Ur (Genesis 11:28). Abraham was born at Ur about 2161 B.C., as the city was rising to the height of its power under the powerful third dynasty of Sumerian kings. Archeological excavations have made Ur a very well-known city. It is possible that Terah was one of the prosperous wool merchants of the town. Houses such as he and his son lived in have come to light through the spade of the archeologist.

Abraham at Haran (Genesis 11:28). As early as Abraham's time, Haran (Assyrian *harranu*, "main road") was an important link in the great east-west trade route linking Nineveh, Carchemish, and Damascus. The city is known from cuneiform sources from the nineteenth and eighteenth centuries B.C. Excavations since 1951 show that it was occupied from at least the third millennium B.C. Terah evidently settled there because he was a devotee of the moon god, who had temples both there and at Ur (cf. Gen. 11:31, 32).

Abraham in Canaan (Genesis 12-17). At about 2086 B.C. Abraham entered Canaan, according to the underlying chronology of the Hebrew Bible. The patriarchal period, then, extends from 2086 B.C. to 1871 B.C. (Gen. 12:4, 5). The highland ridge was then sparsely populated, with ample room for the movement of seminomadic people like Abraham and Lot. Cities such as Shechem, Dothan, Bethel, Gerar, and Jerusalem are archeologically attested for this early period. Abraham's visit to Egypt (Gen. 12:10-20) evidently occurred in the early years of the Middle Kingdom (about 1989 B.C.).

The Invasion of the Mesopotamian Kings (Genesis 14). While the actual kings have not as yet been satisfactorily identified, their line of march on the King's Highway is substantiated, as well as such place names as Ashtaroth-karnaim and Ham.

Sodom and Gomorrah (Genesis 19). The cities of the Plain ("Circle") of the Jordan are proved to have existed during Abraham's period; they were situated at the southern end of the Dead Sea. The valley of Siddim was overwhelmed by a conflagration, probably caused by an earthquake in which the salt and sulfur of the region exploded and the waters of the Dead Sea inundated the burned-out region of oil and asphalt. *Jebel Usdum* ("Mountain of Sodom") is a great salt mass at the southwestern end of the Dead Sea, recalling the fact that Lot's wife was turned into a pillar of salt in this general region.

Patriarchal Customs. Such patriarchal customs as marriage, adoption, the right of the firstborn, and the possession of teraphim (household deities) are mentioned not only in Scriptures (Gen. 12 – 50), but are substantiated by the inscribed tablets recovered from Nuzu (a site near Kirkuk) as well as by the Mari Letters from Tell el Hariri on the Middle Euphrates. In Abraham's time Mari was one of the most flourishing cities of the Mesopotamian world.

Hebrew Residence in Padan-Aram. Terah died in Haran (Gen. 11:31), a town still in existence 60 miles west of Tell Halaf. The city of Nahor, Rebekah's home (Gen. 24:10), occurs often in the Mari Letters (18th century B.C.). Evidence of Hebrew residence in this region also appears in the names of Abraham's forefathers — Serug and Terah.

THE EGYPTIAN PERIOD (1871 TO 1441 B.C.)

The Egyptian Sojourn (Exodus 1 — 6). According to the biblical chronology preserved in the Hebrew Bible, Isaac is to be dated about 1950 B.C., Jacob about 1900 B.C., and the emigration into Egypt about 1871 B.C. (under the Twelfth Egyptian Dynasty of the strong Middle Kingdom, which ruled from 1989 to 1776 B.C. and was headed by Amenemes I-IV and Senwosret I-III). It was apparently under Amenemes I or II that Israel entered Egypt. Elsewhere during this period Hammurabi the Great (1728-1686 B.C.) ruled over the First Dynasty of Babylon (1850-1550 B.C.) Mari was a powerful city-state on the Middle Euphrates during this time.

The Hyksos Invasion (Exodus 1 — 4). The Hyksos were foreign invaders who lodged themselves in the Delta and dominated Lower Egypt in the period of confusion that followed the dissolution of the Twelfth Dynasty. During the Hyksos rule, about 1730-1570 B.C., Israel lived in the Delta and was controlled by these "rulers of foreign countries," as the term Hyksos means. Kamose, the last Egyptian ruler of Dynasty XVII at Thebes in Upper Egypt, began the expulsion of the Hyksos, which was completed by the first ruler of Dynasty XVIII, Ahmose (about 1570-1545 B.C.). Under this famous line of kings Moses was born (about 1520 B.C.). Under this new regime the Israelites were enslaved, perhaps as a reaction against the Hyksos.

The Career of Moses (Exodus 2 — 12). The Egyptian princess who found Moses in the ark of papyrus was perhaps the famous Hatshepsut (1504-1482 B.C.). The name "Moses" is apparently nothing more than Egyptian *Mase*, pronounced *Mose* after the twelfth century B.C. and meaning simply "the child." The interpretation by the sacred writer, however, is connected with Hebrew root *masha*, "to draw out," because Pharaoh's daughter drew the infant out of the water (Exod. 2:10).

The Egyptian Plagues (Exodus 7 — 11). The entire Egyptian sojourn abounds in authentic local color. The miracles consist of events that were natural to Egypt. The supernatural element is seen in the vast increase of their intensity. No phenomena were imported.

The Exodus. The underlying chronology of the Hebrew Bible would indicate that Thutmose III (1490-1445 B.C.) was Israel's oppressor, and that Amenhotep II (1445-1425 B.C.) was the Pharaoh of the Exodus (about 1441 B.C.). Israel was in the desert during the reign of Thutmose IV (1425-1412 B.C.).

THE PERIOD OF THE CONQUEST (1401 TO 1361 B.C.)

The Fall of Jericho (Joshua 6). According to the biblical chronology the fall of Jericho occurred about 1401 B.C. Professor John Garstang, the British excavator of Jericho, agreed with this view. Supporting this position are the chronological notices in Judges 11:26 and First Kings 6:1, as well as the whole time-scheme underlying the body of history from Genesis to Second Kings. In addition, this interpretation has the distinct advantage of allowing at least a partial equation of the Habiru of the Amarna Letters with the Hebrews. These famous letters from Tell el-Amarna in Egypt, discovered in 1887, parallel the period of the Conquest. The Amarna period covers the reign of Amenhotep III (about 1412-1359 B.C.). The letters describe a situation in Palestine that in many respects remarkably coincides with the invasion of the Hebrews. The letters give a first-hand picture of conditions in Canaan. The country was nominally subject to Egypt, but Egyptian control had completely broken down. This condition was ideal for Joshua's invasion and conquest of the land.

The Conquest of Ai (Joshua 8). Identification of Ai with et-Tell is obviously erroneous and has produced confusion. Ai was evidently quite small but nevertheless strategically important as a military outpost (Josh. 7:3). It may have been nothing more than a fort protecting Bethel. Only further archeological research can clear up the situation and vindicate the early date of the conquest.

The Conquest of the Canaanites (Joshua 1 – 11). Archeological evidence from Lachish, Debir, and Hazor supposedly also contradicts the fourteenth century date of the conquest. But the thirteenth-century destruction of these towns should not be connected with Joshua's wars, but rather with the strife and invasions of the later lawless period of the judges.

God's command to exterminate the Canaanites is demonstrated by archeology to be a moral necessity rather than an impugnment of God's justice and goodness, as many rationalistic critics contend. The religious epic literature recovered from Ras Shamra (the ancient Canaanite city of Ugarit in North Syria) since 1929 has revealed the moral viciousness of the Canaanite cults. These documents attest that Canaanite religion revolved around war, violence, and sexual immorality. Depraved male and female deities were worshiped with foul rites that "filled up" the iniquity of the land (cf. Gen. 15:16) by the time of Joshua and the Israelite invasion.

THE PERIOD OF THE JUDGES (1375 TO 1075 B.C.)

The Period and Archeology. Archeology has helped to place the events of this extended period in the framework of contemporary Egyptian,

Aramean, Assyrian, Phoenician, and Hurrian history. Excavations at Megiddo, Bethshan, Lachish, Debir, and Hazor will one day, we believe, vindicate the biblical chronology of this era against the late-date theories of the Exodus that telescope the "dark ages" of Israel's history. *The Judges and the Contemporary Scene.* For the chronology of the period see under the Book of Judges. During the reign of the boy king Tutankhamun (1359-1350 B.C.) and Harmhab (1350-1299 B.C.), when Egyptian influence over Palestine was slight, the Aramean Cushan-Rishathaim invaded Israel. It was at this time that Othniel delivered God's people (about 1361-1313 B.C.; Judg. 3:7-10). Eglon of Moab oppressed Israel 18 years (about 1313-1295 B.C.), until Ehud delivered the nation. Peace followed for eighty years (1295-1215 B.C.; Judg. 3:12-30). This long period of security was made possible by a strong Egypt under Rameses II (1295-1223 B.C.), who ruled all southern Syria after the battle of Kadesh (about 1286 B.C.) and his treaty with the Hittites. His son and successor, Merenptah, alludes to Israel in Palestine on his victory stele (about 1224 B.C.).

Jabin, king of Hazor, overran Israel (1215-1195 B.C.) under the weak pharaohs that followed Merenptah (Judg. 4:1-24). Hazor was a Canaanite kingdom of North Palestine near Lake Huleh. Deliverance by Deborah and a forty-year peace (1195-1155 B.C.) was possible because of a new dynasty in Egypt with the strong Pharaoh Rameses III (1198-1167 B.C.), who was able to maintain order in Asia.

Oppression by the Midianites for seven years (about 1155-1148 B.C.) was due to the decline in Egyptian power under the weak Rameses IV and V, who followed Rameses III (Judg. 6, 7). Under Gideon, however (1148-1108 B.C.), peace prevailed despite decline in Egyptian power, fostering Israel's growing desire for their own king. This resulted in Abimelech's unhappy reign at Shechem for three years (about 1108-1105 B.C.; Judg. 9).

Oppression by the Ammonites (Judg. 10) and Jephthah's judgeship took place about 1105 to 1099 B.C. Coeval with this was the Philistine rise (about 1099-1059 B.C.) and Samson's twenty-year judgeship (about 1085-1065 B.C.) (Judg. 13 – 16). Decline in Hittite, Assyrian, and Egyptian imperial power made possible the rise of the Hebrew monarchy but brought with it also the Philistine threat to Israel.

THE PERIOD OF SAUL (1040 TO 1010 B.C.)
Saul's Initial Exploits. Saul repulsed not only the encroaching Ammonites but the Philistines as well (1 Sam. 11:1-14; 14:1-46). In doing so he was popularized as a hero and became the natural choice for the

kingship, which the threat of the times seemed to necessitate. His early victories over the Philistines weakened the iron-refining monopoly held by this people (1 Sam. 13:19-21). When Saul and David broke the power of the Philistines, the iron-smelting formula became public property, and the stage was set for an economic and political revolution in Israel.

Saul's Fortress at Gibeah. Saul's fortress-palace at Tell el-Ful, about four miles north of Jerusalem, has been excavated. It was more like a dungeon than a royal residence and displays Saul as a rustic chieftain in reference to architecture and other amenities of life. His self-will and disobedience to divine direction through Samuel landed him in occultism and cost him his life and kingdom (1 Sam. 13:13, 14; 15:1-35; 28:3-25).

THE PERIOD OF DAVID AND SOLOMON (1010 TO 971 B.C.)

David's Activity as King. David's magnanimity toward the house of Saul, his brilliant diplomacy with surrounding nations, and his courageous conquests of avowed foes soon won him a strong kingdom. His capture of Jerusalem from the Jebusites (2 Sam. 5:8), making it the religious and governmental capital of the kingdom, was a masterly exploit. Archeology has fully clarified the location of "the city of David" (2 Sam. 5:7) on the eastern hill above the Gihon spring. Though it consisted of a walled space not exceeding eight acres, the city of David was of immense political importance. It became the hub of the united kingdom and, when David moved the ark to Jerusalem (2 Sam. 6:12-15), it became the center of Jewish worship as well.

Archeology has shed a great deal of light on the tabernacle, its ritual, and its sacred music. Now it is quite clear that there is nothing incongruous in the biblical representation of David as the patron saint of Jewish hymnology and the organizer of Temple music. In fact, his skill as a diplomat and prowess as a conqueror combined with his religious zeal to gain him a strong kingdom. His allocation of Levitical cities and cities of refuge cemented his conquests together on a religious basis and helped root out divisions and local feuds. He began the religious and political organization that his son Solomon was to develop so effectively.

Solomon's Power and Splendor. The period of Solomon's reign (971-931 B.C.) was favorable for the Israelite empire because the great powers of the times — Egypt, Hatti, and Assyria — were all in eclipse or abeyance. Solomon used diplomacy on a grand scale to forestall problems in foreign policy. He married the daughter of the then-reigning

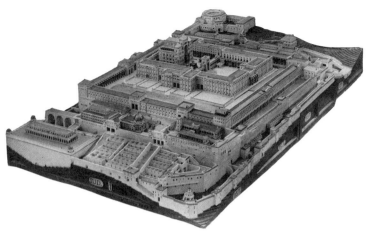

An opulent model of Solomon's Temple (© *MPS*)

Pharaoh (1 Kings 3:1, 2) and followed the general policy of royal marriages (1 Kings 11:1-8) and implemented other ties of amity that prevented war (but led to other evils). Solomon's domestic policy was also designed to foster peace and prosperity. He organized his realm into twelve administrative districts (1 Kings 4:7-20) and initiated various public works and building projects, including the Temple at Jerusalem.

Solomon's industrial expansion was remarkable. He controlled the caravan trade of Syria-Palestine and cultivated the horse-and-chariot commerce between Egypt and Kue (Cilicia) (1 Kings 10:28, 29, RSV), which brought him enormous revenues. He built a fleet of ships at Ezion-geber on the Red Sea (1 Kings 9:26-28) and exploited the copper-rich Arabah in his refinery at Ezion-geber (modern Tell el-Keleifeh, excavated in 1938-40). All of these commercial ventures have been verified and illustrated by modern archeological research, including the magnificent Temple he constructed at Jerusalem. Both the plan and furnishings of the latter are much better understood in the light of recent Near Eastern excavations.

THE DIVIDED MONARCHY (931 TO 722 B.C.)

Rehoboam and Shishak's Invasion. The folly of Rehoboam (about 931-913 B.C.) led to the division of the kingdom. In addition to being weakened by wars between Rehoboam and Jeroboam I (1 Kings 14:30; 15: 6), Judah was invaded by Shishak (Sheshonq I of Egypt, founder of the twenty-second dynasty; 1 Kings 14:25-28). The gold-masked mummy of this pharaoh was discovered in his burial chamber at Tanis in 1938. His triumphal inscription at Karnak (ancient Thebes) includes conquests in both Judah and Israel, despite his previous friendship for Jeroboam (1 Kings 11:40).

Jeroboam and His Idolatry. To strengthen his kingdom and wean his subjects away from the Jerusalem Temple, Jeroboam set up gold calves (bulls) at Dan and Bethel (1 Kings 12:25-53). These were apparently thought to represent the invisible deity enthroned or standing on a bull's back. Ancient Near Eastern iconography shows pagan gods like Baal represented in the form of a bolt of lightning on a bull's back.

Israel and Aram In Conflict. After Solomon's death the Aramean power which was centered in Damascus became a threat to the Northern Kingdom from about 900 B.C. till the fall of Damascus in 732 B.C. In 1940 the inscribed Stele of Benhadad I was discovered in North Syria. It attests "Benhadad, son of Tabrimmon, the son of Hezion, king of Aram" (1 Kings 15:18). This was evidently Benhadad I (about 900-842 B.C.), the foe of Ahab, who was succeeded by the usurper Hazael (2 Kings 8:7-15). Assyrian records declare that "Hazael, son of nobody, seized the throne" after Benhadad's death.

Hazael was a powerful ruler who was God's scourge to Israel during the reigns of Jehu (841-814 B.C.) and Jehoahaz (814-798 B.C.). Benhadad II (about 798-770 B.C.), the son of Hazael, continued his father's oppression of Israel into the reign of Joash (798-782 B.C.). Joash then recouped Israelite fortunes and was able to repel Benhadad. Benhadad II is mentioned in the contemporary stele of Zakir, discovered in 1903. He is represented as heading a coalition of kings against Zakir because of the latter's alliance with Luash. This move upset the balance of power in Syria and precipitated war.

Joash's successes were continued by his son Jeroboam II (782-753 B.C.), who restored Israel to full power and made Damascus a practical vassal of Israel (2 Kings 14:25-28). The resurgence of Assyrian power upon the rise of the great conqueror Tiglathpileser III (745-727 B.C.) gave Ahaz of Judah a chance to pit the Assyrian against Aram and Israel. This resulted in the overthrow of Damascus in 732 B.C. and the death of the last Aramean king, Rezin (750-732 B.C.). These events appear prominently in Assyrian monuments recovered by archeological research.

The Omride Dynasty and Archeology. Omri and Ahab of Israel and Mesha of Moab figure prominently in the famous Moabite Stone set

up at Dibon about 840 B.C. and discovered in 1868. Omri's capital of
Samaria has been unearthed by extensive excavations at the site by G.
A. Reisner, D. G. Lyon, and C. S. Fisher (1908-1910) and J. W. Crow-
foot, Kathleen Kenyon, and E. L. Sukenik (*The Buildings of Samaria*,
1942).

From Omri's time onward Israel appears in cuneiform records as
Bit-Humri ("House of Omri"), and Israelite kings were dubbed *mar-
Humri* ("son of Omri" in the sense of "royal successor of Omri").
Omri's son and successor, Ahab, is mentioned in Assyrian annals in
connection with a western coalition that fought the advance of Assyria
at Karkar in 854 B.C. Ahab is said to have supported the alliance
against Assyria with 2000 chariots and 10,000 men that fought against
the armies of Shalmaneser III (859-824 B.C.).

Jehu and the Advance of Assyria. Jehu (about 841-814 B.C.), the extir-
pator of the house of Ahab and the cult of Baal from Israel, submitted
to Shalmaneser III. The Black Obelisk shows Jehu actually prostrat-
ing himself before the Assyrian monarch. The inscription reads,
"Tribute of Iaua [Jehu] son of Omri. Silver, gold, a golden bowl, a
golden beaker, golden goblets, pitchers of gold, lead, staves for the
hand of the king, javelins I received from him."

The Last Years of the Northern Kingdom. Just at the time of Jeroboam
II's death and the assassination of his son shortly thereafter, the
powerful Tiglathpileser III (745-727 B.C.) resurrected the moribund
Assyrian Empire and advanced westward. Under his popular name,
Pul (Pulu), he placed Menahem (about 752-742 B.C.) under heavy tribute (1 Kings 15:19). The same event is recorded in the Assyrian annals. "As for Menahem, terror overwhelmed him; like a bird, alone he
fled and submitted to me . . . I received . . . his tribute."

Hoshea, the last king of the Northern Kingdom (732-722 B.C.),
was an Assyrian vassal whom Tiglathpileser set over Israel. In the
delusive hope of receiving aid from Egypt Hoshea ceased paying tribute to Assyria. Shalmaneser V (726-722 B.C.) thereupon advanced
against him. Although Hoshea sought to placate his overlord, his be-
lated overtures of submission did not save him from imprisonment (2
Kings 17:3, 4), and his capital was placed under siege by the Assyrians.

The Fall of Samaria. After a stubborn, three-year resistance, Samaria
finally fell to Assyria. Before the overthrow had been accomplished,
however, Shalmaneser V had been succeeded by Sharrukin II (721-
705 B.C.), who assumed the ancient name of Sargon. In the Khorsabad
annals of his reign, the monarch lists the fall of Samaria as the chief

event of his first regnal year. He claims to have deported 27,290 of the capital's inhabitants, set his officers over the city, and exacted tribute. This was probably in the opening months of 721 B.C.

Judah and the Assyrian Menace. The flood of Assyrian power that carried Israel to destruction caused untold anguish to Judah. There is evidence of a Palestinian coalition against Assyria as early as Azariah (791-740 B.C). Tiglathpileser III makes clear reference in his annals to *Azriyau of Yaudu* (Azariah of Judah) in connection with what is obviously such a coalition. Azariah's son Jotham (740-736 B.C.) apparently continued an anti-Assyrian policy. However, Jotham's son Ahaz, an idolatrous apostate, refused to join Pekah of Israel and Rezin of Syria in an alliance to stem Assyrian advance. The result was that Pekah and Rezin invaded Judah, precipitating the Syro-Ephraimite War (about 734 B.C.). Ahaz, hard-pressed, appealed to Assyria for help and introduced a century of vassalage for Judah.

THE KINGDOM OF JUDAH (722 TO 586 B.C.)

Hezekiah and Sennacherib. Hezekiah (716-687 B.C.) inherited the Assyrian menace and did all he could to prepare for an eventual showdown with Assyria. He cleansed out the idolatrous contaminations his father had introduced, strengthened Jerusalem's defenses, and safeguarded the city's water supply by building the Siloam tunnel (2 Kings 20:20).

In 701 B.C. Sennacherib invaded Judah. His account on the Taylor prism represents Hezekiah as the ringleader of the Western revolt. Sennacherib claims to have taken forty-six fortified towns and to have shut up Hezekiah "like a caged bird in Jerusalem, his royal city." Though the Lord intervened to destroy the Assyrian army (2 Kings 19:35-36), Judah suffered a paralyzing blow.

Manasseh and the Assyrians. Manasseh was co-ruler with his father Hezekiah from 696 to 687 B.C. and was the sole ruler from 687 to 642 B.C. His reign witnessed a paganizing movement caused by fear of Assyria and fascination for her cults (2 Kings 21:1-15). The result was an absorption of both Baalism (a cult of Astarte at the "high places") and occult-oriented religionism centering in astrology and star worship. Manasseh's anti-Jehovistic reign was long and cruel.

The name "Manasseh, king of Judah" occurs on the Prism of Esarhaddon and on the Prism of Ashurbanipal, along with twenty-one other tributaries of Assyria. Second Chronicles alludes to Manasseh's deportation to Babylon, his repentance, and his release (2 Chron. 33: 10-13). It is known that a revolt against Assyria took place during

Manasseh's reign, in support of the viceroy of Babylon. Manasseh may well have been involved in it. Necho I of Egypt was captured and subsequently released by Ashurbanipal, as is known from the Rassam Cylinder. (This offers an interesting parallel to the Chronicler's claim concerning Manasseh's deportation to Babylon.) His wicked son, Amon (642-640 B.C.), swept away the superficial reform his father inaugurated before his death.

Josiah and Religious Reform. Josiah (640-609 B.C.) is known as a great and good king who inaugurated a religious reformation in Judah (2 Kings 22, 23; 2 Chron. 34, 35). The climax of this movement was reached in the eighteenth year of Josiah (621 B.C.), when "the book of the Law" was discovered in the Temple. But idolatry had laid such a hold upon the people during the wicked reign of Manasseh that the effects of Josiah's purge were superficial. After Josiah's untimely death in battle with Pharaoh Necho (608 B.C.), the nation reverted to its evil ways and plunged headlong into national ruin.

Jeremiah's prophecies (chaps. 2 — 6) belong to this period. The Lachish Letters (recovered from the town of Lachish or Tell ed-Duweir in southeastern Palestine) bring to life Jeremiah's era, especially just before Nebuchadnezzar's invasion (588-586 B.C.).

The Last Days of Judah. Jehoahaz, Josiah's son, succeeded his father. He reigned only three months before being deposed by Pharaoh Necho, who placed Jehoahaz' brother Jehoiakim (609-597 B.C.) on the throne. But Jehoiakim's evil reign ended in disgrace and death. He was succeeded by his son Jehoiachin, who was carried to Babylon after he ruled for only three months and ten days (2 Chron. 36:9; cf. 2 Kings 25:8-16).

In Babylon Jehoiachin was treated as a royal hostage. His name occurs in Babylonian tablets dated between 595 and 570 B.C. as "Yaukin, king of the land of Yahud." Evil-Merodach, Nebuchadnezzar's successor, set him free from prison in 561 B.C. (2 Kings 25:27-30).

Zedekiah, Josiah's youngest son, was the last king of Judah (597-586 B.C.). Nebuchadnezzar seated him as king and changed his name to Mattaniah as a mark of vassalage. But he rebelled against Nebuchadnezzar and precipitated the siege of Jerusalem. After holding out for 18 months, the city fell in July, 586 B.C. during conditions of horrible famine. Zedekiah and a remnant of his army managed to escape by night from the doomed city. However, they were pursued and captured near Jericho. The king's eyes were put out and he was deported to Babylon. The city and Temple were destroyed. The Chaldeans and the Kingdom of Judah collapsed (2 Kings 24:18 — 25:7).

THE PERIOD OF THE EXILE (586 TO 538 B.C.)

The Chaldean Empire (605 to 539 B.C.). Short-lived but powerful, this kingdom was divinely raised up to chastise God's sinful people; its existence was coterminous with Judah's captivity. Nabopolassar (625-605 B.C.), the governor of Babylon and father of Nebuchadnezzar, threw off the Assyrian yoke. He became an imperial figure with the fall of Nineveh (612 B.C.) and Haran (609 B.C.).

Nebuchadnezzar II (605 to 552 B.C.). His first deportation of Judah (Dan. 1:2) included Daniel; his second, in 597 B.C., included Ezekiel; and the third, in 586 B.C.., resulted in the destruction of Jerusalem and the kingdom of Judah. He ruthlessly conquered the West, desolating Moab, Ammon, Edom, and Lebanon. His siege of Tyre (585-573 B.C) furnishes an example of his tenacity. He invaded Egypt in 568, but little is known of the last thirty years of his reign.

Nebuchadnezzar was a great builder of temples and shrines at Babylon, Sippar, Marad, and Borsippa. He made Babylon the wonder city of the world with the Ishtar Gate, the ziggurat, the processional way, the defense walls, and the canal network. He was very religious, providing regular offerings and garments for the sacred statues. This accords well with the episode of the golden image (Dan. 3).

Evil-Merodach ("The Man Is Marduk") (562-560 B.C.) succeeded his father to the throne. He was the king who released Jehoiachin of Judah from imprisonment (Jer. 52:31; 2 Kings 25:27-30). He was killed by Neriglissar ("Nergal protect the king"), who was apparently an army general married to Nebuchadnezzar's daughter (Jer. 39:3, 13).

Neriglissar (560 to 556 B.C.) reigned only four years. His son Labashi-Marduk was assassinated after a reign of only four months.

Nabonidus (556 to 539 B.C.) was a Babylonian noble who usurped the throne to become the last king of the Neo-Babylonian Empire. His son Belshazzar was coregent with him from the third year of his reign. The very existence of Belshazzar (Dan. 5:1-31; 7:1; 8:1) was doubted until cuneiform accounts chronicling his reign were recovered. Records of both Nabonidus and Belshazzar, however, are fragmentary. Authentication and clarification of the precise details of the fall of Babylon and Belshazzar's death as mentioned in Daniel await further discoveries.

THE POST-EXILIC PERIOD (539 TO 400 B.C.)

The Persian Empire Founded. Cyrus II the Great came to the throne of Anshan around 559 B.C. He soon won supremacy over the Medes and began a career of conquest that founded the Persian Empire. In 546 Lydia was conquered and in 539 Babylon, under crown prince Belshazzar (Dan. 5), fell to him. Unlike most ancient rulers, however, Cyrus was a humane conqueror. Instead of destroying Babylon he won its people over by mercy. He even allowed the Jews to return to their homeland (Ezra 1:1-4).

The spirit of Cyrus' decree of release which is alluded to in the Old Testament (2 Chron. 36:23; Ezra 1:2-4) is confirmed by the Cyrus cylinder. The king records how he permitted the captives of his conquered realms to return to their own lands and rebuild their temples.

Cyrus was slain in battle in 530 B.C. His son Cambyses II (530-522) succeeded him. After conquering Egypt and adding it to the Empire, Cambyses went mad and committed suicide, plunging the empire into revolt.

Darius I and Haggai and Zechariah. Darius I (522-486 B.C.) saved the Empire. He, too, proved to be a very humane administrator. Religiously, Darius I was an ardent Zoroastrian and worshiper of Ahura Mazda, as were later Persian kings Xerxes and Artaxerxes. The beginning of both Haggai's and Zechariah's ministry is dated in the second year of Darius (Hag. 1:1; Zech. 1:1). Likewise, the completion of the restoration Temple is dated in the sixth year of Darius, i.e. 515 B.C. (Ezra 6: 15). Darius I's rock-hewn tomb at Naqsh-I-Rustam (a few miles northeast of Persepolis) bears a trilingual inscription relating his character and achievements. Similar tombs were cut from the cliff for the three successors of Darius – Xerxes, Artaxerxes I, and Darius II.

Darius I and the Behistun Inscription. Carved on a cliff 500 feet above the plain of Karmanshah near the small village of Behistun, the relief depicts and records Darius' victory over the rebellion that inaugurated his reign and his salvation of the Empire. Composed in three languages, Old Persian, Elamite, and Akkadian, the inscription became the key that unlocked Akkadian cuneiform, much as the Rosetta Stone had opened up Egyptian hieroglyphics.

Xerxes and the Book of Esther. Darius I was followed on the Persian throne by his son Xerxes (486-465 B.C.). He is no doubt the Ahasuerus mentioned between Darius and Artaxerxes (Ezra 4:6), the husband of Esther. (Ahaseurus is the Hebrew form of the Persian name Khshayarsha, of which the Greek form is Xerxes.) His invading armies were defeated by the Greeks at Thermopylae and Salamis in 480 B.C.

Artaxerxes I and Nehemiah. The successor of Xerxes was Artaxerxes I Longimanus (465-423 B.C.). Nehemiah's request to visit Jerusalem, according to Nehemiah 2:1, was made in the month Nisan in Artaxerxes' twentieth year. The reference is very likely to Artaxerxes I. The date indicated is therefore Nisan (April-May), 445 B.C.

Archeology confirms generally that Nehemiah had lived at about this time. The Elephantine Papyri, discovered in 1903 on the island of Elephantine at the First Cataract in Egypt and dating from the end of the fifth century B.C., mention two persons connected with Nehemiah in the Old Testament. The first is Sanballat, whose two sons are referred to as governors of Samaria in 408 B.C. Doubtless their father was the leading opponent of Nehemiah (Neh. 2:19, etc.). The second person is Johanan, who was high priest in Jerusalem in 408 B.C., according to the papyri. Nehemiah is said to have been in Jerusalem when Johanan's father, Eliashib, was high priest (Neh. 3:1; 12:23). This also agrees well with the date of 445 B.C. for Nehemiah.

Artaxerxes I and Ezra. It is stated that Ezra the scribe came to Jerusalem in the seventh year of Artaxerxes (Ezra 7:1, 8). This reference is certainly to Artaxerxes I and the date is therefore 458 B.C. This would mean that Ezra preceded Nehemiah. Since Johanan, the son of Eliashib, is mentioned in connection with the work of Ezra (Ezra 10:6), some scholars think that Ezra's mission may have followed Nehemiah's, under Artaxerxes II.

Artaxerxes II and Malachi. Following Artaxerxes I, the Persian throne was occupied by Darius II (423-404 B.C.), Artaxerxes II Mnemon (404-359), Artaxerxes III Ochus (359-338), Arses (338-335), and Darius III (335-331). Malachi's ministry and the close of the Old Testament period took place under either Darius II or Artaxerxes II.

Intertestamental History

THE INTERTESTAMENTAL PERIOD

The era of approximately four centuries between Malachi and John the Baptist (and Jesus) is commonly known as the interbiblical or intertestamental period. Sometimes it is referred to as "the four hundred silent years." During this interval, revelation and inspiration (in the special sense in which this divine operation produced canonical Scripture) was in abeyance.

Unsound higher critical theories deny this position, tending to place books like Esther, Daniel, Chronicles, and even some of the Psalms, during this period, sometimes quite late in the period. However, sound critical scholarship cannot accept these views. Instead, conservative scholarship substantially agrees with Josephus, a prominent Jewish historian of the first century A.D. According to Josephus

Gigantic Temple of El-Khazne (treasure) in Edom's rock-bound Petra (© *MPS*)

the completion of the Hebrew Canon took place in the reign of Arta-xerxes I (465-414 B.C.). (This fact does not mean that other religious literature was not produced. The Apocrypha, Pseudepigrapha, and other religious writings such as those retrieved from the Dead Sea Caves came into being during this general period.)

THE PERSIAN EMPIRE (400 TO 323 B.C.)

THE JEWS UNDER PERSIAN RULE. Malachi, the last Old Testament prophet (about 400 B.C.), ministered under the reign of Darius II (423-404 B.C.), or early in the reign of Artaxerxes II (404-358 B.C.). During the heyday of Persian power Palestine was a tiny province in a mighty Empire that stretched from Asia Minor to India and from Ethiopia to the mountains of Armenia. Palestine fell within the bounds of the Fifth Persian Satrapy. From his capital at Damascus or Samaria the Persian governor (satrap) ruled and administered justice.

Artaxerxes II was succeeded by Artaxerxes III (358-338 B.C.), Arse (338-336 B.C.), and Darius III (336-331 B.C.). During this extended period the Jews enjoyed comparative peace and prosperity under their Persian overlords. Persian power radiated from both Shushan (Susa), the winter capital, located about a hundred miles east of the Tigris River in Anshan, and Achmetha (Ecbatana), the summer capital, located about two hundred miles northeast of Susa in Media. Another center of Persian power was Persepolis, twenty-five miles southwest of Pasargadae, to which Darius I transferred the main capital of Persia. These great capitals with their wealth and splendor were destined to be looted by Alexander the Great.

THE RISE OF MACEDON. Philip II (359-336 B.C.), a military genius, organized Macedonia, the mountainous territory north of Greece, into a strong state. At Chaeronea in 338 he defeated the Greeks and at Corinth in 337 he united them behind himself to fight Persia. He forged the weapons with which his twenty-year-old son, Alexander, was able to conquer the world.

ALEXANDER THE GREAT (336-323 B.C.). In 334 Alexander crossed the Hellespont and defeated the Persian army at Granicus in Asia Minor. His victory at Issus over a huge army of Darius III in 333 opened up Syria, Palestine, and Egypt to his victorious forces. Tyre resisted, but was taken after a seven-month siege in July 332. Gaza, at the entrance to Egypt, fell before him. In Egypt he founded the brilliant city of Alexandria. His contacts with the Jews at this time were amicable.

Alexander advanced eastward, and on October 1, 331 B.C. he clashed with an immense Persian army at Gaugamela, not far from the ruins of Nineveh. Darius III was defeated and fled eastward, only to be treacherously murdered by his own cousin, the satrap of Bactria. Persian power collapsed. Alexander became king of Babylon, looting and destroying the Persian palaces at Susa, Ecbatana, and Persepolis. In 327 he crossed the Indus River into the Punjab, extending his sway to the Hydaspes River, southeast of Taxila. He planned to unite East and West in a world brotherhood predominantly Greek in culture.

Intoxicated by his seemingly limitless power, the youthful world conqueror lived like an Oriental Sultan. But his dissolute life, com-

/,bined with a fever he could not overcome, led to his premature death in Babylon in June, 323 B.C. at the age of 32. His conquests were divided among his generals. Eventually, after the battle of Ipsus in 301, Macedonia fell to Cassander, Asia Minor to Lysimachus, Syria to Seleucus, and Egypt to Ptolemy.

PALESTINE UNDER THE PTOLEMIES
(323 TO 198 B.C.)

PTOLEMAIC PALESTINE AND THE JEWISH DIASPORA. Ptolemy I Soter claimed Palestine along with Egypt at Alexander's death. However, Antigonus, one of Alexander's generals, contested the claim and ravaged Jerusalem, causing thousands of Jews to flee to Egypt. After the victory of Ptolemy I Soter (323-285 B.C.) over Antigonus at Gaza in 312 B.C., 100,000 Jews were deported to Egypt. Alexandria became the greatest center of the Jewish diaspora. (Alexander himself had brought many Jews to his newly founded city.) Within a century after Alexander there were more than a million Jews in Egypt from migrations that took place under Ptolemy II Philadelphus (285-246 B.C.), and Ptolemy III Euergetes (246-221 B.C.). But Ptolemy IV Philopator (221-203 B.C.) was a weakling, and in 198 B.C. Palestine came under Seleucid rule.

Under the Ptolemies the Jews had fared well both in Palestine and Egypt. It is during this period that tradition (preserved in The Letter of Aristeas) places the beginning of the translation of the Old Testament into Greek (the Septuagint). The process of Hellenizing the Jews at Alexandria and in the diaspora all over the Hellenistic world also continued during this period (2 Kings 15:29; 17:6; 24:15; 25:7; 1 Chron. 5:26). The New Testament indicates the importance of the worldwide Jewish diaspora (John 7:35; Acts 2:5-11).

THE RISE OF THE TARGUMS, THE SYNAGOGUE, AND THE SANHEDRIN. During this period Aramaic, the universal language of the time, had begun to supplant Hebrew. Aramaic paraphrases of the Hebrew Scriptures, called Targums, began to be produced for the people. At about 200 B.C. the Phoenician alphabet which had been used in preceding centuries was discarded in favor of the square Aramaic characters found in the Dead Sea biblical manuscripts and in later Hebrew Bibles. This era also witnessed the development of the synagogue and of the Sanhedrin. The former had its origin as a house gathering (Greek *sunagoge*, "an assembly") in homes in Babylonia (cf. Ezek. 8:1;

20:1-3). After the exile the synagogue gradually developed into formal assemblies for public worship and instruction by *sopherim*, or scribes learned in the Hebrew Scriptures. The synagogue became a necessity for Jews in the far-flung diaspora and for those in Palestine who resided at too great a distance from the Temple for regular Sabbath worship. They also became schools and petty law courts.

The Sanhedrin (Aramaized form of Greek *sunedrion*, "a sitting together" or "assembly") was a seventy-member civil and judicial body which came into being during this era and was presided over by the high priest.

PALESTINE UNDER THE SELEUCIDS (198-168 B.C.)

ANTIOCHUS III THE GREAT AND THE MASTERY OF PALESTINE. Because it lay between the Ptolemaic and Seleucid empires, Palestine played the role of a helpless pawn in the incessant intrigues and wars that engulfed the two rival powers on its borders. This era of confusion and turmoil was predicted in detail by the prophet Daniel (Dan. 11:1-35). When Ptolemaic power began to wane under Ptolemy IV and V after 221 B.C., Antiochus III the Great (223-187 B.C.) finally gained control of Palestine in 198 B.C. (Dan. 11:16). He then married his daughter to Ptolemy V (Dan. 11:17). His dreams of further greatness were shattered, however, by his defeat by the Romans at Magnesia (190 B.C.) and his death in 187 B.C. (Dan. 11:18, 19).

His successor, Seleucus IV Philopator (187-175 B.C.), represented a decrease in power from Antiochus III but foreshadowed approaching trouble for the Jews when he attempted to rob the Temple (Dan. 11: 20). At his death his brother Antiochus IV Epiphanes usurped the throne (175 B.C.).

THE JEWISH FAITH AND THE THREAT OF HELLENIZATION. Hellenism, because of its purely humanistic outlook on life, clashed head-on with the theocentric faith and austere moral life of Judaism. The broad-minded liberalism of Greek thought, which fostered a relativistic philosophy (Acts 17:21; 1 Cor. 1:21, 22), presented as serious a threat to Israel's faith as had Baalism and the debauched religion of the Canaanites in a previous era.

While a certain degree of Hellenization was inevitable, the agony of the Hasidim or "pious" was rendered all the more acute by the compromise and capitulation on the part of the Jerusalem aristocracy in order to secure governmental favor. Joseph of the Tobiad family became a leader of this worldly party under Ptolemy IV. Simon, son of Joseph, aided Seleucus IV in his attempt to plunder the Temple. With the accession of Antiochus IV Epiphanes in 175 B.C., the Greek party became more openly active (1 Macc. 1:11-15). In the diaspora the process of Hellenization proceeded further than in Palestine.

THE MACCABEAN UPRISING (168 to 143 B.C.).

ANTIOCHUS IV EPIPHANES AND ENFORCED HELLENIZA-TION. Repulsed from conquering Egypt by Rome in 168 B.C., Antiochus IV in anger determined to unite his empire under Hellenism (Dan. 11:30). He was opposed by the Jews but retaliated by slaughtering the Hasidim in Jerusalem and erecting an altar to Zeus in the Jewish Temple in December, 168 B.C. He outlawed all Jewish customs, including sacrifice, circumcision, Sabbath-keeping, and the dietary laws. To possess a copy of the Law was made a capital offense. Many Jews capitulated (Dan. 11:32), while others fled (1 Macc. 1:62-64; 2 Macc. 7).

THE MACCABEAN REVOLT. Mattathias, an aged priest of the Hasmonean family at Modin, rejected the pagan sacrifices and killed a fellow Jew who had capitulated to this practice. He accompanied this bold act with a ringing declaration of war: "Whoever is zealous for the law, and maintaineth the covenant, let him come forth after me" (1 Macc. 2:27). Mattathias aroused the Hasidim to guerrilla attacks against the Syrians and apostate Jews. He appointed his son Judas to be his successor after his death in 167 B.C.

JUDAS MACCABEUS (167 TO 161 B.C.). By courage, strategy, and divine help Judas won four great victories in 166 and 165 B.C. (Dan. 8:25; Zech. 9:13-17). By December, 165 B.C. he was able to cleanse the Temple and reestablish the daily sacrifice. This great event came to be celebrated annually as "The Feast of Dedication" or "The Feast of Lights" (John 10:22). Antiochus Epiphanes died in 164 B.C., opening up the way for Judas to conquer Idumea, Transjordan, and Philistia (1 Macc. 5).

Despite the defeat of Judas at Bethzacharias in 163 B.C. by young Antiochus V, revolt at Antioch compelled the Seleucid invaders to withdraw, and Judea was granted religious liberty. In 162 B.C. Demetrius I (162-150 B.C.) murdered his cousin Antiochus V and seized the throne of Syria. He appointed Alcimus, a corrupt Hellenizer, as high priest. Judas not only drove out Alcimus but destroyed a Syrian army at Adasa in March, 161 B.C. However, the next month Judas died heroically in battle at Elasa (1 Macc. 9:1-22) in the face of a large invading force of Syrians.

JONATHAN AND SIMON MACCABEUS AND POLITICAL INDEPENDENCE. The brothers of Judas now fought for political liberty. Jonathan (161-143 B.C.) carried on Judas' role as a guerrilla leader and a foe of Hellenizing Jews (1 Macc. 9:58-73). In the struggle among rival claimants for the Seleucid throne, Alexander I, another son of Antiochus IV, appointed Jonathan as high priest in order to gain his favor. Alexander I also defeated and killed Demetrius I in 150 B.C. Demetrius II, the son of Demetrius I, was able with the help of Ptolemy VII to defeat and kill Alexander in 145 B.C. He bestowed upon Jonathan the districts of Samaria to court his favor.

Intrigue, however, continued in the struggle for the Syrian throne, and an infant son of Alexander was now brought forward as Antiochus VI by a general named Tryphon. But the general not only put Antiochus VI to death and arrogated the crown to himself, but treacherously murdered Jonathan as well. However, Tryphon's rival, Demetrius II, granted to Simon Maccabeus (143-135 B.C.) the long-fought-for political independence of Judea (143 B.C.; 1 Macc. 13:36-43).

THE HASMONEAN PRIEST-KINGS (143 to 37 B.C.)

SIMON (143 TO 135 B.C.). Simon was confirmed in the position of King-Priest by the Romans (1 Macc. 14:16-24). While the rivals for the Syrian throne, Demetrius II and Tryphon, fought one another, Simon was able to strengthen Judea and expel the last Syrian garrison from Jerusalem. When Antiochus VII, the brother of Demetrius II, came into power, Simon defeated his attempt to reimpose the Seleucid yoke on Judea (1 Macc. 16:8-10). Simon stabilized the Jewish kingdom until he was treacherously murdered by his son-in-law, Ptolemy, in 135 B.C.

JOHN HYRCANUS I (135 TO 105 B.C.). As the sole surviving son of Simon, John Hyrcanus came to power and drove out Ptolemy. But he was dominated by Antiochus VII (139-129). After the latter's death in 129 B.C. and the ensuing struggle for power in Syria between Demetrius II (who was released by the Parthians) and Alexander II, John Hyrcanus was free to expand his realm, especially since his position had become strengthened by a strong treaty with the Romans. He conquered Idumea, Transjordan, and Samaria. In 128 B.C. he destroyed the Samaritan Temple on Mount Gerizim. He occupied Jezreel in 109 B.C. when he repulsed Antiochus IX.

ARISTOBULUS I (105 TO 104 B.C.). Aristobulus shared the rule with his brother Antigonus I initially, but murdered him as soon as opportunity allowed, thereafter assuming the kingship himself. He was opposed by strict Jews for his cruelties and for his Hellenistic leanings. But he ruled reasonably well nevertheless, and added Galilee to his realm.

ALEXANDER JANNAEUS (104 TO 78 B.C.). A brother of Aristobulus, Alexander Jannaeus, was designated king by Aristobulus' widow, Alexandra, whom he married. He was able to enlarge his kingdom considerably, partly because of the continuing struggle in Syria of rival claimants for the Seleucid throne. However, the rise of Nabataean power under Aretas III put an end to his conquests in 85 B.C.

ALEXANDER (78 TO 69 B.C.) AND THE RISE OF JEWISH PARTIES. Alexander Jannaeus' widow succeeded her husband as regent, though their son Hyrcanus II was high priest. In reality, however, the rule passed into the hands of the Sanhedrin, dominated by the Pharisees. Members of this latter sect were apparently the successors of the Hasidim who had been God's "loyal ones" in the Maccabean era and who had stood true to Judaism against the pressures of Hellenism. They were separatists and strict legalists who stressed prayer, repentance, and charitable giving. They believed in foreordination, immortality, resurrection, angels, judgment, and eternal rewards (Acts 23:8).

The Sadducees were the Zadokite priests and their partisans (1 Kings 2:35). They were principally composed of the aristocratic, worldly-minded priests. They maintained the Temple ritual but were actually more interested in politics than in religion. As worldly followers of the later Hasmoneans they had Hellenistic sympathies. They were the religious rationalists of the day and opposed the traditions of the Pharisees. They laid emphasis on human ability, and denied immortality, the existence of angels, the resurrection, and future retribution. Their religion was anthropocentric (man-centered).

The Essenes were ascetics who withdrew from normal life into monastic colonies in the desert. Their faith was apocalyptic and their morality very severe. Their customs are seen in the Dead Sea Scrolls, especially The Manual of Discipline and the Damascus Document from the Qumran Caves.

ARISTOBULUS II, HYRCANUS II, AND ROMAN SUBJECTION (69 TO 37 B.C.).

The sons of Jannaeus, Aristobulus II (69-63 B.C.) and Hyrcanus II (63-40 B.C.), vied with each other for the throne. Both appealed to Rome for help, which furnished the ideal situation for a Roman takeover. By 64 B.C. Pompey, the Roman general, had already made Syria a Roman province with headquarters in Damascus. When Aristobulus lost the confidence of the Romans and his supporters entrenched themselves in the Temple, Pompey besieged Jerusalem. In 63 B.C. the city surrendered, after three months' siege. Pompey outraged the Jews by entering the Holy of Holies.

Aristobulus II was taken prisoner to Rome. His older brother, Hyrcanus II, was appointed high priest and ethnarch under the Romans. Hasmonean independence came to an end. From that time on the Jews were subject to Rome.

Survey of New Testament History

PALESTINE IN CHRIST'S DAY (4 B.C. to A.D. 30).

THE RISE OF THE ROMAN EMPIRE. After a long period of conquest and expansion from about 500 B.C. Rome entered a period of civil war, beginning with Pompey's conquest of Palestine in 63 B.C. The First Triumvirate (60 B.C.) consisted of Pompey, Crassus, and Julius Caesar. Pompey attacked Caesar, but was defeated at Pharsalus in 48 B.C. and was killed by Ptolemy XIV. Crassus was killed in a campaign against the Parthians (53 B.C.). Caesar's assassination in 44 B.C. opened the way for the Second Triumvirate, consisting of Mark Antony, Octavian, and Lepidus in 43 B.C. These vied for control of the Empire against opposition led by Brutus and Cassius. The republican forces under Brutus and Cassius were crushed at Philippi (42 B.C.). The final clash between Octavian and Mark Antony eventuated in the defeat of the latter and the emergence of the Roman Empire under Octavian ("Augustus Caesar"), who reigned as sole ruler from 31 B.C. to A.D. 14.

THE RISE OF HEROD THE GREAT (37 TO 4 B.C.). Herod was the son of Antipater, the native governor of Idumea under Alexander Jannaeus and the power behind Hyrcanus II (63-40 B.C.). After Pharsalus (48 B.C.), Antipater was awarded the official procuratorship of Judea (47-43 B.C.) for assisting Julius Caesar. Antipater then appointed

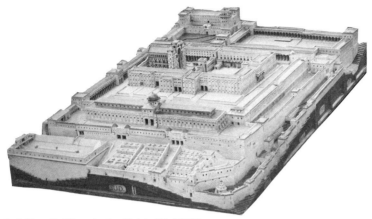

Model of Herod's Temple, by Shick (© *MPS*)

his son Phasael as governor of Jerusalem and his son Herod as governor of Galilee. After Antipater's death by poisoning, both Phasael and Herod gained the favor of Mark Antony and were made tetrarchs over Palestine.

When Antigonus II (40-37 B.C.) took Jerusalem with Parthian help and deposed Hyrcanus II, Phasael committed suicide. Herod, however, fled to Rome, ostensibly to promote the cause of the last of the Hasmonean princes, young Aristobulus III (36-35 B.C.). Instead, he was himself made king of Judea by grant of the Roman Senate. He then married Mariamne, the Hasmonean princess and sister of Aristobulus III, to help strengthen his new position of power.

HEROD'S ADMINISTRATION. Herod had a long and energetic rule. But he was hated by his subjects as an Idumaean or "half Jew" and as a fawning friend of the Romans. In character he was a jealous, crafty monster. No one was safe from his cruelty and suspicion. His slaughter of the male children at Bethlehem (Matt. 2:13, 16) is consistent with his reputation for murder. On the merest suspicion he slew members of his own immediate family, putting to death his favorite wife, Mariamne, and also her brothers, Aristobulus and Alexander. Just five days before he died he ordered the death of his son Antipater. No wonder Augustus said, "It is better to be Herod's hog than to be his son!"

However, Herod ruled fairly well overall, and peace and prosperity resulted. He loved Hellenic culture and architecture and had numerous temples, palaces, theaters, and baths constructed throughout his realm. At the site of ancient Samaria he built Sebaste in honor of Emperor Augustus. On the coast he built the brilliant Hellenistic city of Caesarea, which was to become the capital of the country.

Herod's most magnificent building enterprise was the splendid Temple at Jerusalem begun in 20 B.C. It was constructed in strict conformity with Jewish principles. Herod himself refrained from going into the inner sanctuary, the precinct of the priests. The edifice proper was finished in only one year and six months, though other construction continued for as long as forty years. Only about seven years after its final completion the entire Temple was destroyed in the razing of Jerusalem in A.D. 70.

THE SONS OF HEROD. Of the sons of Herod's ten legal marriages, several had perished in intrigues or had been executed by their father. Thus three younger sons were destined to inherit the kingdom.

Herod Antipas (4 B.C. to A.D. 39). He was the younger son of Malthace and became tetrarch of Galilee and Perea. His capital was built on the western shore of the Sea of Galilee and was called Tiberias in honor of the then-reigning emperor, Tiberius Caesar (A.D. 22). Antipas divorced his first wife, the daughter of King Aretas IV of Nabatea, to marry Herodias, the wife of his half-brother, Herod Philip. John the Baptist was imprisoned and executed by Antipas (Mark 6:14-28) because he denounced this second marriage as unlawful. Jesus once described Antipas as "that fox" (Luke 13:31-33). He also had a brief encounter with Jesus when the latter was sent to him by Pilate for judgment (Luke 23:6-12). Aretas IV avenged Herod's insult in A.D. 36 by defeating him in war. Antipas ended up in banishment in Gaul when deposed from his tetrarchy by Emperor Caligula.

Archelaus (4 B.C. to A.D. 6). He was the older son of Herod by Malthace and received the principal part of Herod's kingdom, comprising Judea, Samaria, and Idumea. His father intended him to have the title of king, but he was actually made only an ethnarch. He was a violent, cruel, and incompetent administrator and was consequently banished to Vienne in Gaul in A.D. 6. When Joseph took Mary and the infant Jesus from Egypt to return to the land of Israel, Joseph was afraid to go into Judea because Archelaus was on the throne. (Joseph withdrew to Galilee instead—see Matthew 2:22, 23).

Herod Philip (4 B.C. to A.D. 34). He was Herod the Great's son by Cleopatra and became tetrarch of regions north and east of the Sea of

Galilee (Gaulonitis, Trachonitis Batanea, and Ulatha). He ruled well for thirty years, and, like his father, was a builder. At the sources of the Jordan he rebuilt the city of Panias, calling it Caesarea in honor of the emperor. Its full name was Caesarea Philippi (Matt. 16:13; Mark 8:27) to distinguish it from Caesarea the capital of Judea, on the Mediterranean coast. He also enlarged and adorned Bethsaida near the spot where the Jordan River enters the Lake of Galilee. He called it Bethsaida Julias after Augustus Caesar's daughter Julia.

LOCAL RULE OF THE JEWISH PARTIES. Five prominent parties in Judaism vied with Roman authority for a voice of power in affairs in Judea in the days of Jesus. The *Sadducees* dominated the priesthood (Acts 5:17) and had a disproportionately large voice in the governing council, the Sanhedrin (Acts 4:1). Influential *Pharisees* also tried to control this supreme legislative body. They opposed the Herods, but were willing to co-exist peaceably with the Romans (John 11: 48). Christ condemned their hypocrisy and self-righteous legalism (Matt. 23:13-36). Infuriated, they plotted his death under the pretense of loyalty to Caesar (John 19:12-15).

The *Herodians* were partisans of Rome and supporters of Rome's puppets, the Herods, and of Hellenism (Mark 3:6; 8:15). The *Zealots* were those Jews fired with messianic hope and hatred of Rome. They were ready to make Christ a revolutionary leader (John 6:15). From the *Essene movement,* illustrated from the discoveries at Qumran, may have come John the Baptist (Luke 3:1-4, 15, 16). Rigid separation and call to reformation constituted the battle cry of this group. Each of these sects had a part in preparing for Christ's advent and ministry. Yet all of these parties became off-balance and extremist. Only in Christ could their central truth find complete fulfillment.

JUDEA UNDER ROMAN PROCURATORS (A.D. 4 TO 66). When Herod's son Archelaus was banished in A.D. 6, his territory became a Roman province ruled directly by the Emperor through a governor of the equestrian order called a *procurator.* This governor could receive help from the legate who governed the imperial province of Syria. His residence was at Caesarea, but he could occupy quarters at Jerusalem when special need arose. From A.D. 6 till the Jewish war with Rome (with the exception of the period A.D. 41-44, when Agrippa I was a Jewish king) Judea and Samaria were governed by a series of Roman procurators.

THE PROCURATORS OF CHRIST'S DAY. Of the Roman procurators of Christ's day by far the most important from the standpoint of Christ's life was Pontius Pilate (A.D. 26-36). In A.D. 26 Tiberius Caesar appointed him to be the fifth procurator of Judea. In accordance with a recent reversal in the policy of the Roman Senate (A.D. 21), Pilate took his wife with him (Matt. 27:19). As procurator he had full control in the province, being in charge of detachments of cavalry and infantry stationed at Caesarea and in the fortress of Antonia at Jerusalem. He had jurisdiction over life and death and could reverse capital sentences passed by the Sanhedrin, which had to be submitted to him for ratification. He also named the high priests and controlled the temple and its funds. At the festivals the procurator took up residence in Jerusalem and brought in additional troops to maintain order.

Pilate had a reputation for giving offense to the Jews. An example of his cruelty is the otherwise unknown act of violence referred to in Luke 13:1, in which he mingled the blood of certain Galileans with that of their animal sacrifices. He took money from the Temple treasury to build an aqueduct to Jerusalem and mercilessly beat down the crowds protesting this act. Later he put inscribed shields in Herod's palace. These were taken down only when the Jews appealed to Tiberius Caesar. His atrocities against the Samaritans led to complaint to Vitellius, the legate of Syria, and ultimately resulted in his replacement.

THE PERIOD OF THE EARLY CHURCH
(A.D. 30 to 65).

THE BIRTH OF THE CHURCH. The death and resurrection of Christ resulted in the gift of the Spirit at Pentecost in A.D. 30 and the formation of the Church. Although the Church was at first composed only of regenerated Jews (Acts 1 – 7), it soon began to include racially mixed Samaritans (Acts 8) and eventually included even Gentiles (Acts 10). The settled order of the new age was established when Jew and Gentile were made one in a new entity that exemplified God's purpose: "to visit the Gentiles to take out of them a people for his name" (Acts 15:14, 15). The Church spread rapidly because it had a vital redemptive message for *all* mankind through the sacrificial death of Jesus Christ, God incarnate.

THE CHURCH AND JEWISH PERSECUTION. The unbelieving part of the Jewish nation rejected and persecuted Christ's Church much as it had rejected and persecuted Christ himself. Judea was the scene of fierce persecutions of the early followers of Jesus (Acts 4 – 7).

These trials, however, served to scatter Christian witnesses far and wide and were an important factor in the Church's growth throughout the Empire.

A bust of Tiberius Caesar, as he may have appeared on the penny handed Jesus *(Russ Busby photo)*

THE CHURCH AND THE ROMAN EMPERORS. Tiberius (A.D. 14-37) was succeeded by his nephew Caligula (A.D. 37-41), who was appointed emperor by the Praetorian guards. A cruel, insane tyrant, he alienated everyone and was eventually murdered by the guards. Claudius (A.D. 41-54), Caligula's uncle and successor, is mentioned in the New Testament. He banished the Jews from Rome (Acts 18:2), but later restored them. During his reign there was a severe and widespread famine (Acts 11:28). Claudius was murdered by his niece, the mother of Nero. Nero (A.D. 54-68) was Claudius' adopted son and, like Caligula, was appointed to the imperial power by the Praetorian guards.

Nero was educated by the famous philosopher Seneca. Yet despite this fact he became a profligate monster. Among his atrocities was a fearful persecution of Christians, whom he accused of burning Rome in A.D. 64. Numerous Christians suffered martyrdom at this time, including the Apostle Peter and the Apostle Paul. Deserted by the Praetorian guards, Nero took his own life.

Civil war followed Nero's death. The army took control, appointing in succession several military figures to supreme power — Galba of

Spain, Otho of the Praetorians, and Vitellius of the Rhine (A.D. 68-69). None of these proved long-lasting. Vespasian (A.D. 69-79), commander of the Syrian legions, left his son Titus in the East to put down the Jewish uprising in Palestine. He himself hastened to Rome to make a bid for the emperorship. He was successful, founding the Flavian dynasty and establishing a stable and just administration.

THE CHURCH AND THE LATER HERODS. Herod's sons, Archelaus, Herod Antipas, and Herod Philip, figure prominently in the background of the lives of Jesus and John the Baptist. The later Herods, Herod Agrippa I and Herod Agrippa II, color the history of the early Church.

Herod Agrippa I, King of Judea (A.D. 41 to 44). He was a grandson of Herod the Great and was sent to Rome to be educated in the family of emperor Tiberius. His extravagant living reduced him to poverty, and he was compelled to return to Judea. His sister Herodias secured him employment with Herod Antipas. But he quarreled with both Antipas and Flaccus, the legate of Syria. Eventually he returned to Rome to become a personal friend of Caligula and to support the latter's rise to power.

Tiberius had replaced Pilate as Procurator of Judea with Marcellus (A.D. 36-37). When Caligula became emperor, he appointed Marullus (A.D. 37-41) to the procuratorship of Judea and rewarded Agrippa with the tetrarchy of Trachonitis, giving him the title of king (A.D. 37). Herodias, the wife of Herod Antipas, in envy prevailed upon her husband to also seek the kingly title over Galilee. Agrippa, anticipating this rivalry, used his influence with Caligula to have Antipas banished to Gaul, and he himself received Galilee (A.D. 39). Being in Rome at the time Caligula was murdered, he urged Claudius to assume the emperorship. As a result Claudius awarded him Judea and Samaria. He was now king of all the territory once held by Herod the Great.

Herod Agrippa I skillfully placated the Jews. This policy involved him in the murder of the Apostle James, the brother of John, and the attempted murder of the Apostle Peter (Acts 12:1-19). He came under the severe judgment of God for accepting divine honors (Acts 12:20-23).

Herod Agrippa II. He was the son of Herod Agrippa I and was in line for the kingship. However, this was precluded by his youth, as he was only seventeen years of age. As a result the procuratorship was reinstituted. In A.D. 48, after his uncle Herod's death, Claudius gave him the kingdom of Chalcis in Lebanon. In A.D. 50 Agrippa II was given Trachonitis and parts of Galilee, with the accompanying title of king. In this way Agrippa became Agrippa II, the last of the Herodian line.

Agrippa II's sister, Drusilla, married the procurator Felix (A.D. 52-60). Felix heard Paul's case, expecting a bribe (Acts 24:1-26). Festus (A.D. 60-62), the most just of the procurators, also heard Paul's defense, together with Agrippa II and Berenice, the latter's corrupt sister-mistress (Acts 25:13 – 26:32). This event shows the deference Rome was prepared to pay to a puppet king, who was a typical Herod of the better sort—regal, intelligent, and pro-Roman but sympathetically understanding toward Judaism, which he saw as the key to the history of his land. With Agrippa II ended the line of the Herods, whose adroit pro-Roman policy went far to postpone the inevitable clash between Rome and the Jews. As a result peace was maintained in the crucial formative years of the Christian Church in Palestine.

THE JEWISH-ROMAN WAR (A.D. 66 to 70).

THE INEVITABLE CLASH WITH ROME. The rejection and crucifixion of Jesus Christ displayed the moral and spiritual deterioration to which the Jewish people had sunk. It was this spiritual decay which led the Jews to their national ruin. Although their Roman overlords were frequently oppressive and corrupt, the real cause for the impending clash with Rome was the inability of the Jews themselves to preserve tranquility, the one thing upon which Rome insisted.

Unrest mounted dangerously under the latter procurators. Extreme zealots called "Sicarii" murdered innocent people, including the high priest, Jonathan, for his policy of moderation. A fanatical Egyptian who claimed to be Messiah led a mob of Sicarii out of Jerusalem (Acts 21:38). Felix killed or captured most of these, but the leader escaped. Severe Jewish-Gentile riots in Caesarea led to the recall of Felix. Even under a good procurator such as Festus (A.D. 60-62), the threat of the Sicarii increased. Albinus (A.D. 62-64) unscrupulously encouraged lawlessness for self-enrichment.

Ananus, the Sadducean high priest, had James the brother of Christ executed in A.D. 62. Gessius Florus (A.D. 61-66), the last procurator, was unprincipled, and precipitated a hopeless situation. Race riots were rampant. Florus demanded money from the Temple treasury. The Jews refused. When soldiers attempted to seize the money, the Jews drove them back. The war was underway.

THE EARLY CAMPAIGNS OF THE WAR. Cestius Gallus, the

Syrian legate, sent Agrippa II to mediate the quarrel. The Zealots, however, would not listen to reason. But the Pharisees wanted to avoid all-out war and so appealed to Agrippa for troops. His forces captured part of Jerusalem, but were unable to take the Temple and eventually deserted or surrendered. Cestius Gallus brought a force against Jerusalem but was thoroughly repulsed in A.D. 66. The Sanhedrin then appointed Flavius Josephus, an educated Pharisee, as governor of Galilee.

Rome undertook to quell the Jewish revolt by sending one of its best generals, Vespasian, and his son Titus. Josephus was forced to yield to Rome in A.D. 67 as a result of heavy sieges and disloyalty of Zealots within the Jewish ranks.

THE DESTRUCTION OF JERUSALEM (A.D. 70). Vespasian in A.D. 68 proceeded to subdue all Judea. Jerusalem, however, held out, despite the fact that within the city rival zealot factions fought each other. For five months the city was besieged against fanatical resistance fanned by popular expectation of messianic intervention. In August, A.D. 70, Titus, the son of Vespasian, took the city. Roman legionary standards were set up in the Temple, and the victorious soldiers presented sacrifices to them. The Temple and the city were destroyed and the Jews were slaughtered in great numbers. With the fall of Jerusalem the Jewish nation came to an end, and the Jew began his weary worldwide exile that has lasted till the modern revival of the Jewish state in 1948.

BOOK-BY-BOOK SURVEY

Summary of Old Testament Books

ORDER OF BOOKS IN THE HEBREW BIBLE

The Jews arranged their sacred books in a threefold division:

The Law (Torah), comprising Genesis, Exodus, Leviticus, Numbers, and Deuteronomy—the five books of Moses.

The Prophets (Nebhiim), comprising Joshua, Judges, First and Second Samuel, First and Second Kings, Isaiah, Jeremiah, Ezekiel, and the twelve Minor Prophets.

The Writings (Kethubim), consisting of 1) Psalms, Proverbs, and Job; 2) Song of Solomon, Ruth, Lamentations, Ecclesiastes, and Esther; and 3) Daniel, Ezra, Nehemiah, and First and Second Chronicles.

BASIS OF THE HEBREW ARRANGEMENT

Although a number of factors led to the threefold division of the Hebrew Scriptures, the main reason is probably to be found in *liturgical usage*. The Torah or Pentateuch held a special place in the minds and hearts of the Jewish people because it had been divinely given through Moses, the great lawgiver and founder of the Hebrew theocracy. The Torah was also considered the basis of the Jewish state and the foundation of everything written in the Prophets and the Writings. For these reasons it was placed first in the Hebrew Canon. The Torah was divided into fifty-four sections called *Parashioth*, which were read on consecutive Sabbaths throughout the Jewish year.

The Prophets were likewise subdivided into consecutive Sabbath

Michelangelo's Moses, in a church in Rome *(Russ Busby photo)*

readings. These were called *Haphtaroth* or "dismissals" because they were read immediately before the close of each public service. In the ninth century A.D. these were further subdivided by the Massoretes into verses. Chapter divisions, ascribed to Stephen Langton, Archbishop of Canterbury, came into use in the thirteenth century. The Massoretic division into verses was then combined with the chapter divisions and passed from the Latin Vulgate into English through the Geneva Bible in 1560.

The Writings were read less frequently than the Torah and the Prophets. The devotional books were used in the synagogue services, the Psalms and Proverbs weekly, and Job at most of the great fasts.

The Scrolls (the so-called "Five Rolls" — Song of Solomon, Ruth, Lamentations, Ecclesiastes, and Esther) were read at special festivals. The remaining books (Daniel, Ezra, Nehemiah, and Chronicles), formed a sort of appendix, read upon various special occasions.

ORDER OF BOOKS IN THE ENGLISH BIBLE

The books are conveniently arranged according to their subject matter.

The Pentateuch — the five books of Moses, Genesis to Deuteronomy.

The Historical Books — Joshua to Esther.

The Poetic and Wisdom Books — Job to Song of Solomon.

The Prophetic Books — Isaiah to Malachi.

The Pentateuch

TITLE

The term *Pentateuch* is the Greek name given to the first five books of the Old Testament. The word means "the five-volume Book." The Pentateuch apparently existed originally as one book in scroll form. If this was the case, its fivefold division became necessary in the course of history for liturgical reasons, to facilitate the reading of the Law (Torah) in the synagogue service. This was because ancient "books" were in the form of scrolls. The Jews employed the standard-size rolls, about thirty feet long, sufficient to accommodate the unvocalized text of Genesis or Deuteronomy. They did not use the huge scrolls employed by the Egyptians, sometimes over four times this length, as in the case of the Book of the Dead and the Papyrus Harris.

The Pentateuch has also been referred to by various other terms descriptive of its contents. These include "the law" (Josh. 1:7; Matt. 5:17), "the book of the law" (Josh. 8:34), "the book of the law of Moses" (Josh. 8:31), "the book of the law of God" (Josh. 24:26), "the law of the Lord" (Luke 2:23), and "the law of Moses" (Luke 2:22).

AUTHORSHIP

The traditional view is that the Pentateuch is the product of one author, Moses. This position was universally held by the ancient Jewish synagogue, the inspired New Testament writers, the early Christian Church, and virtually all commentators until comparatively recent times.

Modern critical theory, however, contends that the Pentateuch was pieced together from a number of documents written by various authors several centuries after the time of Moses, though containing Mosaic traditions. The so-called "Yahwist document," designated "J," is dated in the ninth century B.C., the "Elohist document" (E) in the eighth century B.C., and the combining of these two documents in the seventh century B.C. Deuteronomy is dated 621 B.C. and the addition of the Priestly Code (P) around 500 B.C. These documents were allegedly pieced together by "redactors" or editors who gave the Pentateuch the order and arrangement it now has.

Several lines of evidence converge to refute this unsound theory.

The Pentateuch itself bears explicit witness to its Mosaic authorship. The legal codes (Exod. 24:4; 25:1; Lev. 1:1; 4:1; Num. 1:1; Deut. 31:9, 24-26) as well as the narrative sections (Exod. 17:14; Num. 33:2) claim to be written by Israel's great lawgiver.

The remainder of the Old Testament also testifies to Mosaic authorship of the Pentateuch (Josh. 1:7; 8:32; 22:5; Judg. 3:4; 1 Chron 15:15; 1 Kings 2:3; 2 Kings 18:12; 23:25; Dan. 9:11, 13; Ezra 3:2; 6:18; Neh. 1:7, 8; Mal. 4:4).

The New Testament likewise attests Mosaic authorship of the Pentateuch (Mark 12:26; Matt. 8:4; 19:7; Mark 1:44; 10:31; Luke 5:14; John 1:17; 5:46, 47; 7:19; 2 Cor. 3:15; Acts 15:21).

Tradition also confirms the same view. The Samaritan Pentateuch (fifth century B.C.) proves that both Jews and Samaritans had believed for many years that Moses wrote this portion of the Bible. The apocryphal book of Ecclesiasticus (45:5) as well as Second Maccabees (7:30) attest the same view, as do Philo (*Life of Moses* 3:39) and Josephus (*Antiquities* IV:8, 48), and all the early lists of canonical books.

Internal evidence and local color also confirm Mosaic authorship. The Pentateuch was written in the desert (Deut. 12:1-10) by an eyewitness-author who knew Egypt intimately (Deut. 11:10; Exod. 5:1-14). By certain archaic expressions of thought and by the elemental nature of its doctrinal teachings the Pentateuch bears witness that it belongs to an early period in God's progressive revelation to man.

IMPORTANCE

The Pentateuch's intrinsic worth as divinely-inspired Scripture is enhanced by its antiquity and its position of primacy in both the Jewish and Christian Canons of Scripture. *Doctrinally* it is the seed plot for every other teaching of Scripture, forming the foundation for all divinely revealed truth. *Cosmically* it presents God as the Creator of the heavens and the earth and of all plant, animal, and human life, in sublime contrast to the naive polytheistic creation stories of antiquity. In presenting the universe as the creative act of one God, the Pentateuch sets forth a concept which is totally beyond the grasp of unaided human thought. *Historically* the Pentateuch provides the foundation for every accurate appraisal of the human race and for every realistic account of its progress. It outlines the essentials of redemptive history, incorporating human events only as they are necessary for this purpose. In this respect it is absolutely unique in all the literature of the world.

MOSAIC UNITY

The conservative scholar upholds the Mosaic unity of the Pentateuch, that is, 1) that this portion of Scripture is historical and originates from the time of Moses; 2) that Moses was its only human author; and 3) that though it may have been revised and edited by later inspired writers, these revisions and/or additions are just as fully inspired of God as are the other portions (see Deut. 34:5-12; Exod. 11:3; Num. 12:3). The documentary theory denies without adequate evidence the Mosaic unity and hence the historicity and reliability of this foundational portion of divine revelation.

Genesis

TITLE

Genesis is a word derived from the Septuagint (the Greek version of the Old Testament) and means "origin" or "beginning." This is indeed a most appropriate title for this first book of the Bible, for it is in a most distinctive sense the *book of beginnings*. Important beginnings described are 1) the beginning of the earth as man's habitation (Gen. 1:1 – 2:3); 2) the beginning of the human race (Gen. 2:7-25); 3) the beginning of human sin (Gen. 3:1-8); 4) the beginning of redemptive revelation (Gen. 3:9-24); 5) the beginning of the human family (Gen. 4:1-15); 6) the beginning of civilization (Gen. 4:16 – 9:29); 7) the beginning of nations (Gen. 10:1-32); 8) the beginning of human languages (Gen. 11:1-9); and 9) the beginning of the Hebrew race (Gen. 11:10 – 50:26).

IMPORTANCE

As the "book of beginnings" Genesis constitutes an indispensable introduction to the entire Bible. It forms the foundation of all revealed truth. For this reason and because of its antiquity, no historical work in existence can be compared with it.

The three primary names of deity (*Elohim, Jehovah,* and *Adonai*) and the five most important compound names of God occur in Genesis as part of the progressive self-revelation of God to man.

Of the eight great covenants which regulate human life on earth and outline man's salvation, four of these – the Edenic, Adamic, Noahic, and Abrahamic – are found in Genesis.

OUTLINE

A. The Early History of Man (chapters 1 – 11)
  1. The creation (chapters 1, 2)
  2. The fall to the flood (chapters 3 – 5)
  3. The flood (chapters 6 – 9)
  4. The flood to Abraham (chapters 10, 11)
B. The Patriarchal History of Israel (chapters 12 – 50)
  1. Abraham (12:1 – 25:10)
  2. Isaac (25:11 – 28:9)
  3. Jacob (28:10 – 36:43)
  4. Joseph (37:1 – 50:26)

KEY WORD

The key word of Genesis is *election* Divine electing grace pervades the book. Genesis records a number of family histories in which God personally chooses individuals through whom he will work out his redemptive plan for the fallen race. Of Adam's posterity, Cain drops out and Seth is chosen instead. Of Noah's progeny, Ham and Japheth are passed over and Shem is selected. Of Terah's family, Nahor and Haran drop out and Abram is called. Of Abram's sons, Ishmael is rejected and Isaac is chosen. Of Isaac's sons, Esau is bypassed and Jacob comes into the line of blessing. Of Jacob's sons, Judah is selected to perpetuate the line of Messiah (Gen. 49:9, 10). Underlying the divine plan of redemption in its progressive unfolding is eternal election (Eph. 1:4).

PROBLEMS

Among the difficulties presented by Genesis are the date of creation and the age of the earth, the antiquity of man, the fall of man, and the historicity of the flood.

THE DATE OF CREATION AND THE AGE OF THE EARTH. Many conservative scholars have held that Genesis 1:1-31 describes the original creation of the universe alluded to in Job 38:1-6, John 1:3, and Colossians 1:16. Yet this position is an interpretation rather than an exegetical necessity. It actually fails to explain certain crucial facts, such as the vast age of the earth, the origin of sin and Satan (Gen. 3), the existence of chaos (Gen. 1:2), and the six apparently literal days of creation (often interpreted as geological ages).

The interpretation that sees in these verses not the original creation of the universe but the re-creation of a judgment-ridden earth for the latecomer man is exegetically sound and solves many of the scientific and theological problems of the passage. It recognizes the fact that Genesis does not date the creation of the earth or the universe. It also recognizes that long before the creation of man the earth was inhabited by Lucifer and other angelic beings (Isa. 14:12-14; Ezek. 28:12-15). These denizens of the earth rebelled against God, thereby introducing sin into a universe that was originally sinless as it came from its Creator's hand (Job 38:4-7; Isa. 45:18; John 1:3; Col. 1:16).

THE ANTIQUITY OF MAN. Both science and the Genesis account agree that man is a latecomer on the earth. The only disagreement is *how late?* The Bible permits a date of probably no earlier than 10,000 B.C., and gives the lie to the very much earlier datings of the evolutionist.

However, the re-creation of the earth and the creation of man (Gen. 1:1 – 2:25) cannot be dated at about 4004 B.C., as did Archbishop Ussher by using the genealogies of Genesis chapters 5 and 11. These lists, which trace human descent from Adam to Abraham, are abbreviated and skeletal, as is now generally recognized by conservative scholarship. Symmetry and beauty are aimed at, rather than unbroken succession of father to son. Evidently *extreme brevity* characterizes these two short lists, for they apparently cover as many as eight or ten millennia between Adam and Abraham.

The terms "beget," "bear," "father," and "son" are employed in Semitic languages to mean not only a direct father-to-son relationship but also a more distant relationship of great-grandfather to great-grandson, etc. For example, Jacob's offspring were known as "the sons of Jacob" centuries after the death of the patriarch (Mal. 3:6). Usage extends to tribes and countries (Gen. 10:2-32) and even (in the case of royalty) to non-blood descendants. On the Black Obelisk of Shalmaneser III Jehu is styled "son of Omri" by the Assyrians even though he was actually the founder of a new dynasty in Israel, with no blood relationship whatever with the house of Omri.

The standard genealogical formula of Genesis 5 and 11 reads as follows: "A lived ____ years and begat B. And A lived after he begat B ____ years and begat sons and daughters." B might not have been the literal son of A at all, but rather a distant descendant. If so, the age of A was his age at the birth of the child from whom B was descended. *Centuries may therefore have intervened between A and B.* In addition, great longevity was characteristic of pre-flood humanity (Gen. 5:5, 8, 14, 17, 25), a fact amply illustrated by archeology, which demonstrates that traditions of primeval longevity were widespread in antiquity. According to the Weld-Blundell Prism, eight pre-flood kings ruled in lower Mesopotamian cities, the *shortest* of whose reign was 18,600 years. This is obviously a corrupted tradition of the actual historical facts as preserved in the long-lived patriarchs of Genesis 5.

A "tower of Babel" in Babylonia (© *MPS*)

THE FALL OF MAN. If Genesis 1:1, 2 describes the original creation of a *sinless* universe, how can the chaos of Genesis 1:2 be explained? How can the presence of Satan's tool, the serpent, and the existence of evil be accounted for in chapter 3, as well as the fallen angels in chapter 6? How can man's fall, calling forth God's redemptive plan in Christ, be established if Genesis omits any allusion to the origin of Satan and sin in its opening chapters? The fact is that Genesis does not *omit* these matters but *presupposes* them. It begins with a re-created earth and a new creature—man. Through man God would undo the effects of sin *not only on the earth but also in the universe.* Thus in a certain sense the fall of man in Genesis 3 was a necessity to God's plan and purpose for the ages. This is why Genesis 3 is of such immense theological significance.

THE HISTORICITY OF THE FLOOD. The date of the flood, like the date of the creation of man, can be determined only very approximately, for the genealogical table from Shem to Abraham (Gen. 11:10-30) contains extensive gaps. This is demonstrated by the fact that these tables if taken literally allow only about 4000 years from the creation of man to the birth of Christ. Modern archeology, on the other hand, clearly traces highly developed sedentary pottery cultures, such as the Halafian, well before 4000 B.C. If the Genesis genealogies are used in dating, the Noahic flood would be placed at 2348 B.C., an archeological impossibility. The deluge certainly took place long before 4000 B.C.

Moreover, the flood was a worldwide cataclysm. Theories of a local flood clash with explicit declarations of Scripture (Gen. 6:13; 7:20, 23; 8:21) and are concessions to the false, naturalistic theory of uniformity. The Bible clearly teaches supernatural catastrophism, as shown in the judgmental chaos visited on the earth after the fall of Lucifer and his angels (Isa. 14:12-15; Ezek. 28:13-17) and by the Noahic flood (2 Pet. 3:6).

Geological uniformitarianism, like the naturalistic theory of evolution, is based on false presuppositions. Until geology recognizes supernatural catastrophism, manifested in the destruction and reconstruction of the earth and in the Noahic flood, it will continue to ignore part of the evidence that tells the *complete* story of the earth's crust. It will also continue to deny that such a worldwide flood ever took place. In doing so it utterly fails to explain both the biblical and the extrabiblical evidence of this global event. Significant among the extrabiblical evidences of the worldwide flood are the Sumerian and Babylonian flood epics. Of all ancient traditions that have close affiliation with the Old Testament, none is more striking than the Babylonian-Assyrian flood story, constituting the eleventh book of the Epic of Gilgamesh. If the flood never took place, how can the universal deluge of both the Sumerian and Babylonian accounts be explained, as well as flood traditions of other peoples of antiquity?

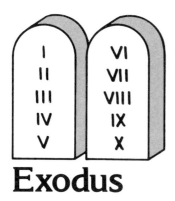

Exodus

TITLE

The name *Exodus* originated from the Greek word employed in the Septuagint Version. It signifies "exit" or "departure," as in Hebrews 11:22. The book narrates the *going out* or *departure* of the Israelites from bondage in Egypt to freedom in the Promised Land. The key word in the book is *redemption*. Man's ruin and God's electing love in Genesis are followed by redemption in Exodus. The need of redemption is seen in the people's condition (Exod. 1, 2). The way of redemption is by blood (Exod. 12) and by God's manifested power (Exod. 14). The law of redemption is the divine will set forth in the Decalogue (Exod. 20) and the Book of the Covenant (Exod. 21—24). The means of redemption is pictured in the tabernacle and priesthood (Exod. 25—40), which point to Christ (Heb. 8:1—10:18).

OUTLINE

A. Subjection: Israel in Egypt (1:1—12:36)
   1. Bondage in Egypt (chapter 1)
   2. Preparation of the deliverer (chapters 2—4)
   3. Contest with the oppressor (chapters 5—11)
   4. Deliverance by the Passover (12:1-36)
B. Emancipation: Israel from Egypt to Sinai (12:37—18:27)
   1. Conduct to the Red Sea (12:37—14:14)
   2. Deliverance through the Red Sea (14:15—15:21)
   3. Leading from the Red Sea (15:22—18:27)
C. Revelation: Israel at Sinai (chapters 19—40)

1. The will of God made known (chapters 19—31)
   (a) In the Law (chapters 19—24)
   (b) In the Tabernacle (chapters 25—27)
   (c) In the priesthood (chapters 28, 29)
   (d) In the service (chapters 30, 31)
2. The will of God flouted (chapters 32—34)
   (a) The great sin (32:1-6)
   (b) The divine anger (32:7—33:23)
   (c) The renewal of the Covenant (chapter 34)
3. The will of God fulfilled (chapters 35—40)
   (a) The Tabernacle commenced (35:1—39:31)
   (b) The Tabernacle completed (39:32—40:33)
   (c) The Tabernacle consecrated (40:34-38)

PORTRAYAL OF THE REDEEMER IN EXODUS

IN MOSES. As a prefigurement of Christ, Moses illustrates how redemption is centered in a man, the man Christ Jesus. Like Christ, he was born under the dire threat of death but was divinely chosen and preserved (Exod. 3:7-10; Acts 7:25). Rejected by Israel, he turned to the Gentiles (Exod. 2:11-15). During the period of rejection he took a Gentile bride (Exod. 2:16-21; Matt. 12:14-21). Later he appeared again as Israel's deliverer and was accepted (Exod. 4:29-31; Rom. 11:24-25).

IN THE PASSOVER LAMB (EXOD. 12:1-28; JOHN 1:29; 1 COR. 5:6, 7; 1 PET. 1:18, 19). The Lamb was *without defect* (Exod. 12:5; John 8:46) and was *slain* (Exod. 12:6; Heb. 9:22). The applied *blood* shielded from judgment (Exod. 12:13; Heb. 9:11-14). The Passover feast speaks of Christ, the Bread of Life (Matt. 26:26-28; 1 Cor. 11:23-26).

IN THE TABERNACLE. The life of the nation was conducted in direct relationship to the tabernacle, every part of which speaks of Christ, the true gathering place of his redeemed (Matt. 18:20). The ark of acacia wood overlaid with gold points to Christ as both human and divine (Exod. 25:10-22). It held a pot of manna, envisioning Christ as Life-Sustainer; the Ten Commandments, portraying Christ as Cherisher of God's law; and Aaron's rod that budded, pointing to Christ as resurrected Redeemer (Num. 17:10). The mercy seat pictures Christ as the way of access to God. The veil between the holy of holies and the holy place symbolizes Christ's human body (Matt. 27:51; Heb. 10:20). The table of showbread typifies Christ as the Bread of Life (John 6:32-

58). The golden lampstand typifies Christ as our Light (Exod. 25:31-40). The golden altar of incense presents Christ in his intercession (Exod. 30:1-10; John 17:1-26; Heb. 7:25). The laver comprehends Christ cleansing his people from defilement (Exod. 30:18-21; John 13:2-10; Eph. 5:25-27). The brazen altar prefigures Christ enduring the wrath of God in the place of his redeemed (Exod. 27:1-8; Heb. 9:14).

IN THE PRIESTHOOD. Aaron, the high priest, typifies Christ in the exercise of his office after the Aaronic pattern, the holy garments for "glory and beauty" representing Christ's glory and beauty as our High Priest (Exod. 28:1-5). The breastplate of precious stones engraved with the names of Israel's tribes illustrates Christ's continual intercession, in which he bears his saints on his heart in God's presence (Exod. 28:15-29). The robe of the ephod of blue portrays the present heavenly priesthood of Christ (Exod. 28:31-35). The golden headplate inscribed with "Holy to the Lord" (RSV) is a reminder of the unsullied purity of Christ's priestly ministry (Exod. 28:36-38).

Aaron's consecration by washing (Exod. 29:1-4) symbolized regeneration, in which Aaron took part because he was a sinner and required cleansing. Our Lord as the spotless Lamb of God (Heb. 7:26-28) did not need cleansing, yet nonetheless yielded to John's baptism in order to identify himself with sinners, thus fulfilling the Aaronic pattern (Matt. 3:13-17). Aaron's clothing and anointing are symbolic of Christ's glory and anointing with the Spirit (Matt. 3:16). Aaron, prefiguring the sinless Christ, was anointed *before* the blood was shed (Exod. 29:5-25).

Mummy of Rameses II, possibly the pharaoh of the exodus (*Russ Busby photo*)

It should be noted that while only two chapters are occupied with the story of creation, fourteen chapters are devoted to the tabernacle. This shows the importance which God places on the work of redemption and on Christ as the center and object of the Holy Spirit's revelation.

CHRONOLOGY

Explicit scriptural statements require the date of the Exodus to be about 1441 B.C., since it occurred 480 years (1 Kings 6:1) before the fourth year of Solomon's reign (about 961 B.C., according to conservative scholarship). In this case 1871 B.C. becomes the year in which Israel entered Egypt, since the sojourn lasted 430 years (Exod. 12:40, 41). Present-day theories that argue for the date of the Exodus a century and a half later (1290 B.C., W. F. Albright) or over two centuries later (1225 B.C., H. H. Rowley) reject not only the specific biblical statements but also the whole chronological arrangement underlying the books of Joshua and Judges. This is done as the result of inferences from inconclusive archeological evidence.

Leviticus

TITLE

The book of Leviticus gets its name from the Septuagint and the Latin Vulgate, where the titles *Leueitikon* and *Leviticus* are used. These mean "relating to the Levites." The aptness of the title "Leviticus" is borne out by the contents of the book, for Leviticus is essentially a handbook of laws and ceremonies regulating the services of the Tabernacle by members of the sacred tribe of Levi, who were divinely appointed as substitutes for the natural priests (the firstborn male of every tribe).

BACKGROUND

Man's ruin and God's electing love in Genesis, opening the way for redemption in Exodus, is followed by communion in Leviticus.

COMPARISON OF EXODUS AND LEVITICUS	
Exodus	*Leviticus*
God's approach to us	Our approach to God
Begins with sinners	Begins with saints
People brought near to God	People kept near to God
The fact of atonement	The doctrine of atonement
Christ presented as Savior	Christ operative as sanctifier
Guilt removed	Defilement cleansed
God as love	God as holiness and light
Brought into union with him	Introduced to communion with him
Offers pardon	Calls to purity
Delivered from world, flesh, and Satan	Separated and dedicated to God
God speaks out of the mountain	God speaks out of the tabernacle
Unsaved man condemned by the moral law of God	Saved man enabled to keep God's law
Keynote: redemption	Keynote: separation, communion
The way of salvation	Provisions for holy living

OUTLINE

A. Access to God (chapters 1–10)
  1. By knowledge of Christ's sacrifice (1:1–6:7)
    (a) The burnt offering – Christ perfect in death Godward (chapter 1)
    (b) The meal offering – Christ perfect in life manward (chapter 2)
    (c) The peace offering – Christ the Bestower of peace (ch. 3)
    (d) The sin offering – Christ removing guilt Godward (ch. 4)
    (e) The trespass offering – Christ atoning for the injury of sin (5:1–6:7)
  2. By appropriation of Christ's sacrifice (6:8–7:38)
    (a) The burnt offering (6:8-13)
    (b) The meal offering (6:14-23)
    (c) The sin offering (6:24-30)
    (d) The trespass offering (7:1-10)

(e) The peace offering (7:11-38)
3. By appropriation of Christ's mediation (chapters 8–10)
   (a) As typified in the consecration of the priests (chapter 8)
   (b) As typified in the ministry of the priests (chapter 9)
   (c) As typified in the regulation of the priests (chapter 10)
B. Communion with God (chapters 11–27)
   1. By separation from uncleanness (chapters 11–15)
      (a) Instructions regarding food (11:1-23)
      (b) Instructions regarding personal cleanliness (11:24–12:8)
      (c) Instructions regarding leprosy (chapters 13, 14)
      (d) Instructions regarding personal defilement (chapter 15)
   2. By cleansing through atonement (chapter 16)
   3. By sanctification in holiness of life (chapters 17–27)
      (a) In food (chapter 17)
      (b) In social conduct (chapters 18–20)
      (c) In priestly relations (chapters 21, 22)
      (d) In public worship (chapter 23)
      (e) In one's whole life (chapter 24)
      (f) In economic affairs (chapter 25)
      (g) In recognition of God's covenant claims (chapter 26)
      (h) In performing vows (chapter 27)

THE OFFERINGS AND THE PERSON OF CHRIST

Offering	Typical Significance
Burnt Offering	Christ offering himself spotless to God (Heb. 9:11-14; 10:5-7). The ox (Phil. 2:5-8), sheep (Isa. 53:7; John 1:29), and dove (Isa. 38:14; Heb. 7:26) portray the yieldedness and innocence of Christ in death. Fire (God's holiness) wholly consumes this offering (2 Cor. 5:21).
Meal Offering	Christ's sinless humanity (fine flour) anointed with the Holy Spirit (oil–Luke 3:21, 22) was fragrant Godward (frankincense). Baking speaks of Christ's testings and sufferings.
Peace Offering	Christ's atonement procuring peace–God propitiated, the sinner reconciled (Eph. 2:14, 17; Col. 1:20; Rom. 5:1).
Sin Offering	Christ bearing the sins of his people (2 Cor. 5:21), thus vindicating the claims of the Law through substitutionary atonement.
Trespass Offering	Christ atoning for injury of sins committed against God or man.

THE PRIESTHOOD AND CHRIST'S MEDIATION	
Person	*Symbolism*
The High Priest	Christ as High Priest effecting redemption, thereby opening communion with God. Two features distinguish the High Priest (Christ) from ordinary priests (prefiguring believers). 1) He was anointed *before* the consecration sacrifices were slain, thus picturing the sinlessness of Christ. 2) Only upon him was the anointing oil poured (John 3:34; Heb. 1:9).
Ordinary Priests	They were first washed, symbolizing regeneration (Tit. 3:5; Exod. 29:1-4; Lev. 8:6), for they were sinners. Then they were clothed, symbolizing Christ's righteousness. Next they were anointed with oil (the Spirit). All believers are priests with direct access to God because of their relation to Christ, as Aaron's sons were related to Aaron.

PROVISIONS FOR HOLY LIVING

Leviticus is a manual for holy living. Leviticus says "Get right with God" (the message of the five offerings; Lev. 1–7), "Enjoy communion with God" (the provision of priesthood; Lev. 8–10), and "Walk with God in holiness of life" (the call of Lev. 11–27). Leviticus is the book of *holiness*. This keynote is sounded 87 times. "Be ye holy, as I am holy" is God's command in Leviticus 11:44, 45; 19:2; 20:7, 26.

A walk with God is based on holiness, which is achieved by sacrifice (Lev. 1–7), priestly communion (Lev. 8–10), separation from sin and defilement (Lev. 11–15), accomplished atonement (Lev. 16), and a dedication to God that results in virtuous living (Lev. 17–27).

THE FEASTS AND UNFULFILLED PROPHECY	
The Feast (Leviticus 23)	*The Prophetic Symbolism*
The Sabbath	Not actually one of the seven feasts of Leviticus 23:4-44, but basic to the entire festival cycle and covenant relationship (Exod. 31:12-17).
The Passover	Redemption from Egypt (Exod. 12:1-13; 1 Cor. 5:7; 1 Pet. 1:19). First feast, basic to all the rest. Spiritual blessing rests on Christ's redemption of sinful man (Hebrew *Pesah*, "a passing over").

Unleavened Bread	Redemption is to be followed by a holy life and walk (1 Cor. 5:7, 8; 2 Cor. 7:1; Gal. 5:7-9). Communing with Christ, the unleavened Bread, will result in separation from evil (leaven).
Firstfruits	The resurrected Christ (the firstfruits) and the saints who will be resurrected at his coming (1 Cor. 15:23).
Pentecost	Advent of the Spirit at Pentecost (Acts 2) to unite the "two loaves" of the Jew (Acts 2) and Gentile (Acts 10) in the Church, the new meal offering (1 Cor. 12:13). Leaven is included because the Church is seen unglorified.
Trumpets	Picture of Israel's end-of-the-age regathering to her homeland after her worldwide dispersion between the advents (Matt. 24:31; Ezek. 37:12-14; Rom. 11:25-36).
Day of Atonement	Repentance and conversion of Israel at Christ's second advent (Lev. 16:1-34; Zech. 12:10 – 13:1). Spiritual highlight of cycle.
Tabernacles	Israel's kingdom rest after regathering and conversion. Commemorates redemption out of Egypt and is prophetic of the restoration of the kingdom.

Numbers

TITLE

The book receives its name from the Septuagint *Arithmoi*, "Numbers," and the Latin *Liber Numeri*, "Book of Numbers." These "Numberings" refer to the dual census of the Hebrew people (Num. 1 – 3, 26).

BACKGROUND

The book of Numbers continues the history of Israel as a "kingdom of priests and a holy nation" where Exodus leaves off. As Genesis is the book of election, Exodus the book of redemption, and Leviticus the book of worship and communion, Numbers is the book of the service and walk of God's redeemed people.

IMPORTANCE

Numbers narrates the continuation of the journey begun in Exodus, commencing with the events of the second month of the second year (Num. 10:11) and concluding with the eleventh month of the fortieth year (Deut. 1:3). The interval of 38 years and 9 months records the disobedience and failure of God's people under testing. In spite of every provision for their welfare and speedy entrance into their promised inheritance, the people failed miserably at Kadesh-Barnea (Num. 14). Their punishment by defeat and death in the desert (Num. 20:1 – 33:49) presents a warning to God's people of every age of the peril of unbelief and disobedience to God's Word. The wanderings of a rebellious people are to be contrasted with the journeyings of a people yielded to the will of God. The book of Numbers presents this contrast.

OUTLINE

A. Preparations for Departure (1:1 – 10:10)
   1. The numbering of the people (chapter 1)
   2. The arrangement of the camp (chapter 2)
   3. The instruction of the priests and Levites (chapters 3, 4)
   4. The provision for cleansing from defilement (chapter 5)
   5. The law of the Nazarite (chapter 6)
   6. The gifts of the princes (chapter 7)
   7. The lighting of the lamps (8:1-4)
   8. The cleansing of the Levites (8:5-26)
   9. The observance of the Passover (9:1-14)
   10. The guidance for the journey (9:15-23)
   11. The signals for action (10:1-10)
B. Mount Sinai to Moab (10:11 – 21:35)
   1. Traveling in unbelief (10:11 – 14:45)
   2. Wandering in discipline (chapters 15 – 19)

3. Starting afresh (chapters 20, 21)
C. The Plains of Moab (chapters 22 – 36)
   1. The episodes of Balaam (chapters 22 – 25)
   2. The additional instructions (chapters 26 – 31)
   3. The distribution of territories (chapter 32)
   4. The review of the journey (chapter 33)
   5. The instructions for entry (chapters 34 – 36)

THE CENSUS

The two numberings of the people (Num. 1:1 – 2:34; 26:1-65) had several purposes. The Sinai count of 603,550 males 20 years of age and over and the Moab count of 601,730 males of the same age illustrates the order God's people are to have. The two registrations indicated not only God's promises of blessing and increase but also his warnings of chastisement for disobedience. Of the more than two million Israelites in the desert only Joshua and Caleb entered the land. These records also facilitated the assignment of territory to the various tribes as they entered Palestine. In addition they made it possible for later generations to trace the genealogy of the coming Redeemer.

Liberal critics reject the biblical figures as grossly exaggerated. They maintain that it would be impossible for a company of two million or more to exist in the desert without continuous miraculous intervention by God. Conservatives accept the figures on this very basis in accordance with the claims of Scripture, as no flaws in the numbers themselves can be proved.

THE ARRANGING OF THE CAMP

The camp of God's people was divinely arranged and ordered. In the center was the tabernacle, demonstrating that the worship and service of God were to be first in importance. Each tribe had its particular location around the tabernacle (Num. 2:1-34). Priests, illustrating believers in priestly capacity, ministered in the tabernacle before the Lord (Num. 3:1-4). The Levites, portraying believers watching over the precious things of the faith (Jude 1:3), were assigned to guard and transport the holy things of the Lord through the wilderness (Num. 3: 5 – 4:49). Everyone was to be at his post and perform his divinely assigned task. Compare the New Testament figure of the body and its members (1 Cor. 12:12-27).

Absolutely essential to the camp was separation from sinful defilement, typified by leprosy, physical secretions, and death (Num. 5:1-4). This illustrates the necessity of thoroughly judging sin in order to be free to serve the living God (Heb. 9:14). Injunctions covering restitution for wrongdoing (Num. 5:5-10) and avoidance of adultery (Num. 5: 11-31) further show how necessary it is for God's people to keep themselves morally clean. The need for a holy walk is emphasized by the Nazarite. This was a person who voluntarily dedicated himself to the Lord. The Nazarite became a visible token among the people that those who serve the Holy God must themselves be holy (Num. 6:1-27). Such separation from evil and devotion to God are beautifully portrayed

THE CENTRAL PLACE OF THE TABERNACLE
Christ To Be Accorded First Place

	DAN	ASHER	NAPHTALI	
BENJAMIN		MERARITES		JUDAH
MANASSEH	GERSHONITES	THE TABERNACLE	PRIESTS LEVITES	ISSACHAR
EPHRAIM				ZEBULUN
	GAD	KOHATHITES / SIMEON	REUBEN	

by the gifts of the princes (Num. 7:1-89) and the consecration of the Levites (Num. 8:1-26) based on Passover redemption (Num. 9:1-14). Resulting guidance for the redeemed is seen in the blowing of the silver trumpets and the orderly movement of the camp from Sinai (Num. 10:1-36).

UNBELIEF AND FAILURE OF GOD'S PEOPLE

The book of Numbers emphasizes the truth that although people may have faith to apply redemptive blood (Exod. 12:28) and quit Egypt (the world), they may still lack faith to enter Canaan rest (Heb. 3:1—4:16). The first intimation of defection was the murmuring at Taberah (Num. 11:1-3) and the rejection of the manna (Num. 11:4-9). God sent quail, but punished the lusting people with a plague (Num. 11:31-35). Miriam and Aaron's criticism of Moses (Num. 12:1-16) was still another evidence of sin in the camp. Sin showed itself again in the adverse report of the spies sent to explore Canaan (Num. 13:1-33) and the rebellion of the people at Kadesh-Barnea (Num. 14:1-45).

What an illustration of many believers! They have faith to trust God to save them from the penalty of sin, but refuse to trust him for deliverance from the power of sin. They wander fruitlessly in the desert of murmuring and defeat under the control of the old, sinful nature. They reject Canaan victory and rest because of imaginary difficulties. As a result they die in defeat like the whole generation of Israelites who disbelieved Caleb and Joshua at Kadesh-Barnea.

THE REBELLION OF KORAH

The sin of Korah and his followers (Num. 16) was the rejection of Moses' authority as God's mouthpiece and the flagrant intrusion into the authority of the priesthood, an honor which no one was to assume except "he that is called by God, as was Aaron" (Heb. 5:4). The insurgents tried to create a priestly order without divine sanction (Heb. 5:10). The punishment (Num. 16:20-50) was so extremely severe because the Levitical priesthood was instituted to bear the iniquity of the people (Num. 18:1-7), and Korah's rebellion threatened the spiritual security of the entire nation. If it were not for the priestly service, all Israel would have been destroyed by the wrath of God. Similarly Christ, our Great High Priest, always lives to make intercession for us in order to guarantee our salvation (Heb. 7:25). Ecclesiastical priestism that denies or encroaches upon the priesthood of every believer is a modern analogy of Korah's sin.

The budding of Aaron's rod was the divine attestation of the Levitical priesthood (Num. 17), for only in Aaron's rod did God cause life to spring up. Thus Aaron became a picture of Christ, who through resurrection was exalted as High Priest (Heb. 4:14; 5:4-10).

THE ORDINANCE OF THE RED HEIFER

This symbolism (Num. 19) beautifully illustrates Christ's sacrifice as the basis of the cleansing of the believer from sinful defilement contracted in his earthly walk (John 13:3-10; 1 John 1:7 – 2:2). The choice of the blemish-free heifer (Num. 19:2) portrays Christ's sinlessness (Heb. 9:13, 14). The choice of the yoke-free heifer (Num. 19:2) bespeaks Christ's total freedom from compulsion in undergoing the sufferings involved in redemption (Psa. 40:7, 8; Heb. 10:5-9). The heifer killed "outside the camp" (Num. 19:3) looks forward to the one who suffered "outside the gate" (Heb. 13:12). The blood sprinkled seven times toward the tabernacle (Num. 19:4) speaks of full atonement. The ashes of the heifer (Num. 19:9) were the memorial of an accepted sacrifice. Death (Num. 19:11-22) typifies the polluting effect of sin as it renders the conscience of the saint defiled and unworthy to serve the living God (Heb. 9:14).

THE BRONZE SERPENT

The bronze serpent (Num. 21:1-9) portrays sin judged in the cross of Christ (John 3:14, 15; 2 Cor. 5:21). (The serpent as Satan's tool in the fall of man became God's illustration in nature of the effects of sin.) Bronze suggests judgment – in the bronze altar of divine judgment and in the bronze laver of self-judgment. Looking at the serpent of bronze for healing from the snake bite (Num. 21:8, 9) speaks of believing in the Christ of Calvary for spiritual healing from the venom of sin.

BALAAM'S PROPHETIC PARABLES

Four in number, these magnificent prophecies envision Israel as God's eternally elect nation, destined for unforfeitable blessing, and incapable of being cursed (Num. 23:1 – 24:25). The reason for the certainty of Israel's blessings is that she had an immutable standing before God as a redeemed people despite her morally reprehensible condition. God chastised his people for their sins but could not call down curses upon them (Num. 23:1-30; Rom. 11:29). God remained *for* Israel and *against* Balak (Num. 23:23; Rom. 8:31). Balaam's allusion to blessing upon those who bless Israel and cursing upon those who curse her recalls the Abrahamic Covenant (Gen. 12:3).

The fourth parable contains a splendid messianic prophecy. The "Scepter out of Israel" and the "Star out of Jacob" (Num. 24:17; Gen. 49:10) looks beyond David to David's Lord, who at his second advent restores the kingdom to Israel (Acts 1:6; Isa. 11:6-16).

Deuteronomy

TITLE

The name "Deuteronomy" is derived from the Septuagint translation of Deuteronomy 17:18: "And he shall write for himself this *repetition* of the Law." The Hebrew actually means "and he shall write out for himself a *copy* of the Law." However, the inaccuracy upon which the English title rests is not serious. Deuteronomy is in a very true sense a *repetition* of the Law to the new generation about to enter Canaan.

AUTHOR

The book itself *most explicitly* declares its authorship by Moses (Deut. 31:9, 24-26, 30). This Mosaic authorship is also sustained by Deuteronomy's close similarity to the other books of the Pentateuch and by evidence of early authorship (about 1410 B.C.) indicated in other books of the Old Testament. The critical theory that postulates Deuteronomy's origin during Josiah's reign (about 621 B.C.—2 Kings 22) makes the book nothing more than a pious fraud. Such a hypothesis, built upon specious presuppositions, is utterly at odds with internal evidence and the whole fabric of revealed truth and cannot be supported by sound scholarship.

Reputed Mount Sinai (also Horeb) towers over shepherd and sheep. (© *MPS*)

IMPORTANCE

As the last of the five books of the Pentateuch, Deuteronomy was called the "five fifths of the Law" by the Jews. The book has been a target of critical attack, which attempts to date it late and label it a forgery. No critical questions, however, can lessen the moral and spiritual value of this great book, with its words of Moses in the Plains of Moab. It has been aptly categorized as "literature of power," and is one of the most spiritual books of the Old Testament.

In its relation to the other four books of the Pentateuch, Deuteronomy has been likened to the relation of John to the Synoptic Gospels, for both John and Deuteronomy interpret spiritually the historical facts of the books which precede them. The dominating notes of the preceding books are all here — the *choice* of Genesis, the *deliverance* of Exodus, the *holiness* of Leviticus, and the *guidance* of Numbers.

Taken as a whole, Deuteronomy is an exposition of the first and greatest commandment, "Thou shalt love the Lord thy God with all thy heart, and with all thy soul, and with all thy might." It was from this book that our Lord summarized the whole of the Mosaic Covenant in a single sentence (Matt. 22:37; Deut. 6:5). From it he drew his weapons to rout the tempter (Matt. 4:4, 7, 10; Deut. 8:3; 6:16; 6:13).

OUTLINE

A. Moses' First Address: Historical (1:1−4:43)
   1. Introduction (1:1-5)
   2. Review of travels (1:6−3:29)
   3. Appeal to keep the Law (4:1-40)
   4. Note on cities of refuge (4:41-43)
B. Moses' Second Address: Legal (4:44−26:19)
   1. Superscription (4:44-49)
   2. Exposition of the Decalogue (chapters 5-11)
   3. Exposition of the special laws (chapters 12-26)
C. Moses' Third Address: Prophetic (chapters 27-30)
   1. The distant future of Israel (chapters 27, 28)
   2. The near future of Israel (chapters 29, 30)
D. Historical Appendices (chapters 31−34)
   1. Final exhortations (chapter 31)
   2. The song of Moses (32:1-47)
   3. Final events (32:48−34:12)

THEMES

The great central truth that underlies Deuteronomy is the uniqueness of the Lord and his relationship to his uniquely chosen people

(Deut. 6:4). Israel's one God is to be worshiped at one central sanctuary (Deut. 12:1-32). The motto of the book may be said to be "one God, one sanctuary."

THE LORD, THE UNIQUE GOD. The Lord (Yahweh) is the only God. "There is none beside him" (Deut. 4:35, 39; 6:4; 32:39). He is the absolute and peerless Lord and God (Deut. 10:17). He is the one *living* God (Deut. 5:26), all other "deities" being imaginary or "dead." He is "the faithful God who keeps the Covenant" (Deut. 7:9). To him idolatry in any form is an insult (Deut. 7:25, 26; 12:31; 13:13-15; 18: 12). He is Creator and Possessor of the universe (Deut. 10:14), Ruler of nations (Deut. 7:19), with a fatherly relation to Israel (Deut 32:6). Being the *only* God, he is justly outraged by would-be rivals (Deut. 7: 4; 29:24-26; 31:16, 17). Idolatry must be rooted out and the pagan worship of the Canaanites completely exterminated (Deut. 7:1-5; 12:2, 3; 20:16-18).

ISRAEL, A UNIQUE PEOPLE. God's chosen people were elected in Genesis, redeemed in Exodus, set apart in Leviticus, led in God's way in Numbers, and instructed in the blessings of obedience in Deuteronomy. An elect people, they were redeemed to be a chosen nation at Horeb (Exod. 19:6). The new Israel born in the desert were to inherit the blessings promised their fathers (Deut. 4:31; 7:12; 8:18; 26:16-19; 29:1). Even though the nation would apostatize and go into captivity, Israel would be regathered from Babylon and from her final worldwide dispersion to be reinstated in kingdom blessing under Messiah (Deut. 30:1-10), through whom the nation would become a medium of salvation to all nations and the means of the redemption and restoration of the earth itself to a sinless eternal state.

THE LORD AND ISRAEL IN A UNIQUE RELATIONSHIP. Israel was chosen as a nation in order to be an example to all the other nations of the value of serving the one true God (Exod. 19:5-7). Other nations *feared* their phony deities. Israel was expected to adhere to her Lord out of *love* as well as respect (Deut. 6:5; 10:12; 11:1; 30:6). Israel was given the highest possible privileges through her covenant blessings. All other peoples were to be considered strangers and foreigners, to be admitted only by special permission (23:1-8).

PROPHETIC ELEMENTS

Deuteronomy contains some of the most striking predictions in the Pentateuch.

CONCERNING CHRIST. Deuteronomy forecasts the coming of the unique Prophet, greater than Moses, yet like him (Deut. 18:15-10). That this allusion is to our Lord is attested by the New Testament (John 1:21, 45; 6:14; Acts 3:22, 23; 7:37).

CONCERNING THE ELECT NATION ISRAEL. The Palestinian Covenant (Deut. 30:1-10) predicts dispersion as a punishment for disobedience (Deut. 30:1; cf. Deut. 28:63-68), the future repentance of Israel in dispersion (Deut. 30:2), the return of the Lord (Deut. 30:3; cf. Amos 9:9-15; Acts 15:14-17), restoration to the land (Deut. 30:5; cf. Hos. 2:14-16), the judgment of Israel's foes (Deut. 30:7; cf. Isa. 14:1, 2; Joel 3:1-8; Matt. 25:31-46), and national prosperity, (Deut. 30:9; cf. Amos 9:11-15).

No passage of Scripture is more remarkable in its prophetic scope or in its confirmation of prophecy in the events of history than Deuteronomy chapters 28 to 30. From A.D. 70 onward the Jewish nation has been dispersed worldwide because of disobedience and rejection of Christ, experiencing exactly the punishments foretold by Moses. In the present century initial steps toward the prophesied restoration of the exiled people to Palestine have been witnessed. The punishment and blessing of Israel have followed precisely the predictions of Moses in these three remarkable chapters.

The Historical Books

THE ENGLISH ORDER

In English Bibles the order of the historical books is as follows: Joshua, Judges, Ruth, First and Second Samuel, First and Second Kings, First and Second Chronicles, Ezra, Nehemiah, and Esther. This order is entirely different from the Hebrew arrangement, having been influenced by the Septuagint and other ancient versions and by the content of the books themselves. The period covered by these books extends from the death of Moses (about 1400 B.C.) to the end of Old Testament history (about 400 B.C.), a period of approximately a millennium.

The long period covered by the historical books falls into three main divisions: 1) from the death of Moses to the accession of Saul (1400-1020 B.C.); 2) from the accession of Saul to the fall of Judah

(1020-586 B.C.); 3) from the fall of Judah to the end of Old Testament history (586-400 B.C.)

THE NATURE OF OLD TESTAMENT HISTORY

The Old Testament historical narrative is history with a religious purpose. This purpose determines inclusion or omission of facts and is true of the Pentateuch as well as the historical books. The millennium covered by the historical books was a period of mighty empires, great conflicts, and stirring events. Yet this whole fascinating story has no place in the Bible record except as these powers and persons interact with God's elect nation, Israel. Even much of the history of Israel itself is passed over briefly, including many events which the secular historian would consider historically important. On the other hand, events which at first glance seem relatively unimportant are recorded at length. The reason for this is that the purpose of Old Testament history is not journalistic. As the account of God's self-revelation for the redemption of the human race, Bible history is *moral and spiritual. All omissions and inclusions must be evaluated in this light.*

Herodotus (fifth century B.C.) is known as the father of history. Yet the Hebrews wrote history a millennium before Herodotus was born! The historical portions of the Old Testament were penned by different authors who wrote in different places and at various times. They nevertheless present a coherent and constructive account of many centuries of history. Divine inspiration was at work, even as the Scriptures themselves declare (2 Tim. 3:16).

Joshua

TITLE

The name Joshua means "The Lord is deliverance (salvation)." The Greek form of this name is "Jesus" (Acts 7:45; Heb. 4:8). The book takes its title from the great leader whose exploits it recounts.

AUTHOR

The title would not necessarily prove that the book was personally written by Joshua. Yet internal evidence indicates that the book was written either by Joshua himself or by someone who lived during or shortly after Joshua's time. Thus the history it contains is authentic. Some of these internal evidences are as follows: 1) Large parts of the book were apparently written by an eyewitness (Josh. 1 – 10); 2) Numerous evidences in the narrative show that it was written very early (Josh. 6:25; 15:63; 16:10; etc.).

BACKGROUND

Critics commonly deny that the book is a literary unit, distinct in authorship from the Pentateuch. They place it in a so-called "Hexateuch," alleging that it originated from the same late and unreliable literary sources as the Pentateuch. That the term Hexateuch, however, is a pure critical invention is demonstrated by the following considerations: 1) It is part of the entire unsound documentary theory of the Pentateuch and is based on the same false literary, historical, religious, and philosophical presuppositions; 2) Evidence that Joshua was ever considered by the ancients as belonging to the Pentateuch is non-existent; 3) Certain distinct linguistic peculiarities found in the Pentateuch are absent from the book of Joshua.

OUTLINE

A. The Conquest of the Land (chapters 1 – 12)
1. The commissioning of the leader (1:1-9)
2. The preparation for the crossing (1:10 – 2:24)
3. The crossing of the Jordan (chapters 3, 4)
4. The circumcision of the people (chapter 5)
5. The conquest of Jericho (6:1 – 8:29)
6. The erection of the altar (8:30-35)
7. The reception of the Gibeonites (chapter 9)
8. The conquest of the south (chapter 10)
9. The conquest of the north (11:1-15)
10. The summary of the conquest (11:16 – 12:24)
B. The Apportionment of the Land (chapters 13 – 22)
1. The instruction of Joshua (13:1-7)
2. The assignment of the eastern tribes (13:8-33)
3. The assignment of the western tribes (chapters 14 – 19)
4. The provision of the cities of refuge (chapter 20)
5. The allotment of Levitical towns (chapter 21)
6. The dismissal of the eastern tribes (chapter 22)
C. The Last Words of Joshua (chapters 23, 24)

MIRACLES

The miraculous element is conspicuous in Joshua, as is also true of the Pentateuch. This is to be expected, since as redemptive history the book continues those events that illustrate God's salvation of the human soul (1 Cor. 10:11). The detailed redemptive typology of the Pentateuch, recording Israel's deliverance out of Egypt, is expanded in Joshua to include the consummation of redemption into the Promised Land, the sphere of victory and blessing. In a sense Joshua is to the Old Testament what Ephesians is to the New Testament. Canaan was to the Israelite what "the heavenly places" (Eph. 1:3) are to the Christian—not a figure of heaven, but an experience here and now of conflict and victory through God's manifested power (Eph. 6:10-20).

Rationalistic critics, who have never experienced redemption, quite naturally regard the large number of miracles in the book (and in the Pentateuch as well) as legends and seek to explain them away by the documentary theory of late and historically unreliable sources. The Christian scholar, however, has every reason to believe in miracles, since he has already experienced the greatest miracle of all — new birth through Christ Jesus.

THE MEANING OF "THE SUN STOOD STILL"

The miracle that has caused the most controversy in the book is that recorded in chapter 10, verses 12 to 14. The common interpretation has been that God prolonged daylight for from ten to twelve (or more) hours, "about a whole day" (Josh. 10:13). God in his omnipotence could, of course, have performed such a stupendous miracle, involving the entire solar system. However, the pertinent question is whether this is truly the correct interpretation.

That the miracle performed in answer to Joshua's prayer (Josh. 10:12) involved not *more* light and heat but rather alleviation from it is shown from the following considerations.

There is no word of such an extended day in ancient history or astronomy — a completely inconceivable fact had the event actually occurred.

There is no *clear* reference to such an extended day in the rest of the Bible (Habakkuk 3:11 is inconclusive), a remarkable silence if the event had taken place, since it would have involved a more stupendous miracle than the crossing of the Red Sea or the Jordan River, events celebrated as climactic of the manifestation of God's power in the Old Testament.

God has established an orderly universe. He does not display his miraculous powers wastefully, but only in sufficient measure to bring bona fide honor to himself.

What Joshua needed and prayed for was not more *sunshine* with its intense midsummer heat (it was about July 22), but rather *shielding* of his men, already taxed by 17 hours of forced march from Gilgal. For the sun to cease in the rainless season would be miracle enough. But God also answered by a cooling storm that not only refreshed Joshua's army but crushed and delayed his enemies with hailstones. The idea that the sun "stood still" — in other words, that the earth temporarily ceased rotating on its axis — has arisen from the unfortunate rendering of the Hebrew *dom* as "stand thou still" (Josh. 10:12). The word means basically "to be dumb, silent, or still" and secondarily "to cease or desist" (from usual activity), as in Job 30:27; 31:34; Psalm 27:7; Lamentations 2:18. Thus in *poetical* language the sun is said to be "dumb" when not emitting light (its words or speech being its world-wide shining and universal heat—Psalm 19:2-6). Hence the root *dm* in Babylonian astronomical texts has the connotation "to be darkened."

Likewise the synonym *ʿamad*, translated "stayed" and "stood still" (Josh. 10:13) frequently has the meaning "to cease" (Gen. 30:9; 2 Kings 4:6; Jonah 1:15). So Joshua's request may be rendered "O sun, be dumb (darkened) at Gibeon, and thou moon, in the Valley of Ajalon. And the sun was dumb (darkened) and the moon ceased (to shine), until the nation took vengeance on its enemies—is it not written in the Book of Jasher—for the sun ceased (to shine) in the midst of the day, *and yet* it did not hasten to set about a whole day."

The violent storm obscured the scorching sun at high noon and sent darkness and death upon Israel's enemies. The clause "and (the sun) did not hasten to go down about a whole day" is adversative in Hebrew. Instead of declaring that the sun and moon "stood still," this clause declares *exactly the opposite*. The sun ceased (to shine) at high noon, *"but* (yet) it did *not* hasten to set." That is, it went on its *normal* course from its rising at that time of the year (about 5 A.M.) till its setting at 7 P.M. But the Lord nevertheless darkened it and made it stop shining in order to refresh his people, so that they could exterminate their foe completely.

Judges

TITLE

The book of Judges takes its name from the charismatic military leaders who rescued Israel from invading foes and ruled over her tribes in her national youth. The Hebrew word "to judge" *(shafaṭ)* includes the thought of "settling a dispute by maintaining justice" as well as the idea of delivering or liberating. The Hebrew judges consequently discharged a twofold task. First, when the nation was only a loose confederacy, lacking a stable central government and subject to enemy incursion, the judges delivered their people from foreign oppression. Second, they ruled over the tribes and dispensed justice. In their governing function they were like the *Shufetim* of Phoenicia and the *Sufetes* of Carthage, who in turn resembled Roman Consuls.

AUTHOR

Rationalistic higher criticism regards the book as a compilation of old hero tales taken from two independent sources. These two sources were supposedly combined in the seventh century B.C. and infused with religious teachings by a "Deuteronomist" in the sixth century B.C. This theory is to be rejected because it is founded upon the same unsound presuppositions as the partition theory of the Pentateuch and Joshua.

The book was probably written by Samuel or a member of the prophetic school around 1020 B.C. The book displays the unity of a single author-editor. The religious motif is no doubt due partly to the influence of the book of Deuteronomy, written 400 years earlier. It is obvious, however, that the author was in large measure a compiler, since the events extended over several centuries. His use of the early poetic "Song of Deborah" in chapter 5 after the prose account of chapter 4 illustrates this. He emphasized the stories of Gideon, Jephthah, and Samson because of their valuable spiritual lessons.

The book contains evidence of belonging to the time of Saul at the beginning of the monarchy. The time was clearly before the reign of David, who captured Jerusalem (Judg. 1:21; 2 Sam. 5:6-8) and before Israel had a king (Judg. 17:6; 18:1; 19:1; 21:25).

IMPORTANCE

The preeminent interest of the author is spiritual edification and admonition. He recounts the history of the Lord's chosen people from the time of Joshua (about 1375 B.C.) to the time of Samuel (about 1075 B.C.). However, the account is not a record of Israel's past for its own sake. The avowed purpose is to use the events and experiences of adversity as a text from which to inculcate religious warning and instruction. The author demonstrates that unbelief and apostasy could lead only to anarchy, for "every man did that which was right in his own eyes " (Judg. 17:6; 21:25). The result of this state of lawlessness was servitude and punishment. Repentance alone could bring deliverance and restoration.

The events included in the narrative illustrate this spiritual principle. The Jews were therefore correct in including this book among the prophetic writings, for it is a book of prophecy as much as a book of history. It displays and reinforces lessons that are useful to all generations of men, teaching the righteousness, justice, and love of God as well as the hopelessness of man apart from God.

OUTLINE

A. Introduction (1:1 – 2:5)
  1. Existing political situation (chapter 1)
  2. Existing religious situation (2:1-5)
B. The Administration of the Judges (2:6 – 16:31)
  1. Description of the people (2:6 – 3:6)
  2. Description of the judges (3:7 – 16:31)
    (a) Othniel (3:7-11)
    (b) Ehud (3:12-30)
    (c) Shamgar (3:31)
    (d) Deborah and Barak (chapters 4, 5)
    (e) Gideon and Abimelech (chapters 6 – 9)
    (f) Tola (10:1, 2)
    (g) Jair (10:3-5)
    (h) Jephthah (10:6 – 12:7)
    (i) Ibzan (12:8-10)
    (j) Elon (12:11, 12)
    (k) Abdon (12:13-15)
    (l) Samson (chapters 13 – 16)
C. Postlude (chapters 17 – 21)
  1. Idolatry of Micah (chapters 17, 18)
  2. Crime at Gibeah (chapters 19 – 21)

CAUSE OF ISRAEL'S SUFFERING

The failure of the Israelites to drive out the Canaanites (Judg. 1) and their refusal to separate themselves from these people with their vile worship (Judg. 2:1 – 3:4) constituted the source of the sadness,

THE OPPRESSORS AND THE JUDGES				
Oppressing Nation	Duration of Oppression	Delivering Judge	Duration of Deliverance	Approximate Dates
Mesopotamians	8 years	Othniel	40 years	1300 B.C.
Moabites Ammonites Midianites	18 years	Ehud	80 years	1280-1182 B.C.
Canaanites	20 years	Deborah Barak	40 years	1182-1122 B.C.
Midianites	7 years	Gideon Abimelech Tola Jair	40 years 3 years 23 years 22 years	1122-1075 B.C. 1075-1072 B.C. ⎰same general ⎱period
Ammonites	18 years	Jephthah Ibzan Elon Abdon	6 years 7 years 10 years 8 years	1110-1086 B.C. ⎧same ⎨general ⎩period
Philistines	40 years	Samson	20 years	1100-1075 B.C.

bondage, and defeat that characterize the book of Judges and make it such a contrast to the book of Joshua. The book begins in compromise, is filled with confusion, and ends in anarchy. It stands as a perpetual warning of the snare of unbelief and the peril of complicity with evil.

Instead of enjoying the freedom, prosperity, and blessing which the Promised Land offered them in obedience to God's Word and Covenant, the Israelites entered the dark ages of their national existence. They forsook the Lord (Judg. 2:13) and the Lord forsook them (Judg. 2:23).

At Bochim the Lord appeared in angelic form to enjoin complete separation from the Canaanites (Judg. 2:1-5), but the nation disobeyed. Consequently the Lord warned Israel that he would not drive out her foes, but that they would instead become a snare to Israel and a thorn in her side. Israel wept but did not repent, thus forfeiting national prosperity and blessing.

THE PROBLEM OF CHRONOLOGY

Critics who hold the late date of the Exodus (1290 B.C. under Rameses II) are compelled to compress the period of the Judges into less than 175 years. In doing so they must reject the time notice given in First Kings 6:1 and the whole chronological scheme underlying Joshua and Judges. Those who adopt the early date of the Exodus under Amenhotep II (1440 B.C.) place the period of the book of Judges from Joshua's death, about 1375 B.C., to Saul's accession, about 1020 B.C., a span of about 355 years. This allows ample time for the events of the period. (The chronological references in the Book of Judges at first reading seem to indicate a total of 410 years during which Israel was alternately oppressed and ruled in peace by the various judges. But this apparent discrepancy is easily explained by the fact that some of the judgeships, such as Jephthah's and Samson's, were contemporaneous.) The chronological notice in Judges 11:26, specifying an interval of 300 years from Israel's sojourn at Heshbon (Num. 21:25) to Jephthah's judgeship, tallies well with the longer chronology generally accepted by conservatives but contradicts the compressed time scheme proposed by higher criticism.

THE PROBLEM OF JEPHTHAH'S VOW

Did Jephthah, the eighth judge, actually offer as a human sacrifice his only child, an unmarried daughter (Judg. 11:29-40)? On the eve of battle with the Ammonites the warrior had made a vow that whoever was the first to come forth from his house to meet him on his victorious return would be the Lord's, and he would offer him up for a burnt offering. This apparently involved an actual human sacrifice. 1) It fitted in with the lawless spirit rampant in the era of the Judges (Judg. 17:6; 21:25). 2) It was in line with the half-pagan background of Jephthah, who would have been following a pagan custom and would not have known or been deterred by the Mosaic Law forbidding such a practice, especially since his daughter concurred in the decision. 3) Jephthah's excessive grief (Judg. 11:35) bears witness that the sacrifice actually took place. 4) There is no suggestion in the story that his conduct was sanctioned by the Lord. 5) The daughter asked for time to "lament" her virginity (Judg. 11:37), because no greater misfortune could befall a Hebrew woman than to die childless. 6) The notion that her perpetual virginity was a fulfillment of the vow seems to fall short of the scope of the passage.

Ruth

TITLE

This lovely pastoral story takes its name from its chief character, the Moabite woman, Ruth. It is one of only two books of the Bible that bear the name of a woman (the other book being Esther).

AUTHOR

The author is unknown. The book was apparently written during the reign of David, about 1000 B.C. The period of the Judges was past (Ruth 1:1), and the genealogy was terminated at David (Ruth 4:17, 22). Had the book been written after David's death, Solomon's name would be expected. The approximate date of 1000 B.C. is also supported by writing style, vocabulary, and mention of local customs.

BACKGROUND

The book of Ruth appears in the Hebrew text among the five scrolls (Megilloth) in the third part of the Canon—"The Writings" (Hagiographa). The book was removed from this position by the Greek translators and placed after Judges because it describes events contemporaneous with that period. This sequence was adopted in the Latin Vulgate and has since then passed into all modern Bibles.

IMPORTANCE

Ruth is the tale of a friendship between two women. Ruth's avowal of love for her mother-in-law, Naomi, is as eloquent a passage as can be found in the whole range of world literature (Ruth 1:16, 17). The events of the book took place in the period of the judges. But what a contrast the story offers to the sad defeat and tragic lawlessness of the Book of Judges! In Ruth, instead of unfaithfulness we find loyalty; instead of immorality, purity. Instead of battlefields appear harvest fields; instead of the warrior's shout, the harvester's song.

The book is much more than a pastoral tale of love. It has a rich underlying typology that links the romance it narrates with the divine plan of redemption which it unfolds. The story presents in figure our Lord as the great Kinsman-Redeemer, especially in his role of future Redeemer of his people Israel. It also presents an important link in the messianic family, from which the Promised One came some eleven centuries later.

SYMBOLOGY OF REDEMPTION IN RUTH	
Person	*Symbolism*
Naomi	Naomi, the "Pleasant One," portrays Israel, the chosen people, married to Elimelech ("My God is King") and prosperous in the land. Famine pictures spiritual failure. Migration to Moab illustrates Israel's worldwide dispersion and woe. Return to Bethlehem prefigures restoration of the nation in unbelief.
Orpah	Unbelieving mass of Israel electing to remain among the nations.
Ruth	Believing remnant will return and find the Kinsman-Redeemer.
Boaz	Christ as Kinsman-Redeemer (2:20), Lord of Harvest (2:3), Dispenser of Bread (3:15), and Giver of Rest (3:1). Marriage to Ruth represents redemption of both land and people.
Nearer Kinsman	Illustrative of the Law, which could do nothing for the poor foreigner, but instead shut her out as a Gentile (Deut 23:3). Hence Ruth was "Lo-Ammi," "Not My People," until Boaz' redemption.

OUTLINE

A. Deciding by Faith (chapter 1)
1. Naomi's misfortunes (1:1-5)
2. Ruth's decision of faith (1:6-13)

3. Naomi and Ruth in Bethlehem (1:19-22)
B. Serving in Grace (chapter 2)
  1. Gleaning in the fields (2:1-17)
  2. Learning about Boaz (2:18-23)
C. Abiding in Fellowship (chapter 3)
  1. The obedience of fellowship (3:1-13)
  2. The expectation of fellowship (3:14-18)
D. Resting in Redemption (chapter 4)
  1. Renunciation by nearest kinsman (4:1-8)
  2. Redemption by Boaz (4:9-17)
  3. Messianic genealogy (4:18-22)

1 and 2 Samuel

TITLE

These books are so named not because Samuel was the author but because that prophet is the most prominent person in the opening portion and the human agent in the founding of the Hebrew monarchy.

AUTHOR

Critics who hold to the documentary theory of the Pentateuch and Joshua usually postulate two principal sources for the books of Samuel—"J," about the tenth century B.C., and "E," about the eighth century B.C. These documents, supposedly similar but not identical to the Pentateuchal documents, are said to have been combined in the seventh century and to thus account for the problems and difficulties of the books. This critical theory is to be rejected because 1) it is at variance with the evident unity of the books; 2) it requires the compiler or editor to be an incompetent blunderer; 3) it accepts the erroneous theory that differences of point of view are evidences of variety of authorship; and 4) it employs inconclusive evidence based on supposed differences of style.

Although the author of First and Second Samuel is unknown, the writer-compiler was most likely a prophet under the kings and used earlier documents left by Samuel, Gad, Nathan, and others (1 Chron. 29:29). The date of composition was in all likelihood not later than the end of David's reign, with which period the books end.

BACKGROUND

First and Second Samuel are essentially a single work. They are so regarded in the Hebrew Canon. However, the Septuagint translators divided the Book of Samuel and the Book of Kings into four books. They named these the *Books of the Kingdoms*. This fourfold division was followed by the Latin Vulgate under the name *Books of the Kings*. Under Jerome's influence the first two Books of Kings became known as First and Second Samuel. This designation remains with us today.

IMPORTANCE

First and Second Samuel span the period from the closing years of the administration of the judges until the establishment of the kingdom under David. Samuel's career as the last of the judges and first of the prophets (Acts 13:20) is described, including the use of the prophetic office alongside the kingly office. Samuel established the schools of the prophets (1 Sam. 19:20; 2 Kings 2:3-5; 4:38) and anointed Saul and later David, but died before God's chosen king came to the throne. David's reign is one of the prime subjects of the books of Samuel.

OUTLINE

A. Judge Samuel (1 Samuel chapters 1 – 7)
  1. Samuel's boyhood (1:1 – 2:10)
  2. Samuel's call (2:11 – 3:21)
  3. Israel's folly (4:1 – 7:2)
  4. Samuel's ministry (7:3-17)

B. King Saul (1 Samuel chapters 8 – 31; 2 Samuel chapter 1)
  1. Israel demands a king (chapter 8)
  2. God selects Saul for Israel (chapters 9 – 11)
  3. Samuel addresses the people (chapter 12)
  4. Saul fights the Philistines (chapters 13, 14)
  5. Saul disobeys God (chapter 15)
  6. Samuel anoints David (chapter 16)
  7. David kills Goliath (chapters 17 – 23)
  8. David flees for his life (chapters 24 – 30)
  9. Saul dies in battle (chapter 31)
  10. David laments Saul's death (2 Samuel chapter 1)
C. King David (2 Samuel chapters 2 – 24)
  1. The coronation of the king (chapters 2 – 6)
  2. The covenant of God to David (chapter 7)
  3. The wars of David (chapters 8 – 10)
  4. The sin of David (chapters 11, 12)
  5. The crimes of Absalom (chapters 13, 14)
  6. The rebellion of Absalom (15:1 – 19:8)
  7. The resurgence of David (19:9 – 20:26)
  8. The revenge of the Gibeonites (21:1-14)
  9. The war with the Philistines (21:15-22)
  10. The song of David (22:1 – 23:7)
  11. The heroes of David (23:8-39)
  12. The census of David (chapter 24)

PROBLEMS

Numerous problems are found in the books of Samuel, but all of these can be resolved by careful study and spiritually discerning interpretation of the text. The problems are not (as negative criticism maintains) the result of contradictions, duplications, and differences in point of view contained in supposedly unreliable early documents cleverly combined to form the present books.

Who slew Goliath? Second Samuel 21:19 apparently reports that "Elhanan . . . slew Goliath" while Second Samuel 17:50, 19:5, and 21:9 assert that David did so. Moreover, First Chronicles 20:5 reports that "Elhanan the son of Jairi slew Lahmi the brother of Goliath the Gittite." It is quite obvious to the student of the Hebrew text that the solution of this apparent contradiction is purely textual. The text of Samuel is in a poorer state of preservation than that of any other part of the Old Testament, with the possible exception of Ezekiel and Hosea. Evidence furnished by a study of the original text suggests that the reading in Samuel and Chronicles was originally either "And Elhanan, the son of Jairi, slew Lahmi the brother of Goliath" or "And Elhanan, the son of Jairi the Bethlehemite, slew the brother of Goliath." The obvious original text of both passages indicates that David slew Goliath and Elhanan slew Goliath's brother.

Are there diametrically opposed attitudes about the monarchy in the Book? Negative critics assert that this is the case, using First Samuel 9:1-10, 16 and First Samuel 7:2 − 8:22 as evidence. They attribute the supposed divergency of viewpoint to a multiplicity of authors. What the critics fail to understand is God's capacity to condemn Israel for their lack of faith in demanding a king and yet to accede to their demand to the point of blessing the king which he reluctantly chose for them.

Was Saul twice deposed from the throne and yet continued to rule, his legitimacy being unchallenged to the day of his death? Critics assert that this is so, as described by a duplicate account in the narrative (1 Sam. 13:14; 15:26-29). But Saul in the first instance was simply told that his kingdom would not be "established . . . upon Israel forever" (1 Sam. 13:13). In his second and more serious offence he himself was divinely rejected. Instead of remaining unchallenged to the day of his death he continued in office apart from the divine presence − adequate proof of his rejection.

MESSIANIC FLASHES

Hannah's prophetic prayer (1 Sam. 2:1-10), which bears a resemblance to Mary's song ("the Magnificat" − Luke 1:46-55), contains a prediction of Christ as King: "The Lord shall judge the ends of the earth; and he shall give strength unto his king, and exalt the horn of his anointed" (1 Sam. 2:10; cf. Psa. 2:1-9).

The Davidic Covenant (2 Sam. 7:8-17) envisions the future kingdom of Christ as belonging to "the seed of David" (Rom. 1:3). It assures to the posterity of the Davidic house a throne and a kingdom rule on earth. The Davidic Covenant given to David by the oath of the Lord and confirmed to Mary by the Angel Gabriel (Luke 1:31-33) is immutable (Psa. 89:20-37). To him who was thorn-crowned at his first advent God will give the throne of David at his second advent (Acts 2: 29-32; 15:14-17).

PRINCIPAL PERSONALITIES OF FIRST AND SECOND SAMUEL

Person	Description
Samuel	Last of judges, first of prophets. Founded schools of the prophets. Anointed both Saul and David. Reprover of Saul.
Saul	First king of Israel. Displayed serious defect of character in presumptuously intruding into priests' office (1 Sam. 13), disobeying divine orders (1 Sam. 15), treacherously massacring Gibeonites (2 Sam. 21:1-9), and visiting spirit medium at Endor (1 Sam. 28).
David	Born leader, magnanimous, tactful, a man after God's heart. Conquered Jebusite stronghold and founded Jerusalem as central capital city and political and spiritual center. United nation and raised it to a significant power. Had a weak side to his character, shown in adultery with Bathsheba and murder of Uriah. Example of a sinning and chastened saint.
Jonathan	Noble son of an ignoble father. His selfless love for David reveals him as one of the finest characters in the Bible.
Joab	Captain of David's army. Crafty and ruthless. Treacherously killed Abner after the latter transferred allegiance to David. Murdered his rival, Amasa. Yet a man of great valor who did many exploits.
Abner	Cousin of King Saul and commander of Saul's army. Supported Ishbosheth, but later went over to David.

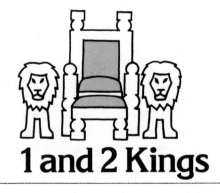

1 and 2 Kings

TITLE

First and Second Kings are entitled the Third and Fourth Books

Hezekiah's tunnel, 500 yards long, brought water into Jerusalem. *(Russ Busby photo)*

of Kingdoms in the Greek Version and the Third and Fourth Books of Kings in the Latin and in Hebrew Bibles since the sixteenth century.

IMPORTANCE

Originally one book, they narrate the history of the undivided kingdom from David's death (971 B.C.) through Solomon's reign (971-931 B.C.) till the divided Kingdom under Rehoboam (931 B.C.). Then the book traces the fortunes of the dual kingdom from 931 B.C. till the demise of the Northern Kingdom in 722 B.C. and the fall of the Southern Kingdom in 586 B.C.

The historian made use of available sources (1 Kings 11:41; 14:19; 2 Kings 24:5). He wrote with a strictly spiritual purpose, evaluating each king according to his loyalty to the Lord and the Covenant relationship, especially as set forth in the book of Deuteronomy. Tradition names the prophet Jeremiah as the author. He could well have been the author, since the scriptural attitude toward idolatry and apostasy emphasized in First and Second Kings coincides with Jeremiah's views as expressed in his life and preaching.

FIRST AND SECOND KINGS AS A WARNING AGAINST APOSTASY

First Kings	Second Kings
Begins with King David	Ends with king of Babylon
Opens with Solomon's glory	Closes with Jehoiachin's shame
Begins with the blessings of obedience	Ends with the curse of disobedience
Opens with the building of the Temple	Closes with the burning of the Temple
Traces the progress of apostasy	Shows the consequences of apostasy
Describes failure to work for God	Records forfeiture of right to rule
Displays the longsuffering of the Lord	Shows the inevitable punishment of sin

THE KINGDOM PERIOD (1010-586 B.C.)
DAVID (1010-971) SOLOMON (971-931) DIVISION (931)

Judah			Israel		
King	Period	Co-Regency	King	Period	Co-Regency
Rehoboam	931-913		1 Jeroboam	931-913	
Abijam	913-911		Nadab	910-909	
Asa	911-870		2 Baasha	909-886	
			Elah	886-885	
			3 Zimri	885	
			Tibni	885-880	
			Omri	880-874	
Jehoshaphat	873-848	873-870	Ahab	874-853	
Jehoram	853-841	853-848	4 Ahaziah	853-852	
Ahaziah	841		Joram	852-841	
Athaliah	841-835		Jehu	841-814	
Joash	835-796		Jehoahaz	814-798	
Amaziah	796-767		Joash	798-782	
Azariah	767-740	791-767	5 Jeroboam II	782-753	793-782
(Uzziah)			Zachariah	753-752	
			6 Shallum	752	
			7 Menahem	752-742	
			Pekahiah	742-740	
Jotham	740-732	750-740	8 Pekah	740-732	
Ahaz	732-716		9 Hoshea	732-722	
			Fall of	722	
			Samaria		
Hezekiah	716-687	729-716	Chronology is that of		
Manasseh	687-642	696-687	Edwin R. Thiele, The		
Amon	642-640		Mysterious Numbers of		
Josiah	640-608		the Hebrew Kings (Grand		
Jehoahaz	608		Rapids: Eerdmans,		
Jehoiakim	608-597		revised edition, 1965).		
Jehoiachin	597		Used by permission.		
Zedekiah	597-586				

CAPSULE HISTORY OF JUDAH AND ISRAEL (931-722 B.C.)			
Judah		*Israel*	
King	*Important Events*	*King*	*Important Events*
Rehoboam (931-913)	Division of Kingdom. Invasion of Shishak of Egypt (Sheshonq I) in 924 B.C.	Jeroboam I (931-913)	Shrines established at Dan and Bethel, precipitating religious anarchy.
Abijam (913-911)	Weak, unworthy three-year reign.	Nadab (910-909)	Unworthy rule of two years.
Asa (911-870)	Good king. Bribed Benhadad I of Syria to attack Israel. Rooted out idolatry.	Baasha (909-886)	Fought with Asa. Cursed because of idolatry and sin.
		Elah (886-885)	Drunkard; reigned 2 years.
		Zimri (885)	7-day reign.
		Tibni (885-880)	Succumbed to rival, Omri.
		Omri (880-874)	Founded new and powerful dynasty. Capital Samaria.
Jehoshaphat (873-848)	Generally godly but made alliance with the godless house of Ahab.	Ahab (874-853)	Sagacious, wicked; married the pagan Jezebel. War with Syria. Conflict with Elijah on Carmel.
Jehoram (853-841)	Married wicked Athaliah.	Ahaziah (853-852) Joram (852-841)	Weak sons of Ahab. Dynasty rooted out by Jehu.
Ahaziah (841)	Slain by Jehu.		
Athaliah (841-835)	Seized the throne.	Jehu (841-814)	Destroyed Baalism.
Joash (835-796)	Hidden in Temple and ruled under the High Priest Jehoiada. Later turned evil and slew Zechariah, son of Jehoiada.	Jehoahaz (814-798)	Weak; Israel reduced by Hazael of Syria.
Amaziah (796-767)	Conquered Edomites and defeated by Israel. Murdered.	Joash (798-782)	Victorious against Syria and Judah. Made Israel a power.

Judah		Israel	
King	Important Events	King	Important Events
Azariah (767-740)	Defeated external foes and brought Judah to great power. Became a leper.	Jeroboam II (782-753)	Victorious over Syria. Lifted Israel to zenith of power.
		Zachariah (753-752)	Last of Jehu Dynasty.
		Shallem (752)	Usurper. Reigned only 6 months.
		Menahem (752-742)	Paid tribute to Assyria.
		Pekahiah (742-740)	Lasted only 2 years.
Jotham (740-732)	Good and powerful king. Builder.	Pekah (740-732)	Assyrian advance.
Ahaz (732-716)	Judah judged by Israel and Aram. Alliance with Assyria. Wicked apostate.	Hoshea (732-722)	Vassal of Assyria. Last king of Israel.
			Fall of Samaria, 722.

THE MIRACLE CONNECTED WITH AHAZ' SUNDIAL

Like the miracle of Joshua's so-called "long day" (Josh. 10:12-14) the return of the shadow ten degrees on the dial of Ahaz in answer to Isaiah's prayer (2 Kings 20:8-11) has occasioned much controversy. In the case of both Joshua and Isaiah, supernatural, divine intervention is unquestioned by believers. The only point of issue is the *extent and scope* of the miracles involved. Those who hold that the sun stood still in one case and went back ten degrees in the other, i.e., that the earth ceased to rotate in the case of Joshua and reversed its rotation in the case of Isaiah, rightly rely on divine omnipotence but fail to take historical and astronomical evidence into consideration.

Since the narrative does not tell us *how* the divinely wrought sign was effected in answer to Isaiah's plea, it is arbitrary to insist that the sun had to back up in its trajectory to satisfy the scope of the passage. That the miracle evidently consisted of *the refraction of the sun's rays* out of the ordinary course of nature is shown from the following considerations.

Having created an orderly universe with consistent natural laws, God is careful to transcend those laws only when it is essential to do so. He does not need to upset the universe to show his power. No testi-

160

mony in ancient history or astronomy attests such an enormous and far-reaching disturbance in the machinery of the heavens. Moreover, Second Chronicles 32:31 apparently restricts the phenomenon to Palestine.

CAPSULE HISTORY OF JUDAH
AFTER FOREIGN CONQUEST OF ISRAEL
PERIOD COVERED: 722-586 B.C.

King	Important Events	Prophets
Hezekiah (716-687)	Wicked Ahaz was still reigning when Samaria fell, but his son Hezekiah was associated with him in rule from 729. Hezekiah cleansed the Temple of idolatry, celebrated the Passover. Withstood Sennacherib's invasion (701). God granted him 15 years extension of life. Embassies sent from Merodach-Baladin, king of Babylon (721-710, 704).	Isaiah— warns against foreign alliances. Micah
Manasseh (687-642)	Became a fanatical idolater. Built altars to Baal, made a symbol of Asherah, worshiped the stars, cultivated occultism, offered his son to Moloch. Was carried to Babylon by the King of Assyria but later restored to his throne. Repented and tried to undo the evil he did.	Isaiah—according to tradition was put to death by Manasseh.
Amon (642-640)	Evil son of Manasseh; slain by officials of his court.	Nahum
Josiah (640-608)	Crowned king at age of 8. Rapid decline of Assyria after death of Ashurbanipal (669-633). Fall of Nineveh in 612 B.C. Finding of Mosaic Law in Temple (622) led to great revival. Josiah killed at Megiddo in effort to stop Pharaoh Necho (609-595) from aiding Assyria. Rise of Chaldeans under Nabopolassar (625-606).	Zephaniah, Jeremiah
Jehoahaz (608)	Third son of Josiah; deposed and taken to Egypt in chains by Pharaoh Necho after 3-month reign.	Jeremiah
Jehoiakim (608-597)	Second son of Josiah; made king by Pharaoh Necho. Oppressive and thoroughly godless. Died in dishonor and was buried in disgrace (Jer. 22:19).	Jeremiah persecuted by Jehoiakim
Jehoiachin (597)	Son of Jehoiakim. Reigned evilly 3 months, then was carried to Babylon by Nebuchadnezzar (605-561), where he spent the rest of his life.	Daniel
Zedekiah (597-586)	Last king of Judah; son of Josiah; set up by Nebuchadnezzar in place of Jehoiachin. Evil ruler. Rebelled against Nebuchadnezzar. Sons killed before his eyes; blinded and carried to Babylon.	Ezekiel

It is not said that the *sun* went back, but that the *shadow* went back (2 Kings 20:10). Isaiah's statement that "the sun returned ten degrees (steps)" (Isa. 38:8) is a perfectly natural idiom employed even today. Ahaz' dial, as the Hebrew indicates, was a series of steps, either circular or running east and west. As the sun sank, the shadow would descend the steps, visible to Hezekiah from his sickroom. The ten "degrees" were ten steps of the stairway.

The theory of J. L. Butler is that the miracle was a "supernatural superior mirage of the sun" (*Journal of the American Scientific Affiliation*, Dec. 1951, p. 13). Some attribute the phenomenon to an eclipse, but it is difficult to see how this could satisfy the scope of the passage. However accomplished, the miracle was proof of divine power to heal Hezekiah's sickness and rescue him from death.

1 and 2 Chronicles

TITLE

In the Hebrew these two books were originally one great historical work. The twofold division made by the Septuagint was not introduced into Hebrew Bibles until the sixteenth century. The name "Chronicles" comes from Jerome (A.D. 400). He suggested that the Hebrew title *Divre Hayyamim*, "Events or Annals of the Times" (1 Chron. 27:24) might better be called "A Chronicle."

AUTHOR

The work was undoubtedly written by Ezra (400 B.C.) and placed last in the third part of the Hebrew Bible. It was put after First and Second Kings in Latin and English versions, following the arrangement of books in the Septuagint.

BACKGROUND

The books of Samuel and Kings are pre-exilic. The books of Chronicles are post-exilic. The former are written from the prophetic outlook and the latter from the priestly viewpoint, emphasizing the implications of true worship and witness. Thus the blessing of God's grace toward David as the establisher of the kingdom (1 Chron. 11 – 21) and the Temple ritual (1 Chron. 22 – 29) is emphasized in First Chronicles. In Second Chronicles Solomon's reign is spotlighted, since this monarch was second only to David in connection with the Temple and its service (2 Chron. 1 – 9).

Although the narrative of Second Chronicles treats both the Northern and Southern Kingdoms, most of the attention is centered on the Southern Kingdom (Judah). The Northern Kingdom is regarded as unrepresentative of true Israel and hence unworthy of major notice in the historical record. Judah was also guilty of gross departures from the true faith, especially in her later years, but God's immutable promises to David, as well as the godly reigns of such kings as Asa, Jehoshaphat, Hezekiah, and Josiah (2 Chron. 10 – 36), retained for the kingdom of Judah a privileged position in the sight of God.

IMPORTANCE

Chronicles was penned for the post-exilic community, to instruct it in the spiritual heritage of the nation and to inspire it in its messianic hope, its Levitical priesthood and sacrificial system, and its fidelity to the Mosaic Covenant.

Chronicles is therefore an interpretive history of the Jerusalem priesthood and its growth and development under the royal line of David. The writer gives prominence only to those aspects of history that illustrate the cultivation of the Mosaic ritual and the observance of the Mosaic Covenant as a medium of spiritual blessing and prosperity in the kingdom.

OUTLINE

A. Genealogies: Adam to David (chapters 1 – 9)
　1. Adam to Jacob (1:1 – 2:2)
　2. Jacob's posterity (2:3 – 9:44)
B. King David (chapters 10 – 29)
　1. The death of Saul (chapter 10)

2. The capture of Zion (chapters 11, 12)
3. The reign of David (13:1 – 22:1)
4. The religion of David (22:2 – 29:30)
C. King Solomon (2 Chronicles chapters 1 – 9)
   1. His wealth and wisdom (chapter 1)
   2. His temple-building program (chapters 2 – 7)
   3. His fame and influence (chapters 8, 9)
D. Kings of Judah (2 Chronicles chapters 10 – 36)
   1. Rehoboam to Zedekiah (10:1 – 36:21)
   2. Cyrus' edict (36:22, 23)

RELIABILITY AND AUTHENTICITY

Since Chronicles evidently represents Ezra's crusade to bring post-exilic Judah back into conformity with the Law of Moses (Ezra 7: 10), many modern critics reject the work as Levitical propaganda, a fiction of "what ought to have happened" (*Interpreter's Bible*, Vol. III, p. 341) rather than what actually took place. Liberal writers, however, with their prior repudiation of the Mosaic origin of Old Testament religion, have rendered themselves incapable of objective evaluation of the work. The repeated validation of the Pentateuchal priesthood and sacrificial system leaves them no alternative but to deny the historicity of First and Second Chronicles.

Yet the religious epic literature recovered from Ugarit, a Canaanite city of Moses' day, amply attests the existence of such contemporary religious practices. Moreover, the reliability of many of the historical statements that are found exclusively in Chronicles has been established by recent archeological discoveries. The fact that the chronicler was interested in those men, institutions, and events which were to be the basis for rebuilding a shattered nation is insufficient reason to reject him as an authentic historian. The writer had a right to highlight the positive virtues of David and Solomon and the succeeding kings of the Davidic line rather than rehearsing their sins. He is not to be demeaned because he magnifies acts of faith, obedience to God's law, and consequent triumphs. As inspired Scripture the books of Chronicles can be expected not only to hold their own in the light of developing research but also to thoroughly vindicate both their historical reliability and their high spiritual value.

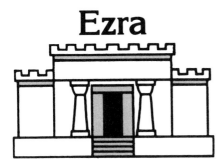

Ezra

TITLE

The book takes its name from its principal character. In both the Hebrew Bible and the Greek Septuagint Ezra and Nehemiah were originally combined into one book, "The Book of Ezra." Around A.D. 400 this book was divided by Jerome into two portions in the Latin Vulgate. Not until the fifteenth century, however, was the division into two books introduced into the Hebrew Bible.

AUTHOR

The book may also get its name from Ezra because of his authorship. Jewish tradition maintains that Ezra was indeed the author. The fact that chapters 7 through 10 are penned in the first person singular while events in which he did not participate are narrated in the third person supports this view. Most contemporary critics, however, hold that an unknown chronicler compiled and edited Chronicles, Ezra, and Nehemiah as one large work between 400 and 300 B.C. Ezra's ministry is to be placed during the reign of Artaxerxes I (465-424 B.C.).

IMPORTANCE

The book of Ezra continues the narrative where Chronicles leaves off. It tells the story of the return from Babylon and the building of the Temple. The author's aim is to show how God fulfilled his promise to restore his people to their homeland. He tells how God raised up such men as Zerubbabel, Haggai, and Zechariah to build the Temple and led Ezra to reestablish the ancient modes of worship and put a stop to compromise with paganism. Whatever does not contribute to this purpose he stringently excludes.

OUTLINE

A. The First Return — Under Zerubbabel (chapters 1, 2)
   1. The edict of Cyrus (chapter 1)
   2. The enumeration of the exiles (chapter 2)
B. The Building of the Temple (chapters 3 — 6)
   1. The construction (3:1 — 6:15)
   2. The dedication (6:16-22)
C. The Second Return — Under Ezra (chapters 7, 8)
D. The Reinstatement of Separation (chapters 9, 10)

CHRONOLOGY OF THE RETURN (ALL DATES B.C.)	
605-536	General period of the Exile
605-597	Deportation of leading citizens, including Daniel and Ezekiel
586	Destruction of Jerusalem and dissolution of kingdom of Judah
538	Edict of Cyrus sanctioning the return
536	Return of 49,897 Jews to Jerusalem
536	Rebuilding of altar, re-institution of sacrifice
535	Initiation of Temple construction
535-520	Economic difficulty, political struggle
520	Call of Haggai to complete the Temple
520-515	Ministry of Zechariah
515	Completion of Temple
458	Return of Ezra
445	Reconstruction of walls under Nehemiah

RISE OF PERSIA	
549	Union of Persia and Media under Cyrus
546	Conquest of Lydia by Cyrus
539	Conquest of Babylon by Cyrus
539-331	Height of Persian Empire
530	Death of Cyrus
530-522	Reign of Cambyses
522-486	Permission for Temple reconstruction
490	Defeat of Darius I
486-464	Epic of Esther and Xerxes I
480	Defeat of Persians by Greeks
464-424	Careers of Ezra and Nehemiah

Nehemiah

TITLE

The book takes its name from its main character and traditional author. The introductory preface is "The words of Nehemiah the son of Hachaliah" (Neh. 1:1).

AUTHOR

The book claims to be "the words of Nehemiah." There is no valid reason to deny authorship to him. Nehemiah 1:1 to 7:5 consists of an excerpt from the author's memoirs, as the first person narrative indicates. Other such passages are Nehemiah 11:1, 2; 12:27-43; and 13: 4-31. The book is to be dated in the reign of Darius Nothus (424-395 B.C.; Neh. 12:22). It is possible that some of the genealogies were amplified by a later scribe (Neh. 12:22).

OUTLINE

A. Nehemiah's Restoration of the Walls (chapters 1 – 7)
  1. Preceding providential events (chapters 1 – 2)
  2. The rebuilding of the walls (chapters 3 – 6)
  3. Watchmen set and a census taken (chapter 7)
B. Ezra and Nehemiah's Religious Reforms (chapters 8 – 13)
  1. Revival and renewal of the Covenant (8:1 – 10:39)
  2. Lists of princes, priests, and dedication of walls (11:1 – 13:3)
  3. Reforms of Nehemiah's second governorship (13:4 – 31)

Esther

TITLE

The book is named from its chief character, Esther. Her Hebrew name, meaning "Myrtle," was changed to a Persian name meaning "star." It is from this Persian word that we derive the name "Esther." In the Hebrew Scriptures the book occurs in the third section among the Five Scrolls (Megilloth) which were read at the great feasts. Esther was read at the Feast of Purim (Lots). Due to a rearrangement of books in the Septuagint and Latin Vulgate, Esther is found among the historical books in English Bibles. Although the name of God does not occur in the book, nor is there any allusion to the story in the New Testament, yet in no other part of the Bible is God's providential care of his people more conspicuous. This divine care is the central theme of the book.

BACKGROUND

There is no valid reason to deny the historicity of the narrative despite the fact that Vashti, Esther, and Mordecai have not as yet come to light in secular history (in the reign of Xerxes I, 485-465 B.C., when the story evidently took place). But it must be remembered that Esther did not become queen till the seventh year of Xerxes' reign (478 B.C.), after his return from defeat by the Greeks at Thermopylae and Salamis (Esth. 2:16). At that time Herodotus records that the king paid attention to his harem (IX:108). Although Herodotus declares that Amestris was the queen, an important monarch like Xerxes must certainly have had a large harem, with many wives and concubines (Esth. 2:14).

Ahasuerus is the Hebrew equivalent of the Persian name, which in the Greek is Xerxes. The portrayal of the Persian king in Esther corresponds with the character of Xerxes as known from history. The author of Esther clearly intended his words as history (Esth. 10:2). He certainly possessed accurate knowledge of Persian life and customs. Even negative critics, who deny the essential historicity of the story, confess that the storyteller knew something of the administration of the Persian kingdom, especially of the palace at Shushan or Susa. Susa was situated in southwestern Iran on the Ulai Canal (Dan. 8:2, 16), which connected the Kerkha and Abdizful rivers. The city and its palaces are well known from archeological research.

OUTLINE

A. God's People in Peril (chapters 1 – 3)
　　1. Esther's rise to royalty (chapters 1, 2)
　　2. Haman's conspiracy to kill (chapter 3)
B. Epic of Divine Deliverance (chapters 4 – 10)
　　1. The courage of the queen (chapters 4 – 7)
　　2. The Jewish revenge (8:1 – 9:19)
　　3. The Feast of Purim (9:20-32)
　　4. The exaltation of Mordecai (chapter 10)

The Poetic Books

THE ENGLISH ORDER

The poetical and wisdom books are Job, Psalms, Proverbs, Ecclesiastes, and Song of Solomon. In the English order these follow the Pentateuch and the historical Books. In the Hebrew, however, the sequence is entirely different. All of these books belong to the third and final part of the Hebrew Bible, the Writings. These are comprised of Psalms, Proverbs, Job and the Scrolls, including (among others) the poetical books of Song of Solomon and Ecclesiastes. The Hebrew order was dictated by liturgical convenience and other criteria that did not have special relevance to non-Jews. The translators of the Septuagint therefore rearranged the order into the sequence that has prevailed in non-Jewish versions.

Besides the books classified as poetical, large sections of poetry are found elsewhere in the Old Testament, as in Exodus 15, Deuteronomy 32, Judges 5, and extensive portions of the prophetic writings.

THE NATURE OF HEBREW POETRY

Parallelism of thought is the basis of Hebrew poetry. Rhythm is not attained by similarity of sound, as in rhymed verse, or by metrical accent, as in blank verse, but principally by the repetition, contrast, and elaboration of ideas. This is called *parallelism*. When the thoughts are essentially the same, the parallelism is *synonymous:*

He that sitteth in the heavens shall laugh,
The Lord shall have them in derision (Psa. 2:4).

When the thoughts are contrasting, the parallelism is *antithetic:*

The young lions do lack, and suffer hunger,
But they that seek the Lord shall not want any good thing (Psa. 34:10).

When the primary idea is developed and enriched, the parallelism is *synthetic:*

And he shall be like a tree planted by the rivers of water,
That bringeth forth fruit in its season,
Whose leaf also shall not wither;
And whatsoever he doeth shall prosper (Psa. 1:3).

By no means does all Hebrew poetry fit precisely into these basic categories. The matching and developing of concepts displays a wide variety and broad adaptation of parallelism that makes Hebrew poetry pleasing to the ear and instructive to the mind. Hebrew words are extremely vivid, and Old Testament poetry abounds in such figures of speech as simile, metaphor, alliteration, hyperbole, and personification. Scholars are also discovering in certain passages of Scripture such structural devices as rythmic beat, stanzas, refrains, and acrostics.

THE NATURE OF WISDOM LITERATURE

This literary style, common not only to the Bible but to the ancient Near East as well, gives instructions for successful living and often deals with the perplexities of human existence. Three of the poetical books—Job, Proverbs, and Ecclesiastes—as well as certain Psalms, such as 1, 10, 14, 19, 37, and 90, furnish excellent examples of wisdom literature. Proverbs deals especially with the practical problems of life, as does Psalm 1. Ecclesiastes grapples with such questions as fatalism, pessimism, and materialism. Psalm 37 wrestles with

170

the tantalizing problem of the prosperity of the wicked, while the book of Job deals with the vexing question of the suffering of the righteous.

Wisdom literature is clearly distinct from speculative philosophy. It is characterized by clear-sighted practicality. It instructs man to have his feet on the ground but his head in the clouds, in communion with the one true God. The emphasis on God's wisdom (Prov. 8) in this body of literature helped prepare for the coming of Christ (John 1: 1-3; 1 Cor. 1:24; Col. 2:3), who is made unto us the wisdom of God (1 Cor. 1:30).

Job

TITLE

The book gets its title from its main character. The name "Job" is found extrabiblically as early as the nineteenth century B.C. in the Berlin execration texts. Job is pictured as a prince of the land of Damascus. In the Amarna Age (fourteenth century B.C.) the name occurs as a prince of Pella (modern Fahil). The biblical Job was a godly man who lived in the steppes eastward or southeastward of Canaan in a region called Uz.

BACKGROUND

Job was a real, historical character, and the events related in the book actually took place. The references in Ezekiel 14:14, 20 and James 5:11 attest this fact. Moreover, there is nothing in the poem itself, in names, places, or circumstances, to suggest that the book narrates anything less than a literal, historical story.

Job is one of mankind's most magnificent dramatic poems. The sublimity of its theme, the grandeur of its thought patterns, and the masterliness of its literary sweep place it in the forefront of the great literature of the world. The value of the book is quite independent of time and its great message is dateless. No doubt this is why it is practically impossible to place it in time or surmise its human author. So little is there in the poem to pinpoint the age in which Job lived that opinions concerning the date of the book vary by as much as a thousand years and more. Yet this uncertainty does not in the least detract from the vibrant, omnitemporal ministry and appeal of the great dramatic poem.

IMPORTANCE

Job deals with the problem of suffering, especially on the part of the righteous and in the light of the providential and ethical government of God. Neither Job, who justified himself, nor his three friends, who charged him with sin, had the answer to this problem. Elihu, who saw Job's suffering as an instance of the divine chastening for the purpose of experiential sanctification, came nearer the truth. The full answer did not come, however, until God himself spoke in his majestic power (Job 38 – 41). Then only did Job, turning from his own goodness, cry out the real answer: "I abhor myself, and repent in dust and ashes" (Job 42:6). It was only then that Job saw himself in true perspective before the infinitely holy God and realized that what he was *personally* was more evil than anything he had ever done. After learning this lesson Job emerged from his suffering into blessing and restoration.

OUTLINE

The Prologue: Job's Testing (chapters 1, 2)
The Drama: Why Do the Righteous Suffer? (3:1 – 42:6)
    Act 1 – The Unsatisfactory Answer: The Righteous Suffer Because of Sin (chapters 3 – 31)
        (a) Job laments, showing need for character development (chapter 3)
        (b) Job philosophizes, but finds no satisfaction (chapters 4 – 31)
    Act 2 – The Partial Answer: The Righteous Suffer to be Refined in Righteousness (chapters 32 – 37)
        (a) Elihu speaks – "God instructs through affliction" (chapters 32, 33)

(b) Elihu speaks again—"God is infinitely just and prudent" (chapter 34)
(c) Elihu speaks a third time—"Piety has advantages despite suffering" (chapter 35)
(d) Elihu speaks a fourth time—"God's greatness shows man's ignorance" (chapters 36, 37)
Act 3—The Ultimate Answer: The Righteous Suffer to Fulfil the Perfect Purposes of God (38:1—42:6)
(a) God speaks—"Creation proclaims God's omnipotence" (38:1—40:2)
(b) Job answers—"I am vile; what shall I answer?" (40:3-5)
(c) God speaks again—"God's power infinitely overwhelms human frailty" (40:6—41:34)
(d) Job answers—"I abhor myself, and repent in dust and ashes" (42:1-6)
The Epilogue: Job's Restoration (42:7-17)

AUTHENTICITY

Critics commonly deny that the prose prologue and epilogue and the speeches of Elihu belong to the original poem. But there is no valid reason for ascribing the prologue (Job 1, 2) and the epilogue (Job 42:7-17) to a later author. It is extremely unlikely that the dialogue had an independent existence, for it presupposes the description of Job's illness (Job 8:4; 29:5) as given in the narrative.

Without the epilogue it would have appeared that Satan had been victorious and that God had abandoned Job. In any case the combination of prose narrative and poetic dialogue is not unusual, having parallels in Egyptian literature.

Because Elihu is not introduced in the prologue or named in the epilogue, and because his speeches are deemed wordy and inferior in style, they are regarded by some critics as ungenuine. But it is purely arbitrary to assume that he had to appear in the prologue. He is not included in the epilogue because he spoke the truth and made a real contribution to the solution of the problem of suffering; thus he needed no rebuke. Far from parroting the words of Job's three friends, he spoke to correct their error (Job 32:3-5). He contributes the important truth that the affliction of the righteous is disciplinary, corrective, and refining (Job 33:16-18; 36:10-12). Elihu's speeches answer Job's problem in part and prepare him for the full answer of the Lord.

Psalms

TITLE

Spiritual experience is the keynote of the Psalter, which the ancient Jews called *Sepher Tehillim,* "Book of Praises." Our English word "Psalms," from the Septuagint *Psalmoi,* means "songs" or "songs accompanied by string music."

AUTHOR

According to the titles of the Psalms the authors were as follows: David, 73 Psalms (37 in Book 1, 18 in Book 2, 1 in Book 3, 2 in Book 4, and 15 in Book 5); Asaph, 12 Psalms (Psa. 50, 73 – 83); the Korahites, 12 Psalms (Psa. 42 – 49, 84, 87, 88); Solomon, 2 Psalms (Psa. 72, 127); Moses, 1 Psalm (Psa. 90); and Ethan, 1 Psalm (Psa. 89).

That David was one of the principal authors of the Psalms is supported by the following facts: 1) he had unusual gifts as a musician and poet (1 Sam. 16:16-18; 18:10; Amos 6:5); 2) he was Spirit-endued (2 Sam. 23:1); 3) his name is connected with the composition and publication of liturgical song (1 Chron. 16:4; 2 Chron. 7:6; 29:30); and 4) the Psalter attests his influence by both the titles and content of many of the Psalms (Psa. 23, 51, 57); his authorship is claimed for 73 of the 150 Psalms.

The great song period of Israel's history was the three centuries from David to Hezekiah. The Psalter contains songs which predate and antedate this era, but the majority are to be placed within these limits. Evidence from the epic religious poetry retrieved from Ras Shamra (Ugarit), stemming from the fourteenth century B.C., demonstrates the antiquity of many of the Psalms. This evidence shows the fallacy of dating the Psalter in post-exilic and Maccabean times, as higher critics have commonly done.

A kind shepherd pours refreshing oil. (© *MPS*)

IMPORTANCE

The Psalms constitute the great devotional treasury of God's ancient people, the Jews. Because they express the experiences of the Lord's people in every age, the Psalms have a universal appeal which make them the hymnbook of God's people even today.

In the English order the Psalms are placed in the poetical and wisdom division after the historical books. But in the Hebrew Bible the Psalter heads the whole third section (the Writings), coming after

175

the Major and Minor Prophets. The importance of the Book of Psalms is attested by the fact that in New Testament times it could represent the entire third part of the Hebrew Canon (Luke 24:44).

Two principal themes dominate the Psalms:

THE SPIRITUAL STRUGGLES AND TRIUMPHS OF SAINTS IN THE PRE-CHRISTIAN ERA. These experiences constitute the basic subject. However, they echo the conflicts of the Lord's people in every age.

THE PROPHETIC ELEMENT. This strand forms the warp and woof of the book, as New Testament allusions and quotations show. Great predictions center in the following: 1) the Messiah (Luke 24:44). This includes his first advent, embracing his incarnation, death, burial, resurrection, ascension, exaltation, and present session (Psa. 2, 8, 16, 22, 45, 69, 72, 89, 110, 118, 132); 2) the nation Israel. Particularly emphasized are the sorrows and sufferings of the believing portion of Israel in the nation's coming time of trouble and the subsequent deliverance and restoration to kingdom glory (Psa. 46, 52, 58, 59, 109, 140); 3) the earth and the nations. Israel's future glories of restoration are stressed, as well as the participation of the nations in these blessings (Psa. 72, 110, 148).

PROBLEMS

More than twenty of the Psalms (e.g. Psa. 35, 69, 109, 139) call down curses upon the godless and pray for the overthrow of the wicked. Such imprecations cause many Christians to wonder how these Psalms ever found a place in the Bible and how they can be reconciled with Christian morality and love. In considering the difficulty the following observations must be made. First, such prayers are uttered by the godly, who identify themselves so closely with God and his cause that they pray with his glory alone in view, totally apart from the human or the personal element. In such a state of identification they realize that God's love can never be separated from his holiness. They must love what God loves and hate what God hates. They must hate sin because God hates it. They must hate sin in the sinner, though not the sinner himself. God loves the sinner, and his love is extended to make the sinner holy. When the sinner rejects God's love and persists in sin, then God's glory can only be realized in the judgment of the wicked and the consequent vindication of his holiness. Imprecatory prayers are uttered upon those who have rejected God's love, for they have become the objects of God's offended holiness and judgment (Psa. 139:21, 22).

Second, we must use the imprecatory Psalms in the light of our Lord's teaching about loving our enemies (Matt. 5:44, 45). We must, like him, hate the sin but love the sinner. Only as the sinner rejects God's love and offends God's holiness to such an extent that divine judgment must fall does God's Spirit impel the godly to pray with imprecations. When human wickedness in the coming period of Israel's trouble reaches its fullness, the godly Israelite remnant, whom the imprecatory Psalms envision, will utter such prayers, for the day of divine wrath and vengeance will have arrived (2 Thess. 2:8-10; Rev. 6: 10, 17).

Proverbs

TITLE

A proverb is a short, pithy saying centering in a comparison or antithesis that strikes the ear and arrests the attention.

AUTHOR

The witness of the book itself concerning its contents attests that it is a compilation principally, but not entirely, of Solomonic proverbs (Prov. 1:1; 10:1). Solomon uttered "three thousand proverbs," in which much of his famous wisdom was enshrined (1 Kings 4:32). However, the collection as we have it today could not have been completed before Hezekiah's time (716-687 B.C.), since many of the Solomonic proverbs were written out and added at that time (Prov. 25:1 – 29:27). The words of Agur (Prov. 30:1-33)and of Lemuel (Prov. 31:1-

9) and the acrostic poem of the virtuous wife (Prov. 31:10-31) were apparently added even later.

IMPORTANCE

Springing out of monotheistic faith and conduct, the Proverbs inculcate practical virtues for successful living and belong to the wisdom literature of the Old Testament (see introduction to the poetical and wisdom books). The sententious sayings that constitute the book of Proverbs are a distillation of the wisdom of the age of the Hebrew monarchy. Mere human wisdom is, however, not the only subject of the book. Divine wisdom — God revealed as the Creator and Goal of all things — is anticipated as well (Prov. 8:22-31). Apart from divinely revealed grace and power, fallen man cannot please God or live a virtuous life. The book of Proverbs shows that in all ages God requires men to live a righteous life.

PROVERBS AND NONBIBLICAL WISDOM LITERATURE

The proverb as a literary style is not confined to the Bible, but is common also to other ancient near Eastern nations beside Israel, notably Egypt. One of the oldest of these wisdom pieces is the *Instruction of Ptah-Hotep*, about 2450 B.C. Important also are the *Instruction of Ani* and the *Wisdom of Amenemope*. In addition the *Story of Ahikar*, (7th cent. B.C.), a tale from Mesopotamia, is embellished with many proverbs that were evidently influenced by the canonical book. Some scholars have tried to prove that the biblical book borrowed from the nonbiblical books. But broad parallels may be expected in any general moral instructions, for they are not the heritage of any one nation.

PROVERBS AND THE NEW TESTAMENT

Our Lord fulfilled not only the Law and the Prophets (Matt. 5:17), but also the wisdom writings. He did so by revealing the fullness of God's wisdom (Matt. 12:42; 1 Cor. 1:24, 30; Col. 2:3; Prov. 8:22-31). But the book of Proverbs has also left its stamp on the New Testament by a number of quotations. (Compare Prov. 3:7 with Rom. 12:16; Prov. 3:11, 12 with Heb. 12:5, 6; Prov. 3:34 with James 4:6 and 1 Pet. 5:5; Prov. 4:26 with Heb. 12:13; Prov. 10:12 with 1 Pet. 4:8; Prov. 25:21, 22 with Rom. 12:20; and Prov. 26:11 with 2 Pet. 2:22). A number of indirect allusions to the book of Proverbs also occur in the New Testament. (Col. 2:3 refers to Prov. 2:4; Luke 2:52 refers to Prov. 3:1-4; Matt. 7:24-27 refers to Prov. 12:7.)

Ecclesiastes

TITLE AND ORDER IN THE CANON

The book of Ecclesiastes takes its name from the Greek version, in which it bears the title *ekklesiastes,* meaning "assembly." The Hebrew title is *Koheleth.* This term has been taken to mean either "one who collects" wise sayings (Eccl. 12:9, 10) or "one who addresses an assembly," that is, a "speaker" or "preacher." The correct interpretation is evidently "one who assembles a group for the purpose of addressing it." In the Hebrew Bible Ecclesiastes appears in the third section of the Canon after Psalms, Job, and Proverbs, among the so-called Five Scrolls (Ruth, Song of Solomon, Lamentations, Ecclesiastes, and Esther). The order in English Bibles follows that of the Septuagint.

AUTHOR

The preacher is distinctly represented as Solomon, "son of David, king in Jerusalem" (Eccl. 1:1), excelling all his predecessors in wealth and wisdom (Eccl. 1:16; 2:7, 9). The book may be regarded either as a writing of Solomon himself in his old age or as words which, though not actually uttered by Solomon, accurately sum up his completed experience. Today most scholars hold that Solomon himself was not the author. Many date it after the Exile. They usually agree, however, that the central figure of the book is Solomon, whom the unknown writer (perhaps himself of the royal line of David) employed as a literary device to convey his message forcefully and dramatically. Those who hold this position insist that there was no intent to deceive and that no one was in fact deceived.

IMPORTANCE

The primary goal of the author is to attest from personal experience that all earthly ambitions and attainments, when pursued as ends in themselves, wind up in emptiness and dissatisfaction. His thematic term is "vanity of vanities" (Eccl. 1:2), a Hebraism denoting "supreme vanity" or "unrelieved emptiness." The man "under the sun" is the secular, unspiritual man, who concerns himself solely with his present life on earth. The author's reasonings and philosophy lay no claim to be revealed truth, but are recorded by inspiration for our instruction, to show us that only God can satisfy the deepest hunger of the human heart, and that living for him in the light of eternity imparts the only true meaning to life.

The sadness and pessimism of the author resulted from unbelief. But after tasting its bitter fruits he returned in faith to God (Eccl. 12: 13, 14). This important theme of the emptiness of life apart from God should be compared with what the Apostle Paul declares about the vanity of the world (Rom. 8:20-25, 28).

OUTLINE

A. The Preacher's Theme: Life without God Is Vain (1:1-3)
B. The Preacher's Proof (1:4 — 3:22)
    1. Everything is transitory (1:4-11).
    2. Evil is everywhere (1:12-18)
    3. Pleasure, wealth, and work are unsatisfying (chapter 2)
    4. Death is inevitable (chapter 3)
C. The Preacher's Elaboration (4:1 — 12:8)
    1. Life is inequitable and oppressive (chapter 4)
    2. Wealth is transitory and unsatisfying (chapter 5)
    3. Death destroys all of life's gains (chapter 6)
    4. Wickedness permeates righteousness (chapter 7)
    5. God's providence overrules all (chapters 8, 9)
    6. Life abounds with disorder (chapter 10)
    7. Without God life is truly empty (11:1 — 12:8)
D. The Preacher's Conclusion: Vanity Can Be Overcome (12:9-14)
    1. Follow the truth (12:9-12)

2. Live for God (12:13)
3. Consider future judgment (12:14)

CANONICITY

The startling nature of some of the statements of Ecclesiastes led certain Jews to question its right to a place among the inspired books. By A.D. 90, however, its right to remain in the Canon was universally accorded. Those who question the book's canonicity forget that the reasonings of a secularist apart from divine revelation are set down by inspiration much as are the words of Satan (compare Eccl. 9:2 with Gen. 3:4, 5 and Job 1:9-11; 2:4, 5). The New Testament contains no direct quotation from the book or unequivocal allusion to it.

Song of Solomon

TITLE AND ORDER IN THE CANON

The designation "Song of Songs" is a literalizing of the Hebrew idiomatic name, denoting the superlative degree, that is, "the best or most exquisite Song." The designation "Song of Solomon" is taken from the data of 1:1. In the Hebrew Bible, the Song of Solomon, like Ecclesiastes, constitutes one of the five *Megilloth* or Scrolls, which were brief enough to be read on festal occasions. The Song heads the list because it was used at the Passover, the first and greatest feast of the year. The English order follows the Septuagint and all later translations.

AUTHOR

The opening verse of the book attributes the Song to Solomon.

The king was as famous for his songs as for his proverbs (1 Kings 4: 32). The Song of Songs was the crowning jewel of his romantic compositions. The Solomonic authorship is attested by internal evidence and local color, though some of the phraseology may have been altered at a later date. This would account for several Persian and Greek words. Since Solomonic commerce was incredibly widespread, there was an inevitable influx of foreign words, which may explain the Aramaic influence.

BACKGROUND

The Song is a unified lyrical poem with the dramatic form of dialogue. Critics who regard it as an anthology of loosely connected love lyrics do not justify its inclusion in the Canon. But they fail to account for the presence of identical imagery and local color in all parts of the Song, the occurrence of the same refrain, and the appearance of the same persons in all parts.

There are three common interpretations of the Song of Solomon.

THE LITERAL INTERPRETATION. This method construes the poem as a representation of chaste marital love without any other meaning. Some who adopt this view justify its place in the Canon by making it a reminder that God, "who has placed love in the human heart, is Himself pure" (E. J. Young, *Introduction to the Old Testament*, 1949, p. 237). Most scholars who hold this interpretation attempt to justify canonicity by resorting to the shepherd hypothesis. Under this supposition a shepherd-lover of the bride is introduced, whom Solomon, villain-like, tries to seduce from her lover. The poem is thus construed as the triumph of pure love over lust. Unfortunately, the shepherd has no tangible existence. He is nothing more than a shadow cast by the person of Solomon.

THE ALLEGORICAL INTERPRETATION. To the Jews the poem represents the Lord's love for Israel. To the Christian it represents Christ's love for his church. The objections to this treatment are mainly that it unnecessarily rules out the actual historicity of the events and lends itself to extravagant, far-fetched interpretations.

THE TYPICAL INTERPRETATION. This is a mediating view between the literal and allegorical views. It avoids the secularity of the literal view and the extravagances of the allegorical view. Since types normally prefigure their antitypes in only a few salient points, the typical view discourages fantastic interpretations of details and recognizes

The Poetic Books

the historical nature of the story. It does not deny that the book is primarily the expression of pure marital love as ordained by God in creation. However, it sees that the secondary and larger interpretation is of Christ and his heavenly Bride, the Church (2 Cor. 11:2; Eph. 5:23-32; Rom. 7:4; Rev. 19:6-8).

The story itself goes somewhat as follows: King Solomon owned a vineyard at Baal-Haman (unknown) and let it out to keepers (Song 8:11), consisting of a mother (1:6), sons (1:6), and two daughters—the Shulamite (6:13) and a little sister (8:8). The Shulamite was the "Cinderella" (1:5), naturally beautiful but unnoticed. Her brothers made her a slave in the vineyard (1:8; 2:5), and so she had little time to care for her personal appearance (1:6). Being so much in the open, she became very sunburned (1:5).

One day a handsome stranger came to the vineyard. It was Solomon in disguise. He took notice of her, and she became embarrassed about her personal appearance (1:6). She thought he was a shepherd, and inquired about his flocks (1:7). He replied evasively, but spoke loving words to her (1:8-10), promising rich gifts for the future (1:11). He won her love and departed with the promise that he would return. She dreamed of him at night and felt him near (3:1). Finally he did come back in all his royal grandeur to take her as his bride (3:6, 7). All this typifies Christ, who first appeared as a humble Shepherd to woo his Bride. Later he will come again as King of Kings, and then the marriage of the Lamb will be consummated.

OUTLINE

A. Rhapsody of Love (1:1—3:5)
 1. Palace musings (1:1-17)
 2. Romance in full bloom (2:1—3:5)
B. Invitation and Acceptance (3:6—5:1)
 1. Bridegroom and bride at Jerusalem (3:6-11)
 2. Bridegroom's delight in the bride (4:1-15)
 3. Bridegroom's anticipation of marital joy (4:16—5:1)
C. Separation and Restoration (5:2—6:3)
 1. Dream of separation (5:2-8)
 2. Reality of restoration (5:9—6:3)
D. Love's Fellowship (6:4—8:14)
 1. Love's laudation (6:4-10)
 2. Love's desire (6:11-13)
 3. Love's devotion (7:1—8:14)

183

The Prophetic Books

NAMES AND HEBREW AND ENGLISH ORDER

In the Hebrew Bible the prophetic books (except Daniel) occur in the second division of the Canon, called the Nebhiim (Prophets). These follow the Pentateuch and consist of the *Former Prophets* (Joshua, Judges, Samuel, and Kings) and the *Latter Prophets* (Isaiah, Jeremiah, and the twelve Minor Prophets). Ruth is joined to Judges and Lamentations to Jeremiah. Following the order in the Septuagint, the English Bible closes with the prophetic books, ending with Malachi. In contrast, the Hebrew Bible closes with the poetical and wisdom books (Psalms, Job, and Proverbs), followed by the Five Rolls (Song of Solomon, Ruth, Lamentations, Ecclesiastes, and Esther) and Daniel, Ezra, Nehemiah, and Chronicles. The Greek-English order is based on logical arrangement of content. The Hebrew arrangement is founded on artificial criteria of limited relevance, including liturgical usage.

NATURE OF THE OLD TESTAMENT PROPHET

Prophets were men raised up by God in times of declension and apostasy to call Israel back to God. They were primarily revivalists and patriots. They were God's spokesmen to the heart and conscience of the nation. But the political and social aspects of the prophets' messages were always secondary. First and foremost the prophet's message was spiritual. He announced the will of God to men. He called for complete obedience to the Word of God. He spoke under inspiration and with divine authority. "Thus saith the Lord" was the theme of his pronouncements as God's spokesman.

The Hebrew terms used to designate a prophet furnish an indication of the nature of the prophet's ministry. He was called a *ro'eh*, "one who sees" (1 Sam. 9:9), a *hozeh*, "one who sees supernaturally" (2 Sam. 24:11), and a *nabbhi*, "one who announces" (1 Sam. 9:9). Usually the "seeing" and "announcing" functions of the prophet pertained to the Word and will of God as they affected the everyday lives of God's people. Sometimes, however, they embraced the future and became predictive.

THE PREDICTIVE ELEMENT IN PROPHECY

Foretelling played a legitimate role in prophecy, but this role was not that of prediction for its own sake. The foretelling of the future was usually not even employed to establish the genuineness of the prophet, although occasionally this was the case, as in Deuteronomy 18:22. Prediction was rather a preview of the future arising from the spiritual circumstances of the present. The purpose was always practical, warning the unfaithful of judgment and encouraging the faithful to persevere in well-doing.

The two great themes of predictive prophecy are the first and second advents of Christ. Associated with the first advent is a suffering Messiah (e.g. Isa. 53:1-9) and with the second advent a reigning Messiah (Isa. 11:1-16). This duality of suffering and glory, weakness and power, and cross and crown presented a mystery which perplexed the prophets (1 Pet. 1:10-12; Luke 24:26, 27). They saw both advents in one blended view. This was the case because the interval between the

THE PROPHETS AND THEIR MESSAGE		
Prophet	*Message*	*Audience and Period*
Jonah	God calls Gentiles (Nineveh) to repent.	To Israel be-
Amos	God will punish persistent sin.	fore the
Hosea	God loves his chosen people, Israel.	Northern Kingdom fell (722 B.C.)
Joel	The day of the Lord and the judgment of the nations.	To Judah in her increas-
Obadiah	Edom's judgment.	ing apostasy
Isaiah	The two advents of the world's Savior and Israel's King	(750-650 B.C.)
Micah	The Bethlehem-born King and his kingdom.	
Nahum	Nineveh and Assyria will be destroyed.	To Judah in
Habakkuk	The Lord's kingdom will triumph.	the last 64
Zephaniah	A remnant will be preserved for blessing.	years before
Jeremiah	The coming Messiah and the New Covenant.	her exile (650-586 B.C.)
Ezekiel	Restoration of Israel and the land.	To the exiles
Daniel	The times of the Gentiles and Israel's kingdom.	in Babylon (606-538 B.C.)
Haggai	Restoration of the Temple and future kingdom.	To the re-
Zechariah	Establishment of the kingdom with Messiah-King-Priest.	stored remnant (538-
Malachi	Second advent of Christ, the Sun of Righteousness	400 B.C.)

advents, revealed in the mysteries of the kingdom (Matt. 13:1-50), had not been made known to them. The formation of the New Testament Church following the rejection of the Messiah was also unknown to the Old Testament prophets. These and other events were "mysteries hid in God" (Eph. 3:1-10), to be revealed through our Lord and the New Testament prophets.

Broadly speaking, Old Testament predictive prophecy is occupied with the fulfillment of the covenants made with Israel, especially 1) the Palestinian Covenant of restoration and conversion of the nation (Deut. 30:1-9), 2) the Davidic Covenant of messianic kingship (2 Sam. 7:8-17), and 3) the Abrahamic Covenant that promises salvation to all mankind (Gen. 12:1-3). Old Testament prophecy therefore centers in Israel. Only the distinctive prophecies of Daniel deal directly with world history. This is because Daniel is the prophet of "the times of the Gentiles."

Isaiah

AUTHOR

The author is Isaiah, the son of Amoz (Isa. 1:1). He is the foremost messianic prophet of the Old Testament. For beauty of style and profundity of prophetic vision he is unequalled among the prophetic writers.

OUTLINE

A. Predictions of Punishment and Blessing (chapters 1 – 35)
  1. Regarding Judah and Jerusalem (chapters 1 – 12)
  2. Regarding foreign nations (chapters 13 – 23)

3. Regarding the future kingdom (chapters 24–27)
4. Regarding Judah and Assyria (chapters 28–35)
B. Ties With the Past and the Future (chapters 36–39)
  1. The invasion of Sennacherib (chapters 36, 37)
  2. The sickness and recovery of Hezekiah (chapter 38)
  3. The imprudence of Hezekiah (chapter 39)
C. The Exile and the Glories to Come (chapters 40–66)
  1. The coming restoration (chapters 40–48)
  2. The coming Redeemer (chapters 49–57)
  3. The coming glories (chapters 58–66)

THE MESSIAH IN THE BOOK OF ISAIAH	
Characteristic of Messiah	Description and Reference
Deity	"A Son is given" (9:6)
Eternity	"Everlasting Father" or "Father of Eternity" (9:6) means "Eternal One"
Omnipresence	40:22
Omnipotence	"The Mighty God" (9:6); see also 40:12
Omniscience	40:12-14
Holiness	"Holy, holy, holy" (6:3) means infinitely holy; "Holy One of Israel" mentioned 22 times
Glory	6:1—compare John 12:41; see also 60:1, 2
Creatorship	40:26; 42:5; 43:1; 45:11, 18
Uniqueness	40:12-18, 25
Humble Service	42:1; 53:1-3
Incarnation	7:14 shows both humanity (virgin birth) and deity (name "Immanuel" means "God with us")
Youth	7:15; 11:1; 53:2
Mildness	42:2; no shouting or other demagogic tactics
Tenderness	42:3; compare Matthew 12:18-20
Obedience	11:2, 3; 42:1-7; 52:13; 53:7
Saviorhood	53:5-7, 11, 12; 60:16
Kingship	9:7; 32:1, 43:15
Exaltation	9:6, 7; 53:12
Peacefulness	2:4; 9:6, 7; 11:6-9
Justifying Power	53:11
Anointing	11:2; 42:1; 61:1; see also John 3:34
Message	61:1, 2
Sufferings	50:6; 52:14; 53:4-7, 10-12
Rejection	53:3-6; compare 49:7
Vicarious Death	53:4-6, 8, 10-12; burial 53:9
Resurrection	53:10-12
Second Advent	9:6, 7; 11:4-16; 42:1-4; 52:13-15; 61:1-6
Judgeship	11:1-5
Spiritual Progeny	53:10, 11

GREAT MESSIANIC PROPHECIES

Isaiah is the messianic prophet of the Old Testament *par excellence*. To him more than to any other Old Testament seer was granted clear and far-reaching foreviews of Messiah. Christ's first coming to redeem and second coming to reign were seen by this prince of Old Testament prophets with a fullness of glory not found in any other book, with the possible exception of some of the great prophetic Psalms and certain passages of Zechariah.

PROPHECIES OF ISAIAH YET TO BE FULFILLED	
Designation	*Reference and Description*
The Day of the Lord	Period of apocalyptic judgments preceding the second advent and establishment of the kingdom (2:10-22; 4:1; 13:9-13; 24:1-23; 63:1-6).
The Restoration of Israel to Palestine	11:10-12; 14:1, 2; 27:12, 13; 35:10; 43:5, 6; 66:20.
The Restoration of Palestine Itself	30:23-26; 35:1-10.
Jerusalem as the Capital of the Earth	1:25-27; 2:3; 52:1-9; 60:1-22; 62:1-7.
The Conversion of the Jewish Remnant	12:1-6; 25:1-12; 26:1-19; 35:10; 44:21-24; 54:1-17.
The Conversion of the Nations	11:10-12; 25:6-9; 60:1-12.
The New Heaven and the New Earth	Isaiah dimly saw the eternal state, but it was blended with millennial conditions (65:17; 66:22).

ISAIAH 53 AND THE QUESTION "IS HEALING IN THE ATONEMENT?"

This great prophecy of Christ's atoning work is frequently taken to teach that physical healing is guaranteed by the atonement. According to Isaiah 53:4, 5, it is claimed, Christ died for all the ills of the body just as he did for all the sins of the soul. On this assumption it is taught that a regenerated believer can by faith in Christ's finished sacrifice expect his body to be healed of sickness just as surely as he experienced the spiritual healing of his soul.

But this kind of healing is not in the atonement. The true healing of the atonement is spiritual, accompanied by the glorification of the body at the rapture and first resurrection. Our present bodies, although redeemed, remain subject to sin, the old nature, infirmity, sickness, pain, and death. These physical impediments *will not be removed* until our redeemed mortal bodies are glorified and made immortal at the first resurrection.

Isaiah's prophecy that Christ would bear our sicknesses and carry our infirmities (Isa. 53:4) was fulfilled in our Lord's ministry of physical healing (Matt. 8:17) and not in his atoning death on the cross. Christ's miracles of healing served to certify him as the Redeemer. They were signs of the greater spiritual healing which he came to bring. They were also pledges of the ultimate full deliverance of the redeemed from all the consequences of sin, physical sickness included. It was in this sense that Isaiah prophesied that Christ would atone for our physical ills.

DOES ISAIAH PREDICT
THE VIRGIN BIRTH OF CHRIST?

Many critics contend that he does not. But the validity of the virgin-birth prophecy (Isa. 7:14, 15) is proved by the following considerations: 1) The sign foretelling this event was *divinely* given: "The Lord himself" (emphatic) gave it. 2) It was given to the Davidic royal house (not to Ahaz—"to you" is plural in Hebrew). 3) It clearly involved a stupendous miracle, for the sign was "deep as Sheol" or "high as heaven" (Isa. 7:11, RSV). 4) It envisioned the preservation of the Davidic house till the sign should be realized. 5) It necessitates a "virgin" (*ᶜalmah*) to satisfy the context and to square with the declarations of inspired Scripture (Matt. 1:22, 23, *parthenos*). The Septuagint translators used this same specific Greek word in their rendering of Isaiah 7:14. Arguments declaring that *ᶜalmah* cannot mean "virgin" not only ignore the emphasis on miraculous intervention in this passage but also overlook the probable meaning of "virgin" for this word in Genesis 24:43, Exodus 2:8, Psalm 68:25, Song of Solomon 1:3, and Proverbs 30:19. 6) The very name "Immanuel," meaning *"with us is God,"* requires the incarnation of Christ, the greatest miracle of the ages. 7) Although the child who was born would be fully divine, he would also be truly human, growing to maturity like other children (Isa. 7:14, 15; Luke 2:52).

The reluctance to accept the virgin-birth prophecy of this passage is sometimes caused by failure to understand that *Isaiah had with him in his arms his own infant son, Shearjashib (Isa. 7:3).* This babe was to constitute the *immediate* sign to unbelieving Ahaz. Verse 16 refers to *this* infant rather than to the messianic child to be born seven centuries later. "Before the child" (the child which Ahaz could see in the prophet's arms) "shall know how to refuse the evil, and choose the good, the land before whose two kings thou art in deadly fear shall be rid of them" (literal rendering). This portion of the prophecy was fulfilled when Tiglath-pileser took Damascus in 732 B.C. and slew Rezin (2 Kings 16:9). Pekah was also slain about two years after this remarkable prophecy.

PROBLEMS

Critics commonly deny that the prophet Isaiah wrote all 66 chapters of the book, despite the fact that the Hebrew Bible attributes them to him. Most of the first part of the book (Isa. 1−39) is attributed by the critics to Isaiah. The second section (Isa. 40−66), however, is ascribed by them to an unknown author (or authors) who lived after 550 B.C., toward the close of the exile in Babylon. Critics argue that differences in literary style and theological concepts support their contention that these two sections of the book were authored by different persons.

A favorite line of reasoning is that the historic function of prophecy is violated by attributing chapters 40 to 66 to Isaiah. (The prophet, according to this reasoning, is supposed to predict the future only from the historical context of his own age.) But the prophet Ezekiel was transferred (Ezek. 40:2) to the idealistic future standpoint of the millennium to see the Temple and the restored nation Israel in the land during the kingdom age (Ezek. 40−48). Why deny Isaiah the possibility of doing the same? Indeed, the essential notion of prophecy−the direct operation of the Spirit of God upon the faculties of man−cannot be circumscribed by time or space or even understood at all apart from the supernatural.

The New Testament witnesses positively to the unity of authorship of the entire book (Matt. 3:3; 8:17; Rom. 9:27-33; 10:16-21). The Dead Sea manuscript of Isaiah indicates no evidence of a "second Isaiah" in the second century B.C. Nor do Jewish or Christian traditions allow room for this theory. The "second Isaiah" is an invention of modern negative criticism.

Jeremiah

AUTHOR

Authorship by Jeremiah is supported by both internal and external evidence. Chapter 36 relates how the prophet dictated his message to his secretary, Baruch. This material, reaching to the fourth year of Jehoiakim, was destroyed by the king (Jer. 36:23). But these prophecies were rewritten with many additions (Jer. 36:32). Then other, later prophecies were added. Chapter 52 was perhaps added by Jeremiah from Second Kings 24:18–25:30, with which it is practically identical.

BACKGROUND

Jeremiah was one of the greatest Hebrew prophets. His birthplace was Anathoth, a town of the tribe of Benjamin located about three miles northeast of Jerusalem. He was a member of a priestly family, his father being Hilkiah (Jer. 1:1). Because of the autobiographical nature of his book, Jeremiah's life and times are better understood than those of any other Hebrew seer. He was called to his career in the thirteenth year of Josiah (626 B.C.). This was five years after the great revival of religion described in Second Kings 23.

Isaiah had prophesied in the heyday of Assyrian power. Jeremiah began his ministry when Assyria was tottering on the brink of ruin. Babylon and Egypt were in a struggle to take over world control. The prophet warned of Babylon's victory and the futility of relying upon Egypt. But when the effects of Josiah's revival wore off, the nation plunged on in unbelief. The prophet was called to warn of impending judgment, particularly during the last two-thirds of his forty-year ministry. The fate of the apostate nation predicted in Deuteronomy 28—30 became inevitable. Judah would be conquered by Babylon. Jeremiah warned that it would be wise to surrender and thus save the city of Jerusalem and many lives in Judah.

This message, coming to men whose desperate nationalism was all they had to cling to, was completely rejected. Jeremiah was looked upon as a meddler and a traitor. He was persecuted by the king and his courtiers, as well as by the people. Jeremiah's immense sorrow at the impenitence of the people gave him the title of "the weeping prophet."

POLITICAL SITUATION DURING JEREMIAH'S MINISTRY	
King	*Political Situation*
Manasseh (696-642 B.C.)	Jeremiah born toward end of reign of this apostate.
Amon (642-640 B.C.)	Wicked son of Manasseh. Murdered.
Josiah (640-608 B.C.)	Godly son of Amon whose 31-year reign temporarily arrested the avalanche of apostasy and ruin. Reforms begun in 627 B.C. and Josiah's great revival instituted in 621 B.C. Scythian invasion, 620 B.C. Rise of Neo-Babylonia and rule of Nabopolassar, 625-605 B.C. Fall of Nineveh, 612 B.C. Fall of Haran, 609 B.C. Josiah killed by Pharaoh-Necho in 608 B.C.
Jehoahaz (608 B.C.)	Deposed by Necho after 3-month reign.
Jehoiakim (608-597 B.C.)	Blatant idolater. Nebuchadnezzar II's rise, 605-562 B.C.
Jehoiachin (597 B.C.)	Exiled by Nebuchadnezzar after 3-month reign.
Zedekiah (597-586 B.C.)	Last king of Judah (Jer. 34—37). Blinded and carried to Babylon, where he died.
Gedaliah (Governor after 586 B.C.)	Jeremiah treated kindly by captors, allowed to remain in Judah. Gedaliah made puppet governor. When Gedaliah was assassinated, the Jews fled to Egypt, compelling Jeremiah to accompany them. There he died an old man.

OUTLINE

A. Introduction: God Commissions the Prophet (chapter 1)
B. God Deals with Judah and Jerusalem (chapters 2—45)
  1. During Josiah and Jehoiakim (chapters 2—20)
    (a) Sermon 1—The Ingratitude of the Nation (2:1—3:5)
    (b) Sermon 2—The Judgment from the North (3:6—6:30)
    (c) Sermon 3—The Warning of Exile (chapters 7—10)

    (d) Sermon 4—The Breaking of the Covenant (chapters 11—13)

    (e) Sermon 5—The Meaning of the Drought, the Sign of the Unmarried Prophet, and the Warning about the Sabbath (chapters 14—19)

    (f) Sermon 6—The Sign of the Potter's House (chapters 18—20)

  2. During other periods (chapters 21—39)

    (a) Zedekiah's punishment (chapters 21—29)

    (b) Kingdom predictions (chapters 30—33)

    (c) Zedekiah's disobedience versus Rechabites' obedience (chapters 34, 35)

    (d) Jehoiakim's sacrilege (chapter 36)

    (e) Jeremiah's experiences (chapters 37—39)

  3. After Jerusalem's defeat (chapters 40—45)

    (a) The ministry of Jeremiah to the remnant (chapters 40—42)

    (b) The ministry of Jeremiah in Egypt (chapters 43, 44)

    (c) The message of Jeremiah to Baruch (chapter 45)

C. God Deals with the Nations (chapters 46—51)

  1. Egypt (chapter 46)

  2. Philistia (chapter 47)

  3. Moab (chapter 48)

  4. Ammon (49:1-6)

  5. Edom (49:7-22)

  6. Damascus (49:23-27)

  7. Arabia (49:28-33)

  8. Elam (49:34-39)

  9. Babylon (chapters 50, 51)

D. Postscript (chapter 52)

  1. Defeat and captivity of Judah (52:1-30)

  2. Release and reinstatement of Jehoiachin (52:31-34)

AUTHENTICITY

The Old Testament contains explicit references to the prophecy of Jeremiah. Daniel refers to Jeremiah's prediction of the 70-year captivity (Dan. 9:2: Jer. 25:11-14; 29:10). The prophecy is confirmed by Second Chronicles 36:21 and Ezra 1:1. The Apocrypha and Josephus confirm the book, as does the New Testament. Jeremiah 31:15 is quoted in Matthew 2:17, 18. Jeremiah 7:11 is quoted in Matthew 21:13, Mark 11:17, and Luke 19:46. Jeremiah 31:31-34 is quoted in Hebrews 8:8-12.

| PROPHECIES OF JEREMIAH YET TO BE FULFILLED ||
Designation	Reference and Description
The Regathering of Israel	Future regathering from worldwide dispersion "to dwell in their own land" (23:7, 8; 30:10).
The Great Tribulation	Future time of "Jacob's trouble," worldwide in scope but centering upon the Jew regathered to Palestine (30:5–8).
The Conversion of Israel	The nation will be "saved" at the second advent by faith in "the Lord our Righteousness" (23:6; 30:10).
The New Covenant with Israel	Benefits of Christ's redemption (Matt. 26:27, 28) as applied to believing Israel at the second advent. It will assure regeneration, forgiveness of sins, and inner heart experience of salvation (31:31-34).
Christ's Kingdom Reign	The "Righteous Branch," the "King," will execute "justice in the earth" (23:5). He is "the Branch of righteousness to grow up unto David" (33:15).

ARCHEOLOGY

The Lachish Letters discovered in 1935 and 1938 at Lachish (Tell ed-Duweir) illustrate Jeremiah's age at the time of Nebuchadnezzar's invasion of Judah in 588-586 B.C. Jehoiachin's exile in Babylon (2 Kings 25:27-30) is confirmed by Babylonian records. "Yaukin of the land of Yahud" ("Jehoiachin of Judah") is listed as one of the recipients of royal rations in Babylon. This text was published in 1940. Jeremiah thrice calls Jehoiachin "Coniah" (Jer. 22:24, 28; 37:1).

TRUE SPIRITUAL RELIGION

God's prophet unfolds the depths of human sin and predicts the interposition of divine grace. He foresees that someday a new and better covenant would replace the old Mosaic one. In that day God's law will be written on men's hearts, bringing them inner spiritual reality (Jer. 31:31-34). God will then bestow "a heart to know him" (Jer. 24:7) upon his renewed people. Jeremiah's confessions (Jer. 10:23, 24; 20:7-18) display the prophet's penetrating comprehension of both his own heart and the hearts of the people around him. His preaching and weeping (Jer. 9:1; 13:17; Lam. 1:16) demonstrate his emphasis on the inner spiritual character of true religion.

Lamentations

TITLE AND ORDER IN THE BIBLE

The full title of this book is *The Lamentations of Jeremiah*. It follows the book of Jeremiah in the English order as the result of the arrangement adopted in the Septuagint and Latin Vulgate. The Hebrew Bible, however, places the work among the five scrolls in the third part of the Canon among the Writings, where it is entitled *ᶜekah* ("How!"), from the initial word of the book. The Septuagint renamed the book *Threnoi* ("Elegies"), followed by both the Latin (*Threni*, "Lamentations") and by the English translations.

AUTHOR

That the book is the work of Jeremiah has been the universal belief of both Jews and Christians from earliest times. The Septuagint, the earliest extant translation of the Old Testament, specifically ascribes the book to Jeremiah in a note prefixed to the first chapter. "And it came to pass after Israel was taken captive and Jerusalem made desolate, Jeremiah sat weeping, and lamented with this lamentation over Jerusalem, and said. . . ." That the book could not have been written long after the fall of the city is clear from the vivid eyewitness account of the horrors of the siege. Critics who deny Jeremiah's authorship can present no satisfactory alternative.

NEW TESTAMENT ALLUSION

The Apostle Paul refers to Lamentations 3:45: "Thou hast made us as the offscouring and refuse in the midst of the people." He applies the passage to the despised condition of himself and his fellow apostles in First Corinthians 4:13: "We are made as the filth of the world, and are the offscouring of all things unto this day."

CONTENT AND FORM OF LAMENTATIONS		
Division	*Poetical Form*	*Subject*
First Dirge (Chapter 1)	Acrostic; each verse begins with next succeeding letter of Hebrew alphabet and has three parts (22 verses total).	Desolation and grief of the city.
Second Dirge (Chapter 2)	Acrostic with same form as first dirge (22 verses).	Jerusalem's destruction the result of sin.
Third Dirge (Chapter 3)	Acrostic; stanzas begin with successive letters of Hebrew alphabet, each stanza having 3 verses (66 verses total).	God's chastening but merciful hand traced in the people's sufferings.
Fourth Dirge (Chapter 4)	Same general form as dirges 1 and 2 (22 verses).	Horrors of the siege and fall of the city.
Fifth Dirge (Chapter 5)	Not an acrostic but contains 22 verses.	Prayer for deliverance.

Ezekiel

BACKGROUND

Ezekiel was *the* prophet of the Exile, as Jeremiah was *the* prophet of the closing years of the Kingdom of Judah. Ezekiel had the tastes and interests of the priest that he was, condemning ritual offenses side

by side with moral offenses (Ezek. 22:8-12). The climax of his prophecy is reached in the prediction of the reinstated Temple worship in the
restored nation during the kingdom age (Ezek. 40 – 48). He was the
champion of established religion. It was his conviction that the best
way to promote true worship was to conserve and purify the Temple
ritual. His name means "God strengthens."

Ezekiel was carried to Babylon in 597 B.C. with King Jehoiachin.
He began his ministry in Jehoiachin's fifth year of exile (Ezek. 1:1, 2)
in 593 B.C., continuing until at least April, 571 B.C. (Ezek. 29:17), the
year of his last dated prophecy. The prophet lived in the town of Tel-
Abib on the Chebar, a canal connecting the Tigris and Euphrates Rivers and running through the city of Nippur.

IMPORTANCE

While Jeremiah was warning the Jews in Palestine of the imminent fall of Jerusalem, Ezekiel was forecasting the same fate to the exiles in Babylonia (Ezek. 1 – 24). However, Ezekiel had a dominant note
of comfort to the discouraged captives. He showed them that the Lord
was justified in sending his people into captivity (Ezek. 8:1 – 33:20).
The complaint of the disconsolate exiles was that "the way of the
Lord is not equal (right or just)" (Ezek. 18:25, 29; 33:17, 20).

Ezekiel's response from the Lord was, "Hear now, O house of Israel, is not my way equal? are not your ways unequal?" (Ezek. 18:25).
The prophet showed that instead of blotting his people out, as God
had done with other nations who had committed similar abominations, his dealings with his own people were preventive and corrective.
His object was to teach them to "know that he was God." The surrounding nations, who were jubilant over Israel's fall, would also be
judged (Ezek. 25:1 – 32:32). Israel, on the other hand, would finally be
restored to the land with all foes conquered and the Temple worship
restored under messianic and kingdom blessing (Ezek. 33:1 – 48:35).

OUTLINE

A. Introduction – Call of Ezekiel (chapters 1 – 3)
B. Condemnation of Judah and Jerusalem (chapters 4 – 24)
  1. Signs, symbols, and prophecies (chapters 4 – 7)
  2. Visions of sin and punishment (chapters 8 – 11)
  3. Inevitability of punishment (chapters 12 – 19)
  4. Final warning (chapters 20 – 24)

C. Judgment of Surrounding Nations (chapters 25 – 32)
1. Ammon (25:1-7)
2. Moab (25:8-11)
3. Edom (25:12-14)
4. Philistia (25:15-17)
5. Tyre (26:1 – 28:19)
6. Sidon (28:20-26)
7. Egypt (chapters 29 – 32)
D. Restoration of Israel (chapters 33 – 48)
1. The preparation for restoration (chapters 33 – 39)
(a) The warning of the wicked (chapter 33)
(b) The promise of the true Shepherd (chapters 34, 35)
(c) The repossession of the land (chapters 36, 37)
(d) The judgment of the aggressors (38:1 – 39:24)
(e) The vision of restoration (39:25-29)
2. The glory of restoration (chapters 40 – 48)
(a) The restored Temple (chapters 40 – 43)
(b) The restored worship (chapters 44 – 46)
(c) The restored land (chapters 47, 48)

THE REALITY OF ISRAEL'S RESTORATION

Many liberal critics deny that chapters 34 through 48 are authentic to Ezekiel and therefore give little authority or credence to their prophetic teachings. Some conservative scholars defend the authenticity of these chapters but deny their literal application to Israel. That the actual nation of Israel is the subject of these chapters and that these prophecies are yet to be fulfilled literally is necessitated by several important considerations.

The details of these prophecies go far beyond any previous fulfillment.

For example, Ezekiel 34:23-30 predicts a restoration in which Israel shall "no more be a prey to the nations." Neither the remnant which returned from Babylon nor their descendants could have fulfilled this prophecy, for they were under continuous Gentile yoke until A.D. 70, when they were driven out from the land entirely. Nor can Ezekiel's description of the Temple be made to fit Solomon's, Zerubbabel's, or Herod's edifices.

Ezekiel's prophecies were not uttered in a vacuum, but dovetail with the covenants and promises made to the nation and with the great kingdom predictions of all the Old Testament prophets.

EZEKIEL'S PROPHECIES OF ISRAEL'S RESTORATION	
Prophecy	*Description*
The Judgment of the Nations (34:1 – 19)	The Lord (the Good Shepherd) will gather the flock and judge between the sheep (the saved Israelite remnant) and the rams and goats (the nations who have abused Israel).
Israel under Messiah, the True Shepherd (34:20-31)	Fulfilled not in Zerubbabel at restoration from Babylon, nor in David raised from the dead at the second advent, but in Messiah, David's name used typically (Jer. 23:5, 6; Hos. 3:5; Isa. 9:6, 7; 55:3, 4).
Israel Restored to the Land (chapter 36)	Assurance of restoration by sovereign "I will" (18 times). Land to be restored and cleansed because Israel is to be regathered and regenerated (chaps. 22 – 29).
Israel Reinstated to Spiritual Blessing (chapter 37)	Vision of the dry bones sets forth Israel's national and spiritual restoration in kingdom blessing. The bones represent the exiles; the valley, their dispersion; and the graves, their national death.
The Destruction of Israel's Last Foes (chapters 38, 39)	Last-day Northern Confederacy headed by Russia in "the uttermost parts of the north" (38:6). Attack on Israel yet future (38:7-23). Defeat is by God and is complete.
Restored Israel in the Land (39:25-29)	Remarkable vision of restored Israel in Palestine during the coming kingdom age.
The Restored Temple (chapters 40 – 43)	A literal future sanctuary to be erected in Palestine during the kingdom age. Details of arrangement are given (chap. 41). The purposes are to demonstrate God's holiness (42:1-20), to provide a dwelling place for the divine glory (43:1-7) and a center for the divine government (43:8-17), and to perpetuate the memorial of sacrifice (43:18-27).
Worship in the Kingdom (chapters 44 – 46)	Ezekiel sees the temporal aspect of the kingdom rather than the eternal, sinless aspect into which it finally emerges (1 Cor. 15:24-28). Hence "the prince" is a mortal man.
Palestine in the Kingdom (chapters 47, 48)	A literal river results from topographical changes. The boundaries and tribal apportionment of the land are given. Jerusalem's status in the kingdom age is described (not its eternal status, as seen by John in Revelation 21:10-27).

See "Time-Periods of the Bible" under "Bible Survey" for the covenants and promises made to Israel (Rom. 9:4, 5). Ezekiel's theme of Israel's restoration is a dominant theme of virtually all the prophets. *If these prophecies are denied literal fulfillment in the nation Israel, there is no other interpretation of them that squares with the facts.* A consistent literal hermeneutic applied to the rest of the Bible must be abandoned in the case of prophecy for an arbitrary, mystical interpretation. Such an interpretation attempts to "explain away" the details but does not actually explain them at all.

History is beginning to authenticate the prophecy of Israel's restoration. The incipient return of the Jews to Palestine, the establishment of the state of Israel, and the role of the Israelis in the world today evidence the eventual setting of the stage for the events predicted by Ezekiel.

IS EZEKIEL'S TEMPLE TO BE CONSTRUED AS A LITERAL EDIFICE TO BE ERECTED IN THE KINGDOM AGE?

The answer to this question must be affirmative. The Temple vision is part and parcel of the reality of Israel's restoration. If the restoration is to be taken literally, the Temple must also be construed in the same way. Non-literal views are inadequate in this regard. They clash with details of the prophecy and violate the context of the entire last third of the book of Ezekiel.

PROBLEMS CONNECTED WITH A LITERAL TEMPLE

These difficulties are significant, but can be adequately resolved. Objections based upon them do not constitute valid grounds for rejecting a literal, futuristic interpretation of Ezekiel's Temple and ritual. The chief charge is that *such a literal Temple, entailing a restoration of Judaistic ritual and animal sacrifice, is at variance with New Testament teaching, particularly the Epistle to the Hebrews.* But this objection fails to reckon with the biblical distinction between the elect nation of Israel and the Christian Church, as well as the time period and divine dealing peculiar to each. The Epistle to the Hebrews and the other New Testament epistles govern the Church in the era between Christ's rejection by Israel at his first advent and his acceptance by Israel at the second advent. When Israel as a nation is saved and brought back into God's favor, the priesthood and kingship will be reinstated. Without doing violence to the Epistle to the Hebrews, the civil and ceremonial Law of Moses will then unfold its spiritual depth and meaning in the worship and constitution of the thousand-year reign under the promises of the Palestinian and New Covenants.

The sacrifices will of course no longer be prospective, as before Christ's finished redemption, but *purely retrospective and commemorative,* like the Lord's Supper in the Church age. Like other Old Testament prophets, Ezekiel envisions a spiritually restored Judaism in the coming kingdom age, with the Sabbath day as its unique sign. Israel will be blessed directly by God, while the kingdom nations will be blessed mediately and indirectly—a situation quite different from that of present-day Christianity.

Another objection against the literal and futuristic interpretation of Ezekiel's Temple and ritual is that it supposedly requires geographical impossibilities and untenable supernatural features. For example, the objection is made that the marvelous river issuing from the Temple could not be an earthly river, but must be interpreted figuratively. From this incorrect premise it is concluded that neither the Temple, the ritual, nor the division of the land can be regarded as literal.

That the river is a literal stream and that the mount of the Temple will be exalted on a high eminence as the result of an earthquake and vast physical changes in the topography of Palestine is foretold by others beside Ezekiel. Zechariah in particular emphasizes this point (Zech. 14:4, 5). God can and will do all that is necessary to make Palestine a suitable scene and focal point for all the glorious events of the kingdom age.

Daniel

TITLE

The historical-prophetical book of Daniel takes its name from its principal character and author. Daniel ("God's judge") was carried away with other promising youths as a hostage by Nebuchadnezzar II (604-562 B.C.). Early in the period of exile he became renowned for godliness and wisdom (Ezek. 14:14, 20).

AUTHOR

Because of its remarkable events and prophecies, the book of Daniel is a battleground between faith and unbelief. The author, date, historicity, and authenticity of the book are frequently disputed by liberal critics. In fact, modern criticism views the establishment of a Maccabean date (about 167 B.C.) as one of its assured achievements. These allegations, however, are based upon fallacious reasoning.

The chief charge is that the author of Daniel makes erroneous statements about historical information belonging to the sixth century B.C. When these alleged inaccuracies are analyzed, however, they usually turn out to be erroneous assumptions based upon arguments from silence or upon faulty presuppositions. When the problems are faced objectively, apart from critical bias, the book stands unimpugned by any testimony that can be produced from any reliable source of information. This does not mean that every difficulty has already been cleared up. Some persist because of lack of pertinent historical or archeological information. Thus in certain details the book can as yet be neither vindicated nor impugned. Meanwhile, faith must take the work at its face value, granting it the authenticity and historical reliability it deserves in the absence of objective proof to the contrary.

It must be said, however, that in numerous instances historical and archeological research has cleared up difficulties that were once employed to deride Daniel's authenticity. The most notable case is that of Belshazzar, whose existence was once denied and his designation as "king" and "son of Nebuchadnezzar" (Dan. 5:1, 2, 11, 18, 22) scoffed at. Archeology has not only attested Belshazzar's existence but has clarified his kingship (it was entrusted to him by his father Nabonidus) and confirmed his relationship to Nebuchadnezzar as a royal "son." (Semitic idiom sometimes uses the word "son" to designate a successor rather than a son by immediate birth.)

It is also sometimes alleged that the literary features of Daniel prove that it was written long after the sixth century B.C. Critics list some fifteen or more Persian words in the book. But certainly it is not far-fetched to expect Daniel to have displayed Persian influence in his book if he wrote it after the Persian conquest of Babylon, particularly

A statue marks the area of Daniel's encounter with caged lions in Babylon. (© *MPS*)

in designating offices, institutions, and the like. Nor does the presence of a few Greek words in chapter 3 prove a late date. Mounting evidence indicates that Greek culture penetrated into the Near East at a much earlier date than had previously been supposed.

The fact that the book is written in two languages (Dan. 2:4 – 7: 28 in Aramaic and the remainder in Hebrew) has also been used as an argument for a late date. The simple explanation for the two languages is that Daniel intentionally employed the two tongues. Since Daniel was the primary prophet of "the times of the Gentiles" (Luke

GREAT PROPHECIES OF THE BOOK OF DANIEL

The Vision	The Meaning
The Colossus Vision (2:31-45)	The colossus itself symbolizes the times of the Gentiles from Nebuchadnezzar (605 B.C.) to the second advent of Christ. The Smiting Stone (2:34, 35), who will destroy the Gentile world system, is Christ. The four metals are four empires — Babylon (head of gold), Medo-Persia (chest and arms of silver), the Roman Empire (legs of iron), and the Roman Empire revived at the end time (feet of iron and clay). Rome is envisioned panoramically, first as it would exist in ancient imperial glory and then as divided in East and West Empires (A.D. 364), as symbolized by the two legs. These two divisions will enjoy a last-day revival, a 10-kingdom European United States composed of dictatorships (iron) and democracies (tile). Then the Smiting Stone will strike and become a mountain (the kingdom restored to Israel — Isa. 2:2; Acts 1:6) which fills the earth. After this temporal kingdom runs its course it will merge into the eternal kingdom (1 Cor. 15:24-28; Rev. 20:4, 5).
The Vision of the Four Beasts (7:1-8)	These trace the same four world empires as the colossus of 2:31-45. The colossus, however, presents the *outward* power and splendor of "the times of the Gentiles" while the four beasts depict the *inner* rapacious and warlike character of the Gentile world governments of the period — Babylon (lion), Medo-Persia (bear), Greece (leopard), and Rome (nondescript iron beast). The ten horns (kings) correspond to the ten toes of 2:40-44. The "little horn" is the last-day Antichrist, the final terrible ruler of the times of the Gentiles. He will be destroyed by Messiah at his advent and kingdom.
The Vision of Messiah's Second Advent (7:9-28)	The "Ancient of Days" is God. "One like the Son of Man" is Christ invested with the kingdom and returning in glory (Rev. 19:16). Messiah's investiture with the kingdom takes place in heaven (7:13, 14) but occurs before his coming (7:9-12). Destruction of the "little horn" is fulfilled at the second advent. "The saints of the Most High," who "possess the kingdom" (7:18, 22, 25, 27), are the saved Jewish remnant. The kingdom will be eternal (7:18), the mediatorial and temporal aspects of it (the thousand years — Rev. 20:4-7) merging into the eternal state when Christ delivers the kingdom to God the Father (1 Cor. 15:24-28). The fourth beast with the ten-kingdom confederation is last-day revived Rome.
The Vision of the Ram, the He-Goat, and the little Horn (8:1-27)	The ram with the two horns (Media and Persia) is the Medo-Persian Empire (539-531 B.C.). The "he-goat" is Macedonian Greece seen in the rapid conquests of Alexander the Great, the "conspicuous horn" of the goat (8:1-7). Four horns (8:8) represent the division of Alexander's empire among his four generals. Out of one division, Syria, came Antiochus Epiphanes (175-163 B.C.), the "little horn" (8:9-14), a foreshadowing of the Antichrist (8:24, 25) and the great tribulation, "the time of the end" (8:17), "the last end of the indignation" (8:19).

The Vision	The Meaning
The Vision of the Seventy Weeks (9:24-27)	The seventy weeks (heptads of 7 years each) equal 490 years. These are divided into a) *7 weeks* (49 years) beginning with the decree of Artaxerxes I to rebuild Jerusalem's walls (Mar.-Apr., 445 B.C.); b) *62 weeks* (434 years), at the end of which "Messiah-Prince" was to be cut off in death and have nothing (no kingdom which was rightly his as king); c) *An unreckoned period* during which the Romans, "the people of the prince that shall come," would destroy the city and the sanctuary" (A.D. 70); since then the Jews have been scattered; d) *A final week* of 7 years as the climax of Jewish history. During the first half of the week the "prince" or "little horn" of 7:8 makes a covenant with the Jews in Palestine, who have by then resumed Temple worship. In the middle of the week the covenant is broken, the Temple worship ceases, and the great tribulation breaks. Christ's second advent consummates this period of desolation, bringing everlasting righteousness to Israel and judgment upon the "desolator," the prince and his armies (Rev. 19:20).
The Vision of the Wars of the Ptolemies and Seleucids (11:1-35)	History has verified the precise fulfillment of these prophecies by the Persian kings (11:12), Alexander the Great (11:3, 4), the Ptolemies of Egypt ("kings of the south"), and the Seleucids ("kings of the north") (11:6-35). The Romans (11:30), Antiochus Epiphanes (prefiguring the Antichrist of the last day), and the Maccabees also had their part in the fulfillment of these prophecies.
The Vision of the End-Time: The Man of Sin (11:36-40a) and The King of the North (Russia) (11:40b-45)	The "wilful king" is the Antichrist, the "man of sin" of 2 Thess. 2:3, 4 and Rev. 13:1-10. The King of the North is Russia, and vv. 40b-45 are parallel to Ezek. 38 and 39, and describe the Russian invasion of Palestine at the end-time.
The Great Tribulation and Israel's Deliverance (12:1)	This terrible period of Jacob's trouble is also mentioned in Jer. 30:5-7 and described in Rev. 12-18. It takes place in the last half of Daniel's 70th week (Dan. 9:27) and is climaxed by Christ's second advent. "Thy people" are Daniel's people, the Jews, who are to be delivered from physical death and regenerated to enjoy kingdom blessing.
The Resurrection of Israel (12:2, 3)	Physical resurrection of the saved Israel into kingdom blessing in fulfillment of Matt. 8:11 and 19:28 and other Old Testament predictions.
The Final Consummation (12:4-13)	The period between Daniel's time and the second advent, especially the latter years (12:4, 9). But the prophecy was to be "sealed up" (not understood) until the end time (12:4). Verses 11 and 12 describe the time of the erection of the image of the Antichrist (9:27) and the duration of great wrath.

21:24), the Spirit of God directed him to use the language then spoken by non-Jews to pen those great prophetic portions that deal primarily with the history of Gentiles.

BACKGROUND

As mentioned previously, Daniel is the prophet of "the times of the Gentiles" (Luke 21:24). This period extends from the captivity of Judah under Nebuchadnezzar to the second advent of Christ and the establishment of the messianic earthly kingdom. During this long era the nations have predominated, and Israel has been an outright vassal of Gentile world powers or has been scattered among them, or has at best been mercilessly exposed to their hatred. The scope of Daniel's descriptions of this long interval makes his visions an indispensable introduction to the study of New Testament prophecy. Daniel's dominant themes are the great tribulation, the revelation of the Antichrist, the second advent of Christ, the resurrections, and the establishment of the millennial kingdom. These are also great New Testament prophetic disclosures. Daniel's prophecies particularly link up with our Lord's Olivet discourse (Matt. 24:15) and the book of the Revelation.

IMPORTANCE

The book of Daniel is *the key to all biblical prophecy.* Our Lord's Olivet Discourse (Matt. 24, 25; Mark 13; Luke 21), as well as the prophecies in Second Thessalonians 2 and the entire book of the Revelation can be understood only through a correct comprehension of Daniel's predictions. The prophetic sweep and import of the book is doubtless a prime reason for the relentless critical attack leveled against it. Conservative scholars, who recognize the strategic place which the prophecy holds in unfolding the divine plan of the ages, realize that it is necessary both to defend the authenticity of the book against negative criticism and to master the prophetic sweep of its predictions.

OUTLINE

A. Early History and Visions (chapters 1 – 6)
  1. Daniel's stand for God (chapter 1)
  2. Nebuchadnezzar's vision of the image (chapter 2)
  3. Daniel's three friends' deliverance from the furnace (chapter 3)
  4. Nebuchadnezzar's vision of the tree (chapter 4)
  5. Belshazzar's feast (chapter 5)

6. Daniel's deliverance from the lions (chapter 6)
B. Later History and Visions (chapters 7 – 12)
   1. The vision of the four beasts (chapter 7)
   2. The vision of the ram and goat (chapter 8)
   3. The vision of the seventy weeks (chapter 9)
   4. The vision of the glory of God (chapter 10)
   5. The vision of the end times (chapters 11, 12)

SPIRITUAL EMPHASES OF THE MINOR PROPHETS		
Prophet	*Period*	*Spiritual Emphasis*
Hosea	755-715 B.C.	God unfailingly loves Israel
Joel	835-796 B.C.	Israel will enjoy latter-day revival
Amos	765-750 B.C.	God's justice must judge sin
Obadiah	850-840 B.C.	Merciless pride must be judged
Jonah	780-750 B.C.	God's grace embraces the world
Micah	740-690 B.C.	Bethlehem-born Messiah will be deliverer
Nahum	630-612 B.C.	Nineveh's sin is to be judged
Habakkuk	615 B.C.	Justification is by faith
Zephaniah	625-610 B.C.	The day of the Lord precedes the kingdom
Haggai	520 B.C.	The Lord deserves top priority
Zechariah	520-515 B.C.	The Lord remembers Israel
(Chaps.		
9 – 14)	after 500 B.C.	The second advent of Christ
Malachi	430-400 B.C.	The wicked will be judged

Hosea

BACKGROUND

Hosea ("salvation") has been styled "the Jeremiah of the Northern Kingdom." Like Jeremiah, he was called to weep and suffer for a decadent nation that was ripening for ruin. His ministry began in the closing years of Jeroboam II's prosperous and morally declining reign and extended on beyond the fall of Samaria (722 B.C.) into the reign of Hezekiah of Judah (Hos. 1:10). Hosea was thus a contemporary of Amos, Isaiah, and Micah.

IMPORTANCE

Hosea is the herald of God's unchanging love for Israel. During his ministry the nation had sunk to the lowest depths of idolatrous immorality. Despite the fact that the people gave every evidence that *they did not love the Lord,* Hosea labored with suffering and tears to show the people that *God still loved them.* Throughout the fourfold theme—the nation's idolatry, wickedness, captivity, and final restoration—God's enduring love for his people is interwoven with a tender strain of sadness.

Israel is portrayed as the Lord's adulterous wife. That Hosea might know the poignancy of God's unrequited love for his own, and that he might be a sign to the unfaithful nation, he was instructed to marry a woman who would prove unfaithful. The children of this marriage were given names symbolic of Hosea's principal predictions. The son's name, Jezreel ("the Lord sows or scatters"), points to judgment on the Jehu dynasty (1 Kings 19:15-17; 2 Kings 10:1-14) as well as to Israel's future restoration (Hos. 2:21-23). Lo-ruhamah ("unpitied"), a girl, would be a living reminder that Israel would no longer be pitied because of her harlotry. Lo-ammi ("not my people"), another boy, would be a living reminder of *why* the Lord would no longer pity—he was temporarily setting aside Israel as his elect people.

OUTLINE

A. Hosea's Home Life Portrays God's Relation to Israel (chapters 1—3)
   1. The children portray the Lord's impending punishment (chapter 1)
   2. The wife portrays the nation's shocking infidelity (chapter 2)
   3. The husband portrays the Lord's undying love (chapter 3)
B. Hosea's Homeland Portrays God's Judgment and Mercy (chapters 4—14)
   1. The guilt of the sinful kingdom (chapters 4—8)
   2. The punishment of the sinful kingdom (chapters 9—13)
   3. The restoration of the repentant people (chapter 14)

THE MORAL PROBLEM OF HOSEA

Did the Lord command Hosea to marry a harlot, or did she become a harlot after his marriage? Or is the incident only an allegory? For centuries commentators have struggled with the difficulty involved. To construe the incident as an allegory is a patent makeshift that dodges rather than deals with the problem. To insist that God commanded Hosea to marry a woman who was already a harlot would be to attribute an unworthy act to an infinitely holy God. To Hosea, too, would be ascribed an act unworthy of a prophet of God.

The best solution to the problem is the interpretation that Gomer became a woman of loose morals sometime after her marriage to Hosea, her future infidelity being foreknown to God. If Hosea delivered his message in later years, he may well have looked back upon his own domestic tragedy as a divinely permitted picture of the sin of God's chosen people. Hence the Lord's initial leading to marry Gomer would have been tantamount to a command.

PROPHECY OF ISRAEL'S FUTURE IN HOSEA

ISRAEL'S PRESENT-DAY CONDITION (HOS. 3:4). Israel is seen deprived of her ceremonial and civil institutions during a period of divine disciplinary actions. The ephod speaks of priesthood, the teraphim of insight into the future, and the king of millennial blessing. All of these the Lord withdrew from Israel, as well as his own personal presence (Hos. 5:15 – 6:3). Her interim affliction will continue until Messiah returns at his second advent (Hos. 5:15). The "two days" (representing a long period of chastisement) will end in "the third day" (Hos. 6:2, 3), the period of regeneration and millennial blessing (Joel 2:28, 29).

THE FUTURE BELIEVING REMNANT (HOS. 6:1-3). The heart-cry of the repentant Israelites of the last days is recorded in Hosea 6:1-3. See also Isaiah 1:9 and Romans 11:5.

THE FUTURE RESURRECTION OF ISRAEL (HOS. 13:14). This is a promise of physical resurrection (1 Cor. 15:55) of saved Israelites preceding the kingdom (Dan. 12:2). This is a sure event (Hos. 13:14).

THE FUTURE RESTORATION OF ISRAEL (HOS. 1:10, 11; ROM. 9:23-26). Lo-ammi ("not my people") prefigures Israel temporarily set aside (Rom. 11:1-5). Ultimately she will be restored and called Ammi ("my people"). Then she will own the Lord as Ishi ("my husband") (Hos. 2:14-23). The full kingdom restoration is predicted in Hosea 14:1-9. Israel as the "lily" and the "olive tree" (Rom. 11:16-24) will flourish in the beauty of holiness.

NEW TESTAMENT QUOTATION

Our Lord quotes Hosea 6:6, "I will have mercy and not sacrifice" (Matt. 9:13), and alludes to the striking metaphor "They shall say to the mountains, Cover us, and to the hills, Fall on us" (Hos. 10:8) in Luke 23:30, as does also John (Rev. 6:16; 9:6). Hosea 11:1 is quoted in Matthew 2:15 and Hosea 2:23 is quoted in Romans 9:25

Joel

AUTHOR

Joel ("The Lord is God") is distinguished from others of the same name only by the name of his father. The precise time of his prophetic career is unknown, for no king or foreign nation that might aid in dating is mentioned in the book. Conservative scholars tend to date Joel either early, during the reign of Joash (835-796 B.C.), or somewhat later, during the reign of Uzziah, Jotham, Ahaz, or Hezekiah.

IMPORTANCE

Joel is the prophet of the day of the Lord, the end-time apocalyptic period preceding the establishment of the kingdom over Israel. During this era the Lord will manifest his power in crushing his (and Israel's) enemies in order to deliver his covenant people for millennial blessing promised them throughout the Old Testament. The locust plague (Joel 1:1-20) is a symbol of this future apocalyptic period (Isa. 2:12-22; 4:1-6; Ezek. 30:3; Rev. 6:1 – 19:21).

OUTLINE

A. Symbols of the Day of the Lord (chapter 1)
  1. Plague and drought (1:1-14)
  2. Starvation and fire (1:15-20)
B. Events of the Day of the Lord (chapters 2, 3)
  1. The army from the north (2:1-10)
  2. The army of the Lord (2:11)
  3. The remnant's repentance (2:12-17)
  4. The remnant's acceptance (2:18-27)
  5. The remnant's blessing (2:28-32)
  6. The restoration of Israel (3:1)
  7. The judgment of the nations (3:2-16)
  8. The establishment of the kingdom (3:17-21)

JOEL'S PROPHECY OF THE DAY OF THE LORD

THE LAST-DAY INVASION OF PALESTINE (JOEL 2:1-10). The terrible destructiveness of the invading host from the North is described. "My holy mountain" (Joel 2:1; see also Psa. 2:6) is Moriah, the Temple hill. The invasion is preparatory to Armageddon (Rev. 16: 13-16).

THE SECOND ADVENT OF CHRIST (JOEL 2:11). The divine intervention of Christ is signaled by the appearance of the Lord's army (Rev. 19:11-16) in the climactic phase of the titanic struggle at Armageddon.

THE OUTCALLING OF THE ISRAELITE REMNANT (JOEL 2:12-27). The Lord calls upon the remnant in Palestine to repent and receive his deliverance (Joel 2:12-14). He promises his fiery jealousy for them instead of his decimating wrath against them, as well as prosperity, military deliverance, joy, and kingdom blessing.

211

THE OUTPOURED SPIRIT (JOEL 2:28-32). This spiritual revival will inaugurate the kingdom age. Peter used this prophecy at Pentecost (Acts 2:16-21) to illustrate that the effusion taking place then was merely a sample of what the Jews could expect when the kingdom was introduced at the second advent. The kingdom outpouring is to be universal (Joel 2:28, 29) and is the climactic phase of the day of the Lord. It will be preceded by signs portending the doom of the wicked enemies of Israel.

ISRAEL'S END-TIME RESTORATION (JOEL 3:1). This great event of the day of the Lord (Isa. 11:10-12; Jer. 23:5-8; Ezek. 37:1-28) is preceded by the judgment of the nations that persecuted Israel.

THE JUDGMENT OF THE NATIONS (JOEL 3:2-16). The basis of this judgment will be the treatment of Israel, illustrated historically by the Phoenicians and Philistines, among others. This judgment connects with Armageddon (Isa. 29:1-8; Jer. 25:13-17; Zech. 1:14, 15; Matt. 25:31-46).

FULL KINGDOM BLESSING (JOEL 3:17-21). Israel finally accepts her Messiah, her rightful King. This is a common prophetic theme, toward which all Old Testament prophets gravitate (Zech. 14:20, 21).

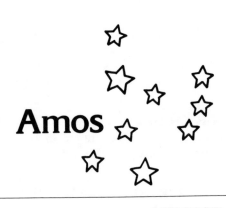

Amos

AUTHOR

Practically all critics concede the substantial integrity of the book. Only a few passages are seriously disputed: the notable messianic passage (Amos 9:11-15), three doxologies (Amos 4:13; 5:8; 9:5, 6), and Amos 1:9-12 and 2:4, 5. These verses are viewed as later glosses on unwarranted theories of Israel's religious development. Objectively considered, however, no proof exists for assigning any part of the prophecy to any author beside Amos.

BACKGROUND

Amos was a fiery and fearless prophet who warned of impending judgment upon a rapidly apostatizing nation. His ministry was conducted in the latter part of the reign of Jeroboam II (782-753 B.C.). This was a period of economic prosperity and luxurious living, with rampant immorality and idolatry. Amos was a simple herdsman and fruit picker (Amos 7:14) from Tekoa, a hill-country hamlet some ten miles south of Jerusalem.

Although Amos was called to be a prophet to the whole house of Jacob (Amos 3:1, 13), his recorded ministry was directed chiefly to the Northern Kingdom (7:14, 15) at the main sanctuary in Bethel (Amos 7:10). There Amos collided with the easy-going, compromising religion of the day, represented by the high priest, Amaziah. Not to be intimidated by Amaziah's threats or the king's displeasure, the prophet continued to thunder forth his warning of approaching judgment.

OUTLINE

A. Indictment of Gentiles and Jews (chapters 1, 2)
  1. Indictment of six Gentile nations (1:1 − 2:3)
  2. Indictment of Judah and Israel (2:4-16)
B. Judgment of the Twelve Tribes (chapters 3 − 8)
  1. Three messages of condemnation (chapters 3 − 6)
  2. Five visions of punishment (chapters 7, 8)
C. Restoration of All Israel (chapter 9)
  1. A rebuilt Tabernacle (9:11, 12)
  2. A revitalized land (9:13)
  3. A reinstated people (9:14, 15)

AMOS'S PROPHECY OF THE FINAL RESTORATION OF ISRAEL (9:11-15)

Amos's theme of impending judgment upon sin thunders in unabated fury throughout the book. Only at the end does judgment melt

Tuthmosis III ruled the entire Near East as well as Joseph's descendants in Egypt. (© *MPS*)

into mercy, like a calm sunset after a tempest. Then Amos's great prediction of future blessing describes 1) the restoration of the Davidic dynasty (Amos 9:11); 2) the conversion of the nations (Amos 9:12); 3) the revival of the land of Palestine (Amos 9:13); 4) Israel's return from worldwide captivity (Amos 9:14); 5) the rebuilding of desolated cities (Amos 9:14); and 6) Israel's permanent settlement in the land (Amos 9:15).

James quoted this great prophecy at the first council of the Christian Church (Acts 15:15-17). On that momentous occasion the Holy Spirit employed it to unfold the divine program for the future *after* the present age of the outcalling of the Church. Then the Lord will return, as Amos foresaw, to reestablish the Davidic dynasty in Christ (Amos 9:11, 12). Millennial prosperity (Amos 9:13) will characterize restored Israel (Amos 9:14, 15).

Obadiah

AUTHOR
Obadiah is completely unknown apart from the meaning of his name ("servant of the Lord"). The date is equally unknown, although a period before Jeremiah seems most likely.

BACKGROUND
The book has the form of a dirge of doom. Its single theme is judgment upon Edom, the nation sprung from Esau. In Obadiah's time Sela (later called Petra) was Edom's capital. The ruins of this ancient city were discovered in 1812. Hewn out of rose-colored cliffs, the remains of Edom's power in the arid region south of the Dead Sea stand as a silent witness to the fulfillment of Obadiah's prophecy.

OUTLINE
A. The Destruction of Edom (1:1-14)
   1. Description of the destruction (1:1-9)
   2. Reason for the destruction (1:10-14)
B. The Day of the Lord (1:15-21)
   1. The judgment of Edom and the nations (1:15, 16)
   2. The exaltation of Jacob and all Israel (1:17-20)
   3. The supremacy of Jehovah as King (1:21)

ISRAEL'S FUTURE
The final verse of the prophecy (Obad. 1:21) is clearly messianic.

Brief as his prophecy is, Obadiah envisions the promise of future deliverance for Israel in the kingdom, as do so many of the other prophets. The "saviors" are deliverers on the earth, as in Judges 3:9, 15. They will serve under the Messiah, the King of kings (Rev. 19:16; 20:4).

Like so many of the prophets, Obadiah also had a vision of the day of the Lord, when all nations, including revived Edom (Obad. 1:18; Isa. 11:14), will be judged for their treatment of Israel (Obad. 1:15, 16, 18). Edom's cruelty to Israel (Obad. 1:10-14) foreshadows the cruelty of the nations to Israel in the great tribulation which precedes the kingdom.

Messiah's deliverance of Israel at the second advent, as well as the nation's regeneration (Rom. 11:26), will result in a holy people and a holy kingdom (Obad. 1:21). Only the Holy One of Israel will be able to set up such a kingdom. Unholy man by himself can never establish it.

Jonah

AUTHOR

Under the view that Jonah is predictive and typical *history* rather than mere fiction or allegory, there is no compelling reason to deny that Jonah himself was the narrator. The miracles of the book, the presence of some Aramaic forms, and a few alleged historical problems are commonly cited as evidence of a date much later than the era of Jonah. But none of these arguments is decisive against traditional authorship by Jonah.

Significantly, the period in which Jonah lived witnessed conditions in Nineveh that were favorable for the prophet's ministry there. Under Semiramis, the queen regent, and her son Adad-nirari III (810-

782 B.C.) there was an approach to monotheism under the worship of the god Nebo. It was either in the latter years of this reign or early in the reign of Assurdan III (771-754 B.C.) that Jonah appeared at Nineveh.

BACKGROUND

Jonah, meaning "dove" in Hebrew, was an actual, historical person and not a fictional character, as some higher critics would suggest. He was the son of Amittai (Jonah 1:1). His home was in Gath-hepher of Zebulun, a few miles northeast of Nazareth in Galilee. He occupies a unique place as the first foreign missionary in the Bible. His ministry reflects Israel's God-ordained mission to the nations. His theme is God's love for mankind and the extension of divine mercy to all peoples. Jonah prophesied under Jeroboam II (782-755 B.C.) that Israel would regain its ancient boundaries (2 Kings 14:25).

The historicity of Jonah is further attested by Christ, who compared Jonah's fish experience and his preaching to his own burial and resurrection (Matt. 12:38-42).

IMPORTANCE

Not only was Jonah himself a historical person, but his book is likewise a narration of actual events. It is neither myth, legend, parable, prophetic allegory, nor fiction, as is sometimes alleged. Both Jewish and Christian traditions maintain that the book is a masterpiece of condensed history. None of the events of the story, including the miracle of the great fish, is incredible to enlightened faith.

Although the book is historical, it is more than mere history. If it were only the recital of events, without a higher moral and spiritual meaning, it would have no proper place among the minor prophets. But the book possesses not only this higher moral and spiritual quality, but also the additional motif of predictive or typical history. It is thus of far-reaching prophetic and typical value.

In one aspect of his ministry Jonah reflects Christ as the One who was sent by the Father, suffered entombment, rose from the dead, and carried salvation to the Gentiles (Matt. 12:39-41; Luke 11:29-32). In another aspect of his mission Jonah foreshadows the nation Israel—a serious trouble to the Gentiles outside its own land, yet meanwhile witnessing to them. Cast out by the nations but miraculously preserved in the future tribulation at the end of the age (Dan. 12:1), Israel finally calls upon Jehovah, finding salvation and deliverance (Rom. 11: 25, 26). The Israelites then become missionaries to the Gentiles in the future earthly Davidic Kingdom (Zech. 8:7-23).

OUTLINE

A. Jonah Disobeys His First Commission (chapters 1, 2)
  1. Disobedience (1:1-3)
  2. Chastisement (1:4-7)
  3. Acknowledgement (1:8-12)
  4. Repentance (1:13-17)
  5. Restoration (2:1-10)
B. Jonah Obeys His Second Commission (chapters 3, 4)
  1. Jonah's preaching (3:1-4)
  2. Nineveh's repentance (3:5-9)
  3. Nineveh's preservation (3:10)
  4. Jonah's anger (4:1-4)
  5. God's reproof (4:5-11)

THE MIRACLE OF THE GREAT FISH

The book has frequently been labeled as allegory or fiction in order to avoid the supposed problem of the swallowing and disgorgement of Jonah by a large marine animal. The story of Jonah and the so-called "whale" has elicited much derision and has for many people negated the important message of the book. In defense of the genuineness of the miracle the following observations are made. The animal in question is described by Scripture not as a whale but a "great fish" (Jonah 1:17). The Greek word *ketos,* translated "whale" in the King James Version of Matthew 12:40, means a huge fish or marine animal, possibly the whale shark or rhinodon. This is the largest of all fish, sometimes attaining a length of seventy feet. Such a sea monster was "prepared" ("appointed" or "ordered") by the Lord to swallow Jonah. We know that there are creatures capable of swallowing a fully grown man, for there are authenticated cases of men who, like Jonah, have been swallowed and disgorged alive. The real miracle is not so much the swallowing as the fact that Jonah was alive when he was vomited by the great fish so many hours later.

Although skepticism has magnified this episode out of all proportion with the other marvels recounted in the book (the storm, the gourd, the conversion of the Ninevites), it is not one whit greater than those which honeycomb all of Scripture: the exodus, the manna from heaven, the water from the rock, or the resurrection of Christ. It is significant that Christ specifies Jonah's fish experience as a prefigurement of his own resurrection (see Matt. 12:39-41; Luke 11:29-32).

Micah

AUTHOR

The name *mikah* is apparently abbreviated from *mikayahu*, "Who is like the Lord?" Micah was a native of the village of Moresheth (Mic. 1:1, 14), located about 20 miles southwest of Jerusalem. Micah was a contemporary of Isaiah and ministered under the reigns of Jotham, Ahaz, and Hezekiah (Jer. 26:18).

BACKGROUND

In Micah's day the Assyrian power was a great threat. The prophet foretold the fall of Samaria (Mic. 1:5-7) and the inevitable desolation of Judah (Mic. 1:9-16), against which his warnings were especially directed. Micah's emphasis was upon personal and social righteousness. His twofold theme was judgment and the coming kingdom.

OUTLINE

A. The Coming Judgment (chapters 1, 2)
1. Judgment of Samaria (1:1-8)
2. Judgment of Judah (1:9-16)
3. Judgment of oppressors (2:1-11)
4. Blessing of the remnant (2:12, 13)

B. The Coming Kingdom (chapters 3 – 5)
   1. Preparatory judgments (3:1-12)
   2. Nature of the kingdom (4:1-5)
   3. Establishment of the kingdom (4:6-13)
   4. Rejection of the king (5:1, 2)
   5. Interval between advents (5:3)
   6. Return of the king (5:4-15)
C. The Final Controversy (chapters 6, 7)
   1. The sin of the people (6:1 – 7:6)
   2. The intercession of the prophet (7:7-20)

GREAT PREDICTIONS OF MICAH	
Prediction	*Description*
Christ's First Advent and Rejection	The Smitten Judge (5:1) who was struck upon the cheek as the height of insult (1 Kings 22:24) is the Bethlehem-born yet preexistent and eternal One (5:2) of the Davidic line. Ephrath was an early suburb of Bethlehem (Gen. 35:19), David's home.
Israel's Condition Between the Advents	Israel is.to be set aside because of rejection of the Messiah. "She who travails" is Israel in tribulation, travailing to bring forth a last-day believing remnant (the remnant of Christ's brethren; 5:3; Matthew 25:31-46).
Christ's Second Advent and Acceptance	The rejected one becomes the Shepherd of Israel (5:4) and the peace of Israel (Isa. 9:7) when he dispenses the peace he has purchased for his restored people (Eph. 2:14, 15). He also attains peace by defeating the northern invader of the end-time (5:6).
The Remnant's Blessing	The remnant dwells securely (5:4) as a witness (5:7) and avenger of wrongs (5:8, 9) in the administration of the kingdom at the second advent.
The Establishment of Christ's Kingdom	Jerusalem is to be the capital of the restored Davidic kingdom (4:1-3; Isa. 2:2-4). The kingdom is to be characterized by justice, peace, security, and loyalty to the Lord (4:3-5). Israel is to be gathered into the kingdom (4:6-8). The intervening Babylonian exile typifies the final regathering (4:9, 10).
Christ's Kingdom Rule	Armageddon is the prelude to the kingdom (4:11-13; Rev. 16:13-16). Jerusalem's victory is assured as she threshes the sheaves (the hostile nations gathered against her). Christ's kingdom rule as supreme King and Lord (Rev. 19:16) is denoted by "the Lord of the whole earth." It is his by virtue of both creation and redemption (Zech. 4:14; 6:5; Rev. 4:11).

Nahum

AUTHOR

Nahum's prophecy is a literary classic. Its poetic descriptions of God's majestic holiness and Nineveh's fall constitute some of the finest poetry of the Old Testament. Critics sometimes deny 1:2 − 2:2 to Nahum, viewing it essentially as a post-exilic, acrostic poem later prefixed to Nahum's poem. But such a view is arbitrary, being based on the theory that the poem had been drastically altered. Even if the acrostic arrangement could be proved, there is no valid reason for robbing Nahum of the credit for it.

BACKGROUND

Nahum (*comfort*) gave consolation to Judah by his prophecy of the fall of Nineveh, the capital of the Assyrian Empire. The destruction of the "bloody city" (Nah. 3:1) meant the fall of the "giant among the Semites," whose tyrannical cruelty periodically scourged the ancient world from 850 B.C. until its fall in 612 B.C. Nahum uttered his oracles between the conquest of No-Amon (Thebes) in Egypt (Nah. 3: 8) in 661 B.C. and the fall of Nineveh in 612 B.C. Nineveh's destruction constituted the vindication of God's holiness, for the infinitely holy God of Israel could not allow such a cruel and bloody nation as Assyria to go unpunished for its crimes and atrocities against humanity.

OUTLINE

A. The Majesty of God (1:1 − 2:2)

1. Superscription (1:1)
2. The fury of the Lord (1:2-11)
3. The mercy of the Lord (1:12—2:2)
B. The Fall of the City (2:3—3:19)
   1. Description of destruction (2:3-13)
   2. Explanation of destruction (3:1-19)

Habakkuk

AUTHOR

Little is known of Habakkuk. He lived, it may be inferred, during the rise of the Neo-Babylonian Empire, about 625-605 B.C. The Chaldeans became a serious threat to Judah after the battle of Carchemish in 605 B.C. Thus Habakkuk probably ministered during the reign of Jehoiakim (608-597 B.C.). His work shows that he, like Nahum and Isaiah, was a great poet. (Chapter 3 constitutes a magnificent lyric ode. It describes a theophany and looks forward to the second advent. See Second Thessalonians 1:7-10.)

IMPORTANCE

Habakkuk deals with a question that has troubled many thoughtful people. How can God's patient tolerance of the wicked be reconciled with his holiness? The answer the prophet gives is valid for all times. God is sovereign. He is holy as well as loving, and both of these attributes must be satisfied. He will therefore deal with evil-doers in his own time and way. Meanwhile the Lord's people must keep in mind that proud sinners like the Chaldeans have no faith, in contrast to God's people, who live by faith. "Behold, his soul which is lifted up is not upright in him but the just (righteous) shall live by his faith" (Hab. 2:4).

Habakkuk therefore announces the great spiritual principle that separates fallen mankind into two categories. Those who exercise faith for their salvation are called "the righteous" and are redeemed by God's grace, while those who rely on their own self-sufficiency for their salvation are regarded by God as unrighteous, and do not obtain eternal life. The proud, overweening Chaldeans were used as an example of the unrighteous. Lacking faith in God, they possessed neither spiritual life (fellowship with God) nor eternal life (escape from eternal death in Gehenna — Rev. 20:11-14).

Habakkuk deals with a question that has troubled many thoughtful people. How can God's patient tolerance of the wicked be reconciled with his holiness? The answer the prophet gives is valid for all times. God is sovereign. He is holy as well as loving, and both of these attributes must be satisfied. He will therefore deal with evil-doers in his own time and way. Meanwhile the Lord's people must keep in mind that proud sinners like the Chaldeans have no faith, in contrast to God's people, who live by faith. "Behold, his soul which is lifted up is not upright in him; but the just (righteous) shall live by his faith" (Hab. 2:4).

Although Habakkuk declared this great truth in reference to the historical situation which he and God's people faced at the time, it is also very correctly used by the Apostle Paul to express the fact of salvation by grace through faith in our time (Rom. 1:17; Gal. 3:11; Heb. 10:38). The essential basis of salvation remains the same through every era of human history.

OUTLINE

A. The Prophet's Perplexity (chapters 1, 2)
  1. The first perplexity (1:1-11)
     (a) Question: Why is Israel's sin unjudged? (1:2-4)
     (b) Answer: The Chaldeans will judge the sin! (1:5-11)
  2. The second perplexity (1:12 — 2:20)
     (a) Question: How can the wicked Chaldeans render judgment? (1:12 — 2:1)
     (b) Answer: The Chaldeans will also be judged for their own sin! (2:2-20)
B. The Prophet's Prayer (chapter 3)
  1. The petition for mercy (3:1, 2)
  2. The vision of God (3:3-15)
  3. The joy of the Lord (3:16-19)

Zephaniah

AUTHOR

Zephaniah ("the Lord hides or protects") was apparently a great-grandson of Hezekiah (Zeph. 1:1). If this is not the case, it is difficult to explain the prophet's departure from the normal custom of mentioning only the father in the superscription. The prophet ministered in the reign of Josiah (640-608 B.C.) and was doubtless instrumental in the revival of 621 B.C. Nahum and Jeremiah were contemporaries.

IMPORTANCE

Zephaniah's message was a warning of impending judgment upon Judah and Jerusalem. The coming invasion of the Chaldeans is treated as a prefigurement of the apocalyptic day of the Lord, in which all earth judgments culminate (Isa. 2:10-22; Joel 1, 2; Rev. 4:1–19:16). Israel's restoration to the kingdom is treated in 3:9-20. The establishment of the kingdom is preceded by the judgment of the nations (Zeph. 3:8-13) and the revelation of Israel's Messiah-King (3:14-20).

OUTLINE

A. The Day of the Lord (1:1–3:7)
    1. Judgment of Judah (1:1–2:3)
    2. Judgment of the Gentiles (2:4-15)
    3. Judgment of the Jewish leaders (3:1-7)
B. The King and the Kingdom (3:8-20)
    1. Judgment of the Gentiles (3:8-13)
    2. Manifestation of the Messiah (3:14-20)

PROPHETIC EMPHASES

THE DAY OF THE LORD IN FIGURE (ZEPH. 1:1–3:7). The scope of this passage encompasses a worldwide judgment of the end-time tribulation. The Chaldean advance under Nebuchadnezzar foreshadows the time of Jacob's trouble (Jer. 30:5-7) which precedes Messiah's second advent (Zeph. 1:14-18).

THE OUTCALLING OF A REMNANT (ZEPH. 3:10-13). "The shameless nation," apostate Israel, is called to repent (Zeph. 2:1-3), prefiguring a call to the Jewish remnant of the end time to separate from the sinful nation.

THE JUDGMENT OF THE NATIONS (ZEPH. 3:8). This event, prefigured by judgment upon surrounding nations (Zeph. 2:4-15), is a necessary prelude to Israel's establishment in kingdom blessing.

CONVERSION OF THE NATIONS (ZEPH. 3:9). The Lord will "turn to the peoples a pure language." This indicates a spiritual transformation of the Gentiles, manifested in their purified speech.

ISRAEL'S RESTORATION (ZEPH. 3:14-20). The call to ecstatic joy envisions the termination of Israel's judgments, her triumph over her foes, and the enthronement of her King-Messiah in her midst (Zeph. 3:15, 17). Regathered, healed, restored, and blessed (Zeph. 3: 19, 20), Israel finds the fulfillment of her predicted destiny as stated in Deuteronomy 26:19.

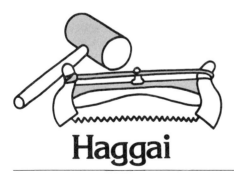

Haggai

AUTHOR

Haggai labored with Zechariah to encourage the returned exiles to finish building the temple. This project had been begun in the second year of Cyrus (535 B.C.), but had been abandoned in despair because of economic difficulties and opposition.

In Darius I's second year (520 B.C.) Haggai delivered four prophetic messages. Parts of these form the present book. The first message (Hag. 1:1-15) was delivered in August-September, the second (Hag. 2:1-9) in September-October, the third (Hag. 2:10-19) in November-December, and the fourth (Hag. 2:20-23) in November-December.

BACKGROUND

Haggai, Zechariah, and Malachi belong to the post-exilic period.

BACKGROUND OF HAGGAI	
Date	Events
549-539 B.C.	Cyrus the Great unites Persia and Media. Conquers Lydia and Babylon. Death of Belshazzar and fall of Babylon.
538 B.C.	Edict of Cyrus.
536 B.C.	Jews return to Jerusalem.
536-534 B.C.	Altar laid. Economic depression.
530-522 B.C.	Cambyses extends Persian Empire. Egypt conquered.
522-486 B.C.	Darius I ascends throne of Persia.
520 B.C.	Haggai ministers.
520-515 B.C.	Zechariah ministers. Temple completed.

OUTLINE

A. A Message of Rebuke (chapter 1)
 1. The neglect of the Temple (1:1-11)
 2. The response of the people (1:12-15)
B. A Message of Encouragement (2:1-9)
 1. "Build the present Temple" (2:1-5)
 2. "Anticipate the millennial Temple" (2:6-9)
C. A Message of Promise (2:10-19)
 1. "Past disobedience brought judgment" (2:10-14)
 2. "Present obedience will bring blessing" (2:15-19)
D. A Message of Prophecy (2:20-23)
 1. Judgment of the Gentile nations (2:20-22)
 2. Establishment of the messianic kingdom (2:23)

PROPHETIC EMPHASES

THE GREAT TRIBULATION. Haggai refers to the period of end-time trouble (Jer. 30:5-7; Dan. 12:1) as "the shaking of all nations" (Hag. 2:7) and "the shaking of the heavens and the earth" (Hag. 2:6, 21). It is preliminary to the restoration of the Davidic kingdom. It is also described as the overthrow of the "throne of kingdoms of the nations" (Hag. 2:22), so that the kingdom of Messiah may be set up. Christ is the "Stone" that smites the image (Gentile world power) and destroys it (Dan. 2:44, 45).

THE SECOND ADVENT. The text of Haggai 2:7 reads, "the desire of all nations shall come." This is an apt prophetic designation of him who is objectively the Desire of all nations. Through him alone can the nations be blessed with that righteousness and peace for which they really yearn.

MESSIAH'S KINGDOM RULE. Zerubbabel the governor was of the Davidic line (Matt. 1:12; Luke 3:27) and typifies Christ as David's son. In the kingdom Christ will receive his Davidic throne and will wear his royal signet ring. The prophecy envisions Christ invested with all rule and authority. Zerubbabel will no doubt himself participate as one of Christ's prime ministers in the kingdom (Dan. 12:2; Matt. 19:28).

THE BUILDING OF THE MILLENNIAL TEMPLE. That the temple ("house") referred to in Haggai 2:7 is not Zerubbabel's but the future kingdom temple is obvious from the context describing the preliminary end-time worldwide tribulation. The Septuagint reads, "The desirable things of all nations shall come," a reference to the costly treasures collected to adorn the millennial temple. "The future glory of this house (the millennial temple) shall be greater than the former" (Solomon's temple—Hag. 2:9). Peace will be bestowed through the Prince of Peace (Isa. 9:6, 7; Mic. 5:5) in that future kingdom of peace (Isa. 11:5-10).

Zechariah

AUTHOR

Zechariah, the son of Berechiah, the son of Iddo (Zech. 1:1) had, like Haggai, a ministry of encouragement for the remnant who had returned from Babylon. His name, meaning "the Lord remembers," suggests his divinely bestowed task of impressing upon the people that in their hardships and testings God had not forgotten them, for they were his elect nation. He would bless them in every way and enable them to complete the temple. He would give them far-reaching assurances of the coming of the Messiah, both as Savior and Redeemer in his first advent and as deliverer-king in his second advent.

Zechariah began his prophetic ministry two months after Haggai, in November, 520 B.C. Their combined preaching brought about the completion of the temple at the beginning of 515 B.C. Haggai's total recorded ministry lasted four months and Zechariah's about two years. His last dated prophecy was given in December, 518 B.C. (Zech. 7:1). Little question exists that Zechariah is the author of chapters 1 through 8.

Chapters 9 through 14 are undated and therefore frequently ascribed to another author. Although they are to be dated much later than the previous chapters of the book (probably after 480 B.C. in the light of the reference to Javan or Greece), there is no decisive reason to reject Zecharian authorship. Zechariah evidently had a long ministry, lasting perhaps fifty years.

OUTLINE

Introduction: The Call to Repentance (1:1-6)

A. The Hope of the Future (1:7 − 8:23)
  1. Visions of comfort and judgment (1:7 − 6:8)
    (a) The man among the myrtles (1:7-17)
    (b) The four horns and craftsmen (1:18-21)
    (c) The man with the measuring line (chapter 2)
    (d) The cleansing of the high priest (chapter 3)
    (e) The lampstand and the olive trees (chapter 4)
    (f) The flying scroll (5:1-4)
    (g) The woman in the ephah (5:5-11)
    (h) The four chariots (6:1-8)
  2. Symbolic crowning of Joshua (6:9-15)
  3. Religion: the true and the false (chapters 7, 8)
B. The Burdens of the Future (chapters 9 − 14)
  1. Messiah's first advent and rejection (chapters 9 − 11)
  2. Messiah's second advent and acceptance (chapters 12 − 14)

CHARACTER OF THE BOOK

Zechariah is by far the most messianic and apocalyptic of all the Minor Prophets. His prophecy contains more prophetic allusions to the person, work, and future glory of Christ than all the Minor Prophets combined. He ranks with Isaiah and Ezekiel in abundance of detail regarding the second advent of Christ and the establishment of the future messianic kingdom.

GREAT PROPHECIES OF ZECHARIAH 9-14

THE FIRST ADVENT OF CHRIST. In contrast to Alexander, the proud world-conqueror (Zech. 9:1-8), the Messiah is lowly, riding upon a humble beast of burden, and righteous, thus validating his Saviorhood (Zech. 9:9).

THE REJECTION OF CHRIST, THE GOOD SHEPHERD. Zechariah performs a symbolic act of prophecy in order to portray "the flock destined for butchery." The nation's abusive treatment of Zechariah prefigures its future treatment of Messiah himself (Zech. 11:4-6). The two rods, "Graciousness" and "Unity" (Zech. 11:7, 8), are broken to picture the cessation of national unity after the rejection of Messiah (Zech. 11:9-11) and his betrayal for "thirty pieces of silver" (Zech. 11:12).

THE ACCEPTANCE OF ANTICHRIST, THE BAD SHEPHERD.
The prophet performs a second symbolic act in order to foreshadow
this tragedy which precedes the second advent. He describes Antichrist's vicious character and doom (Zech. 11:15-17; John 5:43).

ISRAEL'S END-TIME REGATHERING. The presence of Christ is
promised to the remnant, guaranteeing their triumph (Zech. 10:5-7).
Israel will be gathered together to Palestine out of her present worldwide dispersion. Every impediment to her blessing will be removed
(Zech. 10:8-12).

MESSIANIC IMPLICATIONS OF THE EIGHT NIGHT VISIONS

Vision	Interpretation
The Man among the Myrtles (1:7-17)	Hope for scattered Israel, symbolized by the myrtle trees in the deep glen. These express Israel's depressed condition in the world during the times of the Gentiles (605 B.C. to the second advent). The Red-Horse Rider (1:8) is Christ in theophanic form as Redeemer and delivering Warrior. The patrol scouts (angelic agents) ascertain the condition of the earth as it affects Israel's restoration (Hag. 2:21, 22), which was not imminent (1:9-12) because the earth was "quiet."
The Four Horns and Craftsmen (1:18-21)	Israel finally triumphant over her foes. The four horns represent the four great world powers of the times of the Gentiles (Babylon, Persia, Greece, and Rome, the latter to be revived at the end time Dan. 2:37-45; 7:7, 8, 20; Rev. 13:1). The four craftsmen symbolize kingdoms the Lord employs to cast down the persecutors of his covenant people. Three of these (Persia, Greece, and Rome) were horns, which in turn become craftsmen. The fourth horn is Messiah's millennial kingdom, which destroys revived Rome (Rev. 19:15; Dan. 2:44).
The Surveyor (chapter 2)	Jerusalem in kingdom glory. Surveyor is probably the same divine Person as the Red-Horse Rider of vision 1. His measuring activities point to the prosperity of Jerusalem both then and in the kingdom age, as the promises of 2:4-13 demonstrate.
Joshua's Cleansing (chapter 3)	Restoration of Israel as a high-priestly nation. The high priest, Joshua, represents the self-righteous, Christ-rejecting nation (Rom. 10:1-4). The angel (the Lord) effectually rebuffs Satan on the ground of God's sovereign election of Israel. The nation is saved at the second advent (3:4, 5) by accepting the Redeemer-Messiah, the Branch (3:8-10; Isa. 53:1-10; Phil. 2:6-8). He will be the "Stone," a precious carved gem, when Israel receives him at his glorious second advent (Zech. 12:10).

ISRAEL'S CONVERSION. The vision of the crucified Messiah, the Pierced One (Zech. 12:10; Rev. 1:7) results in national conversion and a copious outpouring of the Spirit, fulfilling Joel 2:28-32 and Ezekiel 39:29. Acts 2:16-21 is used as an *illustration* of the Pentecostal effusion that will be fulfilled in the Millennium.

ISRAEL'S NATIONAL CLEANSING. The basis of cleansing is the "fountain" (Zech. 13:1), namely Calvary. Idolatry, occultism, and false prophecy will be removed by Christ (Zech. 13:1-6). The provision for cleansing is Messiah, introduced with dramatic suddenness (Zech. 13:

Vision	Interpretation
The Gold Lampstand (chapter 4)	Israel as the light of the world in fellowship with Christ, the true Light (John 8:12). The lampstand in the midst of Israel (Exod. 25:31-40; John 8:12) portrays the plenitude of the sevenfold Spirit (Heb. 1:9; Rev. 1:4) is prefigured by the seven lamps (fullness of testimony). "The Lord of the whole earth" (Gen. 14:19; Mic. 4:13; Zech. 6:5; Rev. 11:3, 4) is the kingdom name of the victorious King-Priest, who will combine the civil and priestly offices (the two olive trees).
The Flying Scroll (5:1-4)	Messiah's rigid rule in the kingdom. The scroll, illustrating the enforcement of the divine moral law, represents the curse of God against sinners (Deut. 28-30; Gal. 3:10-14). The flying motion denotes the worldwide extent of the curse against all offenders (Psa. 2:9; Rev. 2:27; 12:5; 19:15).
The Woman in Ephah (5:5-11)	Removal of commercial and ecclesiastical wickedness from the millennial earth. The ephah, a Hebrew dry measure (1.05 bushels) represents godless business, the commercial aspects of Babylon (Rev. 18). The talent is also associated with commerce of the Satanic world system. The woman, the personification of wickedness (Matt. 13:33; Rev. 2:20; 17:3-7), represents the religious aspects of Babylon (Rev. 17). Her position in the ephah suggests her complicity with godless business, which ultimately works her undoing (Prov. 5:22).
The Four Chariots (6:1-8)	The judgment of the nations prior to Messiah's kingdom. "The two mountains" (Olivet and Zion) are the locations from which divine judgment goes forth in the horsed chariots. The *red* horses portray blood and war (Rev. 6:4); the *black*, starvation (Rev. 6:5, 6); the *white*, conquest (Rev. 6:2); the *grizzled and bay*, death (Rev. 6:8). The four spirits (angelic ministers) are the celestial agents of judgment who will dislodge the wicked for possession by "the Lord of the whole earth" (6:5).
Finale: Coronation of the High Priest (6:9-15)	*All* eight night visions point to the kingdom restored to Israel under Messiah as the King-Priest (Heb. 7:1-3; Psa. 110:4). The significance of the coronation is that the crown was to be placed *not* upon the head of the civil ruler but upon the head of the high priest, pointing to the kingdom role of Christ as King-Priest.

6). Both his death and deity are described in Zechariah 13:7, where God ("the Lord of hosts" refers to the Messiah as "the man my equal," a strong intimation of the unique divine-human nature of Christ. The prelude to Israel's national conversion is her world wide scattering (Zech. 13:7) and last-day tribulation, resulting in a delivered remnant (Zech. 13:8, 9) that appropriates Christ's redemption (Zech. 13:9).

ISRAEL'S END-TIME DELIVERANCE. Deliverance of the converted remnant will occur at Armageddon and in the future siege of Jerusalem (Zech. 12:1-9; 14:1-3). The enemy is cut down by God at the moment of apparent triumph.

ISRAEL'S NATIONAL HOPE. This centers in the returning Messiah, the "Prince of Peace" (Isa. 9:6). He will bring peace (Zech. 9:10). In prospect of suffering Israel is encouraged (Zech. 9:11, 12). The Maccabean conflict with paganism (175-130 B.C.) was envisioned as an illustration of Israel's final conflict and deliverance (Zech. 9:16 – 10:1).

PERSONAL ADVENT OF MESSIAH. He will come to the Mount of Olives, causing a gigantic earthquake which will produce vast topographical changes (Zech. 14:4). He will come with his angels and saints (glorified men) to deliver his people and destroy their foes (2 Thess. 1:7-10; Jude 1:14, 15).

ESTABLISHMENT OF THE KINGDOM OVER ISRAEL. It is at this time that the restoration of the kingdom which the disciples inquired about in Acts 1:6 will be fulfilled. Because of the absolute lordship of the King (Zech. 14:9), all the blessings of the kingdom center in Jerusalem, his capital of the millennial earth (Zech. 14:10, 11, 16-19). With a retrospective glance Zechariah reviews the destruction of Israel's enemies (Zech. 14:12-15), then climaxes his prophecy with a description of Israel's holiness as a high priestly nation (Zech. 14:20, 21).

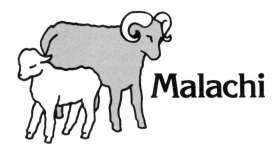

Malachi

AUTHOR

Malachi means "my messenger." This is the prophet's personal name — not an appellation based on Malachi 3:1, as some critics hold. As the last prophetic voice of the Old Testament, Malachi must be placed considerably later than Haggai and Zechariah, including the later portion of Zechariah. The book evidently belongs to a period some time after Ezra's and Nehemiah's reforms, for spiritual decline had set in again. A date between 435 and 400 B.C. would be reasonable.

BACKGROUND

THE WORLD OF MALACHI	
Date	*Event*
522-486 B.C.	Reign of Darius I
520 B.C.	Ministry of Haggai and Zechariah
515 B.C.	Completion of Temple
490 B.C.	Defeat of Darius I at Marathon by Greeks
486-465 B.C.	Reign of Xerxes I (Ahasuerus, Esther's husband)
485-425 B.C.	Life and works of Herodotus, "father of history"
475 B.C.	Later ministry of Zechariah (Zechariah 9-14)
470-399 B.C.	Life and works of Socrates
465-424 B.C.	Reign of Artaxerxes I; "Golden Age" of Pericles
458 B.C.	Return from exile under Ezra
445 B.C.	Rebuilding of walls under Nehemiah
435-400 B.C.	Ministry of Malachi; final message of Old Testament

IMPORTANCE

Malachi rebukes formalism and hypocritical religionism for its total contradiction of God's grace and electing love. In doing this the prophet deals with the sins of the priests of his day. But his emphasis extends far beyond the priestly sins, for these serve only as the background for his prophecies of judgment upon the whole nation. At that coming day of the Lord the wicked will be judged and the righteous will be delivered into the blessings of the restored kingdom. Prerequisite to this climactic event is the coming of the Messiah's forerunner and the Messiah himself at the first advent. This expanded foreview thus includes most of the major themes of Old Testament prophecy.

OUTLINE

A. God's Love for His People (1:1-5)
   1. Disbelieved by Israel (1:1-3)
   2. Demonstrated by Jehovah (1:4, 5)
B. Israel's Sins against God (1:6 — 2:17)
   1. The sins of the priests (1:6 — 2:9)
   2. The sins of the people (2:10-17)
C. God's Warning of Judgment (3:1 — 4:6)
   1. God will send a forerunner (3:1-6)
   2. The people have robbed God (3:7-15)
   3. God will spare a remnant (3:16-18)
   4. Judgment is coming (4:1-4)
   5. God will send Elijah (4:5, 6)

GREAT PROPHETIC THEMES

THE PREDICTION OF MESSIAH'S FORERUNNER. "My messenger" is John the Baptist (Matt. 11:10; Mark 1:2; Luke 7:27). His mission of preparing the way for Christ at his first advent is foretold (Mal. 3:1).

THE SECOND ADVENT OF MESSIAH IN JUDGMENT. He is "the messenger of the covenant," particularly in his second advent to judge (Mal. 3:2-5; Rev. 19:11) in reply to the taunt "Where is the God of Judgment?" (Mal. 2:17). The covenant is the Palestinian Covenant (Deut. 29, 30; esp. 30:3-10).

THE GODLY JEWISH REMNANT. These are the believing Jews

of the end-time, who will be rewarded for their fidelity in times of gross apostasy (Mal. 3:16-18) and be the Lord's peculiar treasure in the day when the Lord separates the righteous from the wicked, previous to the establishment of the kingdom.

THE DAY OF THE LORD. Judgment will be visited upon both the wicked nations and apostate Israel. Evildoers will be purged out by the returning Christ before he sets up his righteous regime (Mal. 4:1).

THE SECOND ADVENT OF MESSIAH IN BLESSING. To the believing remnant who fears his name he will appear as "the Sun of righteousness with healing in his wings." As the "righteousness of God" (1 Cor. 1:30) he will bring to those who believe on him salvation instead of condemnation. As "the Lord our righteousness" (Jer. 23:6) he will bring them healing instead of destruction, blessing and empowering them so that they will be able to tread down their wicked foes.

THE COMING OF ELIJAH. "Elijah" will appear before the onset of "the great and terrible day of the Lord" (Mal. 4:5, 6), when sinners will be punished. He will call out a godly remnant, lest the returning Christ smite the earth with a curse because of its wicked inhabitants (Mal. 4:6).

WHO IS THE ELIJAH OF MALACHI 4:5, 6?

This vexing problem has caused much confusion and called forth many erratic interpretations. That Elijah will not be the Old Testament prophet Elijah returned to earth from heaven but an unglorified member of the godly Jewish remnant in the period of judgment preceding Messiah's second advent is suggested by the following considerations. Our Lord applied the name Elijah to John the Baptist (Matt. 11:14) in his official capacity as a prophet. John was an Elijah in spirit (Luke 1:16, 17), but obviously not the literal Elijah (John 1:21). Preceding Messiah's second advent will be another "Elijah," a man with a preparatory ministry similar to that of John the Baptist. Christ declared that this Elijah (perhaps Elijah will be his real name) will "restore all things" (Matt. 17:3, 11), attesting Malachi's prediction that a prophet would arise in the period of judgment preceding the second advent (Acts 3:21).

That the Elijah predicted by both Malachi and our Lord (Matt. 17:11) is one of the two witnesses of Revelation 11:3-13 seems inescapable. Since both of these two witnesses are first killed for their testimony and then resurrected by God, the Elijah of the Old Testament could not be one of them, for he had long previously been translated to heaven and thus made immune to physical death.

Summary of New Testament Books

RELATION TO THE OLD TESTAMENT BOOKS

The books of the New Testament constitute the capstone of the Old Testament revelation. They also have counterparts in the Old Testament books. Thus the four Gospels correspond to the Pentateuch in showing the need for the Savior and foreshadowing his coming in type and prophecy. The Acts of the Apostles present the early history of God's redeemed people, the Church. They thus correspond to the historical books of the Old Testament (especially Joshua and Judges), since these catalog the story of God's Old Covenant people, Israel.

The twenty-one epistles of the New Testament expound the meaning of Christ's redemption in Christian life. In this way they correspond to the Old Testament prophetic writings, which established the principles of Pentateuchal Covenant and Law that governed God's ancient people. The Book of the Revelation previsions the future of the Church, of Israel, and of the Gentiles and thus corresponds in part to the books of Daniel and Zechariah and the last thirteen chapters of Ezekiel.

DIVISIONS OF THE NEW TESTAMENT

The books of the New Testament may be arranged in the following order:

BIOGRAPHICAL – THE FOUR GOSPELS. These are historical and theological portraits of the person and work of Jesus Christ. Two were written by apostles (Matthew and John) and two by close friends of apostles (Mark and Luke).

HISTORICAL – THE ACTS OF THE APOSTLES. This book is a record of the results of Christ's redemptive work seen in the formation and early experiences of the Christian Church. It forms the link between the biographical and doctrinal portions.

The Golden Gate in the Jerusalem Wall, viewed from the Church Of All Nations (*Russ Busby photo*)

INSTRUCTIVE – THE PAULINE EPISTLES. These epistles unfold the full ramifications of the redemptive work of Christ. They fall into three general categories:

Doctrinal, addressed to churches. These epistles include Romans, Corinthians, Galatians, Ephesians, Philippians, Colossians, and Thessalonians.

Pastoral, addressed to young men with a pastoral gift. These include the epistles to Timothy and Titus.

Special, addressed to an individual (Philemon).

INSTRUCTIVE – THE GENERAL EPISTLES. These are the "non-Pauline" epistles (with the possible exception of Hebrews). They include Hebrews and James (addressed especially to Christians of Jewish background) and the epistles by Peter, John, and Jude (addressed to the Church at large).

PROPHETIC AND APOCALYPTIC – THE REVELATION. The "Revelation of Jesus Christ" (1:1) is the grand consummation of all inspired prophecy.

The Four Gospels

THE DESIGNATION "GOSPEL"

As applied to the four inspired biographies that open the New Testament, the term "gospel" signifies the good news of salvation for lost humanity provided through the life, death, and resurrection of Jesus Christ, the God-Man. The word "gospel" is the Old English rendering of the Greek word *evaggelion,* the Latin *evangelium,* and the English *evangel.* The term is a contraction of "Godspel" and means "news about God." Wycliffe's translation of the Bible (1382) popularized the use of the term. The four Gospels constitute the basis for the gospel message as presented doctrinally in the Pauline Epistles, "that Christ died for our sins according to the Scriptures, and that he was buried, and that he rose again the third day according to the Scriptures" (1 Cor. 15:3, 4). The Apostle shows that the fact of personal salvation is predicated solely upon *faith in what Christ did for the believer* rather than upon anything the believer can do for Christ (Eph. 2:8, 9).

WHY FOUR GOSPELS?

There are four Gospel accounts because a single narrative could never adequately present the glory of the person and work of him who was King of Israel (Matthew), Servant of the Lord (Mark), Son of Man (Luke), and Son of God (John). One pose by a renowned painter could hardly do justice to a great man who was at the same time an educator, a general, a president, and a legislator. How much less could one biographical portrait set forth him who was at the same time a Prophet, Priest, and King and who also combined God and man in one Person!

Neither could a single Gospel narrative adequately meet the varied needs of fallen and lost humanity. Matthew, the Gospel of the "King of Israel," was written for the unregenerate religious man, represented by the nation Israel. Mark, the Gospel of the "Servant of God" – the Gospel of action and miracle – was written for the unregenerate strong man, represented by the world-ruling Roman of Christ's day. Luke, the Gospel of the "Son of Man," was written for the unregenerate thinking man, represented by the intellectual Greek of Christ's day. John, the Gospel of the "Son of God," was written for the unregenerate and insignificant man, represented by the underprivileged Oriental races of Christ's day. These various classes comprise humanity in general in every age.

Matthew

AUTHOR AND DATE

No portion of Scripture displays a clearer impress of divine inspiration than the four Gospels. The Holy Spirit is their obvious Author. Yet each also had, of course, a human agent. The first Gospel is the work of Matthew, a Hebrew, whose preconversion name was Levi. Matthew was a "publican" or collector of tolls and customs imposed on persons and goods crossing the Lake of Gennesaret at Capernaum (Matt. 9:9). He made a great feast at his house in honor of Jesus on the occasion of his call (Luke 5:29). He was among those who waited in the upper room for the promised Spirit just before Pentecost (Acts 1: 13). After this we hear no more of him.

The early Church unanimously ascribed this Gospel to the Apostle Matthew. External evidence abundantly testifies to the early existence and use of the Gospel of Matthew (the *Didache*, the *Epistle of Barnabas*, and many other early sources). Papias, Irenaeus, and Origen comprise a uniform second-century attestation of the genuineness of Matthew's Gospel. Internal evidence also authenticates the Gospel. Since Matthew was not conspicuous among the apostles it would have been strange for tradition to assign the Gospel to him if he had not actually written it.

Conservative scholars date Matthew's Gospel at about A.D. 50.

ORDER AMONG THE GOSPELS

For the following reasons it is appropriate that Matthew stands first in order among the four Gospels: 1) It has historically been considered the earliest Gospel, designed to meet the needs of the earliest Christian converts, who were Jews. 2) Its author was an apostle. 3) The Gospel fulfills the Old Testament in a remarkable way. 4) It bridges the gap between the Old and New Testaments and, like the Book of Hebrews, shows the relationship of Christianity to Judaism and the Law of Moses to the teachings of Christ. For these reasons it is fitting that the Gospel of Matthew not only heads the list of Gospels but also serves as an introduction to the entire New Testament.

PURPOSE

Matthew wrote to supply an account of the life of Christ that would encourage and confirm the earliest Christian converts in their new-found faith. These believers were Jews who turned to the crucified and risen Messiah in the period between Christ's ascension and the outreach of the gospel of grace to the Gentiles (Acts 1-10). In this era, as Peter's sermons in the first part of Acts indicate, the gospel was enunciated primarily in the sphere of the Law, the Prophets, and the

Snows of Mount Hermon (Mount of Transfiguration) to the north furnish water for Sea of Galilee and Tiberias. (© *MPS*)

Psalms, since all believers at this time were either Jews or Jewish proselytes.

While encouraging and confirming these persecuted Jewish believers in their Christian faith, Matthew at the same time undertook to confute their persecutors and to show that in Christ's death and resurrection the promises made to Abraham and David were being fulfilled. A clear presentation of the nature of Christ's person and mission was needed to refute the objections of unbelieving Jews.

PLAN OF MATTHEW'S GOSPEL

The author undertook to achieve his purpose by presenting proof that Jesus was truly the divine-human Messiah and King of Israel prophesied in the Old Testament. Matthew shows that the kingdom he offered, as well as the words he spoke and the works he performed, were those predicted of Israel's Messiah-King. Both the King and his proffered kingdom were rejected by Israel. Israel was consequently rejected by the King. During the time of the nation's rejection the kingdom will assume a new form, existing in concealment during this present age, the outcalling of the Church (13:1-58; 16:16-18). The nation through its leaders murdered the Messiah-King, but his death was nevertheless a ransom for many through resurrection and ascension to heaven. Christ will shortly return to reward his own and set up his kingdom (chaps. 24, 25). Meanwhile his followers are commissioned to carry the gospel to all nations.

OUTLINE

A. Introduction of the King (chapters 1—4)
   1. Qualifications and birth (chapter 1)
   2. Recognition as King-Messiah (chapter 2)
   3. Preparation for ministry (chapters 3, 4)
B. Presentation of the Kingdom (chapters 5—7)
   1. Spiritual principles (5:1—7:27)
   2. Anticipated rejection (7:28, 29)
C. Manifestation and Rejection of the King (chapters 8—12)
   1. The response of Israel's leaders (chapters 8, 9)
   2. The King's messengers to Israel (chapter 10)
   3. The King's rejection by Israel (chapter 11)
   4. The nations rejection by the King (chapter 12)
D. Prophecies of the King (chapter 13)
E. Ministry of the King (chapters 14—23)
   1. Previews of world outreach (chapters 14, 15)
   2. Predictions of death and the church (chapter 16)
   3. Glimpses of the future kingdom (chapter 17)
   4. Descriptions of the kingdom's subjects (chapter 18)
   5. Earthly relationships and the kingdom (chapter 19)
   6. Service and awards in the kingdom (chapter 20)
   7. Final appearances of the King (chapters 21, 22)
   8. Pronouncements of doom (chapter 23)
F. Further Prophecies of the King (chapters 24, 25)

1. The destruction of the Temple (24:1-3)
2. The end-time Tribulation (24:4-51)
3. The testing of Jewish profession (25:1-13)
4. The testing of service (25:14-30)
5. The testing of individual Gentiles (25:31-46)
G. Death and Resurrection of the King (chapters 26 – 28)
1. The betrayal and denial of the King (chapter 26)
2. The crucifixion and death of the King (chapter 27)
3. The resurrection of the King (28:1-9)
4. The commissioning of the disciples (28:10-20)

THE CONCEPT OF THE KINGDOM

Being the Gospel directed to the Jew, Matthew naturally deals with the King and the kingdom. The King is, of course, the Messiah-King so extensively foretold in the Old Testament, and the kingdom is the one described in such detail by the Hebrew prophets. In Matthew the term "kingdom of heaven" occurs thirty-three times; it is peculiar to this Gospel. The expression derives from its use in Daniel (Dan. 2: 44; 4:25, 32) and refers to the rule of the God of heaven over the earth.

The term "kingdom of heaven" is employed in a threefold sense by Matthew. Understanding of this triple usage is essential to the correct comprehension of this important Gospel.

First, the kingdom of heaven is revealed as "at hand," offered in the person of the King (of whom John the Baptist was the forerunner – 3:1-3; 4:17). The biblical expression "at hand" (literally "drawn near") means that the King was then present and that a bona fide offer of the kingdom was being made to Israel on the sole condition of her repentance. The failure of the nation to repent and her rejection of both the King and the kingdom were included in the overall plan of God in order to demonstrate the exceeding sinfulness of sin. This necessitated the King's atoning death as a prerequisite for the future establishment of the kingdom at his second advent. The kingdom offered was the Davidic, earthly, theocratic kingdom promised so glowingly in the Old Testament (2 Sam. 7:4-17; Isa. 11:1 – 12:6; and many other passages).

Second, the kingdom of heaven in Matthew is revealed in its "mystery" form during the long interval when the King and the kingdom are rejected by Israel (Matt. 13). It is designated a "mystery" (Matt. 13:11, 17) because so far as the Old Testament was concerned it was locked up in the secret counsels of God (Eph. 3:3-12). It was to be announced only after the kingdom per se had been rejected by the nation (Matt. 12:1-45). This phase of the rule of God on the earth includes the worldwide preaching of the cross and the outcalling of the Church (Acts 15:14, 15) during the interval between the two advents.

Third, the kingdom of heaven in Matthew is revealed in its future aspect, fulfilled after the second advent of Christ. This is the kingdom offered to Israel by John the Baptist and Jesus but rejected by the nation as a whole. It will be realized as the future millennial kingdom predicted by Daniel (Dan. 2:34-36, 44, 45) and covenanted to David (2 Sam. 7:12-16). It is to be established after the return of the King in glory (Matt. 24:29 – 25:46) and the national conversion of Israel (Zech. 12:1 – 14:21; Acts 15:14-17; Rom. 11:26-36; Rev. 20:4-6).

Matthew does employ the term "kingdom of God" four times. But since he was writing to Jews he usually employed the term "kingdom of heaven" because of its special relevance to the kingdom covenanted to David and the divine plan to be realized through the nation Israel. The kingdom of heaven is similar in many respects to the kingdom of God and is therefore often used synonymously with it in the other Gospels, where the divine rule embraces the larger context of the Church, the nations, and the angels.

GENTILE CONCERN

Despite the fact that Matthew is distinctly addressed to the Jew—presenting Christ as Israel's King and quoting or alluding to the Old Testament no less than sixty-five times—the Gospel also reveals a distinct concern for the Gentiles. This is demonstrated by the following considerations.

Matthew mentions two Gentile women (Rahab and Ruth) in Christ's genealogy (1:5). He includes the story of the Magi (2:1-12). He includes Christ's declaration that many from the east and west will sit down in the kingdom of heaven, while the "sons of the kingdom" (its rightful heirs, the Jews) will be cast out (8:11, 12). He quotes the prophecy that Messiah would proclaim judgment to the Gentiles and that the Gentiles would hope in him (12:18, 21). He includes Christ's disclosure that the mystery form of the kingdom would comprehend Gentiles (13:1-58), that the ministry of the King in rejection and death would bring salvation to the whole world (chaps. 14, 15), and that the Gentiles would enter the kingdom after divine judgment (25:31-46). Matthew also includes the resurrected King's commission to disciple "all nations" (28:19, 20).

Mark

AUTHOR AND DATE

The second Gospel is the work of John Mark. Mark's mother was the Mary whose house in Jerusalem was used as a meeting place for Christian believers (Acts 12:12-17). Mark was apparently Peter's convert (1 Pet. 5:13). In any case Peter was well acquainted with Mark's mother. It was to her home that he went after being miraculously released from prison (Acts 12:12). It seems that Mark assisted Peter, Paul, and Barnabas in their missionary work at one time or another (Acts 12:25; 15:36-39).

Mark labored with Paul at Rome (Col. 4:10; Philem. 1:24), apparently having reconciled the differences that separated them on Paul's second missionary tour (Acts 15:38, 39). In his last epistle Paul urges Timothy to come to him in Rome and bring Mark with him, adding that "he is useful to me for ministering" (2 Tim. 4:11). Mark thus appears to have been a servant rather than a preaching minister, a circumstance admirably in line with his delineation of Jesus Christ as the Servant of the Lord.

That Mark wrote the second Gospel is amply supported by the testimony of early Church Fathers, including Papias, Justin Martyr, Irenaeus, Clement of Alexandria, Tertullian, Origen, and Eusebius. Since Mark was not an especially prominent church leader, there would have been no reason to assign his name to this Gospel if he had not actually written it.

Mark himself was not one of the Twelve. His Gospel, however, has all the earmarks of a firsthand witness. This witness, according to numerous early accounts, was none other than Simon Peter, from

Marker of Tenth Roman Legion, stationed in Jerusalem during Christ's crucifixion
(*Russ Busby photo*)

whom Mark is said to have obtained his information.

Strong evidence points to the fact that Mark's Gospel was written at Rome between A.D 65 and 70, shortly before the fall of Jerusalem. Mark explains Jewish customs because he is writing to Gentiles. He also employs ten Latin words, some of which do not occur elsewhere in the New Testament, thus furnishing additional evidence that he wrote from Rome to Romans.

ORDER AMONG THE GOSPELS

Modern criticism tends to assign to Mark priority in both time and importance. Because Mark has so little material that is peculiar to him, most present-day scholars favor the theory that his Gospel was written first and was employed by Matthew and Luke when they wrote their accounts of Christ's life. It is assumed that the freshness and vividness of Mark's language also suggest that it was written first.

But those who hold to the full inspiration and authority of Scripture and discern the Holy Spirit's obvious superintendence in the four Gospels cannot help being suspicious of such a theory. Why should

Matthew and Luke be so dependent on Mark if the Holy Spirit really led them? Why, too, should Mark be assigned priority in time and importance when it was never placed first in ancient Greek manuscripts and lists or in the writings of the Church Fathers, but was invariably placed second, third, or fourth? Why in the early Church did the Gospel of Mark receive the least attention of any of the four Gospels, if it had priority over the others?

Whatever the exact reasons, the position of Mark after Matthew in the present-day order of the New Testament books is certainly providential. Matthew's thoroughly Jewish emphasis makes it a far more suitable bridge between the Old and New Testaments.

PURPOSE

Mark wrote to supply an account of the life of Christ that would meet the need of the Roman, as Matthew had met the need of the Jew. Thus, while Matthew depicts the Messiah as King of the Jews, Mark delineates him as the Servant of the Lord. This unique Servant displayed a remarkable blending of submission and strength that achieved victory through apparent defeat. Such a portrayal of Christ had a special fascination for Roman Christians.

PLAN OF MARK'S GOSPEL

In presenting Christ as the faithful and obedient Servant, the Holy Spirit through Mark especially fulfills two prophecies by Isaiah: "Behold, my servant . . ." (Isa. 42:1-3) and "Who is blind, but my servant? or deaf as my messenger that I sent? Who is blind as he that is perfect, and blind as the Lord's servant?" (Isa. 42:19).

Mark by the Spirit presents Christ as blind to every object but God's glory and deaf to every call but the voice of God—truly the ultimate example of the perfect Servant! His service, as portrayed by Mark, is distinguished by many beautiful and significant details. For example, his service was undertaken in secret prayer (1:35) and was rendered promptly. Ten times in the opening chapter and forty times in the Gospel we find the Greek word which is translated *immediately, straightway,* or *forthwith,* indicating a rapidity of action which befits an energetically obedient servant (1:12, 21; 2:8; etc.). As if there were scarcely a pause in our Lord's wonderful ministry from first to last, the word "and" occurs over and over in the course of the story of Christ's obedient, unfaltering zeal.

OUTLINE

A. Introduction of the Servant (1:1-13)
   1. The forerunner (1:1-8)
   2. The baptism (1:9-11)
   3. The temptation (1:12, 13)
B. Ministry of the Servant (1:14 — 13:37)
   1. In eastern Galilee (1:14 — 7:23)
   2. In northern Galilee (7:24 — 9:50)
   3. In Perea (10:1-31)
   4. In Jerusalem (10:32 — 13:37)
C. Redemptive Work of the Servant (chapters 14, 15)
   1. Plottings to kill (chapter 14)
   2. Crucifixion and death (chapter 15)
D. Authentication of the Redemption (chapter 16)
   1. Resurrection (16:1-8)
   2. Appearances (16:9-14)★
   3. Commission (16:15-18)★
   4. Ascension (16:19)★
   5. Postlude (16:20)★
   ★Note: These verses are absent from some of the oldest and best manuscripts. Many scholars view them as later additions, assuming that the original ending of Mark was lost at a very early date.

OTHER CHARACTERISTICS

Mark is the shortest of the four Gospels, most of its contents being found in the other two Synoptic Gospels (Matthew and Luke). Christ's death and resurrection receive special emphasis, with over a third of the book devoted to the climactic last week of Christ's earthly career (chaps. 11 — 16). As the Gospel of the Servant of the Lord, Mark is a narrative of action and deeds. Neither a genealogy nor an account of Christ's birth or early years is given since these are not essential to the description of a servant. Although Mark depicts Christ primarily in the servant role, he also mentions his kingly characteristics (11:10; 14:62; 15:2). In contrast, Matthew highlights Christ as King, but also refers to him as a Servant (Matt. 12:18-21). Mark's treatment is concise, straightforward, and chronological throughout, in contrast to Matthew's Gospel, in which chapters 1 — 4 are chronological, 5 — 13 are topical, and 14 — 28 are again chronological.

Luke

AUTHOR AND DATE

The third Gospel is the work of Luke, "the beloved physician" (Col. 4:14; 2 Tim. 4:11; Philem. 1:24). Luke was a Gentile, since he is distinguished from "those of the circumcision" (Col. 4:10, 11). However, it is quite possible that he may have been a Jewish proselyte (a Gentile convert to Judaism). Tradition regards him as a native of Syrian Antioch, in which he displayed a special interest (Acts 6:5; 11:19-27; 13:1-3; 14:26-28; 15:1, 2, 22, 30-40; 18:22, 23). He apparently also lived in Philippi, as the "we" sections of Acts seem to indicate (16:10-17; 20:5-15), and probably studied at the medical school there. He must have been a person of winsome character to have earned the Apostle Paul's adjective "beloved" (Col. 4:14).

The authenticity of Luke's Gospel is well established. Clement apparently alludes to it about A.D. 95. References to it are frequent in the second century (Polycarp, Papias, Marcion, etc.). It is listed as the work of Luke by the Muratorian fragment (A.D. 170) and by Irenaeus (A.D. 180). Such attestation continues into the third century, with Clement of Alexandria, Tertullian, and Origen adding their witness.

The Gospel was probably written about A.D. 58, while Luke was in Caesarea — the city in which Paul was imprisoned (Acts 24, 25, 26). Both the time and the place would have been appropriate for the research which Luke mentions he conducted in order to write his Gospel. Since Luke wrote his Gospel before he wrote the Book of Acts in approximately A.D. 61 (see Acts 1:1 for order of books), it is highly likely that Luke's stay in Caesarea served as his ideal opportunity to pen this Gospel account.

ORDER AMONG THE GOSPELS

The position in our English versions is found in nearly all the Greek and Syrian manuscripts; it was popularized by Eusebius and Jerome. Origen was acquainted with it, though he frequently cites the Gospels in the order Matthew, Luke, and Mark. Occasionally Luke is found in second or fourth place, but never in the first position.

PURPOSE

Luke states plainly that he wrote his Gospel so that Theophilus "might know the certainty" of the things in which he had been instructed (1:4). Theophilus was undoubtedly a Gentile and a person of rank. He was probably a recent convert, perhaps acting as a sponsor for the production of the book.

But a second and far wider purpose for the Gospel was to supply an account of the life and work of Christ that would meet the needs of people at large, especially the Greek-speaking world opened up to Christianity by Paul's missionary tours.

PLAN OF LUKE'S GOSPEL

While Matthew presents Christ as King of the Jews and Mark as Servant of the Lord to the Romans, Luke portrays him as Son of Man to the Greeks. Luke places emphasis upon the perfect humanity of Christ, portraying him as the human-divine Savior, the virgin-born God-Man. Hence Luke lays great stress upon Christ's sinless conception, his genealogy being traced from Mary to Adam. Luke alone tells of Christ's boyhood; he delineates more fully than the other Gospel writers the wonderful prayer life of the pattern Man. He strives to set forth the perfections of the Son of Man as the Friend and Redeemer of men, the Savior of all who will trust in him (1:68; 2:38; 21:28; 24:21).

The term "Son of Man" is a key phrase. Luke 19:10 is commonly designated as the key verse: "For the Son of man is come to seek and to save that which was lost." While beautifully highlighting the humanity of the Divine One, Luke also carefully guards Christ's deity and kingship (Luke 1:32-35). Luke's Gospel is a marvelous exposition of Zechariah's prophecy of "the man whose name is the Branch" (Zech. 6:12). His gospel is emphatically "good tidings of great joy to all people" (2:10), for he tells us how God became man to save a lost and ruined race.

OUTLINE

Introduction (1:1-4)
A. The Son of Man Humanly Related (1:5 – 4:13)
  1. To John the Baptist and Mary and Joseph (1:5 – 2:52)
  2. To John's ministry, the human race, and testing (3:1 – 4:13)
B. The Son of Man in Ministry (4:14 – 21:38)
  1. As Prophet-King in Galilee (4:14 – 9:50)
  2. From Galilee to Jerusalem (9:51 – 21:38)
C. The Son of Man in Rejection and Death (chapters 22, 23)
D. The Son of Man in Resurrection and Ascension (chapter 24)

OTHER CHARACTERISTICS

In this Gospel of Christ's perfect manhood, our Lord is shown in his human development, feelings, sympathies, and powers. The evangelist describes Christ's birth, childhood, growth, and social life. In Luke Jesus is seen rejoicing (10:21), weeping (19:41), praying in agony (22:44), eating with ordinary men (7:36-50), fellowshiping with Mary and Martha (10:38-42), lodging with Zacchaeus (19:1-10), and eating with his disciples after the resurrection (24:41-45).

Glimpses of Christ's sympathy and concern for lost and suffering humanity appear throughout the Gospel. The story of the widow of Nain and her son (7:11-15), the account of the raising of Jairus' daughter (8:41, 42, 49-56), and the parable of the Good Samaritan (10: 30-37) all illustrate the tenderness of Christ.

Praise and thanksgiving are also featured in Luke. Often it is said that men "glorified God" (2:20; 5:25, 26; 7:16; 13:13; 17:15; 18:43). Outbursts of praise are found in the book, such as the Ave Maria (1: 28), the Magnificat (1:46-55), the Benedictus (1:68-79), the Gloria in Excelsis (2:14), and the Nunc Dimittis (2:29-32).

Luke is the longest, the most literary, and the most beautiful of the four Gospels. Its classic introduction (1:1-4) recalls the works of Herodotus and Thucydides. Its general vocabulary and diction show that the author was an educated man. Luke's medical background appears in his many medical terms and in his special interest in the ill and their illnesses. Evidencing his careful research (1:1-4), Luke displays high accuracy in the recording of events, as shown by W. M. Ramsay's work on the archeological backgrounds of the Gospel and the Acts. Luke was truly a historian of the highest rank.

John

AUTHOR AND DATE

The fourth Gospel is the work of John, "the disciple whom Jesus loved . . . who also leaned on his breast at supper" (John 21:20, 24). That this was the Apostle John is evidenced by external and internal evidence as substantial as that for any book of the New Testament. The existence of the Gospel is attested in Egypt before A.D. 150 by the Rylands Papyrus 457, the earliest known fragment of a New Testament manuscript. The use of John as an authoritative Gospel along with the other three Gospels is likewise attested by the Egerton Papyrus 2, also dated before A.D. 150. Tatian also evidences the use of John in the *Diatessaron,* and there are traces of Johannine language in Ignatius (A.D. 115) and Justin (A.D. 150-160). The Gospel was also known and used in heretical Gnostic circles around A.D. 150.

Since 1947 the Dead Sea Scrolls, particularly the *Manual of Discipline* and other Essene materials from the last century-and-a-half preceding Jesus' ministry, demonstrate that "there is no reason to date the Gospel after A.D. 90; and it may be earlier" (W. F. Albright, "The Bible after Twenty Years of Archeology," *Religion in Life,* 21:4:152: 550). Remarkably close parallels to the concepts of John's Gospel are found in the Essenic literature; these parallels support the genuineness of John's Gospel as a true product of a Jew living in Jesus' day rather than a forger from a second-century Gnostic environment.

Irenaeus declares that John, the Lord's disciple, published the Gospel at Ephesus. This tradition is reinforced by Clement of Alexandria (A.D. 200). The Muratorian Canon (A.D. 190) espouses authorship by the Apostle John. Some opposition to the apostolic authorship of

Entrance to the Garden Tomb, possible burial – and resurrection! – site of Jesus Christ
(*Russ Busby photo*)

John developed at the beginning of the third century, apparently because the Gospel had been misused by the Gnostics.

Internal evidence for apostolic authorship by John has received its
classic formulation from B. F. Westcott and J. B. Lightfoot (*Biblical
Essays*, 1893, pp. 1-198) on the well-founded basis that the Gospel was
written by a Palestinian Jew and an eyewitness of the events recorded.
Critical attempts to discount this evidence have been futile, especially
the attempts to prove geographical and historical inaccuracies. The
most recent archeology has attested John's geographical accuracy in a
remarkable manner (R. D. Potter, "Topography and Archeology in the
Fourth Gospel," *Studia Evangelica*, pp. 329-337). The allegation that
John was incapable of writing such a masterful treatise because he was
an uneducated man (Acts 4:13) ignores the fact of divine inspiration.

The date of the fourth Gospel is to be assigned between A.D 85
and 95. This is commonly accepted, especially if early tradition that
connects John with Ephesus and Asia Minor is given credence. A later
date, beyond the limits of the apostolic age, is now untenable in the
face of recent manuscript finds.

ORDER AMONG THE GOSPELS

As noted in the preceding Synoptic Gospels, the present order of the four Gospels was established by early tradition. John was usually placed last because it was thought to have been written last. However, John occasionally appears in all four possible positions. During the third and fourth centuries it sometimes occurred first (in Chrysostom, Tertullian, and Latin Codex k). Codex Bezae (D) and other Western documents generally follow the order Matthew, John, Luke, and Mark, assigning first place to the apostles. But the order based on date of writing generally prevailed.

PURPOSE

The author of the fourth Gospel states his purpose in the most explicit terms in John 20:30, 31. He undertakes to set forth the Messiahship and deity-humanity of Jesus (1:1, 14) as the world's Savior-Redeemer (3:16) by presenting irrefutable proofs of these from Christ's miraculous signs. He does this with the avowed evangelistic aim of persuading men to trust in Christ as their Savior and Redeemer (20:31).

This Gospel was penned for the benefit of all sin-cursed and lost mankind. The aim was that the Jew might be convinced that the historical Jesus was indeed "the Christ" and that the Gentile might accept this same Jesus as "the Son of God," the Savior of mankind. The Gospel of John is thus the "Gospel of Belief" and is directed to all men everywhere — Jew, Roman, Greek, and "whosoever believeth" (3: 15, 16; 4:13, 14; 12:46).

Although John's primary purpose in writing the Gospel was evangelistic, he also had instructive and corrective goals in view. He enunciates clearly the true nature of Christ and shows how the perfections of Christ provide a thoroughly adequate basis for human redemption. Through this positive presentation he refutes wrong views of Christ's person held by unbelieving Jews and Gentile gnostics.

PLAN OF JOHN'S GOSPEL

In accordance with his stated purpose of presenting Christ as the Son of God (20:30, 31), John selects eight of our Lord's miracles, six of which are peculiar to this Gospel. All of these reveal Christ's divine-human nature and the life he came to impart.

Miracle one, turning the water to wine (2:1-11), shows the omnipotence of the Son of God and the exhilarating nature of eternal life. Miracle two, the healing of the nobleman's son (4:46-54), reveals faith as the condition for receiving eternal life. Miracle three, healing the cripple at Bethesda (5:1-9), demonstrates the power available to live the new life. Miracle four, the feeding of the five thousand (6:1-14), discloses the Son of God as the Sustainer of eternal life. Miracle five, walking on the sea (6:15-21), illustrates the miraculous nature of eternal life. Miracle six, the restoration of sight (9:1-41), portrays the Son of God as the Light of life. Miracle seven, the raising of Lazarus from the dead (11:1-44), presents the Son of God as the Resurrection and the Life, displaying the victory of life over death. Miracle eight, the supernatural catch of fish (21:1-14), shows the resurrected Son of God as the ideal Guide, supplying full fellowship in the life he imparts by faith.

OUTLINE

A. The Son of God Revealed to the World (chapters 1 — 12)
  1. Prologue: God the Word becomes incarnate (1:1 — 1:14)
  2. John's witness concerning him (1:15-34)
  3. His witness in public ministry (1:35 — 12:50)
     (a) By his miracles (eight throughout the Gospel)
     (b) By his discourses (eleven throughout the Gospel)
B. The Son of God Revealed to His Own (chapters 13 — 17)
  1. As Savior-Sanctifier (chapter 13)
  2. As Bestower of the Spirit (chapters 14, 16)
  3. As Basis of the believer's union with God (chapter 15)
  4. As Intercessor for his own (chapter 17)
C. The Son of God Glorified (chapters 18 — 21)
  1. By his suffering and death (chapters 18, 19)
  2. By his resurrection (chapter 20)
  3. By his post-resurrection commission (chapter 21)

OTHER CHARACTERISTICS

Christ's birth, genealogy, youth, baptism, temptation, transfiguration, and ascension are omitted from John's Gospel because of the strong emphasis on Christ's deity. By contrast, Luke's Gospel contains all of these important human events. Christ's deity is indicated in many other ways in John's Gospel, notably by the many different titles applied to him, such as the Word, the Only-Begotten, the Lamb of

God, the Son of God, the True Bread, the Life, the Resurrection, and the Vine. Many of these are prefixed by the formula "I am," emphasizing Christ's preexistent and eternal deity.

John's Gospel gloriously presents the good news of grace, by which sinners find regeneration and new life in Christ (3:16; 10:10; 20:30, 31). The evangel which Paul expounds theologically in his epistles is anticipated and illustrated in John's Gospel, with special emphasis on the death and resurrection of incarnate deity.

John's Gospel wonderfully predicts the Spirit's advent and the new people of God to be brought into being at Pentecost (chaps. 13–17). Although the word "church" does not occur in the Gospel, it is prefigured in the new vine and branches, which are to replace the old vine (the earthly people Israel). Jesus himself is the stem from whom life flows to the branches, enabling them to bear fruit (chap. 15). This union of vine and branches was to be effected by the Holy Spirit when he came to unite true believers with Christ and with each other (14:16-20; 16:7, 8, 13). The Holy Spirit was also to personally indwell these believers (14:16, 17). All of this finds historical fulfillment in Acts (1:5; 2:4; 11:14-16) and doctrinal exposition in the epistles (1 Cor. 12:12, 13; Rom. 6:3, 4; etc.). Christ's revelation of himself to his own in John chapters 13–17 is thus one of the most sublime passages in all of Holy Scripture.

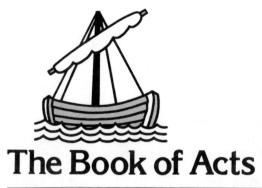

The Book of Acts

TITLE

The title "Acts" or "Acts of the Apostles" is found even in very early manuscripts and refers to the activities of the apostles. Actually only the activities of two apostles are described in any detail—Peter's ministries in chapters 1 — 12 and Paul's evangelization of the Roman Empire in chapters 13 — 28. Acts is therefore not a history of all the apostles but rather a narrative of selected experiences of a few of them. These experiences were selected to show the birth and growth of the Church during the first several decades of Christianity. The title "Acts of the Holy Spirit" has been suggested as an appropriate title for the book, for it is actually the story of the Holy Spirit given as our Lord's ascension gift and working in men to "continue to do and teach" what Jesus merely began (Acts 1:1, 2).

AUTHOR AND DATE

The Book of Acts is the work of Luke, the author of the Gospel of Luke (Luke 1:3, 4; Acts 1:1). The "former treatise" addressed to Theophilus (Acts 1:1; Luke 1:3) is Luke's Gospel. See the biographical sketch of Luke under "Authorship of Luke's Gospel." Luke was a participant in some of the events recorded, indicated by the three "we" passages (16:10-17; 20:5 — 21:18; 27:1 — 28:16).

The evidence for the recognition of Acts as a canonical book does not appear as early or as frequently as the evidence for the Gospels and Paul's epistles, yet sufficient data is available to demonstrate that Acts was early recognized as an authoritative book. The Muratorian Canon, Clement of Alexandria, Tertullian, and Irenaeus all attest the work, and by the time of Eusebius the book was generally acknowledged as part of the Canon.

Internal evidence over and above that given in the discussion of Luke's Gospel is strong for Lukan authorship. The "we" sections in Acts (see above) indicate that the author was one of Paul's companions on his journeys. Similarity of style indicates that the "we" passages were authored by the same person who wrote the rest of Acts. Under no rational hypothesis could these sections in the first person plural be interpolations from some author or source beside Luke. Too, the writer's interest in sickness and the sick and his use of medical language evidence the fact that he was a physician (Col. 4:14).

Scholars date the book either 1) in the decade before the fall of Jerusalem (A.D. 70) or 2) late in the first century or early in the second century. The most probable date is around A.D. 61, soon after the events recorded in Acts 28:30, covering Paul's two-year custody in Rome. The optimistic note on which Acts ends, with Paul being allowed to preach freely in Rome, suggests a period before the outbreak of persecution there in A.D. 64. Scholars who date the book after A.D.

93 surmise dependence of the author upon Josephus. But such dependence is very improbable. If the identification of Theophilus (1:1) were possible, a more precise date for the book could be determined.

PURPOSE

The purpose of the author is first and foremost *historical*. In the Book of Acts Luke continues the account of the origin of Christianity which he began in his Gospel, showing how certain events led to the birth and growth of the Christian Church. Such historical material was needed to show how the life, death, and resurrection of Christ as presented in the Gospels became a vibrant reality in the lives of Christ's followers. This narrative also gives important historical orientation to the New Testament Epistles.

But the historical purpose of Luke is also inseparably connected with a *theological* goal. His history is accurate, even in minute details, but it is not history simply for history's sake. It is the unique history of human and divine interaction, the Holy Spirit working in men through signs and miracles, continuing "to do and teach" what Jesus merely began (1:1). Luke is thus interested in authenticating Christianity as a supernatural regenerating force in a new age in which Christ as Lord operates in and through his people by the Holy Spirit.

In the Book of Acts Luke therefore records the ascension of Christ and his promise to return (chap. 1) as well as the advent of the Spirit and the first historical baptism of the Spirit (chap. 2; see also 1: 5; 11:16). He also records Peter's use of the keys of the kingdom of heaven (see Matt. 16:18, 19) in order to open gospel opportunity to Jews (Acts 2, esp. v. 14), Samaritans (chap. 8, esp. vv. 14-17), and Gentiles (chap. 10, esp. vv. 44-48). Luke traces the spread of the gospel from Jerusalem, Judea, and Samaria to "the uttermost part of the earth" (Acts 1:8).

The purpose of the Acts is also *apologetic.* It supplies proof that the Christian movement was one, whether the believers were Jews, proselytes, Samaritans, Gentiles, or former adherents of John the Baptist. All believed *one* gospel and were baptized by *one* Spirit "into one body" (1 Cor. 12:13), having their oneness *in Christ* (1 Cor. 12:12). Acts likewise presents Paul in the right perspective — not as a renegade and apostate (as his enemies charged), but as God-called and God-approved in his missionary labors. At the same time Acts authenticates the whole Christian movement (Heb. 2:4), connecting it with the redemptive work of the risen and ascended Christ. The author also

Paul ascended Mars Hill to preach the gospel. *(Russ Busby photo)*

shows that Christianity, far from being a menace to imperial law and order, was a peaceful and law-abiding movement. Riots and civil disturbances occurred only when uninformed or prejudiced people (usually unbelieving Jews) stirred up opposition.

OUTLINE

A. Birth of the Church at Jerusalem (chapters 1–12)
  1. The birth of the Church promised (chapter 1)
  2. The birth of the Church effected (chapter 2)
  3. The power of the Church manifested (chapters 3–5)
  4. The persecution of the Church climaxed (chapters 6, 7)
  5. The extension of the Church to Samaritans (chapter 8)
  6. The conversion of the Church's greatest leader (chapter 9)
  7. The extension of the Church to Gentiles (chapters 10–12)
B. Extension of the Church from Antioch (chapters 13–28)
  1. Through Paul's first missionary tour (chapters 13, 14)
  2. Through the decisions of the first Church council (15:1-35)
  3. Through Paul's second missionary tour (15:36–18:22)
  4. Through Paul's third missionary tour (18:23–21:36)
  5. Through Paul's arrest and imprisonment (21:37–28:31)

ARCHEOLOGY

Luke's trustworthiness as a historian has been amply attested by modern archeological research. The author's theological and apologetic interests do not detract from his detailed historical accuracy. These theological and apologetic interests do, however, control his selection and presentation of facts. Luke places his account of Christian origins in the framework of contemporary history. His narrative is replete with references to provincial governors, client kings, city magistrates, etc. These allusions constantly turn out to be correct for the time and place in question. True local color, even of widely differing localities, is reflected in his story. A. T. Robertson has concisely reviewed the evidence for the modern reader in *Luke the Historian in the Light of Research* (New York: Scribner's, 1930), following pioneer work by Sir W. M. Ramsay, the Scottish historian and archeologist, in *St. Paul the Traveller and Roman Citizen* (1895).

THE BAPTISM OF THE SPIRIT

Although the working of the Holy Spirit in the early Christians is a dominating theme in the Acts, the book is *not* a doctrinal treatise on the Holy Spirit, but rather a historical account of the Spirit's operation. That the baptism of the Spirit, *prophetic* in the Gospels (Matt. 3: 11; Mark 1:8; Luke 3:16; John 1:33), became *historical* in Acts on the day of Pentecost (compare Acts 1:5 and 2:4 with 11:14-16) is generally recognized. But what is often forgotten is that the doctrine of the baptism of the Spirit must be formulated *not from the historical account of its occurrence in Acts but from its doctrinal exposition in the Epistles.* There it is revealed to be not an experience but *a position in Christ accomplished by the Spirit for all believers.* It is shown to be an inseparable part of Christ's "so great salvation" (Heb. 2:3), effected upon all believers at the moment they are saved (1 Cor. 12:13; Rom. 6:3, 4; Gal. 3:27).

The baptism of the Spirit was effected on Jewish believers when they were given the gift of the Spirit and introduced to Christ's salvation in Acts 2, upon racially mongrel Samaritans when they were admitted into the same gospel privilege (Acts 8), and upon Gentiles when the gospel opportunity of the new age was extended to them (Acts 10). For each of these ethnic groups the Holy Spirit's baptism was accompanied by his work of regeneration, sealing, and indwelling, at the same time granting each believer the privilege of continual infilling. The infilling, although available to every believer, was to be experienced only by those who comprehend what they are in Christ and act in faith upon that position.

THE CHURCH

Pentecost marked the beginning of the Church, since it occasioned the first historical occurrence of the baptism of the Spirit (Acts 1:5; 2:4; 11:14-16). Only by this operation could the Church be formed, as the Epistles of Paul reveal (1 Cor. 12:12, 13; Rom. 6:3, 4; Gal. 3:27). The Church at first included only believing Jews (Acts 2). Then believing Samaritans were added (Acts 8). When Gentiles were eventually admitted (Acts 10), the normal course of the age was attained. Then Jew and Gentile were constituted *one* in Christ, losing their racial identity (Eph. 3:1-10), and the divine purpose for the age was revealed at the first Church council. God's plan was to visit principally the Gentiles, in order to take out of them the new people of God, the Church; then he would again take up Israel in the kingdom age which followed (Acts 15:14-16).

CHARISMATIC LANGUAGES

Three instances of supernatural utterance of genuine languages unfamiliar to the speaker occur in Acts (2:4; 10:46; 19:6). In each case the miraculous demonstration of the Spirit constituted a sign to the Jews (1 Cor. 1:22). Together with the wind and fire (Acts 2:2, 3), the supernatural languages at Pentecost evidenced to the Jews that the Mosaic age under which they had lived for 1500 years had passed away and that the new age of the Church was dawning. At Caesarea, when Gentiles were admitted to gospel privilege and brought into the benefits of the gift of the Spirit outpoured at Pentecost, the supernatural languages were once again a sign to Peter and the Jews that the Gentiles had not received an inferior salvation to the Jews, but an *identical* gift (Acts 11:17).

The disciples of John the Baptist, who knew only his preparatory baptism in water (Acts 18:25) and nothing at all of the baptism of the Spirit effected by Christ's death and resurrection (Matt. 3:11; Mark 1:8; Luke 3:16; John 1:33), spoke in supernatural languages as a sign to Jews that John's message and baptism had become antiquated. Now that Christ had died, ascended, and given the Holy Spirit from heaven to work out his great salvation in each believer, the Jews must understand that their spiritual heritage included being baptized into union with Christ and with every other believer the moment they believed (1 Cor. 12:12, 13; Rom. 6:3, 4; Gal. 3:27).

IMPORTANCE OF THE BOOK OF ACTS

Acts is a great historical and missionary document and is one of the most indispensable books of the New Testament. It is conceivable that we might get along without one of the Gospels or Epistles. But to be deprived of the Acts would entail irreparable loss. The historical continuity of the Gospels would be broken, the provision of the outpoured Spirit would be largely unknown, the story of the birth and early growth of the Christian church would be an enigma, and the Epistles, especially those of Paul, would exist in an almost total vacuum. In particular, Paul's doctrine of the Holy Spirit would be largely bereft of historical and experiential illustration.

These facts become all the more striking when we remember that the Book of Acts supplies the background for ten of Paul's Epistles (First and Second Thessalonians, First and Second Corinthians, Galatians, Romans, Colossians, Philemon, Ephesians, and Philippians). The book has also blessed the Church with inspiration for missionary and evangelistic fervor, imparting zeal to carry out the great commission of world evangelization and furnishing living illustrations of this outreach in action.

The Epistles of Paul

BACKGROUND

The thirteen letters of Paul and the eight letters by other New Testament writers form a unique collection among the sacred books of the world. Other "Holy Books" — the Vedas, the Zend-Avesta, the Koran, and the writings of Confucius — contain no letters at all. Instead they consist of philosophical discourses, poems, and legendary histories. When Christianity arose in the Greco-Roman world, communication by letters was common in all walks of life. The Apostles thus found an excellent existing means of communicating with the churches they had established.

FORM AND NATURE

Certain features characterize the epistolary form, especially as it was employed by the Apostle Paul: 1) *a salutation or greeting* which identified the author and expressed his well wishes; 2) *an expression of thanksgiving or commendation* for some grace manifested by the specific church addressed; 3) *a main doctrinal section* dealing with some special doctrine or doctrines needing exposition or correction; 4) *a practical instructive section* developed out of the doctrinal portion; 5) *a personal section* containing greetings and brief messages to individuals; and finally 6) *a concise autographic conclusion* authenticating the letter.

CHRONOLOGICAL ORDER

In most versions of the Bible, Paul's thirteen letters are arranged in nonchronological order. The Roman and Corinthian Epistles are usually placed first, apparently because of the size and importance of the cities of Rome and Corinth and because of the length of these Epistles and the significance of their subject matter. But these Epistles were by no means the first written by the Apostle. The probable chronological order of the Pauline Epistles is indicated in the following table:

Epistle	General Period	Approximate Date (A.D.)	Place of Writing
1 Thessalonians	Second Missionary Tour	50	Corinth
2 Thessalonians		51	Corinth
1 Corinthians	Third Missionary Tour	54	Ephesus
2 Corinthians		54	Macedonia
Galatians		55	Corinth
Romans		56	Corinth
Colossians	During the First	61	Rome
Ephesians	Imprisonment	61	Rome
Philemon		61	Rome
Philippians		62	Rome
1 Timothy	After the First	64-66	Macedonia
Titus	Imprisonment	64-66	Uncertain
2 Timothy	During the Second Imprisonment	66-68	Rome

DISTINCTIVES

Two great distinctives characterize the Pauline Epistles. The first of these is the Church's calling, hope, and destiny. The second is the doctrinal exposition of the redemptive work of Christ. The four Gospels describe the one basis of these two distinctive lines of truth—Christ in his flawless person and finished work. The Book of the Acts sketches the results of these historical events in the birth and growth of the Church. The Pauline Epistles expound the doctrinal meaning and theological importance of these events in great detail.

In the parables of the kingdom of heaven in Matthew 13 Christ gave a preliminary revelation about the nature of the era between his rejection at his first advent and his return in glory. However, the union of Jew and Gentile in one new entity, the Church, was not revealed at this time. Instead, it was revealed several years later to the Apostle Paul (Eph. 3:8, 9). In Matthew 16:18 our Lord had preannounced the core of the divine plan regarding the Church, but it was reserved for Paul to expound the position and relationship of the new people of God. Although salvation by grace through faith had always been God's only method of saving fallen men, Paul for the first time expounded this truth in the light of the redemption which Christ had completed on the cross. For the first time in biblical history God's gospel of grace was fully defined by such doctrines as justification, sanctification, and glorification. Paul's Epistles clarify the specific relationship of these doctrines to all believers (Rom. 1—8), to Jews (Rom. 9—11), and to the Law of Moses (Gal. 1—6).

SKETCH OF PAUL'S LIFE

EARLY YEARS (A.D. 5-45). Paul was born at Tarsus (Acts 22:3) about A.D. 5; was educated in Pharisaic Judaism about A.D. 15-25; began his career as a zealous, Christian-hating persecutor about A.D. 25-37; consented to Stephen's death (Acts 7:58) about A.D. 35; was converted near Damascus (Acts 9:3-18) about A.D. 37; resided in Arabia (Gal. 1: 17) about A.D. 37-39; visited Jerusalem (Acts 9:26-29) about A.D. 39; returned to Tarsus (Acts 9:30) in A.D. 39; and ministered at Antioch (Acts 11:25, 26) during A.D. 43-45.

FIRST MISSIONARY TOUR (A.D. 46-47). In A.D. 46 Paul toured both Cyprus (Acts 13:4-12) and Asia Minor—Perga, Pisidian Antioch, Iconium, Lystra, and Derbe (Acts 13:13—14:25). He returned

The Epistles of Paul

to Syrian Antioch (Acts 14:26-28) in A.D. 47 and attended the Jerusalem Council (Acts 15) in A.D. 48.

SECOND MISSIONARY TOUR (A.D. 48-51). Left Antioch by land for Syria and Cilicia (Acts 15:41); revisited Derbe and Lystra (Acts 16: 1-5); evangelized Phrygia, Galatia, Troas, Samothrace, Neapolis, and Philippi (Acts 16:6-40). Proceeded to Thessalonica, Berea, Athens, and Corinth (Acts 17:1 – 18:17). *Wrote First and Second Thessalonians.* Ministered at Ephesus and went on to Caesarea and Jerusalem (Acts 18:18-22), then returned to Antioch (Acts 18:22).

THIRD MISSIONARY TOUR (A.D. 54-58). Revisited and strengthened the churches in Galatia and Phrygia (Acts 18:23) in A.D. 54 and ministered extensively in Ephesus during A.D. 54-57. *Wrote First and Second Corinthians, Galatians, and Romans.* Visited Macedonia, Achaia, Troas, and Miletus (Acts 20:1-38) in A.D. 57. Went on to Jerusalem, where he was arrested (Acts 21:1-36) in A.D. 58.

IMPRISONMENT AND MARTYRDOM (A.D. 58-68). Paul was a prisoner of Rome at Caesarea (Acts 23:23 – 26:32) during A.D. 58-60. The trip to Rome by sea took place in A.D. 60. He was imprisoned in Rome during A.D. 61-63, where he wrote the Prison Epistles: *Colossians, Ephesians, Philemon, and Philippians.* He was apparently released sometime during A.D. 64-67, after which he wrote *First Timothy and Titus.* May have visited Spain, Crete (Tit. 1:5), Asia (2 Tim. 4:13), Macedonia (1 Tim. 1:3), and Greece (2 Tim. 4:20). May have been arrested for a second time in A.D. 67. In any case wrote *Second Timothy* at about this time. Laid down his life for Christ as a martyr in approximately A.D. 68.

Weeds grow in the ruins of the once elegant Roman Forum. *(Russ Busby photo)*

Romans

AUTHOR

The Epistle to the Romans is the work of Paul, the great Apostle to the Gentiles (Rom. 1:1, 7). Internal evidence is strong for Pauline authorship (11:13; 15:15-21). Style, theology, subject matter, and many other factors add their attestation. External evidence is also very abundant, including such witnesses as Clement of Rome, Ignatius, Justin Martyr, Polycarp, Marcion, the Muratorian Canon, and the Old Latin and Syriac Versions. From the time of Irenaeus onward practically all orthodox scholars attest the Epistle as both Pauline and canonical.

BACKGROUND AND DATE

Paul penned the Roman Epistle about A.D. 56, apparently from Corinth during his three-month stay there (Acts 20:2, 3; cf. 1 Cor. 16: 5-7) and near the end of his third missionary tour. The Apostle expressed regret that he had not as yet had the opportunity to visit the believers in the Imperial City (1:10-13; 15:22, 23; cf. Acts 19:21). He reminds the Roman Christians that he must first visit Jerusalem with the money raised for the needy of Judea (Acts 15:25-27). After visiting Rome the Apostle planned a trip to Spain, for which he hoped to enlist the approval and support of the Roman believers (15:24, 28).

IMPORTANCE AND PURPOSE

The Epistle to the Romans heads the thirteen letters of Paul not because it was written first but because it covers the broadest scope of

Christian doctrine. The Roman Epistle can truly be called "The Constitution of Christianity," since it lays the broad foundation upon which the Christian gospel rests. Its subject material, its logical reasoning, its vigorous style, and its relevance to human need accord it a foremost place in divine revelation. In one sense it is a book of great simplicity and clarity and in another sense it is a book of vast profundity. So deep is it, in fact, that it has challenged some of the greatest intellects of the world, men like Augustine, Luther, and Calvin.

"The gospel of God" (1:1) is the subject of the Epistle. This is the good news of the divine redemption of God in Jesus Christ. The gospel of God is the theological exposition of the finished work of Christ. In its broadest sense the term describes the whole body of redemptive truth. Paul designates it "the good news of God" because with God there is no respect of persons (Acts 10:34; Rom. 2:11). He is not the God of the Jews only but of the Gentiles also (3:29). "All the world" is found guilty (3:19), and the salvation presented is as available as the worldwide need. The only human response required in order to obtain this salvation is faith in the finished work of Christ.

Paul's immediate purpose in presenting the gospel of God was to teach the believers at Rome (and throughout the world) the fundamental doctrines of salvation, so that they might be fortified against legalistic perversions of the truths of justification, sanctification, and glorification (chaps. 1 – 8). A further objective in the Apostle's presentation was to explain the unbelief of the majority of Jews and to indicate the nature, extent, and duration of their rejection by God. He shows that the gospel of God does *not* abolish the covenant promises to Israel, but that these will positively be fulfilled after God has completed his Church and has once again reinstated his people Israel (chaps. 9 – 11).

In the light of the glorious provisions of the gospel of God Paul also purposed to urge his readers to appropriate in daily experience the full blessing of the Christian life. This they were to do by surrendering completely to God (chap. 12), by being subject to existing governmental powers and by loving one another (chap. 13), and by exercising forbearance toward the weak (chaps. 14, 15). Paul also had in mind commending Phoebe, the deaconess, to the church at Rome (16:1-4) as well as conveying greetings to many of the friends he had acquired in his evangelistic travels throughout the Empire.

OUTLINE

A. The Gospel of God Expounded (chapters 1 – 8)

1. Introduction and theme (1:1-17)
2. The world's need of the gospel (1:18 – 3:20)
3. The gospel and justification by faith (3:21 – 5:11)
4. The gospel and sanctification by faith (5:12 – 8:39)
B. The Gospel of God and Israel's Rejection (chapters 9 – 11)
1. The tragedy (9:1-5)
2. The justice (9:6-29)
3. The cause (9:30 – 10:21)
4. The extent (11:1-10)
5. The duration (11:11-36)
C. The Gospel of God and its Application to the Believer (12:1 – 15:13)
1. To his dedication (12:1, 2)
2. To his gifts (12:3-8)
3. To his relationship to other believers (12:9-16)
4. To his relationship to unbelievers (12:17-21)
5. To his relationship to the state (13:1-14)
6. To his relationship to the weaker believer (14:1 – 15:13)
D. Conclusion and Greetings (15:14 – 16:27)

THE SAVED AND THE LOST

Are the heathen lost if they have never heard the gospel? Is it possible for good, moral, and religious people, either in pagan or Christian lands, to be lost? If so, what is the basis of being saved or lost? The Book of Romans, as an exposition of the gospel of grace, necessarily deals with these crucial questions. It declares that *all* members of Adam's fallen race are lost sinners, are alienated from God, and are totally unable to save themselves or to stand before God's infinitely holy presence (1:18 – 3:20). They are *all* shown to be under his wrath (the eternal and unchangeable antagonism of God against sin) and under the curse of threefold death – spiritual death (severed fellowship with God), physical death (inevitable death of the body), and eternal death (separation from God for all eternity) (1:18-32). This is true of moral and good-living pagans as well as immoral ones (2:1-29). It is equally true of unbelieving Jews, moral as well as immoral (3:1-8). God's verdict is that *the whole world* of unregenerate mankind stands guilty and condemned before him (3:9-20).

The Book of Romans teaches that *no one* will attain eternal life except persons who have been justified (declared righteous) by God himself (3:21 – 5:11). Such a declaration results not from possessing some supposed personal righteousness based on self-effort or good deeds, but from having God's own righteousness imputed to the believing sinner who puts his entire trust in Christ's completed work of redemption. Before the cross this reckoning was made on the basis of what God's grace *would do* for the sinner through Christ (Gen. 15:6). After the cross the reckoning is made on the basis of what God's grace *has done* for the sinner through the death and resurrection of Christ (3: 24-26).

Accordingly, Romans reveals that *only* those who have God's righteousness actually reckoned to their account are justified by him and possess eternal life (1:17). Conversely, *all* who are so justified are at the same time sanctified (5:12−7:25) and guaranteed glorification (8:30). This constitutes the great dividing line between heaven and hell and the saved and unsaved. Men are placed on either side *solely on the basis of their faith in Christ as God's provision for human sin.*

In the light of these revealed truths, are men really lost? The Epistle to the Romans answers with an emphatic *Yes.* Men are lost not because they are "good" or "bad" by human standards but because they have failed to receive God's perfect righteousness made available to them by faith in Christ.

Are the lost without excuse? This Epistle, as the grand unfolding of the gospel of God, deals with this vexing question. It reveals not only that all unbelievers are lost, but that they are *without excuse* as well. This is true of the unsaved in Christian lands as well as the lost in pagan lands, including those who have never had any chance to hear the gospel. This fact raises serious moral and ethical questions in the minds of finite, fallible men and causes them to question the justice and love of a perfect God. To aid us in grappling with this facet of revealed truth, the Epistle presents the following facts that disclose *why* the lost are without excuse.

The lost are without excuse because they have the revelation of the created universe all around them. The heathen may not have the gospel and the Word of God brought by the missionary, but they have the revelation of the power and deity of God in the book of creation. In this book "that which is known about God is evident" to the pagans and it is "made plain in their inner consciousness, because God (Himself) has shown it to them. For ever since the creation of the world His invisible nature and attributes, that is, His eternal power and divinity, have been made intelligible and clearly discernible in and through the things that have been made−His handiworks. So (men) are without excuse−altogether without any defense or justification" (1:19, 20, *Amplified Bible*).

If pagans read the wide-open book of creation, they will find that "the heavens declare the glory of God, and the firmament shows and proclaims His handiwork. Day after day pours forth speech, and night after night shows forth knowledge. There is no speech nor spoken word (from the stars); their voice is not heard. Yet their voice (in evidence) goes out through all the earth, their sayings to the end of the world" (Psa. 19:1-4, *Amplified Bible*).

If men will read and believe the testimony of God's book of creation and walk in the light which it sheds on their path, God will grant them added light by sending them his book of revelation and redemption through the missionary. If he does not, he will judge each man according to the light with which that man has been favored.

The lost are without excuse because they do not follow the light they have been given in the created universe. Like the ancient heathen, the present-day pagan rejects the testimony of nature. "Because when they" (the heathen who apprehend God through the revelation of creation) "knew and recognized Him as God" (1:19), "they did not honor and glorify Him as God, or give Him thanks . . ." (1:21), *Amplified Bible*). As a result they gradually sank into idolatry. Paganism itself constitutes a witness that God had implanted in the human mind the concept of deity by means of creation, for the concept of a single supreme being appears at the root of all the varied forms of paganistic worship. But instead of receiving the full light of creation, man chose to withdraw his heart and will from it, thereby quenching truth instead of developing it and thus sinking into ever-increasing darkness.

The lost are without excuse because they deliberately and knowingly choose the course of lawlessness and rejection of God. They are guilty because they persist in idolatry and sin and methodically banish the knowledge of God from their thinking (1:28). Despite their realization of the judgment of God upon evildoers, they approve and applaud them (1:32). For this reason God gives them up (1:24, 26, 28) to follow their own sinful course of action to its disastrous end.

The lost are without excuse because they stifle the voice of conscience. The creator has endowed all his creatures with a conscience, that God-implanted inner monitor that tells a man right from wrong. In youth conscience is tender and supple. It responds to truth and light, including God's revelation of himself in his creation. However, when this light is rejected the conscience becomes seared and insensitive. Paul writes that the conscience of the heathen "bears witness" to their actions, "their thoughts the meanwhile accusing or excusing them" (2:15).

Is God unjust and unloving in reprobating the lost? How about those who have never had the opportunity to hear the gospel of saving grace? Is God unjust in condemning these? The answer from the Roman Epistle is *No!* God is not unfair or unloving in condemning *any* lost soul. The Epistle gives the following reasons:

God is not unjust or unloving in reprobating the lost because they are all guilty and without excuse before him. They have no grounds for defense or self-justification because they have rejected the light given to them — that of creation and conscience (see preceding two sections).

God is not unjust or unloving in reprobating the lost because in his sovereign will and long-range purpose he is unimpugnable by finite and erring creatures. He is infinitely holy, just, and impartial as well as infinitely compassionate. "His judgment is according to truth" (2:2). "There is no respect of persons with him" (2:11). He is "faithful, true, and righteous" (3:3-5). He is loving, commending "his love toward us . . . while we were yet sinners" (5:8). He is merciful, yet his mercy is guided by his sovereign will (9:14-24). "He has mercy on whomever He wills (chooses) and He hardens — makes stubborn and unyielding the heart of — whomever He wills" (9:18, *Amplified Bible*).

This manifestation of mercy on the basis of sovereign will appears unreasonable, if not unjust, to sin-blinded men, but only because they cannot discern the full sweep of God's purpose in the case of both saved and the lost. Thus their criticism of God is "Why then does He still find fault and blame us (for sinning)? For who can resist and withstand His will?" (9:19, *Amplified Bible*).

To this objection the Apostle Paul shows that God, being infinitely sovereign and all-wise, is absolutely above the carping criticism of his finite creatures. "But who are you, a mere man, to criticize and contradict and answer back to God? Will what is formed say to him that formed it, 'Why have you made me thus?' " (9:20, *Amplified Bible;* cf. Isa. 29:16; 45:9).

The divine Potter has the absolute right to make of the clay whatever vessel he wishes for whatever purpose he plans. In the final analysis his plan will redound to his eternal glory in the case of both the saved (the vessels unto honor) and the unsaved (the vessels unto dishonor) (9:21). In the case of the saved he will advertise "the riches of the glory" of his love and grace in "vessels of mercy" prepared for glory (9:23). In the case of the unsaved ("the vessels of wrath fitted for destruction"), he will vindicate his holiness and wrath against sin and will reveal his power (9:22).

God is not unjust or unloving in reprobating the lost because he is not obligated to save any, much less all. All members of Adam's fallen race "have sinned and come short of the glory of God" (3:23). Even the best fall short of the divine standard of holiness and hence cannot claim to merit salvation (3:10-23). All of the unsaved are entirely bereft of any righteousness of their own (3:11) and are thus "concluded under sin" (3:9), that is, are completely under sin's dominion and condemnation and are entirely cut off from the love and mercy of God because of his holiness. Only as God freed his love and mercy to act in behalf of fallen men in accord with his holiness could God save *any* of the ruined race. This he did through Christ. Now he can manifest his mercy and grace to save some, in accord with his sovereign will and unimpugnable choice.

God is not unjust or unloving in reprobating the lost because he will judge them and all men on the basis of their works. This must be so, and is revealed to be so, because he is a just, impartial, and fair Judge (2:2, 11; 3:3-5). "For He will render to every man according to his works—justly, as his deeds deserve" (2:6, *Amplified Bible*). God's principles of judgment are outlined (2:1-16). "To those (the saved) who by patience in well-doing seek for glory and honor and immortality, he will give eternal life" (2:7, RSV). They will be rewarded for fidelity in service at the judgment seat of Christ (14:10-12; 2 Cor. 5:10).

"But for those who are factious and do not obey the truth, but obey wickedness (the unsaved), there will be wrath and fury" (2:8, RSV; cf. Rev. 20:11-15). What the sinner does with God's grace revealed in Christ will determine his eternal destiny in heaven (the sin-cleansed universe) or in hell (the one eternal isolation ward for fallen angels and unregenerate men).

God is not unjust or unloving in reprobating the lost because this divine act, like all the divine actions, is regulated by moral law. This moral law, reflected in the Decalogue given to Israel from Sinai (Exod. 20:1-17), is as eternal and unchangeable as God himself, for it is a reflection of his divine being and character. This law, far from saving sinners, shows them their lost and helpless condition (3:19, 20) and drives them to God's grace in Christ so that they can be saved by faith. Nevertheless, even though God's moral law was never meant to be a means of salvation, it is binding upon every human being, both saved and the unsaved, as a way of life.

Man's response to this moral law conditions his actions. Although the unsaved cannot keep the moral law inwardly and vitally, as the saved can, they are nevertheless expected to keep it outwardly in living decent, law-abiding lives. The degree to which they keep this law outwardly determines their degree of punishment in eternal hell. Correspondingly, the degree to which the saved keep this law determines the degree of their reward in heaven.

THE ROMAN EPISTLE, A CRITERION TO DETECT DOCTRINAL ERROR

As a masterful exposition of the salvation purchased by Jesus Christ on the cross, Romans furnishes the criterion by which all basic teachings about the Christian faith are to be tested. Doctrinal subjects which frequently require such examination include the gospel, salvation, justification, sanctification, security, and Christian liberty. These are discussed in the following paragraphs.

THE GOSPEL. The gospel is frequently misrepresented as *something that man does for God*. But in Romans Paul presents the gospel as *everything that God has done for man through Christ*—to be accepted wholly by faith plus nothing (3:24). Another perversion of the gospel is to view it as a matter of *faith plus works*. But Paul shows that works which God can accept follow *salvation*—springing out of it—and never produce it in any degree.

Man often presents only the gospel for the sinner: "Christ died for me." Romans presents the gospel for the saint as well: "I died in Christ and was buried, raised, ascended, and seated with him in the heavenlies" (Rom. 6:1-10). Reckoning on this fact, that is, believing it to be true (Rom. 6:11), enables the believer to obtain daily victory over sin and to enjoy all that has been given to him through Christ (Rom. 8:1-39).

SALVATION. This term includes everything that Christ accomplished on the cross for the sinner (1:16). It is derived from the Greek word *soteria*, meaning "safety," "soundness," or "security," and includes such elements as justification, regeneration, sanctification, glorification, redemption, propitiation, forgiveness, and eternal life. Salvation is a gift received by faith and is totally disconnected from acts of supposed merit on the part of the recipient (1:17; 3:20-24). The gift of salvation contains all of the aforementioned elements and can never be forfeited, either in whole or in part. As a gift from God the salvation of the individual rests securely on the eternal faithfulness of God and cannot be conditioned by human failure.

JUSTIFICATION. Justification is an official act by which God renders a guilty sinner righteous because the condemned one has trusted Christ as his sin-bearer. The individual is not only acquitted of all charges but is pronounced positively righteous (3:22, 24-28; 4:5-8, 22-25; 5:1, 9, 16-21). This foundational element of salvation finds its fullest and grandest exposition in all of Scripture in Romans 3:21−5:21. This vital truth became the clarion call of the Protestant Reformation under Martin Luther.

SANCTIFICATION AND GLORIFICATION. Both of these result from union with Christ by the Spirit's baptizing work in salvation. These too receive their fullest and grandest exposition in Scripture in Romans, in chapters 6−8. This Epistle is the great corrective of common errors on sanctification, presenting this truth in its three aspects — past, present, and future — and inseparably connecting the future aspect with glorification.

SECURITY AND ASSURANCE. Both of these important themes also have their grandest and fullest treatment in Romans, which again serves as the great corrective against popular errors that cluster around these two vital, interrelated themes.

THE FUTURE OF ISRAEL. That God has a future for the nation of Israel in the age to come is most clearly and emphatically taught in this Epistle (chaps. 9−11). This too serves as a corrective for popular errors that deny such a future to the Jewish nation. In dealing with Israel's rejection in the light of Gentile salvation, the Apostle sets forth not only the justice (9:1-29), cause (9:30−10:21), and extent (11:1-10) of that rejection, but its duration as well (11:11-24). He shows that when "the times of the Gentiles" have run their course, the kingdom will be established over Israel (11:25-36).

CHRISTIAN LIBERTY. The entire Epistle to the Romans is an antidote against the poison of legalism which Judaizing teachers were always eager to inject into the grace and truth which Christ had introduced by his salvation. The Christians at Rome and elsewhere were also in danger of becoming enslaved to legalistic issues of conscience and conduct. So the Apostle applies the principles of grace to matters of everyday living: avoid judging fellow believers (14:1-12), discontinue any practice that would offend a brother in Christ (14:13-23), and follow the initiative of love which Christ exemplified (15:1-13).

1 Corinthians

AUTHOR

That Paul wrote First Corinthians is abundantly attested by internal evidence (1:1; 3:4, 6, 22; 16:21) and by the manner in which the book reflects the historical notices of Acts 18:1-18. External evidence of Pauline authorship is also abundant from the first century onward. Clement of Rome, Ignatius, Polycarp, Justin Martyr, and many others attest the genuineness of the Epistle. Clement of Alexandria and Tertullian especially quote extensively from this Epistle.

BACKGROUND AND DATE

In Acts 18:1-11 Luke recounts the circumstances of the founding of the church at Corinth. This metropolis was the most splendid commercial city of Greece, strategically situated just south of the narrow isthmus connecting central Greece with the Peloponnesus. The city was the mecca of trade between the East and West. Its eastern port was Cenchrea (Rom. 16:1) and its western emporium was Lechaeum. The city derived rich income from the transport of cargoes across the narrow isthmus (which was not successfully bridged by a canal until 1881-1893).

As a port city Corinth was both wealthy and immoral. So dissolute was the city that the term "to Corinthianize" was coined to denote the very practice of immorality. If ever the gospel had a place to prove its power (Rom. 1:16, 17), it was at Corinth. It was therefore especially encouraging that "many of the Corinthians, hearing, believed and were baptized" (Acts 18:8). In a night vision the Lord assured Paul that he had "much people in this city" (Acts 18:10). So successful was the gospel outreach at Corinth that the Apostle remained there a year-and-a-half, "teaching the word of God" (Acts 18:11).

Paul probably penned this first letter to the Corinthians about A.D. 54, although a slightly later date is possible. See the discussion under "The Date of First Corinthians and Its Relevance to the Question of Spiritual Gifts."

Revelry is ended and life silenced in Old Corinth. (*Russ Busby photo*)

IMPORTANCE AND PURPOSE

The immediate occasion of the letter was an inquiry from Corinth about marriage and several other matters (7:1). But Paul also used this opportunity to deal with several other problems that were troubling the Corinthian church at this time. What makes the Epistle so vital is that these same problems have vexed local churches in every age, including our own. The following chart lists these problems and the Apostle's directives.

Problem	Inspired Solution
Factions and Divisions (1:10—4:21)	Stop following human leaders and follow Christ instead. Count on him for unity with all believers (1:10-17). Stop relying on human wisdom and rely upon Christ, God's wisdom (1:18—2:16). Avoid carnality (3:1-4); regard service as rendered to God and rewarded by God (3:5-23); regard God's servant as judged by God (4:1-8). Follow only godly apostolic example (4:9-21).
Gross Immorality Accompanied by Indifference (5:1-13)	Offender to be excommunicated and formally delivered to Satan and physical death as the ultimate in chastisement (5:5-13).
Litigation in Pagan Courts (6:1-8)	For a Christian to sue another Christian was shameful enough (6:7), but to take the case to pagan courts was even more shameful. Christians will judge angels and are competent to judge such cases (6:1-6).
General Immorality (6:9-20)	Immorality is totally at variance with the standards of God's kingdom and rewards (6:9, 10) as well as with the believer's position of justification and cleansing (6:11). Temperance and chastity are mandatory because the body is destined for glorification (6:12-14), is joined to Christ (6:15-17), belongs to God as the temple of the Spirit (6:18, 19), and is the vehicle with which God is to be glorified (6:20).
Misunderstanding of Marriage and Celibacy (7:1-9, 25-29)	Celibacy is good (7:1) if one has a special gift from God (7:7), has self-control to avoid sin, and is not inflamed with passion (7:8). If this is not the case, marriage is advocated, but it is to be strictly monogamous and "in the Lord" (7:7, 39, 40). Married couples are not to deny one another intercourse, except for a time and only by mutual consent for prayer (7:3-5). To marry or to remain single is a matter for individual determination before God (7:25). Marriage entails economic responsibilities and worldly troubles (7:26-31). The unmarried state permits a person to serve God without distraction (7:32-35). But marriage is a necessity for those who cannot control their passions (7:36-38).
Misuse of Divorce (7:10-17)	A Christian wife should not separate from her husband. If she does she must either be reconciled or remain unmarried. The husband should not divorce his wife. But if he must, whether or not he has a right to remarry is *not* specified.

Problem	Inspired Solution
Misuse of Christian Liberty (8:1–11:1)	Example: partaking of food offered to idols is in itself harmless, but it becomes a sin if it offends a weaker brother. Hence the practice is to be avoided if it offends (8:1-13). Example: receiving remuneration for Christian ministry is proper and right. Yet Paul would gladly forego this right rather than hinder the effectiveness of his ministry (9:1-14) or be a stumblingblock (9:15-23) or fall in the Christian race (9:24-27). Self-indulgence is to be avoided (10:1-13) as well as all complicity with idol (demon) worship (10:14-22). The law of love is to guide in the exercise of Christian liberty (10:23-33).
Violation of the Order of the Sexes (11:2-16)	The woman is subordinate to the man, denoted by her headdress, as the man in turn is subordinate to Christ (11:2-6). As a token of this a woman should not pray or prophesy with her head unveiled or uncovered. By the same token a man should not pray or prophesy with his head covered or wear long hair like a woman (11:7-16).
Irreverent Participation in the Lord's Supper (11:17-34)	No one is worthy to partake of this ordinance except those who are redeemed. Yet those who are redeemed may partake in an unworthy manner because of unconfessed sin. The penalty is divine chastening of the sinning saint, possibly even to the point of physical death, so that he might not be lost with the world.
Misuse of Spiritual Gifts (12:1–14:40)	Spiritual gifts are given and controlled by the Holy Spirit (12:1-7). Nine such gifts were operative in the apostolic Church (12:8-11). The body of Christ is formed by the baptism of the Spirit and is composed of all believers (12:12-31). The gifts as operative in people are listed in 12:28-31. To be of value these must be exercised in love (13:1-8), which, along with faith and hope, will remain throughout the Church age (13:13). However, three gifts were to be in operation only until the New Testament was completed (13:8-13). These include directly inspired prophecies, knowledge, and supernatural languages (13:8). When the New Testament would be completed and God's full revelation available, these sources of truth would no longer be needed. However, their regulation in the early Church, in which they *were* needed, is indicated in Chapter 14.
Denial of Physical Resurrection (15:1-58)	The denial (15:12) does not take into account the fact (15:1-11) or the necessity of bodily resurrection (15:12-19). Christ's resurrection assures physical resurrection for all who are "in Christ" (15:20-23). The "first resurrection" will be in stages (15:23): 1) Christ's resurrection; 2) later those that are Christ's at his coming (1 Thess. 4:13-18); 3) "the end" (15:24), that is, *the end of the first resurrection.* This is coterminous with the second resurrection of the unsaved (Rev. 20:11-15), after the Millennium. It will involve believers who die during the kingdom age. Paul expounds the logic of the resurrection (15:29-34) and the nature of the resurrection body (15:35-50). The hope of the resurrection forms the secret of Christian confidence (15:51-58).

THE DATE OF FIRST CORINTHIANS
AND ITS RELEVANCE TO THE QUESTION
OF SPIRITUAL GIFTS

First Corinthians was apparently written from Ephesus (1 Cor. 16: 8, 9) during the latter period of Paul's three-year ministry in that city (Acts 20:31; cf. 19:8-22). The spring of A.D. 54 is the most plausible date, though some scholars would date it as late as A.D. 59. It is important to remember that when First Corinthians was written there was practically no New Testament in existence (except the Book of James, addressed to Hebrew Christians, and First and Second Thessalonians). Even these had very limited circulation.

Only in the light of these facts can Paul's instructions on the permanent versus the impermanent gifts of the Spirit in chapter 13 be understood. Love is permanent and all-essential (13:1-8a) and is contrasted with certain gifts that were impermanent and would eventually be superseded. These temporary gifts included direct inspirational prophecy, direct inspirational knowledge, and supernatural languages. Before the New Testament was written and became readily available by circulation, groups of Christians had only the Old Testament to preach and expound when they gathered together for worship and instruction.

Dependence for New Testament truth therefore had to be placed almost completely on the direct ministry of the Spirit through the inspired prophet, rather than on the expositor of Scripture, as is done today. The inspired teacher endowed with the gift of wisdom and knowledge would receive spontaneous revelations from the Holy Spirit during the course of the church service, and would immediately convey the message to the congregation. Often the directly inspired prophet or teacher would present the message supernaturally in a foreign language, which was afterwards translated into the vernacular by someone endowed with the gift of interpretation.

The Apostle envisioned the time when the New Testament Scriptures would be completed. The partial revelation so essential in his time would give way to "that which is perfect" (literally "the complete and final *thing*" — v. 10), meaning the completed Canon of Scripture, as the context shows. Paul then illustrates the early period of the Church, when it had to depend on partial, spontaneous revelation through special gifts. He employs the figures of a child growing to maturity (v. 11) and an indistinct image in a metal mirror. This was the doctrinal situation before the true mirror of the New Testament became available. "Now I know in part," Paul declares of that early period, "but then I shall know even as I am known" — by the Lord himself as revealed in his Word, the New Testament Scriptures.

2 Corinthians

AUTHOR

The intensely personal and autobiographical nature of this Epistle, as well as its distinctive theology and eschatology, plainly stamp it as genuinely Pauline. External evidence for the existence and early use of the letter (especially second-century evidence) is virtually unchallenged.

BACKGROUND AND DATE

Sometime after Paul had sent his first letter to the Corinthians, news apparently reached him of discord perpetrated at Corinth by the Judaizing party (11:4, 5, 12, 13, 20-23). An immediate visit showed that the reports were true, for Paul had apparently been openly flouted by the Corinthian assembly. Returning to Ephesus, he penned a severe epistle (2:3, 4, 9; 7:8, 12) and sent it to Corinth (probably by Titus — 7: 6-8) with the instruction to return with news from Corinth. This severe epistle has not survived, although some scholars imagine that it is preserved in chapters 10 – 13 of Second Corinthians.

Eventually Paul met Titus in Macedonia (2:12, 13). His news was good. The crisis had passed, and the church had been reconciled to Paul. With deep emotion Paul wrote the letter now known as Second Corinthians. It was penned not long after First Corinthians, possibly as early as autumn, A.D. 54, or conceivably a year or so later. Shortly thereafter Paul traveled to Corinth and spent three months there (Acts 20:1-3), during which time he wrote to the Romans.

IMPORTANCE AND PURPOSE

Paul wrote Second Corinthians for at least the following reasons: 1) to explain how God's comfort sustained him abundantly in his trials in Asia (1:3-11); 2) to explain why he changed his plans to return to Corinth (1:12 – 2:4); 3) to give further instructions about the treatment of the offender of First Corinthians (2 Cor. 2:5-11; 1 Cor. 5:1-8); 4) to express his joy at the good news from the Corinthians (2:12, 13); 5) to demonstrate the superiority of the gospel ministry to the Law ministry (2:14 – 6:10); 6) to issue a call for separation from evil and for reconciliation with him (6:11 – 7:16); 7) to urge the Corinthians to consummate the offering for the poor (chaps. 8, 9); and 8) to establish his authority as an apostle (chaps. 10 – 13).

OUTLINE

A. The Glory of the Christian Ministry (chapters 1 – 7)
  1. Concerned for the salvation and welfare of others (1:1 – 2:4).
  2. Concerned for the restoration of offenders (2:5-11).
  3. Concerned for the well-being of churches (2:11-13).
  4. Glorious in service under the New Covenant (2:14 – 7:16).
    (a) Triumphant (2:14-17).
    (b) Accredited (3:1-5).
    (c) Spiritual and non-legal (3:6-18).
    (d) Honest and dynamic (4:1-18).
    (e) Noble in its ambition (5:1-10).
    (f) Exalted in its motives (5:11-21).
    (g) Supernatural in its results (6:1-10).
    (h) Sublime in its appeal for separation from sin (6:11 – 7:1).
    (i) Zealous in its call for true repentance (7:2-16).
B. The Grace of Christian Giving (chapters 8, 9)
  1. Christians first giving themselves (8:1-6).
  2. Christians following Christ's example (8:7-15).
  3. Christians providing for legitimate needs (8:16-24).
  4. Christians realizing no one can outgive God (9:1-15).
C. Paul's Defense of His Ministry (chapters 10 – 13)
  1. Divinely authenticated (10:1-18).
  2. Characterized by godly jealousy (11:1, 2).

3. Fruitful in its warning against false teachers (11:3-15).
4. Free of empty boasting (11:16-33).
5. Authenticated by visions and revelations (12:1-6).
6. Tested by severe physical sufferings (12:7-10).
7. Possessed apostolic credentials (12:11-18).
8. Faithful in exhortation against evil (12:19—13:14).

PAUL'S "THORN IN THE FLESH"

In describing the glory of the Christian ministry and defending his apostolic authority against enemy attack, Paul refers to the visions and revelations which the Lord granted him. He tells how he was caught up to "the third heaven," to paradise, the place of God's abode and manifested glory (12:1-6). Alongside such experiences of God's glory he relates experiences of his testing and chastening, including his "thorn in the flesh." This was some painful affliction in his physical body that had mental, psychological, and emotional repercussions.

The vehicle of suffering is specified only as an "angel" or "messenger" of Satan to buffet him. It was apparently some physical weakness caused by Satanic or demonic power and permitted by God, but not removable by prayer or faith (12:7-10). It had the specific divine purpose of keeping the Apostle humble in the face of all the visions and revelations accorded him. It was also intended to show him that God's grace is completely adequate for his tested servants and that his strength is fully realized only in human weakness. God's servants are therefore to glory in human weakness, so that divine power may rest upon them. They are to remember that when they are weak in themselves they are strong in Christ.

GENERAL CHARACTERISTICS OF THE EPISTLE

Second Corinthians has been aptly described as the Apostle Paul's defense of his life. It contains some teaching, but it is not doctrinal or instructive in the strictest sense of the term. As the most autobiographical of all of Paul's Epistles, Second Corinthians lays bare the heart and soul of one of God's greatest servants. The Apostle here presents the most magnificent portrait of the glory of the Christian ministry to be found anywhere in the Scriptures. The Epistle illustrates the effectiveness of personal integrity and testimony in service for Christ. In alluding to the offering taken for the poor saints of Judea, the Epistle also contains the most extended biblical passage (chaps. 8 and 9) on giving and stewardship.

Galatians

AUTHOR

Both external and internal evidence of the Pauline genuineness of Galatians is abundant from the first century on; by the second century Galatians had become a rather popular Epistle. Irenaeus, Tertullian, and Clement of Rome quote it freely and ascribe it to Paul. It is validated by the Old Syriac, the Old Latin, and the Muratorian Canon.

Internal evidence is also strong. Every sentence of the Epistle clearly reflects the life and character of its author. Twice he calls himself Paul (1:1; 5:2). The historical background of Galatians readily harmonizes with the Acts, and its contents are so presented as to lie far beyond the reach of a forger, even if an adequate purpose could be found for such a forgery. Critical attempts to deny Pauline authorship to Galatians have been dismal failures.

BACKGROUND AND DATE

The Galatians were residents of the Roman province of Galatia. This included not only the territory of Galatia proper, inhabited mainly by Celts from Gaul, but also portions of Lycaonia, Pisidia, and Phrygia, all located toward the south. Paul and Barnabas established churches among these people in the cities of Antioch (of Pisidia), Iconium, Lystra, and Derbe on their first missionary tour (Acts 13, 14). Most scholars hold that these churches were the ones which Paul addressed in Galatians 1:2. Some believe, however, that the Galatian churches were peopled by residents of northern Galatia, the old territorial designation of the Celts' original settlement in the third century

B.C. This included the region in and near the cities of Pessinus, Ancyra, and Tavium (Acts 16:6).

However, Paul's reference to Barnabas (Gal. 2:1, 9, 13) would be unexplainable in a letter sent to northern Galatia. In addition, the Galatians were personal acquaintances among whom Paul had worked (4:13-15). In the south Galatian cities there were Jews who might well have introduced the legalistic error mentioned in the Galatian Epistle (Acts 13:14-51; 14:1; 16:1-3). Moreover, Acts 16:6 gives no hint of a protracted mission in Northern Galatia, as would be required by the Northern Galatian theory. Nor does the view of the Church Fathers lend support to this view. In the second century the Roman province was again restricted to ethnic Galatia, and the double meaning of the term which had been current in the apostolic era disappeared. The Church Fathers simply adopted the designation of their day.

The question of the date and place of writing of this Epistle cannot be answered decisively, and views vary among exponents of the Northern and Southern Galatian theories. The most plausible view is that the Epistle was written about the same time Paul wrote to the Corinthians and the Romans (approximately A.D. 55 or 56) and most likely from Macedonia or Greece on the third missionary tour.

IMPORTANCE AND PURPOSE

The Epistle to the Galatians is the Magna Charta of Christian liberty. Along with the Epistle to the Romans, Galatians became the battle cry of the Protestant Reformation. Martin Luther considered it in a special sense his own Epistle. Under inspiration Paul penned it as a powerful polemic against legalistic teachers who came in to undermine his proclamation of the gospel of the grace of God. These legalists professed to be Christians, acknowledging Jesus as the Messiah. However, they violated the simplicity of the gospel of free grace by insisting that circumcision and obedience to the Mosaic Law must be added to faith in Christ in order to assure salvation (2:16; 3:2, 3; 4:10, 21; 5:2-4; 6:12). Their teaching was a mixture of Judaism and Christianity, based on the false premise that Christianity could operate only within the sphere of the Mosaic Law. Faith in Christ was not sufficient, according to them. Had these legalists gone unchallenged, Christianity would have become a mere sect of Judaism. The challenge called forth a masterpiece of inspired logic and doctrinal truth. With flying colors the Apostle vindicates Christianity on the sole basis of the redemptive work of Christ. Men are both justified and sanctified by what God has done for them in Christ through grace. In no sense is their acceptance in either time or eternity based on works they perform or on rituals they observe. The Book of Galatians echoes the simplicity of justification and sanctification so masterfully expounded in the Epistle to the Romans.

OUTLINE

Introduction (1:1-5)
A. Vindication of Paul's Apostolic Authority (1:6 – 2:21)
   1. The occasion of his vindication (1:6, 7)
   2. The authenticity of his gospel (1:8-10)
   3. The divine origin of his apostleship (1:11-24)
   4. The official endorsement of his apostleship (2:1-10)
   5. The consistency of his conduct (2:11-21)
B. Defense of Paul's Doctrine of Justification (chapters 3, 4)
   1. The defection of the Galatians (3:1-5)
   2. The witness of Abraham (3:6-9)
   3. The redemptive work of Christ (3:10-14)
   4. The Law and the Abrahamic Covenant (3:15-18)
   5. The function of the Law (3:19-22)
   6. The superiority of faith over Law (3:23 – 4:11)
   7. The Apostle's appeal against a return to bondage (4:12-20)
   8. The relation between the Old and New Covenants (4:21-31)
C. Exposition of God's Blessing of Liberty (chapters 5, 6)
   1. Its imperilment by legalism (5:1-12)
   2. Its definition (5:13-15)
   3. Its proper use (5:16-26)
   4. Its practical manifestation (6:1-10)
   5. Its relation to the cross (6:11-16)
   6. Its price (6:17)
   7. Its benediction (6:18)

JUSTIFICATION
AND THE PURPOSE OF THE LAW

Since Paul in Galatians demonstrates that justification is by faith and faith alone (3:1 – 4:31), the question naturally arises, "What then is the purpose of the Mosaic Law?" (3:19a). The Apostle's answer (3:

19b-29) presents the following purposes. The Mosaic law was placed by the side of ("added to") grace (the grace of God shown to men in anticipation of the cross) that had operated from the fall and ever since the fall of man "for the sake of transgressions." It was given to reveal clearly to *all* men through the nation Israel that sin is the transgression of God's moral law as reflected in the Decalogue (Exod. 20:1-17) and that sin involves personal guilt (Rom. 5:13).

Moreover, the Mosaic Law was intended to demonstrate to fallen mankind the incurable sinfulness of the old Adamic nature. The Law not only failed to keep man from sinning but actually provoked him to sin more. This fact was advertised to the fallen race by the priesthood and sacrificial system of the Mosaic system, which pointed to God's forgiving grace to be realized in Christ. Thus the Mosaic Law was to be superimposed only temporarily over the grace which God had permanently covenanted with Abraham and his descendants. The Law was to remain in effect only until "the seed (Christ) should come" (3: 19). In Christ all of God's promises of grace would be fully realized.

The Law of Moses was also added in order to conclude all of mankind under sin (3:22; cf. Rom. 3:19-23). Through the example of the nation Israel it showed sinful men everywhere that salvation by grace through faith is God's only way of saving lost sinners (3:22, 23).

The Mosaic Law as a specific administration of God marked a period of child training for the Jew, and through him presented a lesson to the entire race. The law functioned as a pedagogue, training the Jew with "do's" and "don'ts" appropriate to childhood until he arrived at spiritual adulthood in Christ (3:24, 25). At this point mature and informed love was expected to respond spontaneously to the benefit conferred by grace. In this sense the Law was preparatory to the present age of spiritual adulthood (3:25-29), in which "faith" as the principle of salvation "has come," that is, has been demonstrated by the Law of Moses to be the only way of salvation for guilty sinners in all ages (3:23, 25).

During this present period of spiritual adulthood *all* believers have the mature status of "sons of God" rather than mere "children" (minors) under the Law (3:26). All of them have also been baptized by the Spirit into spiritual union with Christ (3:27) and have thus "put on Christ," thereby laying aside the boyish toga (Mosaic Law observances) for the adult toga (faith in Christ—3:27). Spiritual union with Christ means that all human distinctions are laid aside (3:28) and that the believer inherits through Christ the promises of faith given to Abraham (3:29).

SANCTIFICATION
AND THE PURPOSE OF THE LAW

Since the Apostle demonstrates that sanctification (as well as justification) is by faith and faith alone, the question may be asked, "What relation does sanctification have to the Law?" In dealing with this problem we must remember that the Decalogue given to Israel at Sinai (Exod. 20:1-17) is an expression of the eternal moral law of God, a timeless reflection of God's holy character and attributes. Its particular Mosaic mold and dress (Exod. 20:1-17) was adapted to the nation Israel so that they could be an example of God's dealings in grace with the fallen race as a whole.

The Mosaic Law was given by God to demonstrate to all the world that lost sinners could be neither justified nor sanctified in the sight of God by self-righteousness or law-keeping (5:1-26). Both justification and sanctification are granted to sinners when God imputes the righteousness of Christ to them at the moment of belief. This positional sanctification (in contrast with experiential sanctification) is as changeless and secure as justification, since both rest on God's eternal approval of the person and work of Christ.

In distinction to positional sanctification, which is changeless and secure because it depends entirely on God's faithfulness, *experiential* sanctification (the present-tense aspect of sanctification) is subject to constant change. It depends on the believer's constant exercise of faith in his positional privileges in Christ, as well as on continual reliance on the indwelling Holy Spirit for power to live a holy life. The purpose of the Mosaic Law was to drive men to Christ for both salvation and practical holiness of life.

Thus the Apostle also presents the human responsibility in experiential sanctification. "Walk *by the Spirit*" (5:16, RSV). What this involves is not observing certain ordinances, performing certain good deeds, or "trying harder"; instead, it involves a simple adjustment to the Holy Spirit. Experiential sanctification is produced by the Holy Spirit when we trust God for power to live holy lives (5:16-18). It is accomplished not by "works of the flesh" (5:19-21) but by "the fruit of the Spirit" (5:22-26).

THE BELIEVER
AND HIS RELATION TO THE LAW

But the question remains, "What is the relation of the justified and sanctified believer to the Law of Moses? Does the fact that he could never be saved by the Law mean that the Ten Commandments of the moral law of God no longer have any claim upon him?" By no means. But it does indicate that in their Mosaic mold, as an intrinsic part of the Mosaic Covenant, they do not apply even to saved Jews now, who are "not under the law, but under grace" (2:19; 4:4-7; cf. Rom. 6:14; 7:4). How much less do they apply to saved Gentiles, who were never under the Mosaic Law or Covenant in any sense!

But another problem calls for consideration. Was humanity without God's moral law before the giving of the Mosaic Law to Israel? Was the Gentile world during the legal era without such law? Has the human family since the close of the Mosaic age been without such a legal requirement? Certainly not. (Though the revelation of law was not made as clearly and publicly as it was to Israel.) The fact is that *all* humanity, saved as well as lost, has always been under God's eternal moral law. This will be the basis of God's judgment of the works of the unsaved (eventuating in degrees of punishment in hell—Rev. 20:11-15) as well as the basis of his judgment of the deeds of the saved (eventuating in reward or loss of reward in heaven—2 Cor. 5:10).

Meanwhile, under the New Covenant of grace the Holy Spirit works in the new nature of the believer, making him willing to obey God's will and to comply with his moral law (Heb. 10:16). So far is the life of the dedicated believer removed from the anarchy of self-will that he is described as "inlawed to Christ" (1 Cor. 9:21). The new "law of Christ" (6:2) is now his delight. Moreover, through the indwelling Spirit the righteousness of God's eternal law is fulfilled in him (5:16-18; cf. Rom. 8:2-4). The "commandments" in the distinctively Christian Scriptures refer to those instructions in righteousness which God requires all of his creatures to keep and which his redeemed people are empowered to keep by the Holy Spirit (2 Tim. 3:16, 17; Rom. 13:8-10; 1 Cor. 9:8, 9; Eph. 6:1-3).

FALLING FROM GRACE

Often misunderstood, the phrase "fallen from grace" (Gal. 5:4) means abandoning the true gospel of grace (faith and *faith alone* as the way of salvation) for some admixture of legalism, thereby becoming entangled in the legal yoke of bondage and denying the full efficacy of Christ's atoning work. It involves doing what the Galatians did, namely, being "removed from him that called (them) into the grace of Christ unto another gospel, which is not another; but there are some that trouble you, and would pervert the gospel of Christ" (Gal. 1:6, 7). It has nothing to do with an imagined "losing one's salvation."

CHRISTIAN LIBERTY AND LAW

Christian liberty is an outgrowth of salvation by grace and is realized by the believer in and through Jesus Christ (Gal. 4:3-5). Christian liberty is freedom from the Mosaic Law — not only the yoke of Old Testament ritual ordinances fulfilled in Christ (4:3; Col. 2:20), but the moral law in its Mosaic dress. For example, the fourth Commandment, requiring Sabbath observance, was never imposed upon either the Gentiles or the Church, but only upon the nation Israel. The Decalogue (Exod. 20:1-17) was inseparably bound up with the Mosaic Covenant, and was fulfilled by Christ just as completely as the priesthood and sacrifices of the Mosaic system.

This fact does not imply that Christian liberty means freedom from all moral law, since moral law is a reflection of the eternal character of the Creator. God's law is in the world by virtue of his own personal presence here. Christian liberty is deliverance from the *curse* of both the Mosaic Law and God's eternal moral law. Both condemn every sinner in Adam and confine him to salvation in Christ (3:13).

Christian liberty, far from granting freedom to commit sins, consists of freedom *from* sin and from committing sins (Rom. 6:7, 18). Since he is now "inlawed to Christ" (1 Cor. 9:21 and initiated into "the law of Christ" (Gal. 6:2), the believer as a Spirit-indwelt and Spirit-empowered son (4:1-7) has the inner desire and power to live out the moral law of God. He knows that his response to the eternal moral law of God determines what his works will be. He realizes, too, that he will be judged for his works as a prelude to heaven, even as the unsaved will be judged for theirs as a prelude to hell.

For this reason Christian liberty must never be misused as a cloak for sin. While the believer should guard against any threat to his true liberty under the gospel, he must also constantly keep in mind that his very freedom has brought him into total subjection to Christ, whose bondservant he is and whom he must always obey (Rom. 12:1). This is a paradox. But the Christian discovers that he enjoys his greatest liberty when he is most completely enslaved to the Lord Jesus Christ.

Ephesians

AUTHOR

None of the Pauline Epistles has a stronger chain of evidence authenticating its early and continued use than this Epistle. Clement of Rome, Ignatius, Polycarp, Hermas, Clement of Alexandria, Tertullian, Irenaeus, and others all attest their recognition of the Epistle.

Internal evidence is also strong. The author twice calls himself Paul (1:1; 3:1), and the subject matter and distinctive revelation of Church truths are clearly Pauline. The Epistle is written in Paul's usual epistolary style, including greeting and thanksgiving, doctrinal discussion, practical exhortations, and personal matters. The style and language are clearly Paul's. Nearly every sentence has overtones of what Paul has said elsewhere, especially in Colossians. Scholars have pointed out that of 155 verses in Ephesians, 78 are echoed in Colossians in varying degrees of similarity. The explanation of this similarity undoubtedly lies in the fact that Paul wrote the two Epistles within a short span of time.

BACKGROUND AND DATE

The Epistle was evidently addressed to the church at Ephesus, the most important city in the Roman province of Asia. It was located on the west coast of what is now Asiatic Turkey. The main part of the city, with its theater, baths, libraries, agora, and marble-paved streets, was situated between the mountain ranges of Koressos and the Cayster River, which connected the port with the sea. But the famous Temple of Artemis (Diana), then one of the seven wonders of the

Sheep graze near the tumbled remains of an Ephesian edifice. *(Russ Busby photo)*

world, lay one-and-one-half miles to the northeast, rendering the city a great cult center of the fertility goddess.

Paul founded the church at Ephesus upon returning from his second missionary tour (Acts 18:19-21). Later he spent three years there after returning from his third tour (Acts 19:1 – 20:1). As one of the Apostle's Prison Epistles, Ephesians was apparently written from Rome in A.D. 61 and sent to proconsular Asia with Tychicus (6:21, 22) along with two other Prison Epistles, Colossians and Philemon (Col. 4:7-9; Philem. 1:10).

Although addressed to "the saints at Ephesus" (1:1), the letter was evidently intended to circulate among the neighboring churches as well. The omission of the phrase "at Ephesus" in three of the oldest and most reliable manuscripts (Vaticanus, Sinaiticus, and Papyrus 46) suggests that early copyists were for some reason reluctant to localize the letter when it was intended for reading in other churches in the vicinity. Evidently the Apostle had in some way indicated this universal intent, possibly by a footnote. The early Church, however, construed from the textual evidence that the Epistle was addressed at least principally to the Ephesians. Hence the Muratorian Canon, Irenaeus, Tertullian, Clement of Alexandria, and Origen speak freely of the letter as the Epistle to the Ephesians.

IMPORTANCE AND PURPOSE

Among the Pauline letters none is more sublime and profound than the Epistle to the Ephesians. It expounds the glory of the Church as the "body of Christ" and unfolds the believer's heavenly blessings in Christ. The expression "the heavenlies," which designates the exalted realm of the believer's position in Christ, occurs five times in the letter (1:3, 20; 2:6; 3:10; 6:12).

The letter represents the high-water mark of Church truth as revealed to the Apostle Paul (see 3:1-10). Hence the term *mystery*, denoting truth unrevealed until the proper time for its revelation in the divine program, is found six times (1:9; 3:3, 4, 9; 5:32; 6:19). The fact of the believer's position in Christ permeates the entire thought of the Epistle, occurring about ninety times; the metaphor of the body, describing the believer's union with Christ, occurs eight times (1:23; 2:16; 3:6, 15; 4:4, 12, 16; 5:23). The metaphor "walk," denoting conduct within the body, is the heart of the practical appeal of the Epistle and occurs frequently (2:2, 10; 4:1, 17; 5:15).

The union of the believer with the crucified, risen, ascended, and exalted Christ (1:19-23) is the basis of the believer's standing in grace in the body of Christ, the Church (1:3-14). By *standing* is meant the believer's unchanging position before God, the realm in which the Father sees the believer accepted and exalted in Christ. To these believers Ephesians expresses the sentiment of Matthew 3:17: "This is my beloved Son, in whom I am well pleased."

The believer's position (1:3-14) is related to the triune God. Chosen in Christ by the Father (1:3-6), redeemed by the Son (1:7-12), and sealed by the Holy Spirit (1:13, 14), the believer is placed "in the heavenlies" with Christ (1:13). So wonderful is this placement in Christ that the Apostle pauses in his doctrinal exposition to pray that the believers may experience the power of this incomparable position in their daily lives (1:15-23).

In chapter 2 Paul describes the power of God manifested in our salvation (2:1-10) and its miraculous union of Jew and Gentile into one body, the Church (2:11-22). In chapter 3 the Apostle reveals that he himself is the divinely commissioned messenger of this mystery (3:1-13); then he pauses to pray for the experiential realization of these blessings (3:14-21). This ends the doctrinal portion of the Epistle.

In the practical section (chapters 4–6) the Apostle exhorts his readers to "walk" (live day by day) worthily of their exalted vocation in union with the exalted Christ (4:1–6:9). He realizes that when we understand and depend on our position in Christ we will inevitably precipitate conflict with Satan and his demonic hosts (6:10-20). So he describes the believer's full armor of God. Depending on this armor assures sweeping victory for the believer.

OUTLINE

Salutation (1:1, 2)
A. Union with Christ Expounded (chapters 1–3)
  1. It is effected by the triune God (1:3-14).
    (a) Chosen by the Father (1:3-6)
    (b) Redeemed by the Son (1:7-12)
    (c) Sealed by the Spirit (1:13, 14)
  2. It is realized in human experience by prayer (1:15-23).
    (a) By knowing it (1:15-18)
    (b) By believing it (1:19-21)
    (c) By counting upon the exalted Christ (1:22-23)
  3. It is granted to us in salvation (2:1-10).
  4. It is manifested in the union of Jew and Gentile (2:11-18).
  5. It is illustrated by God's living temple (2:19-22).
  6. It is revealed as a mystery through Paul (3:1-12).
  7. It is apprehended by prayer (3:13-21).
B. Union with Christ Experienced (4:1–6:20)
  1. By a worthy walk (4:1–6:9)
    (a) By a consistent life (4:1-3)
    (b) By striving for unity (4:4-6)
    (c) By the use of the gifts of the risen Christ (4:7-16)
    (d) By a consistent life as a new man in Christ (4:17-29)
    (e) By a walk as a Spirit-indwelt believer (4:30-32)
    (f) By a walk as God's beloved child (5:1-17)

(g) By being Spirit-filled (5:18-21)
(h) By proper family relations (5:22 – 6:9)
2. By a worthy warfare (6:10-20)
    (a) The believer's strength (6:10, 11)
    (b) The believer's foe (6:12)
    (c) The believer's resources (6:13-20)
C. Personal Note and Benediction (6:21-24)

THE PAULINE CONCEPT OF THE CHURCH

In Paul's letters the Church appears in two aspects – the local church (an organized assembly of professing Christians in a particular location) and the universal or true Church (the aggregate of all true believers of this age). The universal Church is that entity referred to in the New Testament Epistles as the *body of Christ*. All believers between Pentecost and Christ's second advent are part of this body.

In Ephesians the Apostle is evidently writing to this universal Church, for he addresses "the saints and faithful in Christ Jesus" everywhere. (The words "at Ephesus" in 1:1 are not found in the oldest manuscripts.) The doctrinal presentation of the mystical Church and the absence of anything about church order confirms the view that the Apostle has in mind the doctrine of the universal Church.

The true Church, as the Apostle presents it in Ephesians, is united with each member and with Christ by the baptism of the Holy Spirit (the "one baptism" – see Eph. 4:4, 5; 1 Cor. 12:12, 13). As the body of Christ, the Church is headed by Christ himself (1:22, 23) and constitutes a holy temple for the "habitation of God through the Spirit" (2:21, 22). It is "one flesh" with Christ (5:30, 31) and is espoused to him as a chaste virgin to one husband (2 Cor. 11:2-4). At Christ's return for the Church its living members will be translated to heaven and its deceased saints will be resurrected with glorified bodies (1 Thess. 4:13-17).

The local church may not be identical with the true Church, for it frequently has unsaved people in its membership. It meets for worship, praise, prayer, fellowship, testimony, the ministry of the Word, discipline, and the furtherance of the gospel to the ends of the earth (Acts 13:1-4; 20:7; 1 Cor. 5:4, 5; Phil. 4:14-18; 1 Thess. 1:8; Heb. 10:25). Every such local church is to be centered in Christ and its regenerated members led by the indwelling Spirit (1 Cor. 3:16, 17). In addition to "saints" (regenerated members), the local church is to include bishops (elders) and deacons (Phil. 1:1; 1 Tim. 3:1-13).

TRUE ECUMENICITY

In an Epistle that expounds the doctrine of the true Church and features the unity of God's people, we could well expect to find specific guidelines for solving the complex problems of unity that have always faced the Church. The Epistle to the Ephesians provides these guidelines, and sheds especially helpful light on the current trend toward religious ecumenicity. In particular, Ephesians presents *right conduct* and *sound doctrine* as the criteria for differentiating between legitimate and illegitimate ecumenicity.

Right conduct is described as behavior worthy of the believer's position in Christ (4:1-3). Basic to the maintenance of working unity within the body of Christ are the virtues of humility, meekness, long-suffering, and forbearing love (4:2). The Holy Spirit alone can produce this real-life unity. Hence it is referred to as the unity of the *Spirit* (4:3). It cannot be successfully imitated by humanly-devised schemes of church amalgamation.

Sound doctrine is basic to the right conduct discussed above (4:4-6). Doctrinal capitulation not only jeopardizes a worthy walk but destroys the foundation of true ecumenicity. Compromise of Christian truth precludes the unity of the Spirit. It substitutes a superficial veneer of man-made harmony in the place of the genuine "bond of peace" (4:3).

The doctrinal essentials that underlie true ecumenicity are clearly specified by the Apostle, and involve the recognition of the following truths: 1) "one body" composed of all who are truly regenerated. Christian unity does *not* embrace unregenerate religionists, no matter what their ecclesiastical or religious pretensions and credentials may be; 2) "one Spirit" — the Holy Spirit of God, who alone inspires and teaches Christian truth (John 16:13). The Holy Spirit must be distinguished from demonic spirits that instigate errors upon which false religions and cults are built (1 Tim. 4:1, 2; 1 John 4:1-6); 3) "one hope of your calling" — the divine calling in Christ "before the foundations of the world" (1:4-6), comprising the saved elect and these alone; 4) "one Lord" — the only Savior, the God-Man, Christ Jesus, the Head of the Body and the center of its unity. Religious teachings that deny or detract from Christ's absolute deity and full saviorhood and recognize other "saviors" and different ways of salvation produce a spurious unity that is artificial and unscriptural; 5) "one faith" in the body of Christian truth "once for all delivered to the saints" (Jude 1:3). This faith centers in the gospel of grace (2:8, 9) and springs out of the death and resurrection of Christ and the great salvation he purchased (2:1-10); 6) "one baptism" — that of the Spirit (1 Cor. 12:13), by which the "one body" is brought into union with Christ, the Head (chaps. 1 — 3; Rom. 6:3, 4); 7) "one God and Father of all (believers), who is above all (created beings), and through all (his own purposes), and in you all (believers)." This is the sevenfold test of Scripture to be applied to all proposals of amalgamation.

THE CHURCH AND SPIRITUAL CONFLICT

The Ephesian letter reveals important information about the Satanic forces leveled against the Church as a whole and against each individual member (6:10-12). Ephesians shows that Satan now attacks Christians in much the same way that he attacked Christ when he was here on earth.

The attacking force is specified as both Satan and his organized army of demon helpers, gradated as "principalities," "powers," "age rulers of this darkness," and "wicked spirits in the heavenlies" (6:12, literal translation). The Christian warrior's resources spring from his position "in the Lord;" he is to "be strong" (literally, "strengthen himself") in the "power" of Christ's "might" (6:10).

The believer's position in Christ constitutes his great resource against the foe; it is described under the figure of a Roman soldier fully equipped for battle (6:13-18). As the believer depends on his secure position in Christ he is pictured as standing against the foe (6:13, 14). As the result of the believer's steadfastness and prevailing prayer the enemy is vanquished and driven from the field (6:18-20). Because the Church is composed of individual members, it enters the spiritual conflict in proportion to their power and victory. Both the individual and group aspects of spiritual conflict and conquest are described in the Ephesian Epistle.

Philippians

AUTHOR

External attestation of the genuineness of Philippians is ample among the Church Fathers. Internal evidence is also strong. Scholars therefore generally recognize its authenticity, though some express doubt as to its unity, alleging that the present letter is a blending of two original letters of Paul addressed to the Philippians. One letter (1:1—3:1; 4:21-23) is supposed to be addressed to the Church in general and the other (3:2—4:20) to more prominent members of it. It is imagined that the Apostle would not have been able to turn abruptly from the grateful and commendatory tone in 1:1—3:1 to a sharply critical one at 3:2, where he inveighs boldly against the Judaizers (as in Galatians). But the Apostle's abruptly critical tone in the last four chapters of Second Corinthians shows that he was indeed capable of changing his tone suddenly when it was called for.

BACKGROUND AND DATE

The church at Philippi was established by Paul on his second missionary tour (Acts 16:6-40) as the result of a clear divine leading, including a supernatural directing vision (Acts 16:6-11). The church was conceived in joy and born in a prison (Acts 16:25-34). This radiant letter, addressed to this same assembly some years later, was also penned from a prison. At the time of the writing of the Epistle the church was well established, as may be inferred from the address. Included are not only "saints in Christ Jesus" but also "bishops" (elders) and "deacons" (1:1).

The immediate occasion of the Epistle was to acknowledge a donation of money from the church. The gift was brought to the Apostle by Epaphroditus, one of the members of the Philippian assembly (4: 10-18). The whole letter is permeated with a spirit of tenderness; it is addressed to a group of believers who were especially dear to the Apostle's heart, having shared his joyful faith and devotion to Christ (2 Cor. 8:1-6).

Paul wrote this gracious Epistle while in prison (1:12-16). Thus Philippians is grouped with Ephesians, Colossians, and Philemon as a "Prison Epistle." The most widely held view is that all four letters were composed during the imprisonment at Rome (Acts 28:30) during the years A.D. 61-62. The allusions to the praetorian guard (1:13) apparently refer to the Emperor's residence on the Palatine. In Rome detachments of the *praetoriani* had charge of prisoners in imperial custody. The reference to "Caesar's household" (4:22) also seems to support Rome as the place of imprisonment.

However, the Emperor's huge staff of domestic and civil servants was somewhat like present-day civil service, and was not confined to the capital. Detachments of *praetoriani* were also sent to the provinces. Therefore some scholars believe that Caesarea, where Paul was in prison for two years (Acts 24:27), was the place of writing. Others hold that it was Ephesus (1 Cor. 15:32). However, if the Prison Epistles were indeed all written at one location, Rome seems to be the most probable site.

IMPORTANCE AND PURPOSE

The Epistle to the Philippians is one of the most intimate and personal of Paul's letters. It is filled with tender affection and spontaneous joy. Its theme is the joy of knowing Christ, the concept of rejoicing occurring no less than sixteen times in the letter. The church at Philippi in ancient Macedonia was the first assembly established by Paul in Europe. It was in a sense his best-loved congregation, for it entered more sympathetically into his sufferings and needs than any other assembly (4:14-20). The church at Thessalonica was also close to Paul's heart, but the ties that bound him to the Philippians were even closer than those that held him to the Thessalonians. The Apostle highly commends the church and expresses no misgivings about its loyalty to him.

Although Philippians is more of a letter than a treatise, it contains a distinct theological emphasis. Christ's person, work, humiliation, incarnation, death, resurrection, and exaltation are expounded in an instructive context and in closest connection with human experience (2:1, 5; 3:10). The doctrines of salvation (2:8-10), the coming of the Lord (3:20), glorification (3:21), and prayer (4:6) are also found among the practical admonitions.

The overall purpose of the Apostle in writing to the Philippians was to present the joy which Christ gives as our life (chap. 1), our example (chap. 2), our goal (chap. 3) and our sufficiency (chap. 4). Other secondary purposes are made to contribute to this primary one. The Apostle's secondary purposes are as follows: 1) to express appreciation to the Philippians for their fellowship and progress in the faith (1:3-11); 2) to share with them his hopes and fears (1:12-26); 3) to exhort them to unity and consistency of testimony (1:27−2:18); 4) to explain his purpose in sending Timothy and Epaphroditus to them (2:19-30); 5) to warn them against legalistic teachers (3:1-14); 6) to urge the reconciliation of two women (Euodias and Syntyche) who were at odds (4:2, 3); 7) to exhort them to joyfulness, prayerfulness, and the pursuit of all that is good (4:4-9); 8) to thank them for their recent gift (4:10-20); and 9) to convey greetings (4:21-23).

OUTLINE

A. Joy in Christ Our Life (chapter 1)
  1. Greetings (1:1, 2)
  2. Thanksgiving, fellowship, and confidence (1:3-7)
  3. Triumph over suffering (1:8-18)
  4. Expectation of deliverance (1:19-30)
B. Joy in Christ Our Example (chapter 2)
  1. Christian humility and its example in Christ (2:1-11)
  2. Christian service and its basis in Christ (2:12-16)
  3. Apostolic burdens and sufficiency in Christ (2:17-30)
C. Joy in Christ Our Goal (chapter 3)
  1. True goal versus false goals (3:1-6)
  2. One goal versus other goals (3:7-14)
  3. One goal and Christian maturity (3:15-19)
  4. One goal and the believer's hope (3:20-21)
D. Joy in Christ Our Sufficiency (chapter 4)
  1. Secret of our steadfastness (4:1-5)
  2. Secret of God's peace (4:6-9)
  3. Secret of Paul's testimony (4:10-20)
E. Closing Greeting (4:21-23)

VICTORIOUS CHRISTIAN LIVING

In Philippians 3:1-14 the Apostle expounds the life of victory in Christ. Such an experience not only *can be* but *ought to be* enjoyed by every believer. Paul shows that to be victorious the believer must first recognize Christ as his true goal in life. Christ then grants joyful victory based on what he accomplished at Calvary. The believer must be careful to avoid false, legalistic goals, for these violate God's grace and detract from the all-sufficiency of Christ's atoning work (3:2, 3). The Apostle employs his own example to warn against trusting legal righteousness in order to find acceptance with God (3:4-6). Christ must be the sole object of the believer's faith for righteousness (3:7-9).

The victorious believer must also understand his position of union with Christ (3:10). His clear-cut aim must be to *know* Christ — not just theologically but in day-to-day joyful living. This incomparable knowledge releases "the power of Christ's resurrection" in the believer, enabling him to walk in "newness of life" (Rom. 6:4; Eph. 1: 19-23) and thereby to overcome sin, self, the world, the flesh, and the devil. But this experience of spiritual victory is inseparable from "the fellowship of Christ's sufferings" (the cross). For resurrection power in the Christian life springs out of Christ's death, to which the victorious saint must be "made conformable." A literal translation would be "constantly molded into the form of" Christ's death.

The victorious believer must rely on his position of union with Christ (3:10). By doing so he experiences the victory called "the resurrection *(exanastasis)* of the dead" (3:11; cf. Rom. 6:11). In this verse the Apostle is not referring to the resurrection of the believer's body *(anastasis)* but is describing victorious Christian living here and now. The Apostle calls this "an out-resurrection from among the dead" because not all Christians take full advantage of Christ's resurrection power.

The victorious believer must constantly press forward toward Christ, the true goal in life (3:12-14). Day-to-day victory in the Christian life cannot be achieved in one climactic experience of permanent triumph; it requires constant pursuit. To this end the believer has been "laid hold of" by Christ (3:12). The Apostle uses his own life as an example of this (3:13, 14). He pressed on toward Christ, the goal, with the utmost concentration of purpose in order to attain and maintain a life of dynamic victory.

CHRISTIAN PERFECTION

The Apostle connects Christian perfection (3:12, 15) with his teaching on victorious Christian living (3:1-14; see the exposition in the preceding section). "Let us, therefore, as many as be perfect, be thus minded" (3:15). To be "perfect" (Greek *teleios*, "mature") means to be "grown up" both doctrinally and experientially. Those who have this maturity understand the doctrines of holiness and sanctification and, as the consequence of faith in God's truth, live the victorious Christian life. As noted previously, the Apostle calls this a *spiritual* resurrection — the "*out*-resurrection" from among those who are dead to sin by virtue of their position in Christ (3:11).

The word "perfect" as Scripture uses it of unglorified men does not refer to sinless perfection. Old Testament characters described as "perfect" were obviously not sinless (Gen. 6:9; 1 Kings 15:14; 2 Kings 20:3; 1 Chron. 12:38; Job 1:1, 8; Psa. 37:37). The Hebrew and Greek words translated "perfect" usually contain the concept of "completeness in all details" (Hebrew *tamem;* Greek *katartizō*) or "reaching a goal" or "achieving a purpose" (Greek *teleios*).

As with sanctification, three stages of perfection are revealed in Scripture: 1) *positional perfection.* This phase is absolute and unchangeable. It is possessed by every believer by virtue of his eternal union with the infinitely perfect Christ (Matt. 3:17; Col. 2:10; Heb. 10:14); 2) *experiential perfection.* This phase is relative, progressive, and changeable. It depends on the believer's knowledge of his position in Christ and on moment-by-moment faith. This is the aspect of perfection which the Apostle deals with in Philippians 3:1-14 and refers to in 3:12, 15; 3) *ultimate perfection.* This is the final phase of perfection and is equivalent to glorification (Phil. 3:20, 21). Positional perfection guarantees ultimate perfection, since both are grounded on what Christ has done for the believer and not on what the believer may do for Christ. Perfection in all its phases is based on faith rather than works. Experiential perfection produces good works, but strictly as the result of the operation of the Spirit in response to faith (Gal. 5:16-26). Perfection is through the Spirit and not the law; Christian character is produced by the Spirit and not by self-effort (John 15:1-5).

PHILIPPIANS VERSUS
THE ERROR OF ANTINOMIANISM

It is significant that the Apostle, having set forth the sound scriptural view of experiential sanctification (3:1-14), should warn against two common erroneous views of it—unsound legalistic perfectionism (3:15; see above for correct view) and dangerous licentious antinomianism (3:17-21).

This latter perversion of sanctification holds that since Christ's obedience and death satisfied the demands of the Law, the believer is free from obligation to observe it. This error overlooks the fact that *only as a system of curse and penalty* and *only in its Covenant associations* has the Law been abolished by Christ's death. As a transcript of the holiness of God the moral law of God is as eternal as is God himself; its demands as a moral rule for *all* mankind are therefore changeless (Matt. 5:17-19, 48; Rom. 10:4; Gal. 3:13).

The antinomian error also ignores the fact that God has imparted to the believer a totally new nature which possesses Christ's spirit of obedience and holiness (Rom. 8:9, 10, 15; Gal. 5:22-25; 1 John 1:6; 3: 6). By giving us the spirit of obedience and sonship Christ liberates us from the Law as an outward compulsion. At the same time he guards against lawlessness by fulfilling the essence of the Law within us through the power of the Holy Spirit.

The Apostle summarizes the error of the antinomian libertines by branding them "enemies of the cross of Christ" (3:18). They are akin to those who say, "We have fellowship with him" while they actually "walk in darkness" (1 John 1:6), or to those who say, "Let us do evil, that good may come" (Rom. 3:8). These errorists are determined to "continue in sin that grace may abound" (Rom. 6:1). Although they claim to belong to Christ they deny being "dead indeed unto sin" or "alive unto God" in union with Christ (Rom. 6:11). In denying the efficacy of the death of Christ to deliver from the power of sin they become enemies of the cross (3:18).

The lawlessness of the lives of these libertines is evident. Their end is "destruction." They invite premature physical death as the ultimate in severe chastening (1 Cor. 5:5; 11:30-32; 1 John 5:16). The Apostle hints at the extreme carnality and licentiousness of their conduct. Their "god is their appetite." Their "glory is their shame." Their joy is in "earthly things." Their tragic error caused the Apostle bitter weeping (3:18).

Colossians

AUTHOR

The Epistle is satisfactorily attested externally by Justin Martyr, Irenaeus, Clement of Alexandria, Tertullian, Origen, the Old Latin and Syriac Versions, and the Muratorian Fragment. Internal evidence is also satisfactory. Paul alludes to himself as author three times (1:1, 23; 4:18), and the style and theological concepts are characteristically Pauline. The Epistle's close affiliations with the Letter to Philemon, which is generally accepted as genuine, also argue for the authenticity of Colossians (cf. Col. 4:10-14 with Philem. 1:23, 24; Col. 4:17 with Philem. 1:2).

BACKGROUND AND DATE

Colossians, like Romans, was written to a church which Paul had not personally founded and apparently had not visited (1:4, 7, 8; 2:1). Paul evidently bypassed the cities of the Lycus Valley of Asia Minor on both his second and third missionary tours. Yet the Apostle considered Colosse, Laodicea, and Hierapolis as his parish, probably because the churches in these towns were indirectly founded by him as the result of his three-year ministry at Ephesus, when he had a powerful evangelistic outlet to the entire province of proconsular Asia (Acts 19: 10, 26).

It is likely that both Epaphras and Philemon were converted under the Apostle's Ephesian ministry (Philem. 1:19, 23). At any rate Paul dispatched Epaphras to preach to the Colossians (Col. 1:7); he in all likelihood evangelized Laodicea and Hierapolis as well (Col. 4:12, 13).

The population of Colosse in Phrygia was composed of native Phrygians, Greek colonists, and Jews. The latter were descended from Jewish families transported from Mesopotamia and Babylon to the provinces of Phrygia and Lydia by Antiochus the Great (223-187 B.C.). It was this Jewish element that was doubtless responsible for the introduction into the Lycus Valley of the Judaic-Gnostic heresy that was causing confusion at Colosse.

During the more than two years of Paul's absence from the province of Asia some apparently Judaistic Christians had introduced erroneous teaching at Colosse. This heresy had a distinctly Jewish element, an ascetic element, and a Greek philosophic (Gnostic) element. The Jewish element appears in the Apostle's reference to circumcision, ordinances, foods and drinks, festal days, new moons, and sabbaths (Col. 2:11-16). The ascetic element shows itself in Paul's reference to ordinances — "touch not, taste not, handle not" (Col. 2:20-23). The speculative element is seen in the warning against "philosophy and vain deceit" (Col. 2:8). There was a denial of the full deity of Christ (2:9; cf. 1:19) and the error of angel-worship (2:18, 19). In Galatia the error consisted of mixing law and grace. At Colosse it consisted of a Judaic-Gnostic-Christian syncretism.

Apparently Epaphras and his fellow-workers at Colosse were unable to deal with the situation and went to Rome to consult Paul about it (1:7, 8). Perhaps the Colossians had hoped for a visit from Paul (2:1-3). Since the Apostle was a prisoner of Rome and a visit was impossible, he wrote a letter. He sent it by Tychicus and Onesimus (4:7-9), since Epaphras apparently could not return at this time (4:12; cf. Philem. 1:23).

Paul was a prisoner at the time but was free to preach (4:10, 18; Acts 28:30, 31). Demas was still with him (4:14; 2 Tim. 4:10). We may conclude, then, that the time of writing was near the close of Paul's first imprisonment at Rome, about A.D. 61.

IMPORTANCE AND PURPOSE

Colossians is a strong polemic against an error that later developed into the heresy called Gnosticism. This false system that threatened the Colossian church assigned to Christ a position subordinate to the true Godhead and undervalued the uniqueness and complete efficacy of his redemptive work. It taught that between the infinitely holy God and this earth there were a host of angelic intermediaries, of which Christ was one. The error included the worship of angels (2:18) and a legalistic asceticism (2:20-22).

In refuting this incursion of error the Apostle presents a masterly exposition of the person and work of Christ that makes the Epistle of tremendous importance. In setting forth the dignity of Christ as the Head of the Church, Colossians is related to Ephesians, which presents the exaltation of the Church as the body of Christ. The Apostle meets the challenge of false teaching at Colosse by positive presentation of the truth rather than by point-by-point refutation. After expressing his apostolic solicitude and concern for the Colossians (1:1-8), Paul breathes a prayer for their spiritual welfare (1:9-23) in which he presents the nature of redemption (1:13, 14), the glory of Christ's person (1:15-19), the all-sufficiency of Christ's work (1:20-23), and the overall glory of Christ as proclaimed by the Apostle in his ministry (1:24-29). The Apostle proceeds to show that Christ is the answer to doctrinal error (2:1-7), including the peril of philosophy (2:8-13), the peril of legalism (2:14-17), the peril of false mysticism (2:18, 19), and the peril of asceticism (2:20-23).

The Apostle demonstrates that Christ is also the answer to dynamic Christian living (3:1–4:18). Union with him is the basis of a heavenly walk (3:1-4). It enables the believer to pronounce death on a sinful life (3:5-7), to put on the new man (3:8-17), and to conduct a heavenly walk in all relationships of life (3:18–4:6). It is also the basis of Christian fellowship (4:7-18).

OUTLINE

Introduction: Apostolic Solicitude (1:1-12)
A. The Person and Work of Christ (chapter 1)
   1. All-sufficiency of Christ's redemption (1:13, 14)
   2. Supreme glory of Christ's person (1:15-19)
   3. Completeness of Christ's work (1:20-23)
   4. Glory of Christ proclaimed in Paul's ministry (1:24-29)
B. Refutation of Doctrinal Errors (chapter 2)
   1. Conflict of error (2:1-7)
   2. False philosophy (2:8-13)
   3. Legalism (2:14-17)
   4. False mysticism (2:18, 19)
   5. Asceticism (2:20-23)
C. Exposition of Christian Living (chapters 3, 4)
   1. Heavenly walk with Christ (3:1-4)
   2. Conquest of sin through Christ (3:5-7)

3. New life in Christ (3:8-17)
4. Godly behavior from Christ (3:18 – 4:6)
5. Fellowship with believers in Christ (4:7-18).

THE PROBLEM OF RELIGIOUS RELATIVISM

Though Colosse was a comparatively small and insignificant town when Paul wrote to it in the first century A.D., the issues in the church there were vitally important. Moreover, it is becoming increasingly evident that the problem in the Colossian community is peculiarly pertinent to our own day of religious pluralism. The world is rapidly opening up to embrace the so-called Gnostic notion of Christ, namely, that he fits in with all religions and systems. As Ephesians presents the Church as the body of Christ and furnishes the divine criterion for distinguishing true ecumenicity from false, so Colossians furnishes the gauge to test true religion from false.

The Colossian errors are also today's errors. In the face of a Babel of cults on one hand and an infidel "liberalism" within the fold of professing Christianity on the other hand, the crucial question again needs to be answered, "What think ye of Christ? Whose son is he?" (Matt. 22:42).

Paul answers this question by proving the uniqueness of the Christian faith and its inevitable clash with all other systems of religion and human philosophy. This uniqueness is bound up in the *person* of Christ and his redemptive *work*. With Paul, arguments over such questions as Christ's virgin birth, sinless life, vicarious death, bodily resurrection, ascension, glorification in heaven, and second coming have no place. The Christ whom Paul presents is very God of very God (1:15a), the eternal Creator and Sustainer of the universe (1:15b-17), the God-Man who is Head of the Church (1:18a), the crucified and risen Redeemer, the Firstborn from among the dead (1:18, 19), and the Reconciler of lost and estranged humanity (1:20-23).

The Apostle eliminates all pretenders to Christ and his position of supreme exaltation. He refutes those who would impose upon salvation any requirement except faith in the finished, redemptive work of Christ. He sounds the death knell to all human formulations of doctrine (2:8). He repudiates all those who would in any way depreciate Jesus Christ. He does so by declaring that "the fullness of the Godhead" dwells in him (2:9, 10). He is "the mystery" revealed (1:27; 2:2). In him are "all the treasures of wisdom and knowledge" (2:3). Christian maturity and practical sanctification rest solely on union with Christ (3:1–4:6).

The Epistle to the Colossians furnishes the answer to the religious relativism of today, which would make Christ *a* Savior instead of the *only* Savior and *a* way to God instead of the *only* way to God. The Apostle gives the lie to the popular pluralism of the hour that sends missionaries not to win the heathen to Christ but merely to share mutually the common residuum of truth claimed to underlie all religions, and that does not view the gospel as centering in Christ at all, but in the notion that each man may find God in his own particular religion.

1 Thessalonians

AUTHOR

External evidence for Pauline authorship is adequate from before the time of Clement of Alexandria. Marcion included the Epistle in his Canon, and it is found in the old Syriac and Old Latin Versions. The Muratorian Canon includes First Thessalonians. Irenaeus quotes it by name, and Clement of Alexandria ascribes it to Paul. After this period frequent references to the Epistle occur.

Internal evidence points clearly to Pauline authorship. Twice the writer calls himself Paul (1:1; 2:18). The historical allusions dovetail with Paul's life as set forth in the Book of Acts (cf. 2:2 with Acts 16: 22, 23; 2:17 with Acts 18:5; 3:4 with Acts 17:5). The Epistle itself is a mirror reflecting the life and character of the Apostle. It shows Paul's deep concern for his converts (3:1, 2), his consuming desire for their spiritual welfare (3:8-11), his great tenderness (2:7), his joy at their steadfastness (3:6, 7), and his deep sympathy in their distress (4:13-18).

Ruins of Caesarea, Mediterranean port used by the Apostle Paul *(Russ Busby photo)*

BACKGROUND AND DATE

The general events accompanying the founding of the church at Thessalonica on Paul's second missionary tour are outlined by Luke in Acts 17:1-9. Thessalonica was the capital of the Roman province of Macedonia. It was a free city, governed by its own officials, called "politarchs" (Acts 17:6, 8). The three-week synagogue ministry there (Acts 17:2) was apparently only an initial phase of Paul's work in this important town, for he refers to the believers there as Gentiles (1:9; 2: 14; cf. 2:9 and 2 Thess. 3:8 with Acts 17:4). How long Paul stayed on his first visit is conjectural — possibly several months. Implacable hatred and venomous persecution by the local Jews drove the Apostle to Berea (Acts 17:5, 10).

Because he had to leave in such haste, the Apostle was deeply concerned about the welfare of the Thessalonian converts; thus he sent Timothy back to see how they were faring. Timothy brought back good news when he returned to the Apostle at Corinth (cf. Acts 18:5). The Thessalonians were standing true (1:3-10; 2:14; 3:6-9), though they had certain problems. Some of these were ethical, with special reference to sexual matters (4:3-8), but the main difficulty was prophetic. They were concerned about the coming of the Lord for his own (4:13-

18). They were under the misapprehension that those believers of their number who had died would be at a disadvantage as compared with those who were alive when the Lord returned. They also had difficulties regarding the day of the Lord (5:1-11).

To allay their misgivings Paul wrote to the Thessalonians immediately, expressing his joy at Timothy's good news and explaining that his abrupt departure from them was through no choice of his own (as his enemies had alleged). He described the coming of the Lord and explained why the deceased saints would suffer no disadvantage. He also distinguished this prophetic event from the day of the Lord.

It would appear from the Book of Acts that First Thessalonians was written during the latter part of Paul's second visit to Corinth. The year A.D. 50 (or perhaps 51) is the most probable date. Second Thessalonians was written shortly thereafter.

IMPORTANCE AND PURPOSE

First Thessalonians is important because it is not only the earliest of Paul's thirteen letters but, with the possible exception of the Epistle of James, it is probably the earliest writing of the entire New Testament. The Epistle is also significant because of its theme of Christ's return. In fact the second advent is such a prominent theme in both First and Second Thessalonians that together they have been called "the eschatological Epistles of Paul." First Thessalonians is also important because of the clear picture it presents of the Apostle Paul's ministry and of the life of an early Christian church.

OUTLINE

A. The Exemplary Church (chapter 1)
  1. Its faith, hope, and love (1:2-4)
  2. Its faithful discipleship (1:5-7)
  3. Its clean break with idolatry (1:8-10)
B. The Exemplary Pastor (chapter 2)
  1. The apostolic example (2:1-12)
  2. The response of the Thessalonians (2:13-16)
  3. The apostolic concern (2:17-20)
C. The Exemplary Individual (chapter 3)
  1. The apostolic solicitude (3:1-8)
  2. The apostolic intercession (3:9-13)
D. The Exemplary Walk (chapter 4)

1. Demands moral purity (4:1-8)
2. Demonstrates brotherly love (4:9, 10)
3. Displays integrity and honest industry (4:11, 12)
4. Derives dynamic from the Lord's coming (4:13-18)
E. Exemplary Watchfulness (chapter 5)
1. The day of the Lord and the need for vigilance (5:1-11)
2. Practical exhortations (5:12-22)
3. Prayer for experiential sanctification (5:23-24)
4. Conclusion (5:25-28)

THE LORD'S COMING (4:13-18)

In this passage the Apostle presents the central paragraph in all of Scripture dealing with Christ's coming for his own. Some have termed this important event the "rapture" or "catching away" of the Church. The Apostle discloses with incisive clarity certain revealed truths about this important phase of Christ's second advent.

The rapture is the blessed hope of the believer (4:13; Tit. 2:13).

The believer is exhorted in the light of the rapture not to grieve over the death of loved ones in the same way as do unbelievers, who have no hope beyond the grave. For a believer, death is only "falling asleep" as far as the body is concerned. At the coming of the Lord the body will be resurrected in the sense of being awakened from the sleep of death. This vital truth had been so subject to ignorance and misunderstanding that the Apostle had to declare concerning it, "I would not have you ignorant" (4:13).

The coming of the Lord is only for those who have believed the gospel (4:14).

At the heart of the gospel is the vicarious death and physical resurrection of Jesus Christ (1 Cor. 15:2-4). On this basis (1 Cor. 15:20, 52) God will bring with him through Jesus those who have "fallen asleep in death" (4:14, *Amplified Bible*). When Christ returns, God will bring the soul and spirit of all believers with him to be united with their risen and glorified bodies (4:14). The Christian dead will be united to the living and glorified Christ in glory. They will not miss the coming of the Lord, for God has promised to bring them with Christ when he returns (3:13).

These truths of the Lord's coming constitute a divine revelation from Christ to the Apostle Paul (4:15). It is by the Lord's own authoritative word (John 14:1-4) that Paul declares that those who are alive at Christ's coming will have no advantage over the Christian dead except that they will never have passed through physical death. The Apostle refers to this in First Corinthians: "Take notice! I tell you a mystery — a secret truth, an event decreed by the hidden purpose or counsel of God. We shall not all fall asleep (in death), but we shall all be changed (transformed)" (1 Cor. 15:51, *Amplified Bible*). The saints who are living at the time of the Lord's coming "shall in no way precede (into His presence) or have any advantage at all over those who have previously fallen asleep (in Him in death)" (4:15, *Amplified Bible*).

The coming of the Lord will involve the descent into the upper air of the glorified Lord himself (4:16).

This has been called "a secret coming," but it will be secret only to the unsaved. To those who are "in Christ" it will be exceedingly grand and glorious. The "shout" (the cry of triumph over death — 1 Cor. 15:54-57), the voice of the Archangel (Michael, who apparently figures prominently in the stages of the first resurrection — Dan. 12:1, 2; Jude 1:9), and the trumpet of God (1 Cor. 15:52) are all connected with the first resurrection to life. The unsaved, living or dead, have no part in this. This is emphasized by the Apostle when he declares that the dead *in Christ* will rise at this time. Because believers are united to the risen Lord by the baptism of the Spirit (Rom. 6:4; Col. 3:1-4) they fall asleep "in Jesus" when they die and thus constitute "the dead in Christ."

The coming of the Lord will occasion the resurrection of deceased believers and the simultaneous translation of living saints (4:17).

"Then we, the still living who remain (on the earth), shall simultaneously be caught up along with (the resurrected dead) in the clouds to meet the Lord in the air; and so always — through the eternity of the eternities — we shall be with the Lord!" (4:17, *Amplified Bible*). The expression "caught up" comes from a Greek word (*harpazō*) which literally means "to seize upon, to claim for oneself eagerly, to snatch out or away, to carry off speedily." To accomplish this grand event the living saints will immediately receive a sinless, deathless body like the resurrected one which our Lord now possesses (Rom. 8:23; 1 Cor. 15:50-53; Phil. 3:20, 21). The deceased saints will receive this same kind of glorified body by the act of resurrection — the raising of their mortal bodies from the grave.

The coming of the Lord for his own as revealed here must not be confused with his coming with his own (4:17b).

The rapture described here is the first stage of the Lord's coming. He does not at this time actually come down to the surface of the earth. "Clouds" and "air" imply simply the lower atmosphere *above* the earth. His resurrected and translated saints are snatched up from the earth to meet him *in the air*, after which they receive their rewards. His coming *with* his saints is *after* their rewards have been dispensed; it is then that they come to reign with him as he sets his feet upon the earth and conquers his enemies (Zech. 14:1-4; Rev. 19:11-16).

The coming of the Lord is the basis of solid comfort for the Christian (4:18).

The curtain of the future has been lifted enough to make our hearts leap with joy and hope. The Apostle's exhortation is practical, loving, and nonspeculative. "Therefore comfort and encourage one another with these words" (4:18, *Amplified Bible*).

FIRST THESSALONIANS AND THE DAY OF THE LORD (5:1-11)

Having just described the coming of the Lord for his own, the Apostle distinguishes it from the day of the Lord, which *follows* this event. While the coming of the Lord for his own inaugurates "the day of Christ" in heaven, with rewards for the glorified Church saints (1 Cor. 1:8; 5:5; 2 Cor. 1:14; Phil. 1:6, 10; 2:16), it ushers in "the day of the Lord" on the earth. By contrast, the day of the Lord concerns the earth judgments which take place prior to the establishment of the kingdom over Israel (Acts 1:6, 7; 3:19-21). Church saints will not participate in it because they will previously have been removed from the earth (4:13-18).

The earth judgments of the day of the Lord will eventuate in "the times and seasons" of Israel's restoration. The nation's repentance and conversion will bring "the times of refreshing" from the presence of the Lord and "the . . . times of restitution of all things, which God hath spoken by the mouth of all his holy prophets since the world began" (Acts 3:19-21). Because this was a well-known revelation of the Old Testament (Isa. 2:6-22; 11:1 – 12:6; Jer. 30:5-9; Zech. 14:1-21), the Apostle declares that he had no need to write about it to the Thessalonians (5:1). They knew perfectly well from the Old Testament that that day would come upon the wicked "as a thief in the night" (5:2).

Expecting world peace, the godless of earth will at that time be swiftly engulfed in the cataclysmic judgments described in Revelation chapters 6 – 19. They are "in darkness," in contrast to believers, who are of the light (5:4-8). Believers will be taken out of the world at the coming of the Lord for his saints (4:13-18); this event marks the beginning of the day of the Lord.

The Apostle emphasizes this truth by declaring that "God hath not appointed us" (believers) "to wrath but to obtain salvation by our Lord Jesus Christ" (5:9). That the "wrath" is God's manifestation of judgment against sinners *on the earth* during the day of the Lord (cf. Rev. 6:17; 14:10; 16:1) rather than eternal condemnation in hell is plain from the context. That the "salvation" is the climax of the coming of the Lord for his own (4:13-18) is demonstrated by 5:10: "Who died for us, so that whether we are still alive or are dead (at Christ's appearing) we might live together with Him and share His life" (*Amplified Bible*). This we believers will do at the Lord's coming for us, either by resurrection (if we have died in Christ) or by translation (if we are still living when he returns).

THE LORD'S COMING AND SANCTIFICATION

The Apostle wrote to the Thessalonians not only to correct erroneous views concerning the Lord's coming but to exhort them to moral purity (4:3-8) and holiness of life (4:9-12) in the light of the sanctifying effect of this "blessed hope" (1:9, 10; 2:12, 19; 3:13; 4:1-12, 5:4-11, 23, 24). Paul is in full accord with the Apostle John in emphasizing the fact that "everyone who has this hope in him *purifies himself, even as he is pure*" (1 John 3:3). The Apostle Paul, however, points out that "purifying oneself" is the result not of self-effort or legalistic fleshly striving but of adjustment to the Holy Spirit, so that God actually does the sanctifying rather than the believer.

Sanctification is the work of God and not an attainment of man; it is by faith and not by works (5:23a). "The very God of peace" (literally "the God of peace *himself*") "sanctify you wholly." Paul is viewing sanctification as a whole in all three tenses — past, present, and future. Not only is the sanctifying operation emphatically *all* of God in *all* its aspects ("God himself" is intensive), but it is also the gateway to a deeper peace: "The God *of peace himself* sanctify you wholly."

Sanctification comprehends the entire man (5:23b). It involves man's spirit, that higher part of man by which the regenerated man knows God (1 Cor. 2:11). It also comprehends man's soul (the seat of his intellect, affections, and will), which becomes consecrated to God in salvation and used by him in dedication. Sanctification also extends to the body, which as God's holy temple is indwelt by the Spirit. The body is to be presented to God (Rom. 12:1) in order to glorify him (1 Cor. 6:19, 20).

Sanctification is God's provision to keep us blameless in our life in this world (5:23c). The entire man may be preserved blameless until death or translation at the Lord's coming for his own (3:13; 4:16, 17; 5:10). "Blameless" means "free of specific moral or spiritual fault."

Sanctification has its incentive in God's faithfulness (5:24). God's character guarantees sanctification: "Faithful is he." God's call assures sanctification: "Faithful is he who calls you" (cf. Rom. 8:30). God's power effects sanctification: "who also will do it." Those who seek the power for holy living in themselves and their own faithfulness are doomed to failure and disappointment. For victorious living, occupation with self must give way to occupation with Christ; self-effort must yield to faith in God's provision in Christ and human strength must be displaced by divine power. Then a holy life will be the spontaneous result.

2 Thessalonians

AUTHOR

The external evidence for the early use and Pauline authenticity of Second Thessalonians is even earlier and more extensive than for that of First Thessalonians. Justin Martyr, Irenaeus, Tertullian, Clement of Alexandria, the Muratorian Canon, the Old Syriac, the Old Latin, and Marcion's Canon evidence its authenticity. The internal evidence reinforces the external evidence. Twice the writer names himself as Paul (1:1; 3:17). The vocabulary, style, and theological and eschatological concepts are all Pauline. Attempts by critics to establish Second Thessalonians as a forgery have been dismal failures.

BACKGROUND AND DATE

Apparently neither Paul nor any of his associates had returned to Thessalonica since the sending of the First Epistle. But the new teaching concerning the day of the Lord had caused great confusion. Whether it arose from a forged letter purporting to come from Paul, an alleged revelation from the Spirit, or a miscomprehension of Paul's First Epistle is not certain. In any case news of increased persecution against the Church, misunderstanding of Paul's teaching regarding the return of the Lord, and the idleness and dreamy expectation of some of the Thessalonians (3:6-12) prompted this letter to them.

The interval between the writing of the two Epistles was scarcely more than six months — a year at the very most. The condition of the Thessalonian church as described in both Epistles is practically identical. The same excitement prevailed concerning the coming of the Lord; Silas and Timothy were still with the Apostle (2 Thess. 1:1); the same group in the church continued in fanatical neglect of their everyday work (cf. 2 Thess. 3:6-14 with 1 Thess. 2:9; 4:10-12). It is very likely, therefore, that Paul wrote Second Thessalonians while still in Corinth, not more than a year later than First Thessalonians. This would place the date at late A.D. 50 or early A.D. 51.

IMPORTANCE AND PURPOSE

Second Thessalonians has much in common with First Thessalonians. Both are prophetic and deal with the coming of the Lord for his own and the day of the Lord following it. However, the Second Epistle was written to correct apparent misunderstanding of certain prophetic themes in the First Epistle. The Thessalonian believers had somehow gotten the erroneous notion that the trials they were going through were those of "the day of the Lord" (2 Thess. 2:1, 2). The Apostle had told them in First Thessalonians that they were to wait for the coming of the Lord for his own, and that as believers they were to be "delivered from the wrath" to be manifested in the day of the Lord (1 Thess. 1:10). He had also instructed them that as "sons of light" believers were not to experience "the wrath" of the day of the Lord; this was reserved for the unsaved, who were in darkness (5:1-8). Instead, God's people were to be taken out of the world by rapture (5:9, 10) before the events of that time of judgment would take place on the earth.

To clarify the wrong ideas which the Thessalonians had gotten about the coming of the Lord, whether from misunderstanding his first letter, from false teaching, from a forged letter (2:2), or from forgetting what he had taught them while he had been with them (2:5), the Apostle in his second letter to them clearly presents the removal of the Church *before* the day of the Lord. In addition he describes the events of the day of the Lord, the Man of Lawlessness, the latter-day demonic delusion (2:1-12), and the coming of the Lord in glory (1:5-10).

The Apostle also continues the theme of sanctification and holy living which he began in the first Epistle (2:13-15). Particularly singled out are the idle and disorderly (cf. 1 Thess. 4:11, 12); these are exhorted to work while awaiting the Lord's return (3:6-15).

OUTLINE

Salutation (1:1-4)
A. The Lord's Coming and Comfort (1:5-12)
   1. The reasons for their sufferings (1:5, 6)
   2. The basis for their comfort (1:7-10)
   3. The prayer for their blessing (1:11, 12)
B. The Lord's Coming and the Day of the Lord (2:1-12)
   1. The rapture and the day of the Lord (2:1-5)
   2. The rapture and the Holy Spirit (2:6, 7)
   3. The rapture and the man of sin (2:8, 9)
   4. The rapture and demonic deception (2:10-12)
C. The Lord's Coming and Christian Living (2:13 – 3:15)
   1. Believers are chosen to salvation and sanctification (2:13-17)
   2. Believers are chosen for a prayer ministry (3:1-5)
   3. Believers are to practice disciplinary separation (3:6)
   4. Believers are to be exemplary in life (3:7-9)
   5. Believers are to seek to cure disorders (3:10-15)
D. Conclusion (3:16-18)

THE TIME OF THE RAPTURE

Three present-day schools of interpretation exist. *Pretribulationism* holds that the removal of the Church will occur *before* the great tribulation. *Midtribulationism* maintains that this removal will take place *in the middle of* the great tribulation. *Posttribulationism* equates the rapture with Christ's second advent in glory and holds that it occurs *at the end of* the great tribulation.

Posttribulationism cannot be squared with the Apostle's teaching in Second Thessalonians, for the whole point of Paul's correction of the Thessalonian misconception is that the coming of the Lord for his own occurs *before* the day of the Lord (2 Thess. 2:1-5). Paul buttresses this teaching by revealing that the day of the Lord is *followed* by Christ's coming with his own in power and glory (2 Thess. 2:8).

Midtribulationism, while differentiating the rapture from the coming of Christ in glory, cannot be reconciled with Paul's clear revelation that the rapture occurs *before* the day of the Lord. The events of the first half of Daniel's seventieth week are part of the day of the Lord and are open and public, so that the truth of the imminency of the rapture as taught in the New Testament would be nullified by midtribulationism.

Paul is evidently arguing for a pretribulation rapture in Second Thessalonians 2:1-5. The Apostle describes the first phase of Christ's coming as the personal appearance of Christ in the clouds coupled with our gathering together to him (2:1; 1 Thess. 4:13-18). The apostasy occurs *before* the apocalyptic judgments of the day of the Lord burst upon a Christ-rejecting world (2:3). Then the Man of Lawlessness, the Antichrist of the end-time, is to be revealed (Dan. 11:36; Zech. 11:15-17; Rev. 13:1-10; 19:20; 20:10). He will arrogate to himself divine honors and deceive the nation Israel (2:4; Dan. 9:27).

THE RAPTURE OF THE CHURCH AND THE DEPARTURE OF THE SPIRIT

At Pentecost the Holy Spirit came and took up residence in the newly formed Church (John 16:7, 8, 13; Acts 2:4; 1 Cor. 6:19; Eph. 2:22). In the same sense in which he came when the Church began, he will leave when the Church is completed and raptured to heaven. This means that the Spirit will resume his pre-Pentecostal presence, as in Old Testament times. This important truth is revealed by the Apostle. He who has been indwelling the Church (John 14:16; 1 Cor. 6:19; Eph. 2:22) and has been restraining evil will continue to do so until "he is taken out of the way" (literally "comes out of the midst"). This takes place when the Church, indwelt by the Spirit, is glorified and caught up to meet Christ in the air (1 Thess. 4:13-17). Only when the divine Restrainer departs with the glorified Church can and will "the apostasy" take place (2:3) and "the lawless one" and "the mystery of iniquity" be revealed. Paul reveals clearly that the Church will be caught up before the day of the Lord and the unbridled demonism and deception of that time (2:8-12).

THE TWO PHASES OF CHRIST'S SECOND ADVENT

Not only does the Apostle in the Thessalonian letters differentiate between the two aspects of Christ's advent, but the rest of the New Testament likewise does so (John 14:1-3; Tit. 2:13; 1 John 3:1-3). The first or "rapture" phase is most fully expounded in First Thessalonians (see especially 4:13-18). This is Christ's coming *for* his saints. The second phase of Christ's advent is *with* his saints to judge the ungodly and destroy the Man of Lawlessness. This aspect is touched upon in First Thessalonians 3:13 and 5:1-6 and in Second Thessalonians 1:7-10 and 2:1-12. The latter aspect, with its accompanying judgments, climaxes the Old Testament day of the Lord (cf. Isa. 2:6-22).

Apparently because of the severity of their persecutions (1:4-7), the Thessalonians had begun to wonder whether they had failed to qualify for the rapture and whether the day of the Lord had already come (2:2). It is because of this uncertainty that Paul urged the Thessalonians to remain steadfast in their belief in the pre-tribulation rapture. The following chart will illustrate the New Testament teaching on the second advent.

THE TWO PHASES OF CHRIST'S SECOND ADVENT	
Phase 1 — the Rapture	*Phase 2 — the Revelation*
Christ's coming *for* his Church (1 Thess. 4:13-18). He comes to resurrect and translate his saints (4:16, 17).	Christ's advent *with* his Church (Rev. 19:11-16). He comes to slay his foes and set up his earthly kingdom (Acts 1:6).
Christ does not actually come to the earth but instead meets his glorified saints in the air (1 Thess. 4:17). This coming is hidden from the unsaved.	Christ's feet stand on Olivet (Zech. 14:4). He comes as a glorious Conqueror and King (Rev. 19:16). This coming is public to every eye (Rev. 1:7).
This coming is imminent, expected and awaited by the Church (1 Thess. 1:10; Tit. 2:13). No prophetic event will intervene. Occurs *before* the day of the Lord (2 Thess. 2:1-5).	This advent is not imminent but is preceded by definite signs (Matt. 24:29-31), although it will come upon sinners like a thief. Occurs following the day of the Lord (2 Thess. 2:8).
Not revealed in the Old Testament because the Church was not made known there except in types, which were unrevealed until the antitype appeared (Eph. 3:1-10).	Emblazoned on the pages of the Old Testament as a part of the day of the Lord and the prediction of the Davidic millennial kingdom (Dan. 7:9-12; Zech. 14:3-7; Mal. 3:1-6).
Precedes the revelation of the Antichrist (2 Thess. 2:3) and the final great apostasy (2:2). Precedes the consummation of "the mystery of iniquity" and worldwide rebellion (2:7).	Follows the career of Antichrist and is the means of his destruction (2 Thess. 2:8-10; Rev. 19:20; 20:10). Crushes the final apostasy and rebellion.

The Pastoral Epistles

First and Second Timothy and Titus are commonly called "Pastoral Epistles." This eighteenth-century designation, though practical, is not entirely accurate. The letters furnish invaluable instructions for pastors and important directions for the conduct and administration of local churches, but Timothy and Titus were not pastors in the usual present-day sense of that term. They were rather the Apostle's special envoys dispatched to act in a pastoral capacity in order to meet a specific need or to carry out a special assignment.

Modern criticism has shown a marked tendency to deny Pauline authorship to the Pastoral Epistles, despite clear statements of Pauline authorship in the three letters (1 Tim. 1:1; 2 Tim. 1:1; Tit. 1:1) and other objective internal evidence. Arguments against Paul's authorship are largely inferential, with objective proof lacking. The arguments, involving alleged variations in style and vocabulary between the Pastorals and the other Pauline letters, are tenuous and inconclusive. The claim that the theology is different and that grace is no longer central is unsupportable (cf. 1 Tim. 1:14; 2 Tim. 1:9; Tit. 3:4-6). It is true that good works as the *fruit* of faith are featured in the Pastorals, since the *nature* of faith and its *precedence* over works of Law had been thoroughly expounded in preceding letters.

The contention that the errors exposed in the Pastorals belong to the second century and that these letters could therefore not have been authored by Paul is far-fetched. It is claimed that the Pastorals controvert second-century Marcionism (e.g., 1 Tim. 6:20), a heresy with erroneous views of Christ's person. But this and other supposed allusions to second-century "isms" have no objective foundation, since the errors are essentially the same as in certain other Pauline Epistles. The allegation that the church organization in the Pastorals is too advanced for the first century is purely imaginary. The chronological argument—that no place for the Pastorals occurs in the Acts or in the life of Paul, and that they are therefore not genuine—is an argument drawn largely from silence and is thus inconclusive.

The Book of Acts points toward Paul's release rather than his execution (Acts 23:12-35; 28:21, 30, 31), as do Paul's Prison Epistles (Phil. 1:25-27; 2:24; Philem. 1:22). Clement of Rome and Eusebius bear witness to two Roman imprisonments, with ample room for the writing of the Pastoral Epistles in the interval between the two.

As to internal evidence, the epistolary form of the Pastorals and the Apostle's descriptions of himself are similar to the other Pauline letters. All of the objective evidence favors Pauline authorship.

1 Timothy

AUTHOR

See the preceding comments under "The Pastoral Epistles."

BACKGROUND AND DATE

Released from his first Roman imprisonment and apparently on his way to Asia Minor, Paul left Titus on the island of Crete to complete the organization of its churches (Tit. 1:5). At Ephesus the Apostle was joined by Timothy, who had evidently returned from Philippi (Phil. 2:19-23). Paul left for Macedonia, instructing Timothy to stay on at Ephesus in order to meet a great need there (1 Tim. 1:3, 4). From Macedonia Paul wrote his First Letter to Timothy in Ephesus and a letter to Titus in Crete. The most likely date for these would be A.D. 64-66.

IMPORTANCE AND PURPOSE

The central theme of the Epistle is stated in 3:15: "That thou mayest know how thou oughtest to conduct thyself in the house of God, which is the Church of the living God, the pillar and ground of the truth." Hence the letter concerns itself with church organization, the qualification and duties of various church officers, and the general conduct and responsibility of church members. Local churches were rapidly increasing in number during the close of the apostolic era, and these assemblies needed clear teaching about such matters as order, creed, and discipline. The Pastorals supply this important need.

Paul had four main goals in addressing this Epistle to Timothy: 1) to encourage him to expose false teaching (1:3-7, 18-20; 6:3-5, 20, 21); 2) to furnish the young pastor with written credentials authorized by Paul himself (1:3, 4); 3) to instruct Timothy in the organization and management of the local church (3:14, 15); and 4) to exhort him to pastoral diligence and fidelity (4:6 – 6:2).

OUTLINE

Salutation (1:1, 2)
A. Importance of Sound Doctrine (chapter 1)
  1. The pastor and unsound teachers (1:1-7)
  2. The Law and the gospel of Christ (1:8-11)
  3. The gospel and evangelism of sinners (1:12-17)
  4. The admonition to faithful pastoral work (1:18-20)
B. The Importance of Prayer and Public Worship (chapter 2)
  1. The Church and public prayer (2:1-8)
  2. The order of women in Christian society (2:9-15)
C. The Importance of Church Government (chapter 3)
  1. The qualifications of elders (3:1-7)
  2. The qualifications of deacons (3:8-13)
  3. The Church and revealed truth (3:14-16)
D. The Importance of a Faithful Pastor (chapters 4 – 6)
  1. The faithful pastor and error (4:1-6)
  2. The faithful pastor and self-discipline (4:7-16)
  3. The faithful pastor and various Christians (5:1-22)
  4. The faithful pastor and apostolic advice (5:23-25)
  5. The faithful pastor and social classes (6:1-5)
  6. The faithful pastor and materialistic gain (6:6-10)
  7. The faithful pastor as a man of God (6:11-16)
  8. The faithful pastor and wealthy believers (6:17-19)
  9. The faithful pastor and an appeal to watchfulness (6:20, 21)

THE RELATION OF THE LAW TO THE GOSPEL

The Apostle deals briefly but incisively with this momentous question as he faced the errors of the legalists at Ephesus (1:8-11). In

Galatians Paul had dealt with the justification and sanctification of the believer in relation to the Law. Now in First Timothy he relates the Law to the gospel of grace. He first declares that *the Law itself is good* (1:8a; cf. Rom. 7:12): "We know the law is good." It is good because it reflects the holiness of God. However, *the Law must be used lawfully*, that is, for the purpose for which it was designed (1:8b). The Apostle declares that it was never intended to make bad people good, but rather to convict bad people of their sinfulness and to drive them to Christ to be saved (Rom. 3:21-28; Eph. 2:8-10). Therefore, the Law is not to be misused in the case of the "righteous (justified) man" as a means of either justifying or sanctifying him. The Law was *intended for the sinner, to reveal to him his sin and its penalty apart from Christ* (1:9, 10).

The Law must be used properly, *in accord with the gospel of grace* (1:11). Although the Law can neither justify, sanctify, nor glorify the believer, the gospel of Christ accomplishes and guarantees all of these things. It is therefore fitly called "the gospel of the glory of the blessed God." Because every believer has been given a new nature at the moment of conversion and is securely indwelt by the Holy Spirit, he manifests the ethics of God's eternal moral law in his upright way of life (2 Cor. 3:11; Rom. 8:1-15). This holy life is not the result of the works of the flesh or of legalistic strivings, but is "the fruit of the Spirit" (Gal. 5:22, 23).

THE ORDER OF WOMEN
IN CHRISTIAN SOCIETY

The Apostle treats this important aspect of Christian living and public worship in First Timothy 2:9-15. The Christian woman's demeanor and dress are to be consonant with her position in Christ and are never to violate Christian propriety (2:9, 10). In her relation to her husband she is to be characterized by a spirit of teachableness and quiet submission (2:11). In the first Corinthian letter Paul had dealt with the order of the sexes (1 Cor. 11:1-16). There he pointed out that the woman is subordinate to the man (denoted by her headdress), even as the man is subordinate to Christ. As a token of this a woman should not pray or prophesy with her head unveiled or uncovered.

In prescribing proper conduct in the Church and in Christian circles, the Apostle resumes the subject of the order of the sexes in his instructions to Timothy. He indicates that any lack of teachableness or quiet submission on the part of a Christian wife toward her husband is highly improper, particularly in a woman professing godliness. The

Apostle hints at the confusion which results when women forget their proper place in public worship and teach men or usurp authority over them (2:12). Women have a wide sphere of teaching, but not where men are directly involved. New cults have been started or abetted by women who refused to abide by God's Word on this point.

The Apostle establishes the doctrinal basis for the Christian ideal of subjection in First Timothy 2:13-15 (compare Genesis 3:16); it is a strikingly relevant issue in our own day, when the "liberation" of women is a militant cause and when the need for Christian balance is especially needed. Paul points out that Adam was created as the federal head of the race before Eve was formed (Gen. 2:7, 18; Rom. 5:12). Eve was formed from Adam and not Adam from Eve (Gen. 2:18-22). The woman rather than the man was deceived (Gen. 3:1-6) and is still particularly vulnerable to doctrinal deception. The woman will be "saved," that is, rescued or preserved from insubordination, deception, doctrinal error, and other evils or improprieties that threaten her, by the queenly grace of motherhood.

A Christian mother who possesses the essential qualities of "faith and love and holiness with sobriety" (3:15) can make a priceless contribution to the work of Christ and the upbuilding of the Church. The marriage that is strengthened by these hallowed virtues results in God-fearing youth who further the health and growth of the Church and the well-being of society.

THE DIVINE CRITERION TO DIFFERENTIATE FALSE RELIGIONS FROM TRUE

After relating the local church to revealed truth (1 Tim. 3:14-16) and tracing the origin of error, cultism, and false religion to demonism (4:1-6), the Apostle pauses to set forth the doctrinal norm or standard by which the countless varieties of religious teaching can be tested. This doctrinal touchstone is found in First Timothy 3:16: ". . . Great is the mystery of godliness: God was manifest in the flesh, justified in the Spirit, seen of angels, preached unto the Gentiles, believed on in the world, received up into glory." By this doctrinal formula all the cults of Christianity, as well as Judaism and all the non-Christian faiths of the world, can be evaluated and their truth or falsity determined.

This criterion of truth summarizes the essential verities of the Christian faith. It shows how lost and ungodly sinners can be restored to "godliness" (God-likeness) by being accepted before an infinitely holy God on the basis of the finished work of Christ. It contains the following elements: 1) the incarnation. "He who (God, the eternal Word) was manifest in the flesh" (cf. John 1:1, 14); 2) Christ's death and resurrection. He was "justified in the Spirit," that is, he was personally vindicated by the Holy Spirit by the act of physical resurrection; 3) Christ's divine person and complete redemptive work as attested by the unfallen angels. He was "seen by angels"; 4) the evidence of Christ's saving power. He was "believed on in the world"; 5) the divine validation of Christ's redemptive work. He was "received up into glory."

How good of God not to abandon us to our own fallible judgment in a realm so baffling as the religious! In a day of apostasy and false ecumenism how grateful we ought to be for the divinely revealed standard by which all doctrinal error can be exposed!

THE SOURCE OF DOCTRINAL ERROR AND FALSE RELIGIONS

Having presented the criterion of truth (3:16), the Apostle proceeds to reveal the origin of error. He shows that heresies spring from *doctrines of demons* (4:1, 2). This disclosure is of the utmost importance to the Church in her function as the "pillar and ground" of the truth (3:14, 15). The Holy Spirit declares that error is instigated not primarily by false teachers but by evil spirits or demons who inspire susceptible human beings. The result is called "doctrines of demons" (4:1).

As an illustration that false doctrine is demon-originated the Apostle chooses a type of legalistic asceticism current at the time (4:3, 4). It forbade marriage and thereby incriminated God by implying that this God-ordained institution was evil. It likewise disallowed certain foods created by God to be received with thanksgiving and prayer. The demonic impress in this error, illustrative of many that Satan tries to introduce, is apparent. It displays Satan's pride (Isa. 14:12-14), his slander of God's goodness (Gen. 3:5), and his treacherous falsehood (Gen. 3:4).

2 Timothy

AUTHOR

Refer to the comments under "The Pastoral Epistles."

BACKGROUND AND DATE

Paul was a prisoner in Rome (1:8, 16, 17; 2:9), with martyrdom facing him (4:6-8). Severely tested by loneliness (4:10, 11), he wrote to Timothy, who was presumably at Ephesus (since Priscilla and Aquila—4:19; cf. 1 Tim. 1:3—as well as Onesiphorus—1:16-18; 4:19— were apparently residing there).

After Paul had written First Timothy and Titus (evidently from Macedonia), he proceeded to Nicopolis, where he intended to spend the winter (Tit. 3:12). Nicopolis was the capital of Epirus; it lay north of Achaia on the west coast of Greece. Nicopolis was a Roman colony, like Philippi, and Paul may have planned to use it as a base for evangelizing Epirus. Although there were other towns named Nicopolis ("city of victory"), this was the only one of sufficient standing to warrant Paul's residence through an entire winter. In addition, its geographical location northwest of Crete would favor a meeting with Titus.

At Nicopolis Paul was apparently arrested and taken to Rome (1:16, 17). There in prison he wrote Second Timothy. Soon afterward, according to tradition, the noble Apostle died a martyr's death on the Ostian way, west of the capital. Paul seems to have been executed shortly before Nero's death on June 8, A.D. 68. Second Timothy was clearly written shortly before Paul's martyrdom. The Epistle may therefore be dated in the autumn of 67 or the spring of 68.

IMPORTANCE AND PURPOSE

Paul's Second Letter to Timothy is undoubtedly the Apostle's last in a total of thirteen that have come down to us. In this noble Epistle he displays the fortitude and resiliency of character that mark a great warrior and missionary of Christ. Although the Apostle was now a prisoner without human hope, he was courageously resigned to an inevitable death sentence. Paul's faith, subject to the utmost test, proved to be completely adequate. His message is a farewell from a man of indomitable spirit. In the Epistle he urges others to "endure hardship, as a good soldier of Jesus Christ" (2:3). Meanwhile he himself became the great exponent of what he challenged others to be. His triumphant spirit in the face of martyrdom has moved countless souls to take up their cross and follow Christ bravely and dauntlessly to the end.

But despite his approaching death, Paul did not ignore the specific needs of his younger co-worker. In writing this Epistle Paul charted the course of the faithful pastor in a day of doctrinal declension (chap. 1) and warned about the spiritual conflict which a good soldier of Jesus Christ must engage in if he would remain true to his call (chap. 2). He described the apostasy (3:1-5) and outlined its dire results (3:6-9) in persecution and suffering (3:10-13), together with the all-important role which the inspired and fully authoritative Word plays in the battle (3:14-17). The remedy for apostasy is the preaching of the inspired Word (4:1-4); this will be accompanied by rewards for the faithful preacher (4:5-8). Advice and instructions are given concerning fellow workers (4:9-13), as well as a warning concerning evil workers (4:14, 15). The faithful pastor must not lose heart at man's failure (4:16). He must rely instead on God's faithfulness (4:17, 18).

OUTLINE

Introduction (1:1, 2)
A. Pastoral Fidelity in Apostasy (chapter 1)
   1. Commendation of Timothy's faith (1:3-5)
   2. Encouragement to continued faithfulness (1:6-14)
   3. Warning against disloyalty (1:15)
   4. Reassurance in fidelity (1:16-18)
B. Spiritual Conflict in Apostasy (chapter 2)
   1. Standing true to grace (2:1, 2)
   2. Striving for mastery (2:3-10)
   3. Relying on God's faithfulness (2:11-19)

4. Separating from sin (2:20-22)
5. Avoiding foolish strife (2:23, 24)
6. Cultivating positive virtues (2:25, 26)
C. Defense of the Word in Apostasy (chapter 3)
   1. Prediction of apostasy (3:1-9)
   2. Apostolic warning (3:10-13)
   3. Believer's resource (3:14-17)
D. Faithfulness of God in a Day of Apostasy (chapter 4)
   1. He is Judge — therefore preach the Word (4:1-5)
   2. He will reward fidelity — therefore trust him (4:6-8)
   3. He never fails — therefore put confidence in him (4:9-18)
Conclusion (4:19-22)

THE CHRISTIAN'S RESOURCES
IN TIMES OF APOSTASY

The Apostle indicates these resources as 1) faith (1:5); 2) the Holy Spirit (1:14); 3) the Word of God (3:14-17); 4) the grace of Christ (2:1); 5) the Lord's faithfulness and power (2:13, 19; 4:17, 18); 6) separation from heretics and apostates (2:20, 21); and 7) the Lord's sure reward (4:7, 8).

APOSTASY AND CHRISTIAN PROFESSION

The term "apostasy" comes from the Greek word *apostasia*, "a falling away," which in turn comes from *aphistasthai*, "to stand away from." It denotes a professed Christian who deliberately rejects the central facts of Christianity and turns away from Jesus Christ and his atoning sacrifice (1 John 4:1-3; 2 Pet. 2:1). Apostasy, unlike error or heresy, is never associated with regeneration and true saving faith. Error may be caused by simple ignorance (Acts 19:1, 2), and heresy may be traced to demonic delusion and Satanic deception (1 Tim. 4:1, 2; 2 Tim. 2:25, 26). Either of these may at times be true of regenerated believers. Apostates, however, deliberately depart from the faith (Jude 1:3) which they once professed intellectually but never enjoyed experientially. They forsake the *faith* of a Christian but not the *outward veneer and profession* of Christianity. They have "a form of godliness" but have denied (renounced) "the power of it" (2 Tim. 3:5).

Paul graphically describes apostates as rejecting "sound doctrine" and instead "after their own lusts heaping to themselves teachers, having itching ears." They "turn away their ears from the truth" and have "turned unto fables" (2 Tim. 4:3, 4). The Apostle Peter fully exposes apostates (2 Pet. 2:1-22), demonstrating that they are unsaved, having never experienced regeneration and the new nature. He graphically portrays their old nature under the figure of a dog and a sow: "But it is happened unto them according to the true proverb: the dog is turned to his own vomit again; and the sow that was washed to her wallowing in the mire" (2 Pet. 2:22; cf. Prov. 26:11).

Apostasy is irremediable; it awaits divine judgment (2 Thess. 2: 10-12; 2 Pet. 2:17-21; Jude 1:11-15; Rev. 3:14-16). God's judgment is seen in the case of the angels that fell (Matt. 25:41; Jude 1:6), in the case of Israel (Deut.28:15-68; Isa. 1:5, 6; 5:5-7), and in the case of Christendom (2 Thess. 2:10-12). Of course, no sinner is beyond the reach of the grace of God in Christ. But an apostate must come as a lost sinner in order to accept the Savior for salvation. This means that he must renounce his apostasy and thus cease to be an apostate.

INSPIRED SCRIPTURE AND APOSTASY

The great bulwark against error and apostasy is the Word of God. The recognition of the Bible as the fully inspired and completely authoritative guide in matters of doctrine and morals is the believer's protection against error and apostasy. In times of doctrinal declension this or that doctrine of the faith may come under attack and be denied. But in a day of apostasy, as in both Paul's day and today, the Bible is rejected as the inspired and authoritative voice of God; as a result the very foundations of the faith are rejected. Once the full inspiration and authority of Scripture are renounced, the whole structure of doctrine is threatened with collapse.

The Apostle realized these important facts. Hence in Second Timothy, his Epistle that combats and exposes apostasy, he gives us the classic passage on the inspiration of Scripture (3:14-17). He sets forth the pivotal role which the Scriptures played in Timothy's life from childhood (3:14, 15; cf. 1 Tim. 1:1, 2; 2 Tim. 2:1, 2). God's Word, he points out, has the power to make one "wise to salvation" through faith centered in the person and work of Christ (3:15). Then he sets forth the inspiration and usefulness of Scripture (3:16, 17).

The correct rendering of this pivotal passage is: "All Scripture is God-breathed and profitable. . . . " This teaches that 1) *the entire Bible is fully inspired by God.* The inspiration of the Old Testament is indicated by direct assertion and the rest of canonical Scripture by clear implication. 2) *All Scripture is a product of God* — it is "God-breathed" (*theopneustos*). Not only was it breathed *into* the human agents, but through them it was breathed *out* by God. Without depriving the human authors of intelligence, individuality, literary style, or personal feelings, God supernaturally directed the writing of the Sacred Oracles. As a result the Scriptures recorded his comprehensive and infallible revelation to man with perfect accuracy. 3) *Since it is God-breathed, all Scripture in the original autographs is inerrant and fully authoritative.*

Having expounded the full inspiration of the Word, the Apostle outlines the usefulness of Scripture, particularly as the antidote against error and apostasy. He shows that all of Scripture is useful 1) "for *doctrine*" (teaching and systematizing Christian truth); 2) "for *reproof*" (censure of wrongdoing); 3) "for *correction*" (setting right what is wrong); 4) "for *instruction in righteousness*" (both God's own intrinsic righteousness and the righteous conduct which he requires of his saints); and 5) that "the man of God may be perfect," completely furnished "for all good works."

THE PREACHING OF THE WORD AND APOSTASY

As the antidote against apostasy, the Apostle solemnly enjoins the heralding of the Word (4:1, 2). Realizing how essential this activity is, the Apostle stresses the accounting which Christ's servants will be required to give regarding their treatment of God's truth. "Preaching the Word" means proclaiming it both authoritatively and systematically. A task of such unparalleled importance must be performed both "in season" (conveniently, opportunely) and "out of season" (inconveniently, inopportunely).

The Apostle leaves no doubt about the reason for his solemn charge to preach the Word constantly (4:3, 4). It is that the Word of God exposes and counteracts apostasy. Apostates cannot tolerate sound doctrine. They multiply teachers who will cater to their illegitimate desires. They have "itching ears," eager to be entertained by some novel error or unsound theory. They knowingly turn their ears from the truth of the Word. The result is that they adopt myths and fables (2 Thess. 2:10-12).

THE LORD'S COMING AND APOSTASY

In times of apostasy the faithful minister is to encourage himself with the prospect of the Lord's coming for his own (John 14:1-3).

"Henceforth there is laid up for me a crown of righteousness, which the Lord, the righteous Judge, will award to me on that day, and not only to me but also to all who have loved his appearing" (4:8). The Scriptures inculcate in believers an eager expectation of the Lord's coming for his own (1 Thess. 4:13-18).

Titus

AUTHOR AND DATE

Paul apparently wrote the Epistle to Titus from Macedonia between his Roman imprisonments during A.D. 64-66. See comments under "The Pastoral Epistles."

BACKGROUND

Though he is not mentioned in the Acts of the Apostles, Titus is referred to quite frequently in Paul's Epistles, particularly in Second Corinthians and Galatians. He was born of Gentile parents (Gal. 2:3) and was a member of the delegation from Antioch who accompanied Paul and Barnabas to the first Church Council (Acts 15:2; Gal. 2:1-3). During the third missionary tour Titus was twice dispatched on urgent missions to Corinth, in which he was quite successful. It is not strange that he should be entrusted with an important assignment in the island of Crete. After the completion of this assignment he is said to have gone to Dalmatia, a region on the eastern coast of the Adriatic Sea (2 Tim. 4:10).

IMPORTANCE AND PURPOSE

Paul's letter to the young pastor Titus is much like his first letter to Timothy in that it features church order and sound doctrine. Titus had proved his ability in previous assignments and was charged with considerable responsibility on the island of Crete. He was given authority to appoint elders in the various churches there (1:5), to rebuke insubordinates (1:13; 3:10), to teach sound doctrine (2:1), and to exercise general oversight over the churches.

The Apostle's purpose in this letter is much the same as in his first letter to Timothy. After his first imprisonment in Rome Paul evidently stopped at Crete, for he left Titus there to carry on the work. Crete is a mountainous island about 156 miles long and 7 to 35 miles wide; it lies at the southern end of the Aegean Sea. Cretans are mentioned among those present at Pentecost (Acts 2:11).

After a lengthy salutation (1:1-4), Paul deals with scriptural church organization, urging Titus to complete the task facing him in Crete (1:5). The Apostle lists the qualifications to be required of elders (1:6-16). He then proceeds to outline proper pastoral ministry toward various groups, including the aged (2:1-3), the young (2:4-8), and servants (2:9-15). He then relates pastoral ministry toward Christian living that adorns the gospel (3:1-11). He closes with greetings and instructions concerning good works (3:12-15).

OUTLINE

Salutation (1:1-4)
A. The Church Adorning the Gospel (1:5-16)
1. By proper organization (1:5)
2. By qualified elders (1:6-9)
3. By a firm stand against false elders (1:10-16)
B. The Pastor Adorning the Gospel (2:1-15)
1. By his teaching ministry to the aged (2:1-4)
2. By his teaching and example to the young (2:5-8)
3. By his teaching and example to servants (2:9, 10)
4. By his teaching and experience of the gospel of grace (2:11-15)
C. The Church Members Adorning the Gospel (3:1-11)
1. By exemplary behavior before the world (3:1, 2)
2. By comprehending the grace of God (3:3-7)
3. By a life of good works (3:8-11)
D. Closing Greetings and Instructions (3:12-15)

SCRIPTURAL CHURCH ORGANIZATION

Both First Timothy and Titus give invaluable instruction about the need for scriptural organization of the local church. In Crete the problem was not the absence in the local church of persons having the qualifications of elders, for the Holy Spirit raises up and equips such (Acts 20:28). The problem was instead *the recognition and appointment* of qualified and Spirit-prepared elders. Whether Titus was to appoint such men or the church to elect them under his supervision is not stated. The important thing is not *how it is done* but that it *actually be done*, and that the qualified and Spirit-prepared men be duly installed in their important office.

The terms "elder" (Greek *presbuteros*, "an elderly man") and "bishop" (Greek *episkopos*, "overseer") apparently denote the same person, for they are used interchangeably (cf. Acts 20:17, 18; Tit. 1:5, 7). The term "elder" seems to refer to the office and the term "bishop" to the elder's general duty of overseeing the flock of God.

Eldership in the New Testament always occurs in the plural. The idea of *one* elder ruling or officiating over the church in the sense of an ecclesiastical dictatorship is foreign to Scripture. This practice is nevertheless sometimes found in churches that otherwise regard themselves as Bible-centered.

The functions of elders are clearly outlined in Scripture. These include 1) teaching and preaching (1 Tim. 5:17); 2) guarding the faith from error and distortion (Tit. 1:9); and 3) overseeing the spiritual interests of the local church (1 Tim. 3:4, 5; 5:17; John 21:15, 16, 17; Acts 20:28; Heb. 13:17; 1 Pet. 5:2). Not every elder will necessarily perform all these functions. Often these duties are distributed among the several elders.

THE GOSPEL OF GRACE AND GODLY LIVING

In combating the tendency to loose living and general immorality among the Cretans (1:12, 13), the Apostle penned one of the most comprehensive and concise New Testament summations of the relation of the gospel of grace to a godly life (2:10-14). In doing so he achieves a perfect balance of doctrine and practical living. The believer who accepts "the grace of God that bringeth salvation" (2:11) will in his life "adorn the doctrine of God, our Savior, in all things" (2:10). The Greek word translated "adorn" means "to decorate, to embellish." A consistent, godly life is an adornment to the grace of God which appeared to us in salvation.

Beginning with the incarnation ("the grace of God . . . hath appeared" — 2:11), this doctrine is related to a life that denies evil and does good here and now (2:12). The doctrine of the return of Christ is made the incentive for godly conduct ("looking for that blessed hope" — 2:13). The great truth of redemption is presented as God saving us, not *in* our sins (cf. Matt. 1:21) but *from* our sins and "all iniquity" in order to purify for himself a people for his own possession, "zealous of good works."

The doctrinal significance of this great passage as a refutation of both lawless abuse of grace and legalistic self-righteousness can scarcely be overstated. The Apostle in his great doctrinal Epistles (especially Romans and Galatians) had expounded the far-reaching truth of justification and sanctification by God's grace *alone*, apart from the works of the Law. Now he shows that such salvation, far from leading to license, is inseparably wedded to a pure, holy life produced by the Holy Spirit in the believer.

JUSTIFICATION AND GOOD WORKS

The second great doctrinal passage in the Epistle to Titus (3:4-8) complements the first one (2:10-14; see above) and likewise relates God's grace to a holy and useful life. However, there is this difference: the first passage features God's grace as manifested in salvation in general. The second passage relates divine grace specifically to justification and good works. In previous writings the Apostle had repeatedly propounded the far-reaching truth of justification by God's grace through faith, *totally* apart from works of law or self-effort. Did this mean that the justified believer was free to live a loose or lawless life, devoid of good works? Of course not. The Apostle's reply is, "This is a faithful saying, and these things I will that thou affirm constantly, that they who have believed in God might be *careful to maintain good works*. These things are good and profitable" (3:8; cf. Eph. 2:8, 9 with Eph. 2:10).

But it is significant that the Apostle in exhorting to good works does not in one iota minimize God's grace in salvation or justification ("being justified by *his grace*" — 3:7). Instead, he extols the all-sufficiency of divine grace, totally apart from works, to save and sanctify the lost. This he does in a passage which meets or exceeds in grandeur anything he had ever penned in Romans or Galatians about God's unmerited favor manifested in justification.

However, in relating justification apart from works to a justified life *that produces good works,* the Apostle stresses the fact that God saved us by the "*washing* of regeneration" in order to deliver us from the penalty and power of sin and by the "*renewing* of the Holy Spirit" in order to provide the inner dynamic for a holy life of good works (3: 5). That this inner dynamic is completely adequate for the production of such good works is also emphasized: ". . . which he *shed on us abundantly* through Jesus Christ our Savior" (3:6).

Philemon

AUTHENTICITY

This priceless letter demonstrates the power of the gospel of grace and the blessing of Christian fellowship in action. Marcion's Canon and the Muratorian Fragment (the earliest existing lists of Pauline writings) contain Philemon even though they omit the Pastoral Epistles. In the fourth century Philemon was questioned not so much for its authenticity as for its supposed triviality. Most scholars, however, have placed a high value on the tact, grace, delicacy of feeling, and Christian affection which adorn this letter, and have regarded it worthy of canonicity in the highest sense.

The letter is much more than a mere chance correspondence between two people. If we look beyond its personal and informal nature we see careful composition and observance of literary forms. It is important to note that both individuals and a church were recipients of this letter by the Apostle (1:2). Although Philemon is specifically named, his family and church are presumably linked with him, as in Romans 16:5 and Colossians 4:15.

BACKGROUND AND DATE

Paul is imprisoned (vv. 9, 10). The occasion is the same as that in the Epistle to the Colossians. Onesimus is to accompany Tychicus, the bearer of the Colossian letter (Col. 4:9). Paul's party in Philemon 1:23, 24 is almost identical with that in Colossians 4:10-14. The place is evidently Rome, during Paul's first imprisonment, in A.D. 61 or 62. Some scholars, however, single out Ephesus as the place of writing and date the Epistle at about A.D. 55. Rome was a haven for displaced persons of every description, and Ephesus too was large enough to get lost in. It is very unlikely that Onesimus would have stayed in proconsular Asia, knowing the stiff penalty which his defection as a slave involved.

This stone found at Caesarea bears the name of Pontius Pilate. *(Russ Busby photo)*

IMPORTANCE AND PURPOSE

The core of the Epistle is an appeal by Paul on behalf of a runaway slave from Colosse named Onesimus (Col. 4:9). Onesimus' conduct was in sharp contrast to his name, which means "useful" (v. 11).

By some means, possibly through his fellow-townsman Epaphras (Col. 4:12), the renegade slave had been brought into contact with Paul in prison. The result was a radical conversion. Not only so, but a deep love was engendered in Paul for his new "son" in the faith, in whom the veteran saw great potential.

Onesimus was in grave danger of severe punishment from his offended owner, Philemon. Under contemporary law frightful penalties could be imposed not only on derelict slaves but also on those who harbored them. It was at this point that the Apostle interposed with Philemon, a brother in the Lord (vv. 7, 20). He does not command but earnestly entreats (vv. 8, 9) that the master will receive his returning slave as he would Paul himself (v. 17). Paul solemnly offers to underwrite all the slave's debts (vv. 18, 19).

It is possible that Paul is asking for more than clemency. Some scholars think the Apostle is asking for Onesimus himself (v. 10), rather than merely pleading in his behalf. The request would then mean that Paul is asking that Onesimus be released to him for Christian service (vv. 11-14). The slave would from then on stand in an unspeakably closer and more permanent relationship than the old domestic one (vv. 15, 16). In any case Philemon owed his own introduction to Christ to Paul (v. 19).

OUTLINE

Introduction: Greeting to Philemon (1-3)
A. Commendation of Philemon (4-7)
  1. His love and faith (4, 5)
  2. Paul's prayer for him (6, 7)
B. Intercession for Onesimus (8-19)
  1. Plea for a runaway slave (8-10)
  2. Defense of a servant of Christ (11-16)
  3. Illustration of the principle of imputation (17-19)
C. Expression of Confidence (20, 21)
  1. Request of confidence (20)
  2. Assurance of confidence (21)
Conclusion (22-25)

AN EXQUISITE ILLUSTRATION OF DIVINE IMPUTATION

Paul's eloquent intercession for Onesimus breathes the spirit of Christ's intercession for his own before the Father. Moreover, his plea for the runaway slave, now a servant of Christ (vv. 17, 18), perfectly illustrates imputation: "Receive him as myself; if he has wronged thee or owes thee anything, put that on my account."

In imputation (Gen. 15:6; James 2:23) the sinner's sins are reckoned or imputed to Christ's account, and Christ's righteousness is credited or imputed to the sinner's account, all on the basis of faith. As a result the sinner is not only forgiven and discharged of any sin or debt but is credited with the infinite righteousness of Christ and the riches of his salvation.

How exquisite that the Apostle should use this lofty and powerful appeal to Philemon, who had himself had his sins imputed to Christ and Christ's righteousness reckoned to him! Let Philemon deal with his runaway slave as God had dealt in grace with him!

CHRISTIANITY AND THE ISSUE OF SOCIAL INJUSTICE AND INEQUALITY

The Epistle of Philemon not only beautifully illustrates the liberating gospel of Christ and its central feature of imputation, but it also illustrates how this liberating message works to set enslaved humanity free from its social ills and injustices.

Philemon, the slave owner, became converted to Christ. Then his unsaved slave, Onesimus, robbed him and ran away. Converted to Christ, the recreant slave now sustained to his master the new relationship of "brother beloved" (v. 16). This new relationship was bound to affect the old relationship drastically, if not eventually dissolve it altogether. This was especially true under the influence of so strong a protagonist of Christ as Paul, who next to his divine Lord was the greatest emancipator of the human race that has ever been produced.

In the Epistle to the Galatians, the "Magna Charta of Christian Liberty," Paul the Emancipator penned these soul-stirring words that sound the death knell to prejudice, tyranny, and injustice, and show that in Christ's redemptive work lies the answer to the social problems that agitate present-day society. "For ye are all the sons of God by faith in Christ Jesus. For as many of you as have been baptized into Christ have put on Christ. There is neither Jew nor Greek, there is neither bond nor free, there is neither male nor female; for ye are all one in Christ Jesus" (Gal. 3:26-28).

"In Christ Jesus . . . there is *neither bond nor free*." Slavery was one of the curses of the ancient world, especially in the Greco-Roman world of the first century A.D. Pagan people saw no more wrong in possessing slaves than we see in having domestic servants. Estimates of the slave population of the Roman Empire have been as high as sixty million! Under the provisions of Roman law, a slave was usually considered as property owned by another, possessing no rights at all, and, like any other form of personal property, disposable at the owner's whim. For the smallest offense a slave might be scourged, mutilated, thrown to the wild beasts, or otherwise inhumanly treated.

It is quite natural that some of the early Christians had slaves (see Eph. 6:9; Col. 4:1). The fact that the New Testament does not directly inveigh against slavery as a social evil does not mean that it condones the practice. Like the Epistle to Philemon, the New Testament as a whole exemplifies the Christian way of dealing with a grievous social evil. It does not advocate force or violence as the method of rooting out an injustice or inequality like slavery. It viewed the practice of slavery as a part of the order of the world that was passing away and which could not be eradicated instantly. It announced principles of righteousness and provisions of the gospel of redemption that would set men free in Christ and gradually and spontaneously cause the institution of slavery to vanish of itself. In the last resort the fraternity of the sons of God would see all its members free of their bonds. Even men outside this fraternity would come to see the essential injustice of an institution that treats human personality as so much chattel property and robs man of his dignity and right as a self-determining individual.

The Jewish-Christian and General Epistles

NATURE OF THE EPISTLES

The Jewish-Christian Epistles, which in most English versions follow the Pauline Epistles, consist of Hebrews, James and First Peter. These inspired books are addressed directly to Jewish believers. In the case of Hebrews the purpose is to expound the all-sufficiency and absolute finality of Messiah's redemptive work on the cross. It constitutes a warning to Jewish Christians of the peril of abandoning complete trust in Christ and going back to the fulfilled ritualism and legalism of Judaism as a means of either justification or sanctification before God.

The Epistle of James is a very early letter, having been written to Jewish believers before the gospel went out to the Gentiles and before the distinctive truths of the Church were revealed through the Apostle Paul. It instructs believers in the death, resurrection, and ascension of Christ in practical terms familiar to Old Testament saints.

First Peter is also addressed largely to Jewish believers of the Dispersion. Although it resembles James, it shows more advanced Christian truth than this very early Epistle. First Peter displays knowledge of most, if not all, of the Pauline Epistles, though these truths are molded to meet the needs of Jewish converts throughout the Roman Empire. Second Peter and Jude are more general, like the so-called General Epistles of First, Second, and Third John.

DIFFERENCE FROM PAUL'S EPISTLES

The Jewish-Christian and General Epistles differ significantly from the Pauline Epistles. The difference, however, is not that of conflict or disagreement but rather that of development and extension. Both present the same Savior, the same salvation, and the same hope. But as the Apostle to the Gentiles, Paul received the great spiritual revelations of the Church—an entity composed predominantly of saved Gentiles. The distinctive elements of this revelation, such as the nature, position, and destiny of the Church, are presupposed in the non-Pauline Epistles but are not expounded in any detail. The Epistle to the Hebrews, for example, expounds "so great salvation" from the viewpoint of its fulfillment of the Mosaic Covenant and its superiority to Judaism.

By way of further contrast, the inculcation of Christian living in the non-Pauline Epistles is grounded in the basic doctrines of Christianity, while in the Pauline Letters this same conduct is based on the more complex information of the believer's positional association with Christ in his death, burial, resurrection, and present session in glory (Rom. 6:1-11; Eph. 1:1-14; Col. 3:1-4).

Hebrews

AUTHOR

The Epistle is plainly anonymous and divinely intended to be so. All attempts to identify the author have been little more than futile guesses. Ancient traditions regarding the matter consisted of two divergent opinions, one (Tertullian's) attributing it to Barnabas and the other, the more dominating tradition (that of Clement of Alexandria and Origen), attributing it to Paul. The question of authorship was of greater importance in the early Church than it is today, for upon this issue depended the canonicity of the Epistle. The prevalence in Alexandria of the idea of Pauline authorship was responsible for early recognition of canonicity in the East; in the West canonicity was recognized by the time of Jerome and Augustine (about A.D. 400).

By the time of the Reformation, however, Erasmus, Luther, and Calvin were again disputing the Pauline authorship of the Epistle. Luther suggested that Apollos was the author. Other suggestions by later scholars include Philip the evangelist and Aquila and Priscilla. Scholars would do well to abide by Origen's caution and to leave the author incognito, as he was intended to be.

BACKGROUND AND DATE

The Epistle was evidently sent to Jewish Christians in Jerusalem and the surrounding regions. It seems clear that the Temple was still continuing (8:4, 13; 10:1, 8, 11; 13:10, 11). The readers had evidently been Christians for a long time and had suffered severely. A date of about A.D. 67-69 would thus seem to fit the internal evidence. Scholars who date the Epistle at A.D. 80-90 do so on insufficient evidence.

IMPORTANCE AND PURPOSE

From the standpoint of doctrinal contribution and literary excellence Hebrews stands among the greatest of the New Testament books. The work is unique in its explanation of the transition from Mosaic Law to Christian privilege and in its interpretation of the Old Testament symbols of Christ.

The writer especially undertakes to show the relationship of Christianity to Judaism. This problem had been a lively issue among Christians since the death, resurrection, and ascension of Christ and the giving of the Spirit, which marked the beginning of the Church age. To accomplish this goal the author expounds the superiority of the Son of God to everyone and everything else — to prophets and angels (1:4 — 2:18), to Moses and Joshua (3:1 — 4:13), and to Aaron and the Aaronic priesthood (typified by the Melchizedek priesthood — 5:1 — 8:5). He continues by demonstrating the superiority of the New Covenant to the Old Covenant (8:6 — 10:39) and the overall superiority of faith in God and his redemptive grace in Christ (11:1 — 13:17).

The author realizes the severe pressure upon Hebrew believers to turn back because of either fierce persecution from fellow Hebrews or the allurement of legalistic ordinances practiced by the nation for fifteen centuries. He therefore intersperses his masterly argument with periodic warnings against defection to legalism, each time prompting the Hebrew believer to press on in the grace of Christ (2:1-4; 5:11 — 6:12; 10:19-39; 12:12 — 13:17). Often the correct meaning of these passages has been missed by failing to keep this important consideration in mind.

OUTLINE

Introduction: The Son, God's Final Revelation (1:1-3)
A. Christ's Superiority to the Angels (1:4 — 2:18)
    1. In his person and work (1:4-14)
    2. Parenthesis — warning against drifting (2:1-4)
    3. In his authority and perfect humanity (2:5-13)
    4. In his conquest of sin and death (2:14-18)
B. Christ's Superiority to Moses (3:1-19)
    1. As Son in contrast to a servant (3:1-6)
    2. Parenthesis — warning against unbelief (3:7-19)
C. Christ's Superiority to Joshua (4:1-13)
    1. In the rest he gives (4:1-8)
    2. In the redemption he provides (4:9-13)

D. The Superiority of Christ's Priesthood to Aaron's (4:14 – 10:39)
1. Because of its redemptive accomplishment (4:14-16)
2. Because of its higher qualifications (5:1-10)
3. Parenthesis – warning against defection (5:11 – 6:12)
4. Because of its superior order (6:13 – 7:22)
5. Because of its efficacy and perpetuity (7:23-28)
6. Because it is ministered in the heavenly sanctuary (8:1-5)
7. Because it is ministered under the New Covenant (8:6 – 10:18)
   (a) It is superior to the Old Covenant (8:6 – 9:10)
   (b) It brings reality (9:11-14)
   (c) It is sealed by Christ's blood (9:15-22)
   (d) It assures a better sanctuary (9:23, 24)
   (e) It is based on a better sacrifice (9:25 – 10:10)
   (f) It involves a finished redemption (10:11-18)
8. Parenthesis – appeal to faith in Christ (10:19-39)
E. The Superiority of Faith in Christ (11:1 – 13:17)
1. Faith that envisioned Christ defined (11:1-3)
2. Faith that envisioned Christ illustrated (11:4-38)
3. Faith of Old Testament saints and ours compared (11:39-40)
4. The race and goal of faith described (12:1-4)
5. The disciplines of faith explained (12:5-11)
6. Parenthesis – warning from Esau's example (12:12-17)
7. Results of faith indicated (12:18-24)
8. Parenthesis – warning against refusal to hear God's voice (12:25-29)
9. Faith expressed in conduct (13:1-9)
10. Faith attested in separation from Judaism (13:10-14)
11. Faith exercised in spiritual worship and obedience (13:15-17)
Concluding Request and Benediction (13:18-25)

THE UNIQUENESS AND FINALITY OF CHRISTIANITY

The uniqueness of Christ and Christianity is the great theological contribution of the Epistle to the Hebrews. The author presents not *a* revelation of God, but *the* final and perfect revelation of God. This means not only that *Christianity supersedes all other faiths* (including Judaism) but that *Christianity itself can never be superseded*. Its salvation is eternal (5:9). So also is its redemption, its inheritance, and its covenant (9:12, 15; 13:20). Christ's offering is described as being "through the eternal Spirit" (9:14). The perfection and finality of the

Christian faith imbues the whole Epistle and furnishes the key for the comprehension of all its major themes.

Like the Pauline Epistles (notably Colossians), Hebrews gives the lie to present-day religious relativism and ecumenical pluralism, which make Christianity just another religion among the various religions of the world and just another way of salvation among many. In masterly fashion the writer to the Hebrews presents the person and work of Christ, demonstrating his superiority to *all* other intermediaries — prophets, angels, Moses, Joshua, and Aaron.

THE PERSON OF CHRIST. The opening chapter of the Epistle strikes the positive and exalted note of Christ's divine sonship. He is eternal, uncreated deity (1:2) — the Word who was with God and was himself God, but who became man (John 1:1, 14). The Son's role as eternal heir, exact replica of God's nature, and creator and sustainer of the universe is declared, as well as his role as redeemer of fallen man (1:2, 3). The Son is superior to the angels in his person and accomplishment (1:4-14), in his authority (2:5-9), in his perfect humanity (2:10-13), and in his conquest of sin and death (2:14-18).

The incarnation of the divine Son is emphasized. He was made a little lower than the angels (2:9), taking upon himself human nature (2:16, 17), and was made subject to all of the temptations which sinless humanity could be exposed to (4:15). His earthly life comes into focus in his temptations (2:18; 4:15), his agony of prayer (5:7), his perfect obedience (5:8), his teaching ministry (2:3), and his endurance of opposition (12:3). Christ's humanity is emphasized in his fulfillment of the Aaronic pattern; his deity is stressed in the fulfillment of the Melchizedek order (5:1 – 10:39).

THE WORK OF CHRIST. Christ's work in creating and sustaining the universe (1:2, 3) is presented as a prelude to his work in human redemption (1:3; 5:1 – 10:39). He is presented as the Redeemer-Priest who surpasses the two greatest Old Testament priests — Melchizedek and Aaron. He thoroughly fulfills both the eternal order of Melchizedek and the temporal and typical order of Aaron. It is against the background of the inadequacies of the Aaronic order that the writer to the Hebrews expounds the superiority of Christ's atoning work. The major superiorities are 1) the *personal nature* of the offering: he offered himself (9:14); 2) the *spiritual character* of the offering: he offered himself "through the eternal Spirit" (9:14); 3) the *permanent results* of his priestly work: he "obtained eternal redemption for us" (9:12); and

4) the *finality* of Christ's offering: he offered himself and entered the holy place once and for all (7:27; 9:12, 28; 10:10).

THE ISSUE OF THE BELIEVER'S SECURITY

In view of the eloquent presentation in Hebrews of the complete and eternal salvation which the all-sufficient Redeemer grants to the believing sinner, it is ironic that passages from this Epistle are frequently misinterpreted to teach that salvation is forefeitable and may be lost. The passage which is most widely abused in this way is the parenthetical exhortation to maturity and warning against defection recorded in 5:11—6:12. This passage concerns *truly regenerated converts from Judaism* who lapsed back into Mosaic legalism. They are therefore designated as immature (5:11-14), having failed to go on to "perfection" or mature status in "the grace and truth" that "came by Jesus Christ" (John 1:17). Instead, they were going back to the Mosaic Law and trusting in its ritual and precepts. They were occupied with what they were *doing* in order to be acceptable to God instead of relying upon what God *had done* for them in Christ to make them acceptable.

The spiritual declension of these Hebrew believers was due to a threefold cause. They were lingering in elementary truths instead of advancing to the deeper truths of grace. They were re-laying basic foundations instead of erecting the superstructure of grace on the existing foundation (6:1, 2). They were failing to appropriate God's power for gracious living and were instead lapsing back into legalistic self-effort.

The Apostle follows the cause of the sin by a clear analysis of its character (6:4-8). That it concerns genuinely regenerated believers is clearly evidenced (6:4, 5). However, they were Hebrew believers who failed to heed what they had heard from Christ through his Apostles and had neglected "such a great salvation" by reverting back to Mosaic legalism (2:1-4). They had remained in the wilderness of unbelief and self-occupation (although redeemed out of Egypt) instead of crossing over Jordan and entering the Canaan of God's rest by reposing in faith in Christ *alone* for their perfection (chaps. 3, 4). So they remained spiritual babies (5:11-14).

The essence of the sin of these believers was *doctrinal defection from the all-sufficiency of Christ's death* (6:6). It was falling from faith and grace to unbelief and works. It was "falling *along the way*" of grace (Greek *parapiptō*), similar to the "falling from" (*ekpiptō*, falling *out of*) grace in Galatians (5:4), with the difference that the former concerned Gentile believers and the latter Jewish believers. In neither case, however, is the issue forfeiture of salvation. The issue in both cases is leaving the gospel of pure grace for some legalistic admixture of works.

The sin was a contradiction of the Hebrew believers' initial repentance from the "dead works" of Judaistic observances (6:1). Consequently it involved the impossibility of restoration to repentance from "dead" religionism as long as it was persisted in. It was in reality a denial of the complete efficacy of Christ's death to save sinners (John 19:30). In reverting to ritual that had meaning only as it pointed ahead to Christ's sacrifice, this sin was tantamount to putting Christ back on the cross as an impostor and declaring that his death was not a fully sufficient atonement for sin. (In fact, this is the basic implication of all legalistic admixtures with grace.)

Such defection merits severe chastening of the believer (6:7, 8). The issue here is not salvation but rewards for Christian life and testimony (cf. 2 Cor. 5:10). Divine dealing with the believer is necessary because of lack of fruit (6:7), the presence of the curse of sin and the Law (6:8; cf. Gal. 3:13), and divine disapproval (*adokimos*, "not approved" — 1 Cor. 9:27). The cure of the sin (6:9-12) involves faith in God's grace in Christ (in order to show forth "the better things" inseparably connected with salvation — 6:9), keeping in mind God's justice and impartiality (6:10), and pressing on to maturity in grace (6:11, 12).

THE DOCTRINE OF ANGELS

In demonstrating the superiority of the Son over the angels the Epistle gives remarkable prominence to this order of created spirit beings.

ANGELS ARE RELATED TO BELIEVERS. They are "ministering spirits, sent forth to minister for them who shall be heirs of salvation" (1:14). This service evidently refers primarily to the physical safety and well-being of God's children (1 Kings 19:5; Psa. 34:7; 91:11; Dan. 6:22; Matt. 2:13, 19; Luke 22:43; Acts 5:19; 12:7-10). It would seem that this care begins in infancy and continues throughout life (cf. Heb. 1:14 with Psa. 91:11 and Matt. 18:10). Angels are said to observe us (Eccl. 5:6; 1 Cor. 4:9; Eph. 3:10), a fact which should influence our conduct for good. Man is made "a little lower than the angels" (Psa. 8:4, 5; Heb. 2:7). In the incarnation Christ assumed "for a little (time)" this lower place so that he might elevate the believer into his own sphere above the angels (Heb. 2:9, 10).

ANGELS ARE INCORPOREAL CREATURES. Though spirits (Psa. 104:4; Heb. 1:7) are normally invisible to human beings, angels are enabled upon occasion to become visible in the semblance of human form (Gen. 19:1, 5; Num. 22:22-31; Judg. 2:1; 6:11, 22; 13:3, 6; 1 Chron. 21:16, 20; Matt. 1:20; Luke 1:26; John 20:12; Acts 7:30; 12:7, 8; etc.). They are exceedingly numerous (Psa. 68:17; Matt. 26:53; Heb. 12:22; Rev. 5:11). Their strength is far above natural or human power (2 Kings 19:35; Psa. 103:20). Their position is around God's throne as his servants (Psa. 103:20; Rev. 5:11; 7:11). Although referred to in Scripture by masculine pronouns, angels are apparently sexless. They are all direct creations of God and do not marry and propagate like human beings (Matt. 22:30; Mark 12:25).

THE ANGELS WILL ACCOMPANY CHRIST AND HIS SAINTS AT THE SECOND ADVENT (MATT. 25:31; REV. 19: 14). To them will be committed the preparation of the judgment of individual Gentiles among the nations (Matt. 13:30, 39, 41, 42). However, the coming age as a whole will not be subject to them. It will instead be in charge of Christ and his redeemed saints, for whom he was temporarily made a little lower than the angels (Heb. 2:7). Gabriel and Michael are archangels named in Scripture. The former is mentioned in connection with distinguished services (Dan. 8:16; 9:21; Luke 1:19, 26), while the latter is related to the nation of Israel and the resurrections (Dan. 10:13, 21; 12:1, 2; Jude 1:9).

THE REALM OF THE FALLEN ANGELS INCLUDES SATAN AND HIS DEMONS (ISA. 14:12-14; EZEK. 28:11-17). Some of these angels are bound (Jude 1:6; 2 Pet. 2:4), whereas others are free with Satan to do his bidding. The doom of Satan and fallen angels is eternal hell — Gehenna (Matt. 25:41).

THE EXPERIENCE OF REDEMPTIVE REST

The demonstration of Christ's superiority over Joshua furnishes the writer of the Epistle to the Hebrews the occasion to expound the rest into which Christ's salvation brings the believer (4:1-13). The gospel of grace is presented as the source of salvation rest; it is prefigured in the Canaan rest of the Old Testament (Num. 14:1-45; Psa. 95:8-11). Redemptive rest is *full trust* in the finished work of Christ, both for salvation of the soul and sanctification of the life. The gospel, which looked forward to Christ's atonement, was preached to Israel in the Old Testament. But because it was not received by faith (except for

Caleb and Joshua) the Israelites died in the wilderness and thus failed to enter the Canaan rest (Psa. 95:11; Heb. 3:11-19).

God's seventh-day creation rest (Heb. 4:3-8; Gen. 1:31 — 2:3) serves as a picture of the rest which the believer may enter spiritually now, as he fully relies on what Christ has done for him on the cross. Only Jesus, the greater "Joshua," can provide true rest (Heb. 4:8; Matt. 11:28-30). Christ's superiority to Joshua is seen in the redemption rest he provides. It is available for all believers as a "sabbath-keeping" (*sabbatismos*, "a state of cessation from all labor and self-effort"). It calls the believer to rest completely in Christ's perfect work of redemption, even as God rested from his own work of creation (4:10). It ceases from all self-effort, human merit, or legalistic claim as a means of attaining either salvation or sanctification (cf. Eph. 2:8-10). Through faith this God-given rest enjoys a daily experience of victory over Satan, self, and the world.

The rest, the writer shows, is to be diligently realized through faith (4:11). Unbelief robs us of it. The living Word of God is the object of faith which God uses to bring men into this rest (4:12, 13). Our ascended High Priest in the heavens is the guarantee of the rest (4:14-16). Such an approach to a life of victory was peculiarly appropriate to converts from Judaism, for they had been wedded to forms and ceremonies and legalistic observances for over fifteen centuries.

THE NEW COVENANT

One of the major reasons for the superiority of Christ's redemptive priesthood over Aaron's symbolic priesthood is the fact that it was ministered under a new and better covenant. The New Covenant (8:8-12; cf. Jer. 31:31-34; Matt. 26:28; Mark 14:24; Luke 22:20) is a covenant of unconditional blessing based upon the finished redemption of Christ. It secures blessing for the Church (Matt. 26:28; Mark 14:24) from the Abrahamic Covenant (Gen. 12:1-3; Gal. 3:13-20). In addition it guarantees covenant blessings to converted Israel (Jer. 31:31-34), including the promises of the Abrahamic, Palestinian, and Davidic Covenants. The New Covenant is unconditional, final, and irreversible. Its superiority over the Old or Mosaic Covenant appears from the following chart.

THE CONCEPT OF FAITH

One of the featured words of the Epistle is "faith." But it carries a different emphasis than the Pauline concept. Paul, writing mainly to

COMPARISON OF THE COVENANTS	
The Old (Mosaic) Covenant	*The New Covenant*
Based on law and works.	Based on grace and faith.
Given by Moses (John 1:17).	Mediated by Christ (John 1:17).
Set forth in types and shadows (9:1-10).	Revealed in antitype and reality (9:11-14).
Limited, unsatisfactory, not gracious, conditional, enacted on inferior promises. Lacking finality and efficacy (8:6-13).	Unlimited in blessing, gracious, unconditional, possessing finality and efficacy (8:10-13).
Sealed by animal blood (9:15-22).	Sealed by Christ's blood (9:15-22).
Pertains to an earthly tabernacle.	Enacted in heaven (9:23, 24).
Its sacrifices are imperfect, repeatable, not expiatory (10:1-4).	Christ's sacrifice is perfect, final, fulfilling the old order (10:5-10, 15-18).
Inferior because of the inferior position of the Levitical priests (10:11-14).	Superior because of Christ's superior position, work, and present session (10:11-14).
A conditional covenant of works, making it a ministry of "condemnation" and "death" (2 Cor. 3:7-9) designed to lead the transgressor to Christ. Hence it was *ad interim* and temporary. Given solely to the nation Israel.	The covenant of unconditional blessing. Through Christ's redemption it secures blessing *for all mankind,* including the Church, from the Abrahamic Covenant (Gal. 3:13-20). It also secures Covenant blessings to converted Israel, including those of the Abrahamic, Palestinian, and Davidic Covenants.

Gentiles, stressed the dynamic concept of faith that accepts and rests in God's provision of salvation. The writer to the Hebrews, on the other hand, features faith as persevering against the temptation to lapse back into Mosaic legalism or to succumb to virulent persecution.

Faith in Hebrews is therefore defined not in its widest sense but simply as trust in God that holds out and endures to the end (11:1). Such faith enables men to receive divine approval and to understand spiritual truth (11:2, 3). It is illustrated by Old Testament worthies whose trust envisioned "the promise" (Christ) and persevered (11:4-40). They won divine approval as a result of their faith, but did not receive "the promise" in the sense of Christ's complete salvation or the fulfillment of the New Covenant. The perfection of the New Covenant will be realized for both Old Testament and New Testament saints when Christ returns to consummate salvation and to reign as absolute King and Lord (11:39, 40). Persevering faith is compared to a race with a goal (12:1-4). It is related to testings and chastenings (12:5-17). The results of persevering faith are specified. It delivers from the terror of the Law and introduces the believer to the blessings and relationship of grace (12:18-29). Such faith expresses itself in gracious, godly living (13:1-6), in a stable testimony (13:7-9), in a clear-cut separation from legalism (13:10-14), and in spiritual worship and obedience (13:15-17).

THE CONCEPT OF THE CHURCH

In the Epistle to the Hebrews the Church is related to the completed salvation which Christ has accomplished and the fruition of the persevering faith which the writer has expounded (12:18-24). The Church is seen glorified in the sinless eternal state, co-inhabiting the New Jerusalem with the glorified elect of every age (cf. Rev. 21:10—22:5; John 14:1-3). The writer declares that Abraham looked for this heavenly city (11:10), which God has prepared for his people (11:16) and which will be permanent (13:14). It is called "Mount Zion . . . the city of the living God, the heavenly Jerusalem" (12:22).

Inhabiting this celestial city as a part of its eternal splendor will be the glorified saints of this age, called "the church of the firstborn enrolled in heaven" (12:22, 23, literal translation). "The firstborn" is a reference to Christ (Rom. 8:29; Col. 1:15, 16; Heb. 1:6). The Church is the entity described by Paul as the Body of Christ, whose members are citizens of the heavenly city (Eph. 2:19; Phil. 3:20). The writer to the Hebrews relates the Church to the rest of glorified humanity (Heb. 11:39, 40). These others are designated "just men made perfect" (Heb. 12:23), and include perfected saints of the Old Testament, tribulation, and kingdom eras. Also inhabiting the City will be God in his unveiled glory (Rev. 21:3), as well as "Jesus, the Mediator of the New Covenant" (Heb. 12:24) and an uncounted host of unfallen angels (Heb. 12:22).

James

AUTHOR

Not until the Third Council of Carthage (A.D. 397) did the Epistle of James come to be generally recognized as canonical. Hesitation concerning its acceptance was due to uncertainty about the identification of the author, who styles himself simply as "a servant of God and of the Lord Jesus Christ" (1:1). When it became generally understood that James the brother of the Lord was the most likely author, and that he was called an "apostle" by Paul (Gal. 1:19), opposition against canonicity vanished.

James is referred to in the Gospels (Matt. 13:55; Mark 6:3). Like his brothers, he did not believe in Jesus during our Lord's ministry (cf. Mark 3:21, 31-35; John 7:3-9). After the Ascension, however, Jesus' brothers are found with those who were awaiting the promised Spirit (Acts 1:14). Paul mentions Christ's resurrection appearance to James (1 Cor. 15:7). James must already have shown gifts of leadership, for he soon became head of the Jerusalem Church (Acts 12:17; 15:13; 21: 18; Gal. 1:19; 2:9, 12).

BACKGROUND AND DATE

James wrote his Epistle for Christian Jews in the Dispersion (1:1). Representatives of this far-flung Jewish population in the Greco-Roman world were present at Pentecost, when the Spirit came and the Christian Church began (Acts 2:9-11). Some of these doubtlessly carried the gospel back to their native lands. It must be remembered that Jewish believers were the first Christian missionaries. The Christian movement was well on its way toward a wide outreach among the Jews of the Roman Empire *before* any Gentiles were admitted to gospel privilege (cf. Acts 4:36, 37; 9:2, 10, 14; 11:19, 20; 1 Pet. 5:13).

If the writer was indeed James, the Lord's brother, his Epistle was written before A.D. 62, the date of James' martyrdom, according to Josephus (*Antiquities XX*, 9, 1). That it was actually written much earlier, between A.D. 45 and 48 and before the first Church Council, is suggested by the following facts: 1) the Church order and discipline of the Epistle are very simple. The leaders are called "teachers" and "elders"; no reference is made to "bishops" (overseers) or "deacons." Believers still congregated in the synagogue (2:2). 2) The doctrine of the Epistle is also very elementary. There is a total absence of information about the character and destiny of the Church or the deeper theological meaning and implications of Christ's death. Even more significant is the absence of any information covering the relation of Gentiles to gospel privilege. All of the foregoing provides evidence that the Epistle must have been written about A.D. 48 or 49, before the Jerusalem Council.

IMPORTANCE AND PURPOSE

James is without doubt the most Jewish book in the New Testament—more so than even Matthew, Hebrews, or the Revelation. The letter is concerned mainly with the practical aspects of the Christian faith. It consists of maxims and advice for everyday conduct and is reminiscent of the wisdom literature of the Old Testament, especially Proverbs. There are practically no references to any of the central doctrines of the Christian faith. If the two passages referring to Christ were omitted (1:1 and 2:1), the whole Epistle might just as properly have appeared in the Old Testament.

The Epistle is addressed to Jewish believers, called "the twelve tribes scattered abroad" (1:1). It apparently circulated among the first converts to Christianity before the Gentiles came into gospel privilege and the great truths of the Church were revealed to Paul.

James in all likelihood intended his Epistle for all Christian Jews, wherever they were. Peter also wrote in part to the Jewish Dispersion (1 Pet. 1:1), but he evidently had the Western Dispersion especially in mind, since he wrote to Jewish believers in Asia Minor. The believers there would perhaps be less likely to know the Epistle of James.

These Jewish believers were undergoing intense persecution from their fellow countrymen and were being discriminated against. Their spiritual state was low. Strife, faction, and bitter speaking were common. Many acted as if knowing the truth were sufficient, as if faith without works met all requirements. Temptation to materialism was great and oppression of the poor was a common evil. These conditions among his fellow Jewish believers prompted the strict and righteous James to write this Epistle.

James presents a living faith in Christ as the panacea for the trials and ills that faced his Jewish brothers in the Dispersion. Such a vital trust would enable his brothers in the Christian faith to meet persecutions and testings courageously and victoriously. It would also rid them of their erroneous notion that a mere intellectual assent to Christian truth was sufficient. Living faith, in contrast to such "dead" (ineffective and nonexistent) faith, would change their lives and make them productive of good works. This would turn out to be the cure for their spiritual ills.

OUTLINE

Salutation (1:1)

A. Living Faith Tested by Trials (chapter 1)
　　1. The purpose of trials (1:1-4)
　　2. Wisdom for trials (1:5-12)
　　3. God's role in trials (1:13-18)
　　4. God's Word and trials (1:19-25)
　　5. Genuine religion and trials (1:26, 27)

B. Living Faith Attested by Works (chapter 2)
　　1. Dead faith is manifested in partiality (2:1-9)
　　2. Dead faith results in judgment (2:10-13)
　　3. Dead faith is useless (2:14-20)
　　4. Living faith attests a man's righteousness (2:21-26)

C. Living Faith Evidenced by Conduct (chapters 3 – 5)
　　1. Living faith controls the tongue (3:1-12)
　　2. Living faith manifests heavenly wisdom (3:13-18)
　　3. Living faith resists worldliness (4:1-5)
　　4. Living faith demonstrates humility (4:6-10)
　　5. Living faith avoids slander (4:11, 12)
　　6. Living faith counteracts secularism (4:13-17)
　　7. Living faith courageously meets persecution (5:1-11)
　　8. Living faith shuns swearing (5:12)
　　9. Living faith is exercised in prayer (5:13-18)
　　10. Living faith maintains a diligent witness (5:19, 20)

JAMES AND TRUE RELIGION

The subject of true religion is especially timely today because so many people have (in Paul's terminology) "a form of godliness" but have denied (renounced) "the power of it" (2 Tim. 3:5). In James' terminology such religionists do not practice "true religion" (1:26, 27). James points out what false religion is. It is, according to him, the expression of "dead works" produced by the flesh and the result of "dead" (nonexistent) faith.

Because man has been created religious he remains so even in his fallen state. As a result the world is full of empty religion, not only in the non-Christian faiths of the world but also within the fold of professing Christianity. James cites an example of such false religion by describing an unruly tongue that yields itself to slander and backbiting while claiming to be religious.

When religion (*outward* religious service) is genuine, it is the expression of a true *inward* faith. James cites an illustration of this. Such true religion is manifested 1) *in social consciousness* (looking after such helpless people as orphans and widows) and 2) *in separation from sin*. A truly religious person keeps himself clean of the world's smut and taint.

Many Christians today practice scriptural separation from apostasy and sin but are woefully deficient in a sense of social obligation and involvement. On the other hand, many professing Christians are extremely lax in scriptural separation from evil but are nevertheless vocal and active in social activity, some even to the extent of renouncing the gospel of redemption for a so-called "social gospel."

THE RELATION OF JUSTIFICATION TO WORKS

James shows that faith unverified by works is a "dead" faith—not really faith at all, but simply intellectual assent. Such a faith cannot save a man. It is just as useless as telling a destitute person to be fed and clothed but doing nothing to help him (2:14-16). James is here demonstrating that works and saving faith are inseparable. He does not question that faith is the way of salvation and *the only way*. But he does question that such living faith can ever be divorced from the works which prove its very existence. To offer God a faith separated from good works is to rise little higher than the demons, who believe and shudder but nevertheless remain incorrigibly wicked (2:17-19).

"Living" faith, that is, faith wedded to works, proves a man righteous. It attests that a man has been justified (declared righteous before God). Two examples of living or saving faith (faith with works) are given—Abraham, the classic man of faith in Scripture (2:21-24), and Rahab, the harlot (2:25). James teaches that Abraham was justified (vindicated) by works when he offered up Isaac (Gen. 22:9-12). Since

Abraham had already been justified by faith in the sight of *God* (Gen. 15:6), his supreme act of faith in offering his only son provided incontrovertible vindication of his faith in the sight of *men* as well.

In similar manner Rahab's saving faith was demonstrated before *men* when she hid the spies, sent them back by another route, and hung out the scarlet cord (Josh. 2:1-21; Heb. 11:31). James further illustrates this important principle with the analogy of the death of the body. When the body dies the spirit departs. Likewise, when faith is separated from works it is a dead, lifeless thing which can neither secure our righteous standing before God nor demonstrate our justification before men.

JAMES'S AND PAUL'S DOCTRINE OF JUSTIFICATION COMPARED

Martin Luther contended that James contradicts Paul on the matter of justification. He called James's letter "a right strawy Epistle" and held that it was not on a par with other canonical books. However, this personal judgment of the great reformer is not supported by any patristic evidence or sound exegesis. That James does not contradict Paul, who declares that Abraham was justified by faith apart from works (Rom. 4:2-5), appears from the following chart.

JUSTIFICATION COMPARED	
Justification in the Pauline Epistles	*Justification in the Epistle by James*
Paul employs the term "justified" in the sense of being *judicially declared righteous before God*. Paul is speaking *Godward*.	James uses the term in the sense of being *proved righteous before men*. James is speaking *manward*.
Abraham enjoyed justification by faith apart from works (Gen. 15:6) long before he offered up Isaac.	Abraham was justified (vindicated) by works when he offered up Isaac (Gen. 22:1-12) because he was already justified by faith.
Paul sets forth the truth itself.	James offers the corrective for the abused truth.
Paul's Epistles are beamed toward Gentiles, lost in sin, with no legal righteousness to offer to God.	James's Epistle is aimed at Jewish believers tempted to substitute a head knowledge of the Law for a heart experience of grace manifested in a holy life.

JAMES'S TEACHING ON DIVINE HEALING

Instructions for the physically ill (5:14, 15) direct that the sick Hebrew believer was to call for the elders of the assembly and ask them to anoint him with oil and pray for him. The Talmud shows that using oil for anointing the sick was generally practiced among the Jews. Our Lord and his disciples adopted the practice (Mark 6:13). Oil was also commonly used for medicinal purposes in the ancient Near East (Isa. 1:6; Luke 10:34). Its use here in James may symbolize either the employment of medicinal means for healing or, more likely, the healing power of the Holy Spirit.

James's stress, however, is not on the oil but on the "prayer of faith"; it is this which "saves the sick." This special type of prayer is *breathed by the Holy Spirit* through the human agent and is *always in God's will.* Since it is *not* always God's will to heal, this special "prayer of faith" is not always given; healing by God's power is thus *not* always effected. Chastening, testing, refining, and other factors influence the Lord's healing of a believer's illnesses (cf. 1 Cor. 11:30-32; 2 Cor. 12:7-9; 1 Tim. 5:23; 2 Tim. 4:20). Consequently, those who pray for the sick need the gift of "discerning of spirits" to ascertain the state of the ailing saint *in relation to the will of God* (1 Cor. 12:10). They also need "faith by the same Spirit" and "gifts of healing" (1 Cor. 12:9) in order to pray the prayer of faith after the will of God has been determined in each case.

For so-called "faith healers" to insist that it is *always* God's will to heal a believer who is in right relation with God is extremely perilous. Healings that are forced under the halo of the will of God may turn out not to be in the will of God at all, but instead may prove to be the "faith healer" forcing his own will under the disguise of God's will. Demonic spirits are waiting to take over when God's will is flouted, either consciously or unconsciously, deliberately or ignorantly. When demonic healings occur, there is *always* a price tag. The malady may be transferred from the physical to the mental, emotional, or spiritual realm, or there may be ensnarement in error or cultism or bondage to fanaticism of some sort.

DIVINE HEALING TODAY

God can and *does* heal today, but *not always.* James' passage on healing has often been misused by "faith healers." The fact that James 5:14-16 was never addressed to a Gentile church (James 1:1) and dates *very early* (A.D. 45-48 — before Gentiles were admitted to gospel privilege) is often overlooked. The nation Israel had not yet been set aside (cf. Acts 28:17-29), and the passage is based on a healing covenant made with Israel (Exod. 15:26). Under this covenant James 5:14-16 guaranteed Hebrew believers instantaneous and complete healing in response to faith in Christ (cf. Acts 3:6, 16; 4:30; 5:12-16; 6:8; 8:7, 8). This efficacious faith for healing was divinely imparted to the *apostolic* Jewish Christian elders in response to their claim upon the promises of Israel's healing covenant.

But the all-important point for the correctly instructed Christian minister to see is that now that the nation Israel and her healing covenant have been set aside while the great Gentile Church is being called out, the "prayer of faith" is divinely given and operative in the established Gentile Church *only when it is God's will to heal.* This is the reason why *nowhere* in any of the Church Epistles is anything said about anointing the sick with oil (cf. 2 Cor. 5:7). When "the prayer of faith" is prayed, however, and God heals the sick today, it is *always* on the basis of the divine will. God's will must be determined in each case and the petition offered in accordance with his divine purpose. Healings that flout this principle run the risk of being effected by demonic power, with perilous results to the one who is "healed." This is true no matter how sincere, well-meaning, or even godly the "faith healer" may be.

1 Peter

AUTHOR

The author is "Peter, an apostle of Jesus Christ" (1:1). Everywhere in the Epistle there are reminiscences of Peter's personal acquaintance with our Lord; he claims to have been "a witness of the sufferings of Christ" (5:1; cf. 3:18 and 4:1). He writes with deep per-

A street scene in the old part of Jerusalem (*Russ Busby photo*)

sonal feeling about the person of Christ and his sufferings (2:19-24). He pleads with his readers to remember that they are sharing in the sufferings of Christ (4:13). His admonition to "feed the flock of God"

(5:2) recalls Christ's own words to Peter, "Feed my lambs" and "Feed my sheep" (John 21:15-17). His injunction "Gird yourselves with humility" (5:5) apparently has in mind Christ's girding of himself with a towel when he washed the disciples' feet (John 13:3-5).

Scholars have also noted a correspondence between Peter's speeches in Acts and his words in the Epistle. Acts 10:34 recalls First Peter 1:17. Acts 2:32-36 and 10:40, 41 recall First Peter 1:21. Acts 4: 10, 11 brings to mind First Peter 2:7, 8. Internal evidence strongly indicates that Peter wrote the Epistle toward the end of his career. The same recognition of the equality of Gentile and Jewish Christians that appears in the latter part of the Acts is found in the Epistle.

Attestation of the genuineness of the Epistle appears in its recognition in the early Church as a true work of the Apostle Peter. Its acknowledgement in the Second Epistle (2 Pet. 3:1) is amply corroborated by the early Church Fathers, especially Polycarp and Irenaeus.

Peter simply and unpretentiously introduces himself to his readers as "an apostle of Jesus Christ" (1:1). There is nothing in his two Epistles or in his early or later career that would substantiate the notion that he was the founder of the church at Rome or its first bishop. In the book of Acts Peter appears as the chosen instrument (Matt. 16:16-18) to present "such a great salvation" of the new age (Heb. 2:3) to Jews (Acts 2). Somewhat later he and John healed the crippled man (Acts 3:1-11) in the Temple and preached the sermon on the future fulfillment of Israel's covenants (Acts 3:12-26). He and certain other Apostles were arrested and tried before the Sanhedrin (Acts 4:1-22). As a leader of the Jerusalem Church, Peter was faced with disciplining Ananias and Sapphira (Acts 5:1-11).

Following a period of spectacular power in the early Church, Peter and other apostles were again subject to persecution and imprisonment by Jewish officials (Acts 5:12-40). After Stephen's martyrdom Peter introduced gospel opportunity to the half-Jew Samaritans (Acts 8:1-15) and later to pure Gentiles (Acts 10:1-48). He was imprisoned under Herod Agrippa I (A.D. 41-44) and miraculously released (Acts 12:7-11). Following Paul's first missionary tour, Peter took a leading role in the first Church Council in Jerusalem (Acts 15:7-11).

At Antioch Peter was reprimanded by Paul for hypocritically withdrawing from fellowship with Gentile believers (Gal. 2:11-14). Peter traveled extensively in the later years of his life, often with his wife (1 Cor. 9:5). He apparently had an extensive ministry in Asia Minor, especially in Pontus, Cappadocia, and Bithynia, areas Paul did not visit. His martyrdom was predicted by our Lord (John 21:18, 19).

BACKGROUND AND DATE

Peter addressed his Epistle to Christians who resided in the Roman provinces of Pontus, Galatia, Cappadocia, Asia, and Bithynia in Asia Minor (1:1). These provinces are probably listed in the order which the messenger, Silvanus (5:12), was to follow in delivering the letters to the churches concerned. "The exiles of the dispersion" (1:1, RSV) are evidently "elect" believers in general. James wrote to "the twelve tribes in the dispersion" (James 1:1, RSV), who were Jewish Christians outside Palestine, apparently of the Eastern dispersion (see under James).

However, Peter does not address his readers as "the twelve tribes." He evidently had Gentile as well as Jewish believers in mind (cf. 1:14; 2:9, 10; 4:3-5). His readers were "aliens and exiles" (2:11) in the sense of pilgrims and sojourners on earth (cf. Heb. 11:13-16; 13:14). He regarded Christians as dispersed among the heathen. Some scholars think that this statement may refer literally to members of the Roman church dispersed to the provinces as a result of Nero's fanatical persecutions.

The Epistle was written from "Babylon" (5:13), which some think is a pseudonym for the city of Rome (cf. Rev. 14:8; 18:2, 10, 21). However, numerous scholars believe that the literal city on the Euphrates is intended. Since Peter died in perhaps A.D. 66 or 67, this Epistle was in all likelihood written as late as A.D. 65, for it shows acquaintance with Colossians, Ephesians, and Philippians. Recent attempts to date First Peter in the reign of Emperor Trajan during the persecutions under Pliny's governorship of Bithynia-Pontus (A.D. 110-111) have not been very successful.

IMPORTANCE AND PURPOSE

First Peter is the Epistle of triumphant suffering and radiant hope. Seven different words are used for suffering in the letter. Hope in the midst of suffering is produced by the prospect of a glorious future inheritance (1:4, 5) to be realized in the advent of the Chief Shepherd (5:4). The sufferings of Christ provide the foundation of the Epistle (1:11; 2:21, 23; 5:1), and our suffering Lord is held up as an example to all of God's suffering children (2:21; 4:1, 2).

The Apostle warns God's people to expect suffering (4:12), for it is often consonant with the will of God (4:19). Saints are not to be upset by adversity (3:14), but are to bear it patiently (2:23; 3:9), even joyfully (4:13), knowing that fellow-believers also suffer (5:9). Peter is careful to show the value of suffering righteously (1:6, 7; 2:19, 20; 3:14; 4:14). But he warns against suffering as an evildoer (2:20; 4:15). The Epistle is thus more practical than doctrinal.

OUTLINE

A. Present Suffering in View of Future Glory (1:1-25)
  1. Suffering in the light of assured salvation (1:1-12)
  2. Suffering in the light of the Lord's coming (1:13-22)
  3. Suffering in the light of the Word of God (1:23-25)
B. Present Suffering in View of Christ's Passion (2:1—4:6)
  1. Suffering in view of Christian growth (2:1-3)
  2. Suffering in view of identity with Christ and his own (2:4-10)
  3. Suffering in view of Christian character and conduct (2:11-20)
  4. Suffering in view of Christ's example (2:21-25)
  5. Suffering in view of God's order for the home (3:1-7)
  6. Suffering in view of harmonious living (3:8-12)
  7. Suffering in view of a good conscience (3:13-17)
  8. Suffering in view of Christ's triumph (3:18-22)
  9. Suffering in view of Christ's example for victory (4:1-6)
C. Present Suffering in View of Christ's Advent (4:7—5:11)
  1. Suffering and impending judgment (4:7-19)
  2. Suffering and reward for service (5:1-4)
  3. Suffering and vigilant conduct (5:5-9)
  4. Suffering and Christian maturity (5:10, 11)
Concluding Greeting (5:12-14)

FOREKNOWLEDGE, ELECTION, AND FOREORDINATION

The Apostle Peter describes believers as "elect according to the foreknowledge of God" (1:2). Foreknowledge is that attribute of God by which all things are known to him from the beginning. Consequently, God knew from eternity who would be saved from the fallen human race. Election is that gracious and sovereign act of God by which from eternity certain are chosen from the human race for himself (John 15:16, 19; 1 Thess. 1:4; Eph. 1:4; 1 Pet. 1:2; 2 Pet. 1:10). Election is based on God's sovereign purpose or decree (Rom. 9:11; Eph. 1:11) and is in accordance with his foreknowledge (1 Pet. 1:2). However, nowhere does Scripture reveal exactly how God's foreknowledge determines his elective choice. This is the realm of the infinite; it is unfathomable to the finite human mind. In any case the Scriptures teach both that men bear moral responsibility for their choices and that the sovereign God works out all things according to his infinite wisdom and good pleasure.

Peter speaks also of foreordination. He declares that Christ the Savior "verily was foreordained before the foundation of the world," but was manifested in his Saviorhood "in these last times" for the elect (1:20). Foreordination is that operation of God's will in which everything he has decreed from eternity past is brought to realization in time. It is the believer's assurance that what God has predetermined for his own saints (the elect) will not be nullified. In this latter sense it is tantamount to predestination (Rom. 8:29, 30; Eph. 1:5, 11).

REDEMPTION

Peter declares that believers "were not redeemed with corruptible (perishable) things, like silver and gold . . . but with the precious blood of Christ" (1:18, 19). The word translated "redeemed" (*lutroō*) means "ransomed," that is, "bought back from bondage." The necessity for redemption springs out of the fact that the sinner is enslaved to Satan and sin (John 8:34; Rom. 6:17, 20). Redemption itself is God's undertaking on the basis of free and unmerited favor and choice. It is made possible by Jesus Christ, the Redeemer (1 Cor. 1:30; Gal. 3:13; 4:45; Eph. 1:7; Tit. 2:14). The basis is the shed blood of Christ. Redemption is both past and future. The price has been paid once, and believers are thereby redeemed for all time. However, they wait in expectation for the final fulfillment of that which is already theirs by faith (Rom. 8:23). Those who are redeemed (ransomed, delivered from bondage) once belonged to Satan as slaves. Now they belong to God as free men (1 Cor. 6:20). Their chief purpose in life is now to glorify their Redeemer (2:9).

THE PRIESTHOOD OF THE BELIEVER

Peter teaches that believers are "a holy priesthood, (offering up) spiritual sacrifices, acceptable to God by Jesus Christ" (2:5). He calls *all* Christians "a royal priesthood" (2:9; cf. Rev. 1:6). He emphasizes that every believer, being made one with Christ himself by faith, is constituted a priest before God in the tabernacle in heaven. In the Old Testament economy a priest had to mediate between God and the people by serving at the altar. A high priest also mediated for them in the Holiest Place before the Shekinah glory of the divine presence. But Christ himself has now become the believer's high priest (Heb. 4:14; 5:10; 7:27; 9:11). Through Christ alone the humblest believer may now obtain access into the immediate presence of God. How ironic that the Apostle Peter, who declares so plainly that the only valid New Testament priesthood is that which includes every believer, should be connected by men with a hierarchical system of ecclesiastical priestism that would shut the believer out of his God-given privilege of access to God through Christ alone!

Never in the New Testament is the term "priest" (*hierus*) applied to an apostle or an ordained elder in the Church except as he shared in the universal priesthood of all believers. Recovery of this great New Testament truth furnished one of the great emancipating impulses of the Protestant Reformation and brought multitudes back to fellowship with God.

VICARIOUS ATONEMENT

The Apostle Peter presents the vicarious, atoning work of our Lord in one of the clearest and most incisive passages on the subject in the Bible. He declares that Christ "his own self bore our sins in his own body on the tree, that we, being dead to sins, should live unto righteousness; by whose stripes ye were healed" (2:24). Vicarious atonement means substitutionary reconciliation. The term "vicarious" derives from the Latin *vicarius*, meaning "substituted," "delegated." The expression "atonement" is from the Greek *katallagē*, denoting "an exchange," " a reconciliation," and "restoration to divine favor" (Rom. 5:11; 11:15; 2 Cor. 5:18, 19). It comprehends the thought of appeasing God's infinitely holy wrath against sin by a sufficient and satisfying sacrifice substituted for the guilty sinner. Christ, the "lamb without blemish and spot" (1:19), who died as a vicarious (substitutionary) sacrifice for sin, took the place of and died in the stead of the sinner. Thus he made atonement by reconciling the guilty sinner to God.

Three great facts underlie the doctrine of substitutionary atonement: 1) the sinner lies under the wrath of God and is therefore utterly undone and lost (Rom. 1:18; 3:19; 6:23); 2) by God's grace Christ willingly offered himself as a sin-bearer and substitute (Isa. 53:6; 2 Cor. 5:21); and 3) God willingly accepted the atoning death of Christ, so that the sinner thereby secures the benefits of reconciliation and fellowship with God (Rom. 5:1-11).

In the old economy the blood sacrifices had to be repeated because they were typical and educatory and could not really remove sin forever. When offered by faith, however, these sacrifices were acceptable because they envisioned the future death of Christ and drew in advance upon the merit of his atonement (Rom. 3:25). Since the time of his death there has been absolutely no need for further sacrifice (Heb. 9:11-15; 10:1-14).

THE BROTHERHOOD OF MAN

The Apostle Peter speaks of honoring "all men" and loving "the brotherhood" (2:17). In a day when the humanistic notion of "the brotherhood of man and the fatherhood of God" has become a popular slogan in ecumenical Christianity, the concept involved must be clearly understood within the limits imposed by Scripture. There is a sense, of course, in which all men are brothers; it is the sense in which they are descended from Adam as the father of the race. But the fall of man and the entrance of sin into the human family destroyed that brotherhood and alienated men not only from God as their Father but also from their fellow men as their brothers.

For this reason Scripture is silent concerning a supposed brotherhood that includes the unsaved (Malachi 2:10 was spoken only to Jews within the covenant relationship). Exponents of the "brotherhood" of fallen man ignore not only the fall and its consequences but also the necessity of Christ's redemptive work in restoring alienated humanity to God. Scripture does speak, however, of a brotherhood which is the result of regeneration and adoption into the family of God. This new spiritual relationship is emphasized by Peter (1:2, 23; 2:2, 10; etc.) and by all the New Testament writers (e.g. John 3:3-5; Gal. 3:27; etc.). Through Christ believers are brought back into right relationship not only with God but also with one another as God's children and heirs (1 John 3:2; Gal. 3:26). Only those who have believed on the Lord Jesus Christ are accounted as God's children in the scriptural sense. Because of this they are brothers to all who confess the same Father and Lord.

THE NOTION OF A "SECOND CHANCE"

The idea that the Lord Jesus between his death and resurrection descended into Hades and there preached to the unsaved dead, giving them a second chance, has sometimes been erroneously attributed to the Apostle Peter. "Being put to death in the flesh but made alive by the Spirit, by whom also he went and preached unto the spirits in prison, who at one time were disobedient, when once the longsuffering of God waited in the days of Noah, while the ark was preparing, in which few, that is, eight souls, were saved by water" (3:18-20, *New Scofield Bible*).

"Quickened" or "made alive by the Spirit" refers to Christ's physical resurrection and not to a supposed quickening of his human spirit, since his spirit did not and could not die and therefore needed no quickening. Only his human *body* could die, and this was what was made alive by the Holy Spirit (Rom. 8:11). Through the Holy Spirit Peter declares that Christ "went and preached unto the spirits in prison." The preaching was not done by Christ personally, but by "the Spirit of Christ," who was in Old Testament prophets (1:11). Just as the Spirit of Christ testified through these prophets about Christ's future sufferings and glory, so the Spirit of Christ preached through Noah (Gen. 6:3) to the antediluvian sinners for 120 years while the ark was being built. Hence "the spirits in prison" were not in prison when Christ preached through Noah by his Spirit, but were living men in Noah's day.

BAPTISM

Peter declares that "corresponding" to the ark in which eight persons "were brought safely through the water . . . baptism now saves you — not the removal of dirt from the flesh, but the appeal to God for a good conscience — through the resurrection of Jesus Christ" (3:21, *New American Standard Bible*). That Peter is referring *primarily* to Spirit baptism and only secondarily and figuratively to water baptism is shown by the following facts.

Only Spirit baptism can save. The unanimous testimony of Scripture is that no mere external rite can place one "in Christ." Therefore, Peter *must* be referring to the spiritual reality when he declares, "baptism now saves you." Peter was well acquainted with Paul's Epistles and the truth of Spirit baptism as revealed to the Apostle to the Gentiles (cf. 2 Pet. 3:15, 16).

Water baptism saves figuratively rather than actually. Peter uses the flood as an illustration. How were "the few, that is, eight" souls of the preflood generation "saved"? It was *by* or *through* water. The flood water was that which cut them off from the sinners of that day, who were doomed under divine judgment. In the same way we are saved by spiritual baptism through removal from the sphere of sin and condemnation.

But this aspect of spiritual baptism is only negative. If this were the total picture, the eight antediluvians would have perished *in* the water rather than being saved *by* or *through* the water. They were saved by *entering the ark*. The believer is saved by Spirit baptism not because he is merely cut off from a state of sin and judgment, but because he is positively placed in the antitypical ark, Christ, by the Spirit's baptism. Likewise, the Israelites were saved from Egypt (the world) and Pharaoh (Satan) by the waters of the Red Sea, having been "baptized into Moses (picturing Christ) in the cloud and in the sea" (1 Cor. 10:2). Paul expounds the same truth in Romans. Spirit baptism *disconnects* the believer from his lost position "in Adam" (Rom. 5:12-21) before joining him to Christ (Rom. 6:3, 4).

No mere external rite can save. Peter is extremely careful to point this out by the qualifying definition, "Baptism now saves you — *not the removal of the dirt of the flesh.*" Then he adds the positive statement, ". . . but the appeal to God for a good conscience."

Spirit baptism directly connects with Christ's resurrection. "Baptism now saves you . . . through the resurrection of Jesus Christ." The intervening words are a parenthesis. Spiritual baptism (but not ritual baptism) has the most *direct* connection with Christ's resurrection. There was not, nor could there be, any spiritual baptism until after Christ's resurrection, ascension, and giving of the Spirit (Acts 1: 5; 11:14-16). Water baptism is intended to portray outwardly what spiritual baptism has *already* accomplished inwardly. It pictures the believer's separation from sin and union with Christ.

2 Peter

AUTHOR

Considering external evidence, Second Peter has less historical support for its genuineness than any other New Testament book. This is because it is a brief Epistle, addressed to no specific person or church, and contains little new doctrinal information. Internal evidence, however, is substantial. The writer calls himself Simon Peter (1:1). The autobiographical allusions are true to the facts, as in the case of the transfiguration (1:16-18) and Christ's prediction of Peter's martyrdom (1:12-14; cf. John 21:18, 19). Noah is spoken of as a preacher of righteousness (2:5), which is also the correct meaning in First Peter 3:18-20.

The allusion to Paul's Epistles (3:15, 16) does not necessarily imply that all thirteen had already been written. Peter simply includes the letters he had come to know. There is no evidence that the error which Peter exposes and denounces belongs to a later period than Paul's. The earnestness, the apostolic tone, and the lofty, chaste character of the teaching render it impossible to believe that the Epistle is a second-century forgery, as some critics contend.

BACKGROUND AND DATE

It seems clear that Second Peter was written to the same people as First Peter (cf. 3:1 and see 1 Peter). When the Apostle alludes to the recipients of his letter as those who "have obtained a like precious faith with us" (1:1), he most assuredly included at least some Gentile Christians. In 3:15 Peter probably had Paul's Epistles to the Galatians, Colossians, and Ephesians in mind (cf. 1 Pet. 1:1). He distinguishes between the things Paul wrote specifically to them (3:15) and the rest of Paul's Epistles (3:16). Believers, mainly Jewish converts scattered throughout "Pontus, Galatia, Cappadocia, Asia, and Bithynia" (1 Pet. 1:1), are apparently the addressees.

A philosophical Gnosticism with intellectual and antinomian characteristics (chap. 2) had gained entrance. Its unsound teachings were producing lawless and immoral living (2:10, 13, 14, 18, 19-22). The danger was spreading and posed a real threat (2:1-3, 18, 19). The Apostle Paul had been confronted with this heresy at Colosse and had dealt with it in the Colossian letter. But the error still persisted. Precisely what relationship Peter sustains to his readers is not clear. Perhaps he had visited them. Along with others, he had made known to them "the power and coming of our Lord Jesus" (1:16). His concern for them led him to pen this Epistle, especially since false teachers were flouting the truth of Christ's second advent (chap. 3).

Second Peter was written before the Epistle of Jude, since Jude apparently alludes to Second Peter (2:1 – 3:3; cf. Jude 1:4-16). This is more probable than that Peter cites Jude, since the latter quotes from tradition or possibly the apocryphal books of the Assumption of Moses and of Enoch, while Peter scarcely quotes at all. Jude (1:17, 18) almost certainly alludes to Second Peter 3:1-3, the unusual word "mockers" *(empaiktēs)* being found in each passage. Moreover, the false teachers in Second Peter are in a sense still future (2:1, 2, 12). In Jude they are already present (1:4, 8, 10-13, 16).

Apparently, then, Second Peter was written not long after First Peter and before the Epistle of Jude. The years A.D. 66 or 67 would seem to meet requirements.

IMPORTANCE AND PURPOSE

The subject of First Peter is *suffering* and its purpose is *consolation*. The theme of Second Peter is *false teachers and false teachings* and its purpose is *warning*. The Apostle's antidote for false teaching is true spiritual knowledge (cf. John 16:12, 13). The words "know," "knowledge," etc. are found no less than sixteen times in the Greek text (1:2, 3, 5, 6, 8, 12, 14, 16, 20; 2:9, 20, 21 (twice); 3:3, 17, 18). In six of these instances is found an intensified form of the word denoting full or complete knowledge (1:2, 3, 8; 2:20, 21). The knowledge *(epignōsis)* which Peter describes springs out of faith that rests on facts; it is imparted to the believer in fullness and precision by the Holy Spirit.

The golden text of Second Peter may be taken as 3:18: "But grow in grace and in the knowledge of our Lord and Savior, Jesus Christ." The Apostle shows that true knowledge is understanding God's grace in Christ. As a result of faith which brings such knowledge, believers are empowered to overcome sin and to confirm their call and election. The Christian faith is not founded on myths or man-made legends. It rests on the personal witness of those who saw the glory and majesty of Christ (chap. 1).

True knowledge of Christ's grace is perennially threatened by false teachers. By their lawless lives and unsound doctrine they deny the Redeemer. They promise freedom, but all the while they themselves are enslaved by lust. Their punishment is inescapable (chap. 2).

True knowledge of the future is perverted by false teachers; they reject the truth of Christ's second coming and misconstrue God's patient delay of judgment. But Christ's return to judge is inevitable. The destruction of the ungodly and the renovation of the earth by fire are likewise certain. Knowledge of this inspires God's own to live righteously.

OUTLINE

Salutation (1:1, 2)
A. True Knowledge from God (chapter 1)
    1. Centers in Christ (1:3-5)
    2. Promotes spiritual growth (1:6-9)
    3. Confirms Christ's call and our election (1:10, 11)
    4. Is based on eyewitness testimony of Christ's glory (1:12-18)
    5. Is founded on the authoritative Word (1:19)
    6. Is communicated by the Holy Spirit (1:20, 21)
B. False Knowledge from False Teachers (chapter 2)
    1. Inroads of their error (2:1-3)
    2. Punishment of their error (2:4-10)
    3. Their character and conduct (2:11-16)
    4. Dire consequences of their deception (2:17-22)
C. True Knowledge of the Future (chapter 3)
    1. Denied by rejectors of Christ's second advent (3:1-4)
    2. Centers in God's set plan for the future (3:5-7)
    3. Finds explanation in God's forbearance toward sinners (3:8, 9)
    4. Will be realized in cataclysmic judgment (3:10)

5. Fosters a holy life (3:11, 12)
6. Will eventuate in a sin-cleansed eternity (3:13)
7. Furnishes the basis for godly exhortation (3:14-18)

DIVINE ELECTION
AND CHRISTIAN CONDUCT

The Apostle insists on the validation of the believer's "calling and election" by the cultivation of Christian virtues (1:4-14). "Therefore (because of the peril of falling into spiritual ignorance and sin), brothers, be all the more diligent to make certain about his calling and choosing you" (literal translation). From God's point of view the Christian's election is certain. It is subject to no contingency, since it is the result of God's sovereign and immutable choice and is based on the total efficacy of Christ's finished work of redemption (cf. Eph. 1:4-6).

However, believers have the responsibility in life and testimony *to make their calling and election certain and assured before men.* This can be done only by employing the spiritual resources they are endowed with in grace (1:2-4), thus manifesting maturity (1:5-10). If they validate and confirm God's call and election before men by a virtuous life, Peter declares that they will *"in no wise"* (emphatic negative) "fall" (stumble so as to fail the grace of God bestowed on them).

ENTRANCE INTO GOD'S KINGDOM

If believers validate their divine calling and election before men by a virtuous life (1:5-10), the Apostle declares that "an entrance shall be ministered (to them) abundantly into the everlasting kingdom of our Lord and Savior, Jesus Christ" (1:11). Believers spiritually enter the kingdom of God when they are born again (John 3:3-5).

The entrance which Peter speaks of is the literal entrance into the eternal kingdom at the resurrection and glorification of the redeemed body (1 Thess. 4:13-18; Phil. 3:20, 21). Spiritual regeneration on the basis of faith in God's grace *assures* entrance to *every* born-again believer. Validating our calling and election before men by faithful service and a virtuous life will assure an abundant, full, and victorious entrance, with honors and awards for the faithful (1 Cor. 3:9-15; 9:27; 2 Cor. 5:10).

The prospect of this glorious future easily becomes dimmed. Thus Peter did not wish to be "negligent" in reminding God's people of "these things," though they knew them and were "established in the present truth" (1:12). Peter had in mind those gospel truths which were formerly promised to Old Testament saints but are now present with believers as an arrived reality.

INSPIRATION AND AUTHORITY OF THE WRITTEN WORD

It is highly significant that, in dealing with the general theme of true knowledge from God as opposed to false knowledge from apostate teachers, the Apostle Peter should touch upon the pivotal subject of the source of authority in matters of spiritual knowledge. This is always a crucial issue in times of apostasy — today as in the days of the Apostles.

In expounding this subject Peter first lays the foundation by demonstrating *the authority of the apostolic testimony* (1:16-18). The inspired witness of the apostles precludes deception or imposture. They did not follow "cunningly devised fables," that is, man-concocted myths. Their witness is supported by divine revelation and the first-hand evidence of eyewitnesses (1:16; Matt. 17:1, 5). They saw the transfigured, glorified Christ on the mountain. Peter saw with his own eyes "that great One's majesty" (this is the emphasis of the Greek). Significantly, too, they had a personal revelation of "the power and coming of our Lord Jesus Christ," since the transfiguration was a portrayal in miniature of the second advent (Matt. 17:1-8; Mark 9:2-8; Luke 9:28-36). Peter also heard the voice of "the majestic glory" (God) with James and John in the "holy mountain" (1:17, 18).

Having established the authority of the apostolic testimony, Peter then declares *the inspiration and authority of the written Word* (1:19-21). The written Scriptures not only contain and preserve the authority of the apostolic testimony, but are themselves attested through fulfilled prophecy. "And we have the prophetic word (the Old Testament Scriptures) made more sure" (literal translation). In other words, Old Testament prophecies concerning Christ's first advent were fulfilled by the events of the New Testament era. Prophecies about the second advent received a foretaste of their fulfillment in Christ's transfiguration, which Peter, James, and John witnessed.

Through the Holy Spirit Peter declares that the Scriptures are of divine origin — that they are directly inspired by God (1:20, 21). An expanded translation of the Greek text has this emphasis: "For *not by the will of man* (emphatic) was any prophecy ever borne to us, but, on the contrary, men being borne along by the agency of the Holy Spirit spoke *from God* (emphatic)" (1:21).

Since Scripture is composed of the words of God spoken through human authors as directed by the Holy Spirit, no part of it is "of any private interpretation" or "its own interpretation." It is not to be isolated from what the Scripture declares elsewhere. Scripture is to be interpreted by both its own context and other relevant passages of Scripture, that is, by both the *immediate* connection in chapter and book as well as the broadest connection of all sixty-six books that make up the Bible. God's voice must not be stifled by the interjection of man's voice. God must be allowed to speak by the Spirit in interpretation, even as he has spoken by the Spirit in inspiration. The *authority* of God's voice must be recognized. Before this authority men's ideas and philosophies must bow in utter subjection.

FULFILLED PROPHECY AND INSPIRATION

Peter declares, "We have a more sure word of prophecy" (literally, "the prophetic word made more sure" — 1:19). Prophecy is made "more sure" by fulfillment. As Peter points out, fulfilled prophecy is a remarkable attestation of inspiration. Predictions of future events in the Bible were spoken so long before the events transpired that in no possible way could mere human precognition have foreseen them. Moreover, these predictions are so minute in detail and specific in character as to exclude the possibility of an unusual coincidence or a chance guess.

The Word of God has a large prophetic or predictive element woven into the warp and woof of its fabric. Hundreds of predictions concerning Israel, the nations, and historical personages have come to pass exactly as foretold. Through the power of God these amazing forecasts have been fulfilled by men who were ignorant of them, who disbelieved them, or who struggled in desperation to avoid their fulfillment. These predictions have been so ancient, so unique, so improbable, and so detailed and definite that no human mind could have anticipated them. They prove conclusively that the Scriptures which contain them are beyond any question inspired by God alone.

APOSTATE TEACHERS AND THEIR DOOM

Second Peter and Second Timothy have a great deal in common. Among other similarities, both envision the widespread departure from the faith that will culminate in the great apostasy of "the last days" (2:1 – 3:7, 2 Tim. 3:1-9, 13). The main thrust of Second Peter is the eloquent and comprehensive denunciation of apostasy and apostate teachers (2:1 – 3:5). These men had departed from the Christian faith (Jude 1:3), which they once professed intellectually but never enjoyed experientially. They had abandoned the faith of a Christian but retained the outward veneer and profession of Christianity.

The Apostle outlines the activity and influence of these apostate teachers (2:1-3) and declares their sure judgment. "Their judgment from long ago (in God's purpose and plan) is not idle, and their destruction is not asleep" (literal translation). Their ruin is illustrated by the case of the fallen angels (2:4), the sinners who perished in the flood (2:5), and the wicked inhabitants of Sodom and Gomorrah, who were consumed by fire (2:6-10). The presumption and greed of these false teachers are condemned (2:10-16), their empty intellectualism is denounced (2:17, 18), and their bondage to sin is exposed (2:19-22). Their spiritual ignorance and opposition to the prophetic Word (3:1-7; cf. 1:16-21) lead them to scoff at the truth of Christ's second coming.

THE SECOND ADVENT OF CHRIST
AND HOLY LIVING

The Apostle shows that denying Christ's advent, as the apostate teachers were doing, was in line with their immoral and lawless conduct and was a deterrent to holy living (3:1-7). These "scoffers" walked "after their own lusts" (3:3). They made light of the second advent by espousing a uniformitarian view of history, flouting the idea of supernatural catastrophism suggested by the second advent. They say, "Where is the promise of his coming?" After all these centuries Christ's coming has not occurred, and their sneer is, "It never will!" They assume that all things in the natural world will continue as they have, with no major upset. Their ungodly assumption and their denial of the Word of God are refuted by both *Bible history* – the restoration of the chaotic earth (Gen. 1:1-31) and the flood (3:5, 6; cf. Gen. 6:1 – 8:22) – and *Bible prophecy* – the coming renovation of the earth by fire (3:7, 10-12).

Peter appeals to holy living in view of this fiery catastrophe and the coming dissolution of the old earth in preparation for a "new heavens and a new earth, in which righteousness dwells" (3:13). He is in perfect accord with the Apostle Paul (Tit. 2:11-13) and John (1 John 3:1-3), who also present the Lord's coming as an incentive to a holy life.

THE DAY OF THE LORD
AND THE DAY OF GOD

Peter unfolds a new revelation about the day of the Lord. He relates this extended period to the cataclysm of fire (3:7, 10-12). Old Testament prophecy had clearly related that day to the earth judgments culminating in the advent of Messiah in glory and his subsequent reign over the millennial earth (Isa. 2:6-22; 4:1-6; cf. Rev. 4 — 19).

Peter's new revelation stresses the *consummation* of that day. He calls this climactic and final aspect of it "the day of God" (3:12). This day involves the ultimate and final catastrophe of time, when the earth is consumed in a fire-bath and the "new heavens and new earth" of the sinless state are created. The "day of God" envisions the time when sin, death, and hell are isolated in Gehenna (Rev. 20:11-14) and Christ surrenders the mediatorial kingdom to the Father (1 Cor. 15:24-28; Rev. 20:7 — 22:21).

GOD'S TIMETABLE
AND THE DIVINE PURPOSE

Peter rebuffs those who scoff at the second advent of Christ by showing that human concepts of time are not the limited context in which God accomplishes his purposes for time and eternity. Peter quotes Psalm 90:4 to demonstrate that God operates in eternity, and is not restricted by the time limitations which bind a finite creature like man (3:8).

Peter also shows that, even though God is not bound by time, he is always punctual (3:9). One day with him is "as a thousand years, and a thousand years as one day." He is not "slack" (remiss). He does not delay in the sense of being indecisive or remiss in keeping his promises, as some men erroneously interpret his patience. Instead, God has a purpose in his patience. "He is longsuffering, not wishing that any should perish, but that all should come to repentance" (cf. Gen. 6:3; 1 Tim. 2:4; 1 Pet. 3:20). He gives sinners time to consider their evil ways and to turn from their iniquity.

1 John

AUTHOR

The external evidence for the genuineness of First John is early and strong. Polycarp quotes First John 4:2, 3 in his Epistle to the Philippians. The Muratorian Fragment, the Old Syriac, Irenaeus, and Clement of Alexandria add their evidence, as do Cyprian, Origen, and Dionysius of Alexandria. Eusebius places First John among the books accepted canonically.

The author himself claims to be an eyewitness of Christ (1:1-4; 4:14). He is clearly the same person as the author of the fourth Gospel. Although the author does not state his name in either the Epistle or the Gospel, the early Church on solid grounds of internal evidence attributed both works to the Apostle John. There are striking resemblances between these two works in style, language, and thought patterns. Among the resemblances are the following distinctive words and expressions: *word, light, eternal life, love, new commandment, lay down one's life, take away sins, works of the devil, murderer, overcome the world, pass from death unto life, Savior of the world, Paraclete, begotten of God, joy-fulfilled, bear witness,* etc.

A few technical words, such as *propitiation, anointing,* and *parousia,* occur in only one of the works. But this is no evidence against Johannine authorship. Not even the blindest critic would insist that an author has to use his entire vocabulary every time he writes. The same simple, straightforward Hebraic style with use of parallelism characterizes both the fourth Gospel and the Epistle. Authorship of both by the Apostle John is the only logical conclusion.

BACKGROUND AND DATE

There is scarcely a clue from the testimony of the Epistle itself as to whom the Letter was addressed. The warning against idols (5:21), the sparse reference to the Old Testament, the absence of any reference to Hebraic legalism, and the general address to the family of God would at least indicate that its original readers were not primarily Hebrew believers.

The only significant indication of the original destination of John's First Epistle comes from early Church tradition. Irenaeus writes, "Then, again, the Church of Ephesus founded by Paul and having John remaining among them permanently until the time of Trajan, is a true witness of the tradition of the apostles" (*Against Heresies III:* 3, 4). (Emperor Trajan ruled during A.D. 98 to 117.)

It seems that John was active not only in the church at Ephesus but also in the assemblies of proconsular Asia (Rev. 2, 3). No doubt John visited neighboring districts and organized new churches. What would be more likely than to suppose that he directed First John to these Gentile converts?

John's immediate purpose in writing the Epistle was apparently to refute the twin error of Cerinthian Gnosticism and antinomian Nicolaitanism. The first of these errors was a philosophic perversion of the person and work of Christ. Cerinthus lived during the period A.D. 80-100 and was educated in Egypt, according to Irenaeus. He taught that the world was created not by God himself but rather by a certain power far separated from him. He declared that Jesus was merely the natural son of Mary and Joseph (though more righteous and prudent than other men). At Jesus' baptism "the Christ" as a spirit and in the likeness of a dove descended upon him, endowing him with miraculous gifts. At Jesus' death "the Christ" departed from him, so that Christ did not die, since he was a spirit being incapable of death. Thus only the *human* Jesus died and rose again, according to the Cerinthian heresy.

Although Irenaeus declares that the Nicolaitans were heretical followers of Nicolas ("a proselyte of Antioch" — *Against Heresies I:* 26, 3; *III:* 11, 1), there is no real historical basis for this identification. It is apparently an inference rather than a fact. The same is apparently true of Irenaeus' identification of the Nicolaitans as antinomian libertines. So far, all that we know definitely about the Nicolaitans of John's day is contained in Revelation 2:6. In all likelihood the name there is symbolic (like Jezebel in Rev. 2:20) and refers to the rise of a priestism that placed clergy over laity (*nikao*, "conquer" and *laos*, "people").

To combat the Cerinthian error John outlines the reality of the incarnation (1:1-4). He also delineates the practical aspects of the sin question (1:5 — 2:6) and describes the responsibility of "little children" in the Father's family to love one another (2:7-11) and to avoid being enamored of the evil world (2:12-17). He warns against heretical teaching (2:18-29) and admonishes the little children to live consistently in the light of the Lord's return (2:18 — 3:12) and to prove the reality of their salvation by their testimony before men (3:13-24).

Israel's modern parliament building, the Knesset, in Jerusalem (*IGTO photo*)

John gives the criterion for detecting false teachers (4:1-4) and describes their wordly outlook (4:5, 6). The Apostle presents another urgent entreaty to practice brotherly love (4:7-21). He presents faith as the principle which overcomes the world (5:1-8), gives assurance of salvation (5:9-15), and enables the believer to avoid sinning (5:16, 17). He closes with those things of which the believer has sure knowledge (5:18-21).

The date at which the Apostle John wrote his First Epistle can be determined approximately by the events of early Church history. The destruction of Jerusalem had scattered early believers, some of whom had migrated to Asia Minor. Tradition places John, Philip, and Andrew among these. As noted previously, Irenaeus claimed that John lived to the Trajan era (A.D. 98-117). From these and other considerations conservative scholars conclude that the Apostle wrote his Gospel at approximately A.D. 85-90 and his First Epistle a little later (since the Epistle assumes the reader's acquaintance with the Gospel).

IMPORTANCE AND PURPOSE

First John is best described as a family letter from the Father to his "little children" in the world. An intimate and tender word is employed for "children." It is a diminutive meaning "born-ones" who are beloved and cherished in the family circle. This is only one of many tender touches that make this Epistle one of the most intimate of the inspired writings. In First John the sin of the believer is treated as a child's offense against the Father; it is dealt with as a family matter (1: 9; 2:1). The Epistle is addressed exclusively to believers; hence other ethical and moral problems are hardly mentioned.

OUTLINE

A. Family Fellowship and the Father (chapters 1 – 3)
    1. The basis of fellowship (the incarnation) (1:1-4)
    2. The conditions of fellowship (1:5-10)
        (a) Walking in the light (1:5-8)
        (b) Confessing our sins (1:9, 10)
    3. Christ's advocacy and fellowship (2:1, 2)
    4. Obedience and fellowship (2:3-6)
    5. Brotherly love and fellowship (2:7-11)
    6. Spiritual maturity and fellowship (2:12-14)
    7. Worldliness as a threat to fellowship (2:15-17)
    8. Doctrinal defection as a foe to fellowship (2:18-23)
    9. Abiding in Christ as a prerequisite to fellowship (2:24-29)
   10. Holy living as a prerequisite to fellowship (3:1-10)
   11. Brotherly love as an expression of fellowship (3:11-18)
   12. Christian assurance and fellowship (3:19-24)
B. Family Fellowship and the World (chapters 4, 5)
    1. False teachers of the world destroy fellowship (4:1-6)
    2. Love is the supreme manifestation of fellowship (4:7-18)
    3. Divine love is an incentive to fellowship (4:19-21)
    4. Faith is the ground of fellowship (5:1-5)
    5. The testimony of God's Son and the Spirit produce fellowship (5:6-12)

6. Prayer furthers fellowship (5:13-15)
7. Sin in the saint breaks fellowship (5:16, 17)
8. Assured knowledge fortifies fellowship (5:18-21)

FIRST JOHN AND THE GOSPEL OF JOHN

The Gospel of John describes *the Son of God*. The Epistle discusses mainly *the sons of God*. The Gospel stresses regeneration, while the Epistle stresses fellowship. The Gospel opens with the living Word existing in face-to-face fellowship with the Father "in the beginning"; the Epistle opens with the Word of life moving toward salvation of the Father's chosen ones "from the beginning." The following chart shows further comparisons.

COMPARISON OF JOHN'S GOSPEL AND FIRST EPISTLE	
Gospel of John	*First Epistle of John*
Presents the Son of God	Features the sons of God
Attests the Savior of the world	Instructs those saved out of the world
Stresses regeneration of lost sinners	Emphasizes fellowship in God's family
Written that men might believe and be saved from sin (20:30, 31)	Written that those saved might not go on sinning (2:1)
Presents the believer's Advocate (Chap. 17)	Urges the believer to use his Advocate (2:1)
Christ the Light of the world (8:12)	"Walking in the light" in fellowship (1:7)
Faith to receive life from God (3:16)	A righteous life the proof before men (2:29)
The coming of the Lord as a comfort (14:1-3)	The coming of the Lord as a warning (2:28)
How redemption was provided	How redemption is to be appropriated

JOHN'S WRITINGS
AND THE EPISTLES OF PAUL

In Paul's letters the doctrine of justification is prominent. In John's writings the doctrine of regeneration dominates. Paul presents unsaved men as outside God's favor and under divine wrath. John views them as outside the family of God, separated from the fellowship and joy of the family circle. Paul expounds the full theological perspective of the redemptive work of Christ. He especially stresses the nature, position, and destiny of the Church, the body of Christ. In contrast, John defines the person and work of the Redeemer as a historical event to be applied to the life of the believer in an intimate Father-son-family relationship.

Although John and Paul have different tasks to perform and different emphases to make, there is no disagreement, only perfect accord as inspired recorders of divine revelation. One supplements the other. For each the cross is the foundation of all his teaching. Its provisions constitute the only way a sinner can be saved and begin the Christian life. Its dynamic is the only way that those who are saved can continue on in Christian victory, fellowship, and blessing.

THE INCARNATION AND FELLOWSHIP

True Christian fellowship *must* be based on truth. The foundational truth of Christianity is the incarnation of the eternal Word, who was "with God" and "was God" (John 1:1; Prov. 8:23). In the Gospel John declares that it was God the Word who became incarnate (John 1:1, 14) and that this incarnate Word was the Creator of all things (John 1:3). The Gnostic, Cerinthus, had denied this basic truth. He declared that the world was created not by God himself but by some power far separated from him.

In introducing the incarnate Word the Apostle John refers to him in his eternal, preincarnate deity: "that which was from the beginning" (1:1; 2:13; John 1:1). He then documents his own personal witness to the incarnation of the eternal Word. He especially emphasizes the evidence which the human senses provide in attesting the genuine humanity of Christ: ". . . which we have heard, which we have seen with our eyes, and our hands have handled, of the Word of life." The "Word of life" describes Christ as the eternal Word of God who became incarnate to bring life to people dead in sin (John 3:16). The same Word who was eternally co-existent with the Father became revealed to men in the incarnation (1:2).

The Apostle thus at the outset refutes the error of Cerinthus, who denied the incarnation and substituted a kind of "apotheosis," by which a sinful, fallen man became indwelt by deity in the person of the eternal Word, "the Christ." Cerinthus taught that the eternal Word did not assume humanity by the operation of the Holy Spirit in the womb of the Virgin Mary (cf. Matt. 1:18-25; Luke 1:35; John 1:14) but was rather the natural offspring of Mary and Joseph and consequently a sinner like all of Adam's fallen race. At his baptism "the Christ," a spiritual, noncorporeal being, descended upon and indwelt him. He departed from him at death, since as a Spirit "the Christ" could not die. Only the human Jesus died and rose again.

Cerinthus thereby denied the incarnation—the union of God and man in the person of Jesus Christ. This was accompanied by a denial of Christ's sinless conception by the Holy Spirit (the virgin birth), a denial of the real and sinless humanity of Jesus Christ, and a denial of Christ's redemptive death. The heresy denied every basic teaching of the Christian faith. It offered no real Savior. It destroyed the very basis of the family of God and the fellowship of the Father's children in the family circle. This evil heresy did have one good result, however—it called forth the Apostle John's clear definition of the person and work of our Lord Jesus and the reality of his incarnation.

THE QUESTION OF "SINLESS PERFECTION"

This Epistle has sometimes been misconstrued to teach that a believer can in this life reach a spiritual plateau in which he is immune from the possibility of sinning. First John 3:9 has frequently been used as the basis of this misinterpretation. "Whosoever is born of God *doth not commit sin,* for his (God's) seed (nature) remains in him, and he cannot sin because he is born of God." Does this verse teach "sinless perfection"—that a believer can reach the place where he cannot sin? That it appears on the surface to teach this is due to the fact that the real meaning of the Greek tenses has been obscured in translation.

First John 3:9 may be paraphrased as follows to give the precise meaning of the original: "Whosoever is born of God," that is, who is regenerated and possesses a new nature, "does not go on *practicing* sin." The present tense denotes continuous action. The reason given is "for his (God's) seed," that is, the new divine nature implanted in the believer at regeneration, "remains in him" (present tense, "continues to abide in him") "and he cannot sin" (present tense again, "he is not able to go on practicing sin").

The Apostle shows that the practice of sin as the common custom of life is not possible with the regenerate, as it is with the unregenerate. Nor are they confirmed in the direction of sin, for they have a new divine nature given by God that *cannot* sin. But the question is, Why then do believers sin and require cleansing? The answer is that as long as the believer is still in this world he has the old nature alongside the new divine nature. Although the new nature cannot sin, the old nature can and does sin. However, the new nature cannot allow the *practice* of sin in the believer; through the indwelling Spirit it resists the habitual manifestation of sin.

That sinless perfection is not attainable in our unglorified bodies of this present life is due to the fact that the old nature is not removed until glorification. The Apostle John is careful to point this out. "If we say that we have no sin" (the sin nature as the principle or root of sin) "we deceive ourselves, and the truth is not in us" (1:18). Believers who imagine that they stand above the possibility of sinning are self-deceived. They lose sight of God's unsullied holiness (1:5), the presence of the old nature, their proneness to sin as a result, and their continual need of confession and cleansing (1:7, 9).

If believers say they "have not sinned" (a perfect tense in the Greek, denoting past action *continuing into the present*), they "make God a liar" by denying what his Word teaches and what their own experience should prove to them (1:10). The Apostle warns that the holiest and most mature saint still possesses an old nature. Not only *can* he sin but he must continually "walk in the light" as God is in the light (1:7) in order *not* to sin.

CONFESSION AND FELLOWSHIP

The Apostle teaches that if a believer sins he is to confess it immediately. Otherwise fellowship with the Father is broken. "If we confess our sins he is faithful and just (righteous) to forgive us our sins and to cleanse us from all unrighteousness" (1:9). The problem faced here by the believer who has sinned is not restoration to *salvation* but restoration to *fellowship*. The believer's *salvation* rests securely on the changeless person and merit of Christ. This unchanging basis enables the infinitely holy God, who "is light" and in whom "is no darkness at all" (1:5), to forgive the sins of his saints and yet remain "just" (righteous), totally uncompromising in his infinite holiness. It also enables God to remain "faithful" (cf. 1 Thess. 5:24) to his Word even though the sinning saint may be unfaithful.

While eternal salvation constitutes the unchanging basis upon which the Father-Son-child relationship of God's family rests, *fellowship* in the family is variable and changeable, depending on the believer's confession of sin and his walk "in the light" (1:6, 7).

To "confess one's sins" is to acknowledge them in a spirit of full avowal and admission. The word "confess" is from the Latin *con*, "together," and *fateri*, "to acknowledge," "to avow freely." Confession should be made to God as Father in the name of the Son, since the believer has been constituted a beloved child in the Father's family. God has promised to fully forgive and thoroughly cleanse the believer who confesses his sins (1:9). This promise is to be taken exactly as given. By faith the believer knows that God has forgiven him of his sin as soon as confession has been made. God's promise remains true even if the believer's emotions of guilt linger on. Fellowship with God and with fellow believers is restored, for "if we walk in the light, as he is in the light, we have fellowship with one another, and the blood of Jesus Christ his Son cleanseth us" ("keeps on cleansing us," present tense) "from all sin" (1:7).

CHRIST'S ADVOCACY AND CHRISTIAN FELLOWSHIP

The Apostle presents Christ as the believer's advocate or defense lawyer in the court of heaven. "My little children, these things write I unto you, that ye sin not. And if any man sin, we have" (continually and unfailingly, a present tense) "an advocate with the Father, Jesus Christ the righteous" (2:1). As our legal representative our Lord never assumes the role of a prosecutor—despite the fact that charges are preferred against the believer before the Father's throne by Satan, the accuser of the brethren (cf. Rev. 12:10).

The heavenly Advocate's ministry is twofold. He advocates in behalf of the believer when he sins and intercedes for him in his weakness and immaturity. In the first chapter the Apostle expounds the effect of the believer's sin upon himself. In the second chapter, however, he contemplates the far more serious problem of the effect of the believer's sin upon God.

Recognizing this sin problem, some Christians assume that there is no specific cure for the believer's sin against God and that the saved one who has sinned must be prosecuted by the court of heaven and dismissed from his saved estate. Such a procedure would indeed be absolutely necessary were it not for the present advocacy of Christ. In this ministry our Lord pleads the complete efficacy of his atoning death for the specific sin or sins in question.

As the believer's advocate in heaven Christ pleads the fact that he bore the believer's sins. His resurrected and glorified human body bears witness to God's acceptance of his substitutionary work. Christ's redemptive work and God's acceptance of it therefore guarantee the sinning believer's acquittal and release. Condemnation is a legal and theological impossibility. Christ's complete effectiveness as the heavenly Advocate gains him the distinctive title of "Jesus Christ *the righteous*."

Christ's present advocacy in heaven is an inseparable part of his saviorhood. It is effective for *every* believer at all times. It remains in operation whether or not the believer understands it. Christ's advocacy is therefore not a subject of petition but rather an integral part of our "great salvation" (Heb. 2:3). It should evoke praiseful thanksgiving and confident rejoicing.

PROPITIATION AND FELLOWSHIP

In dealing with the problem of sin within the family circle of God's children, the Apostle sets forth the believer's advocate as his *propitiation*. "And he is the propitiation for our sins; and not for ours only, but also for the sins of the whole world" (2:2). Propitiation is the Godward side of Christ's redemptive work; it is the provision by which the infinitely holy God (1:5) can graciously extend mercy and forgiveness toward sinners. God's character has always been gracious and merciful, but his infinite holiness prevented him from extending this mercy toward fallen men.

But Christ made propitiation by dying on the cross and thus answering the just demands of God's holiness against sin. His own blood was, as it were, sprinkled over his sinless human body, the true mercy seat (Rom. 3:25; Heb. 9:5). God was now morally free to demonstrate limitless mercy and grace to the vilest of sinners.

God's propitious grace extends toward the unsaved as well as toward the sinning saint. "He is the propitiation for our sins: and not for ours only, but also for the sins of the whole world" (2:2). The death of Christ for the sins of the world altered the position of the entire human race in the sight of God. God recognizes what Christ did in behalf of the world whether men appropriate it or not.

The true gospel message is that God is propitious by virtue of what *Christ has done* and not as the result of anything the sinner might do or try to do. Thus all the burden is removed from both the sinner and the Christian, leaving him only to personally accept God's propitiousness through Christ. "Herein is love, not that we loved God, but that he loved us and sent his Son to be the propitiation for our sins" (4:10).

The blood-sprinkled body of Christ on the cross became the mercy seat for the sinner once and for all. There the God of righteousness can meet the sinner with salvation and the sinning saint with restoration to fellowship and joy. What otherwise would be a throne of awful judgment becomes the throne of infinite grace (cf. Heb. 4:16).

THE WORLD AND CHRISTIAN FELLOWSHIP

The Apostle John singles out "the world" (Greek *kosmos*) as the special enemy of God's children and a perennial peril to the destruction of Christian fellowship in the family circle. "Love not the world, neither the things that are in the world. If any man love the world, the love of the Father is not in him" (2:15; cf. Matt. 6:24; James 4:4). John is referring not to the material earth or to humanity in general but to those institutions of men set up in independence of God and headed by Satan. It is this Satanic system organized on principles of greed, selfishness, war, and godless commercialism that God does not love. The believer is likewise warned not to love it. If he does, his love for God will grow cold. This is the peril which the world presents.

Satan uses both this world system and the sin nature of the human body to generate prideful, godless living. This is the kind of life which Christ will destroy when he returns in glory. By contrast, "he who does the will of God remains forever" (2:17). He builds on the solid foundation of God's Word and will and rests securely in the knowledge that his life will stand in the day of judgment.

ABIDING IN CHRIST AND FELLOWSHIP

In John's writings abiding in Christ is presented not as a matter of maintaining *union* with Christ but of maintaining *communion* with him. Our union with Christ is eternally assured by his finished work of redemption. It is this secure relationship which makes fellowship or communion possible (Rom. 5:1-11). The Apostle John does not dwell at length on the believer's eternal union with Christ, because Paul had already expounded this in great detail, especially in the Book of Romans. Instead John challenges the believer to see if he is really "abiding in Christ" in his daily experience. "He that saith he abideth in him ought himself also to walk, even as he walked" (2:6). "He that loveth his brother abideth in the light, and there is no occasion of stumbling in him" (2:10; cf. 3:14). "Whosoever abideth in him sinneth not" (does not sin habitually, does not practice sin—a present tense in the Greek). "Whosoever sinneth" (constantly sins, a present participle) "hath not seen him, neither known him" (3:6). "And he that keepeth his commandments" (the eternal moral law of God) "dwelleth in him, and he in him" (3:24). Good works and holy living are the fruits of abiding.

John, like Paul, teaches that union with Christ is permanent and unchangeable (3:24b). Communion, however, is changeable and variable; it depends on keeping God's commandments and walking in God's light (1:7). In Paul's language it is "reckoning" (depending by faith) upon our union and experiencing it in our daily lives (Rom. 6:11).

TEST OF DOCTRINAL ORTHODOXY

The Apostle John in warning against doctrinal error as a foe to Christian fellowship gives a divine yardstick by which *all* religious untruth can be detected (4:1-6). This passage is comparable to the divine criterion for measuring truth described by the Apostle Paul in First Timothy 3:16, as well as to the pivotal Pauline passage that traces the source of all religious error to demonism (1 Tim. 4:1-6).

The particular demon-instigated and demon-propagated heresy which John refutes is Cerinthian Gnosticism. As discussed earlier, this error denies the true person and work of Christ. John shows that the demons propagate their false doctrines with great aggressiveness (4:1). The children in the Father's family need to remember that demonism is both the source and the dynamic of all false doctrine (4:1-3; 1 Tim. 4:1).

Because of the peril of demonic spirits the Apostle warns God's beloved not to believe every spirit, but to test the spirits, "whether they are of God." Many "spirits not of God" (i.e., demons or evil spirits) speak through false prophets. John warns that "many false prophets" have gone out into the world, parading as teachers of Christian truth but actually energized by demons. Such false teachers abounded not only in John's day but in our own day as well. Thus Paul's warning in First Timothy 3:16 and John's warning in First John 4:1-6 are especially timely for spiritually concerned believers today.

In First John 4:2, 3 John gives the acid test of error. The test centers in Christ's *deity* and *incarnation.* Confession of the truth involved in this basic issue is the touchstone that differentiates between true and false teachers. Every Christian heresy involves some erroneous teaching about the person and work of Christ.

The confession that "Jesus Christ is come in the flesh" embraces our Lord's true humanity. It acknowledges the reality of both his sinless human body before his death and his present resurrected and glorified human body installed at the right hand of the Father. It is the pledge and guarantee that the body of every believer will be glorified in the same way as Christ's body (cf. 3:1-3). This truth is brought out in the tense of the verb: "Jesus Christ *is come*" (*elēluthota*, a perfect tense—not a mere past historical fact but *present* and continuing in its blessed effects). Our Lord's glorified humanity in heaven assures a glorified body for *all* those united to him.

In this clear manner the Apostle John provides the authoritative test for distinguishing truth from error and the Holy Spirit from demon spirits. Together with the Apostle Paul (2 Tim. 3:13-17), he furnishes the criterion which God gives man to judge between the true and the false in the exceedingly complex realm of the religious. Those who heed man's voice instead of God's and ignore this divinely given chart expose themselves to the subtle snare of the Satanic and demonic. This peril often parades as "an angel of light" (2 Cor. 11:14) under the halo of the popular religious fads and cults of the day.

SIN THAT RESULTS IN PHYSICAL DEATH

In discussing prayer fellowship John shows that it is possible for a true believer to fall into serious and scandalous sin (5:16, 17). When a Christian sins a fellow Christian is to pray for him. God will in answer to prayer preserve the sinning Christian's physical life. (The Apostle is not speaking of eternal life, for this cannot be forfeited.) However, such prayer is effective only in instances where the sin is not "unto (physical) death."

"There is a sin unto death," that is, sin of such seriousness that it eventuates in *physical* (not spiritual) death. What the Apostle is warning against is persistent, wilful, deliberate sin that brings such dishonor upon God's salvation and the Savior that "the flesh is destroyed" (physical death occurs) so that "the spirit might be saved" (1 Cor. 5:1-5; Acts 5:1-11; 1 Cor. 11:30). This sin calls forth the ultimate in God's chastening of his own, the last recourse he uses with a disobedient and wilful child. Both Samson and Saul are Old Testament illustrations of this. David illustrates a sinning saint who came perilously close to committing this sin (2 Sam. 12:13; cf. 12:7-12).

The sin that entails physical death is *not to be prayed for.* It involves the operation of a fixed law of God that cannot be altered by prayer. All of the foregoing shows that *sin has different degrees of seriousness.* "All unrighteousness is sin," but there is "sin which is not unto (physical) death," involving less severe disciplinary action (5:17; cf. 1 Cor. 11:30; 2 Sam. 12:7-12).

SIN AND ITS REMEDY (1 JOHN 5:18-20)

John presents a threefold remedy for habitual sin. 1) *The new birth*

(5:18). "We know that everyone who has been born of God does not go on practicing sin" (present tense). This divine life keeps the believer from habitually practicing sin, as the unregenerate do. As a result Satan is unable to touch him. 2) *The believer's new position* (5:19). The believer is born into the family of God. "We know we are of God." By contrast, "the whole world" (the Satanic system of unregenerate humanity) "lieth in the wicked one." The world (the unsaved as a group) is under the power of Satan. 3) *The believer's comprehension of the truth* (5:20). This is an effective deterrent to the practice of sin. The spiritually healthy child of God moves in an atmosphere of truth, love, and light.

2 John

AUTHOR

Both the Second and Third Epistles of John are so similar in style, ideas, and character to the First Epistle that they must have been written by the same author. In the first verse of both the Second and Third Epistles the writer designates himself simply as "the elder" rather than as an apostle. But this is not evidence against authorship by John. Peter calls himself both "an apostle" (1 Pet. 1:1) and "a fellow elder" (1 Pet. 5:1). John could also certainly speak of himself as an elder. He may possibly have used the term in the sense of "advanced in years" or "aged." It is inconceivable that the letter could be a forgery, since a forger would certainly write under the guise of apostleship. There is no sound reason for rejecting authorship by the Apostle John.

BACKGROUND AND DATE

The letter is addressed to "the elect lady." Some scholars have interpreted this designation as a personification of one of the first-century churches. The reference to "some of your children" (v. 4) and "the children of your elect sister" (v. 13), as well as the tone of the letter, seem to indicate that a church is addressed rather than a family. However, many scholars conclude that John addressed the letter to a highly honored Christian matron with whom he was acquainted.

The time and place of writing of all three of John's Epistles are probably about the same, between A.D. 85 and 90 in the city of Ephesus.

IMPORTANCE AND PURPOSE

This extremely brief letter is concerned with God's own children "walking (living) in the truth" (v. 4) according to the "commandments" (the principles of righteousness reflected in God's character and required of all his creatures—v. 6). This is essential to resisting the encroachments of deceivers and false teachers (vv. 7-11). False doctrine is a peril that leads to disaster for any church or Christian. For this reason the author was intensely zealous that the truth of God's Word be wholeheartedly embraced and faithfully practiced in daily living.

OUTLINE

A. A Walk in Truth and Love (1-6)
   1. Greeting in truth and love (1-3)
   2. Commendation in truth and love (4)
   3. Exhortation to truth and love (5, 6)
B. A Threat to Such a Walk (7-11)
   1. Is presented by false teachers (7)
   2. Necessitates the utmost vigilance (8)
   3. Demands the keenest perception (9)
   4. Requires the most clean-cut separation (10, 11)
Conclusion: A Promised Visit and Personal Greetings (12, 13)

SOUND DOCTRINE AND CHRISTIAN LIVING

The urgent message of this significant Epistle centers around the vital dual issue of truth and right conduct. By the term "the truth" the

Apostle refers to both the Bible as God's written revelation of truth and the Lord Jesus Christ as the living embodiment of truth (cf. John 1:17; 14:6).

Orthodox Christian theology is not merely a matter of theory; it determines the way a Christian lives and forms the very foundation of the Christian message and mission. Only sound doctrine can produce sound experience. Rejection of the full inspiration and unquestioned authority of Scripture is the spawning ground for every type of false doctrine and consequent erratic conduct. This short letter provides insights into this problem not only as it threatened early Church life but also as it menaces the Church today.

The Apostle John clearly saw this peril of false doctrine in his day. He understood thoroughly how error dilutes the Christian witness and exerts its baneful effects in the lives of believers. His own love of the truth led him to pen an eloquent plea for a "walk (daily conduct) in truth" (v. 4) on the part of those who "have known the truth" (v. 1). He speaks about "love in the truth" (v. 1) "for truth's sake" (v. 2). His greeting from the triune God is "in truth and love" (v. 3). In the Gospel the Apostle declares, "And ye shall know the truth, and the truth shall make you free" (John 8:32). "New morality" and other errors in the Church today are not setting people free to happiness in right living but are enslaving them in lust and misery.

GOD'S COMMANDMENTS
AND CHRISTIAN LIVING

The Apostle John connects truth inseparably with love and obedience to God's commandments. He speaks of loving *in the truth* (v. 1), of grace, mercy, and peace from God *in truth and love* (v. 3), and of *"walking in truth,* as we have received a commandment from the Father" (v. 4). He also speaks of the "commandment" from the beginning, that we "love one another" (v. 5). He declares "this is love, that we walk after his commandment" (v. 6).

Truth represents doctrine—the Word of God. "Thy word is truth" (John 17:17). The truth of the Word produces genuine love—the queen of all Christian virtues. A believer who loves God loves his fellow man and is, in John's terminology, "walking in truth" (v. 4) and walking "after God's commandments" (v. 6).

These "commandments" represent God's eternal moral law. They are as eternal as God is eternal; they are a reflection of his holy being and character. As given to the nation Israel in the Decalogue of the

Mosaic Covenant (Exod. 20:1-17) they were intended not as a way of salvation but as a means of showing to fallen man God's way of salvation through grace by faith. Yet even in their Mosaic wording the Commandments were summarized by love — love for both God (the first Table) and man (the second Table). See Deuteronomy 6:5; Leviticus 19:18; Matthew 22:35-40.

Now that the Mosaic Law has been fulfilled by Christ's loving sacrifice for fallen man, the new law of love is fulfilled in regenerated hearts by the indwelling Spirit (Rom. 5:5; Heb. 10:16). Our Lord in prospect of his redemptive work and the gift of the indwelling Spirit envisioned this new law of love (John 13:34). It was to be the fulfillment of the moral law of God not only in its Mosaic form in the Decalogue but also in its eternal form as the expression of God's relationship to all of his creatures of all time.

Christ therefore called the new law of love "a new commandment . . . that you love one another; as I have loved you, that you also love one another" (John 13:34). It is a *new commandment* (singular) in contrast to the *old commandments* (plural) of the Mosaic Decalogue; this single commandment of love embodied the essence of all ten of the Mosaic requirements.

The new law of Christ is a command to love with divine love. This love is produced in a believer's heart solely by the operation of the Holy Spirit. Through the Spirit this divine love is manifested spontaneously and without constraint in every believer who is "walking in truth" (v. 4). It is the "law of liberty" of James 1:25 and 2:12.

The Law of Moses, by contrast, was external and "dead" — trying to keep it was both a constraint and a bondage. It was simply beyond the ability of fallen human nature to completely obey it. The Law therefore exposed the depravity of all humanity.

Moses' Law demanded love (Lev. 19:18; Deut. 6:5; Luke 10:27), but Christ's new law of love (1 John 3:18, 23; 4:7-12, 19-21) takes the place of the external law by fulfilling it and supplying the internal reality and dynamic to keep it (Rom. 13:10; Gal. 5:14). Christ's law of love is "written in the heart" under the New Covenant (Heb. 10:16) and displayed in the believer's conduct by the power of the Holy Spirit.

REWARDS AND CHRISTIAN LIVING

In expounding the believer's "walk in truth" the Apostle John is careful to point out the peril of succumbing to error and falling prey to false teachers and deceivers (v. 7). This carries the risk of losing a "full reward" (v. 8). In broaching this subject of rewards the Apostle touches on a very important doctrine of Scripture.

A believer by steadfast faithfulness in service and good works will gain rewards or suffer loss of reward (1 Cor. 3:15). While no true believer can lose his salvation, some believers will receive less than a full reward (v. 8). In Pauline metaphor they will have failed to run the Christian race with full concentration on Christ (1 Cor. 9:27; Phil. 3: 10-14). The Apostle John warns that it is necessary to be constantly vigilant in order to receive a "full reward" at the judgment seat of Christ (2 Cor. 5:10). "Look to yourself" (be cautious and self-critical) in view of "the many deceivers" in the world, who deny the true person and full saving efficacy of Christ's finished redemption (v. 7). These "antichrists" use every possible trick of deception to lure God's people away from a walk of truth and the full reward that follows.

SEPARATION FROM SIN AND APOSTASY

This short Epistle also sheds light on the issue of separation from ecclesiastical apostasy. In our day this issue has been almost as vexing as the question of ecumenicalism (see discussion under Ephesians). Although separatist movements among Christians have often been tarnished by a spirit of censorious criticism and a conspicuous lack of love, it must still be said that Scripture does *not* condone compromise with apostasy and sin. There simply cannot be harmonious fellowship with religionists who deny the true person and work of Christ (vv. 9-11).

John states clearly that anyone who rejects "the doctrine of Christ," that is, the teaching of his full deity and perfect humanity as John has presented it (v. 9; cf. John 1:1, 14; 1 John 1:1-4; 4:1, 2), does not have God (cf. 1 John 2:19, 24). On the other hand, everyone who holds to this basic Christian tenet has both the Father and the Son (1 John 2:23). This admonition identifies apostates and apostasy (see discussion of apostasy in Second Timothy) and enjoins clear-cut separation from them on the part of every believer.

3 John

AUTHOR

The third letter of John is the shortest book of the New Testament. In style, vocabulary, and ideas it closely resembles the other Johannine writings. It was written by "the elder" (1:1; cf. 2 John 1:1), who is certainly John the Apostle, writer of the Gospel of John and First John (see remarks on Second John).

BACKGROUND AND DATE

The letter is addressed to "Gaius the beloved" (v. 1), of whom nothing is known, since the name was very common (cf. Acts 19:29; 20:4; Rom. 16:23; 1 Cor. 1:14). Whoever Gaius was, he was evidently a prominent member of a church in Asia Minor under John's supervision. Trouble had arisen in this assembly because of another influential member named Diotrephes. This domineering individual had refused to recognize messengers of the gospel sent by John to minister to the church. The only reason given for Diotrephes's opposition to these itinerant preachers was that he himself desired the place of preeminence. Perhaps he was ambitious to do all the teaching and was jealous of anyone else who came in this capacity.

The date of Third John is approximately the same as that of the other letters of John, that is, between A.D. 85 and 90.

IMPORTANCE AND PURPOSE

The Apostle penned the letter to voice his esteem of Gaius (v. 1), to assure him of his prayers for his health (v. 2), and to let him know of his joy at his stand for the truth (vv. 3, 4). John also commends him for having received the visiting preachers, urging him to continue this Christian hospitality (vv. 5-8). The Apostle promises to deal with Diotrephes, if he comes for a visit (vv. 9, 10), and commends Demetrius, who was likely the bearer of this Epistle (vv. 11, 12). The Apostle expresses the hope that he may be able to pay the church a visit and see Gaius face to face (vv. 13, 14).

OUTLINE

A. A Godly Life Commended (1-4)
1. Greeting and well wishes (1, 2)
2. Praise of a godly walk (3, 4)
B. Hospitality to Itinerant Ministers Lauded (5-8)
1. Gaius' faithfulness mentioned (5)
2. Gaius' hospitality exemplified (6)
3. Gaius' hospitality encouraged (7, 8)
C. A Domineering Church Worker Denounced (9-11)
1. He resisted the Apostle's authority (9)
2. He insisted on his own way (10)
3. A scriptural guideline set down (11)
D. A Godly Church Worker Praised (12)
1. He is approved by his conduct (12a)
2. He is approved by his doctrine (12b)
3. He is approved by the Apostle (12c)
Conclusion: Intentions and Benediction (13, 14)

THE CHURCH AND THE PROBLEM OF ECCLESIASTICAL DOMINATION

The Third Letter of John anticipates a difficulty that has in varying degrees plagued the Church since Apostolic days. It is the problem of domineering individuals, groups of individuals, or ecclesiastical organizations. Third John presents the problem as crystallized in an individual. Diotrephes was perhaps a layman, but he illustrates the evil of domineering ambition on the part of anyone in the church—pastor, elder, deacon, or lay member. It was this spirit of pride and self-importance that led Diotrephes to slander "with malicious words" everyone who questioned his oppressive domination (cf. Prov. 9:8; 10: 8; 12:1). Diotrephes's objects of slander included the Apostle John himself (v. 10).

Diotrephes intensified his dictatorial tactics by refusing hospitality to itinerant ministers of the gospel recommended by the Apostle John himself and by forbidding other church members to do so. Believers who exercised such hospitality he excommunicated from the church! (See verse 10.)

The Apostle Peter warned elders against being "lords over God's heritage," exhorting them rather to be "examples to the flock" (1 Pet. 5:3). The spirit of self-assertion which Diotrephes showed has crystallized in the Church in the invention of a priestly order that dominates over the so-called laity. It ignores the great truth of the priesthood of all believers, substituting instead the wholly unscriptural notion of a priesthood which is superior to ordinary believers.

The spirit of Diotrephes sometimes finds expression even in a church where the priesthood of all believers is taught and practiced. Occasionally a sound gospel preacher gets the notion that he must "run the church" as a God-ordained dictator. He listens to little advice from elders or deacons (if he has any) and tolerates no opposition. Those who dare to oppose him are put out of the church in true Diotrephene style. He spurns advice from older, more experienced men, as Diotrephes ignored the Apostle John.

The cure for the evil of ecclesiastical domination is rigid adherence to the Word of God and submissive reliance on the Holy Spirit's leading. The Holy Spirit never leads anyone to become an ecclesiastical dictator.

"The well-beloved Gaius" (vv. 1-4) and Demetrius, a believer of fine reputation for living out the truth (v. 12), are the Apostle's answer to unworthy intruders like Diotrephes.

Jude

AUTHOR

Similarities and allusions to Jude occur in the writings of Hermas, Polycarp, Theophilus of Antioch, and Tertullian. Although its canonicity was questioned by some because of alleged citations from the noncanonical books of Enoch and *The Assumption of Moses*, Jude's right to inclusion in the Canon was universally recognized by A.D. 350.

The author (1:1) was apparently the brother of James (bishop of Jerusalem and writer of the Epistle of James) and a half-brother of Christ (cf. Matt. 13:55; Mark 6:3). At first Jude or Judas was an unbeliever (John 7:3-5). Later, however, he became convinced of Christ's deity (Acts 1:14). Some scholars identify the author of the Epistle as the Apostle Judas (Luke 6:16; Acts 1:13), called elsewhere Lebbaeus or Thaddaeus (Matt. 10:3).

BACKGROUND AND DATE

The occasion of the Epistle was the appearance of a philosophic heresy which encouraged moral laxity and lawlessness. It was apparently the Gnosticism exposed elsewhere in the New Testament (notably in Colossians and Second Peter). Gnostic philosophy clashed sharply with Christianity in its assessment of all matter as evil. It denied the biblical doctrine of creation and the true incarnation of Christ, teaching that Christ's body could not have been real without at the same time being evil.

In the realm of Christian ethics the Gnostic philosophy taught a dual error. On one hand it prompted antinomianism (the belief that one is not obligated to keep the moral law) and on the other hand it fostered ascetic abuse of the body in order to promote spirituality. Both of these errors are clearly opposed by the Word of God.

Precisely where or when Jude wrote his Epistle is not known. The Epistle was apparently written not later than A.D. 81, when Domitian became Emperor. Hegesippus in the second century declares that Jude's two grandsons were arraigned before Domitian as descendants of David, but were dismissed as harmless peasants. Had Jude been alive, he too would probably have been brought before the Emperor. Jude apparently knew of Peter's writings. If so, his Letter cannot be earlier than A.D. 66 or 67. A date of about A.D. 75 would probably not be far afield.

IMPORTANCE AND PURPOSE

The Epistle of Jude contends for the faith against unbelief and apostasy. Jude's message is one of the most severe in the New Testament. But its severity is justified by the grave peril which Jude faced and combated. Like Second Peter, Jude concerns itself primarily with false teachers that had infiltrated the Church (cf. vv. 4-16 with 2 Pet. 2: 1 – 3:7). Jude denounces these false teachers in even stronger language than does Peter.

Both Second Peter and Jude deal with conditions that were already developing in their day. But both also envisioned the intensified apostasy that would prevail at the end of the age. In this respect Jude forms a fitting introduction to the Book of the Revelation.

OUTLINE

Salutation (1, 2)
A. Contending for the Faith (3, 4)
    1. Desire to expound salvation (3a)
    2. Necessity to contend for the faith (3b, 4)
B. Examples of Apostates (5-7)
    1. Israel in the wilderness (5)
    2. The fallen angels at the flood (6)
    3. The sinners of Sodom and Gomorrah (7)
C. Condemnation of False Teachers (8-16)
    1. Their presumption outlined and illustrated (8-10)
    2. Their woe predicted (11)

3. Their spiritual sterility indicated (12, 13).
4. Their judgment foretold (14, 15)
5. Their character reviewed (16)

D. Exhortation of God's People (17-23)
   1. To remember apostolic warnings (17-19)
   2. To build up themselves on their holy faith (20a)
   3. To pray in the Holy Spirit (20b)
   4. To keep themselves in the love of God and faith (21)
   5. To show mercy toward the sinner (22)
   6. To abhor the sinner's sin (23)

Concluding Doxology (24, 25)

JUDE AND THE COMMON SALVATION

Jude's original purpose was to write to believers concerning "the common salvation" (v. 3). This is deliverance from the world, the flesh, and the devil through the redemptive work of Jesus Christ. It is "common" in that it is offered to all, being based upon the glorious invitation "*Whosoever* will, let him take the water of life freely" (Rev. 22:17; cf. John 3:16). It is not confined to any particular nation, people, or race. Christ's redemptive work made the entire race salvable. God can justly redeem lost sinners who believe on Jesus.

Jude's exercise of "all diligence" in writing discloses his earnest zeal for the growth of God's people in the truth of the Word. That he felt compelled to write about "contending for the faith" instead of "the common salvation" (his original topic) is clearly providential. Salvation has been fully expounded by several other New Testament writers, notably the Apostle Paul. Jude's special topic has been important to the Church throughout its entire history, and never more so than today.

CONTENDING FOR THE FAITH

When Jude exhorted his readers to "contend for the faith" (v. 3) he employed a strong Greek word meaning "to zealously and earnestly contend" *(epagonizesthai)*. An expanded definition would read, "to fight while standing on a fortress which is being attacked by a determined enemy; to hold the fortress at all costs."

Unfortunately, this concept of "contending strenuously in defense of the faith" has often been abused by sincere and well-meaning Christians. Too often the contending has been conducted in a spirit of pugnacious battling and censorious criticism devoid of meekness and love. Thus intellectual warfare has been waged at the expense of practical Christian living.

The contender for the faith is like a man walking a tightrope. Walking the rope requires two feats. The man must both stay on the rope (keep true to the faith) and move ahead with balance (keep true to the moral life of faith). If either of these endeavors is ignored the believer's testimony is lost. True scriptural zeal in contending for the faith *must* conform to the noble walk to which every believer is called. The militant must demonstrate "all lowliness and meekness, with longsuffering, forbearing one another in love." He must make every effort to "keep the unity of the Spirit in the bond of peace" (Eph. 4:1-3). He is responsible before God to keep the seven unities which the Spirit of God uses to maintain peace and purity in the Church.

These seven unities of Scripture consist of the following: "one body" (the true Church); "one Spirit" (the Holy Spirit); "one hope of our calling" (the hope of glorification); "one Lord" (Jesus Christ our Savior); "one faith" (the faith once-for-all delivered to the saints—Jude 1:3); "one baptism" (Spirit-baptism into Christ, of which water baptism is a symbol); and "one God and Father of all, who is above all, and through all, and in all" (Eph. 4:4-6).

THE CHRISTIAN FAITH

This is described as "the faith which was once-for-all delivered to the saints" (v. 3, ASV, RSV). This "faith" is the entire body of revealed truth which God expects Christians to believe, and is intimately tied to faith in everyday Christian living (Tit. 2:11-15; James 2:12-26). Believers are expected to defend "the faith" by both their sound words and their godly actions.

Jude's definition of "the faith" leaves room for no novel doctrines of any kind—such as the "ungodly men" of verse 4 were trying to introduce. The key word "once-for-all" *(hapax)* is employed of actions that are both final and permanently valid. It is this changeless quality of the Christian faith that Jude emphasizes. The Apostle Paul also stresses the same truth (cf. Gal. 1:8-12; 2 Tim. 3:16).

Today religious pluralism is attempting to "streamline" Christianity into a relativistic, ecumenical mold and to elevate the "good" of every religion and cult in the world to the level of Christian acceptability. Jude's definition of the Christian faith has thus never been more urgently needed. Like Jude, the Christian teacher is responsible to declare the changelessness of Christian principles of faith and practice. Although certain secondary applications of Christian truth vary from generation to generation in order to meet changing needs, *every principle of biblical truth remains forever the same.* This is "the faith delivered once-for-all to the saints" (v. 3).

ASSURED PUNISHMENT OF SIN

In treating the subject of rebellion and sin on the part of false teachers, Jude clearly points out the certainty of divine judgment upon deliberate and wilful sin. He presents three illustrations from history—the Israelites in the desert, the fallen angels at the time of the flood, and the sinners of Sodom and Gomorrah (vv. 5-7).

The first historical illustration involves the Lord's redeemed people (v. 5). Although they had faith to sprinkle the Passover blood (Exod. 12:1-40) and to be delivered out of Egypt, they were afterward destroyed at Kadesh-Barnea (Num. 14:1-45; 1 Cor. 10:1-5; Heb. 3:17-19) because of unbelief. The judgment of the redeemed involved physical death (cf. 1 Cor. 5:1-5; 11:30-32; 1 John 5:16).

The second historical warning relates to the fallen angels who cohabited with mortal women at the time of the flood (v. 6). Their immediate punishment for intrusion into the realm of another order of created beings (Gen. 6:1-4; 2 Pet. 2:4) was imprisonment in Tartarus. Their final doom will be consignment to the lake of fire after the great day of judgment (Rev. 20:11-15).

The third warning from history concerns the sinners of Sodom and Gomorrah (v. 7). Their destruction is intended to warn all transgressors of God's moral laws that punishment for sin is real (Rev. 19:20; 20:10, 14, 15; cf. Matt. 25:41). Jude's warning is especially striking in this day of apostasy, "new morality," and "God-is-dead" theology.

CONTENTION BETWEEN MICHAEL AND SATAN OVER THE BODY OF MOSES (v. 9)

Jude dramatizes the sinfulness of slander by contrasting the attitudes of apostate teachers and the archangel Michael. The apostates did not hesitate to slander exalted personages, possibly even angels ("dignities" literally means "glories"), while Michael refused to slander even a fallen angel (Satan). Jude's pointed contrast shows not only the pride of the apostates but also the seriousness of the sin of slander.

Contention about the body of Moses apparently arose because it was raised before its allotted time to appear in glorified form with Elijah (Matt. 17:3, 4). At the fall of man Satan had obtained "the power of death" over the whole human family (Heb. 2:14; cf. Gen. 2:17). He therefore challenged Moses' right to receive a glorified body *before* Christ's redemptive work had destroyed that power over believers. Michael in response simply claimed the redemptive power of Christ's sacrifice for Moses, as Zechariah had done for Israel in prospect of her future regeneration (Zech. 3:2). Further details about this incident are lacking because Scripture nowhere else mentions it.

RELIGIOUS NATURALISM

The religious naturalism so rampant today has been popularly designated "modernism." Though this name might seem to imply new concepts in religious thinking, the Book of Jude shows that the spiritually barren concepts of this error existed since the days of Cain. "The way of Cain" (v. 11) represents the religious but unsaved man who rejects the blood of Christ and instead attempts to offer his own good works to God (Gen. 4:3-8).

Jude exposes these same religious naturalists as mercenaries who "abandon themselves for the sake of gain to Balaam's error" (v. 11b, RSV; cf. 2 Pet. 2:15; Rev. 2:14). This error is the mistake of assuming that a righteous God could curse his chosen people because they had sinned (cf. Num. 22-24). It rejects the efficacy of Christ's death and ignores the higher morality of the cross, by which God can be righteous and at the same time eternally justify the believing sinner. Thus these false teachers reject the very essence of the Christian gospel.

Jude also denounces these men as partakers of Korah's sin of rebellion against the divine order in morality and religion (Num. 16:1-50; 26:9-11). Korah rejected the divine authority given to Moses as God's mouthpiece and to the Levites as God's priesthood. He demonstrated his rebellious attitude by intruding into the official activities of the priests. It is the mark of *all* false teachers to reject the authority of the Word of God and to pursue religious matters in their own way.

ENOCH'S PROPHECY
OF THE SECOND ADVENT

This prophecy, preserved as tradition in the noncanonical book of Enoch, is apparently cited by the Holy Spirit through Jude as divine truth (vv. 14, 15). Jude reveals that Enoch, "the seventh from Adam"

(Gen. 5:18-24; Heb. 11:5), envisioned the rise of these false teachers even in his day. He foretold that judgment would overtake them at Christ's second advent, when the latter-day apostates would be judged (v. 15).

The question arises, Does Jude ascribe this prophecy found in the apocryphal Book to the Enoch of Genesis 5? He apparently does. The difficulty may be resolved as follows. 1) There are reasons for thinking that the book of Enoch in the form now existing copied from Jude rather than Jude from the book of Enoch. Some later writer may have inserted the quotation in the original Book of Enoch. 2) The original prophecy of the patriarch Enoch may well have been appropriated by the author of the Book of Enoch without giving proper credit. 3) The Holy Spirit guided Jude in using this brief, true quotation from a non-canonical book, even as Paul was guided in referring to certain facts unrecorded in the Old Testament (2 Tim. 3:8; Gal. 3:19; Heb. 11:24) and in quoting certain true statements by pagan poets (cf. Acts 17:28; Tit. 1:12). In any case the earliest biblical prophecies of the Redeemer dwell on his second advent in glory rather than on his first coming in lowliness (cf. Gen. 3:15 with Rom. 16:20).

The Revelation

TITLE

The correct title of this great prophetic book is "The Revelation of Jesus Christ." The term "revelation" is from the Latin *revelatio*, "a revealing or uncovering," and the Greek *apokalupsis*, "an uncovering, a revelation." The phrase "of Jesus Christ" is objective genitive, indicating that the revelation or disclosure was not only *given to* Jesus Christ by God the Father but also *concerns* him (1:1). The great climactic events of history converge in Christ.

The sealed Golden Gate in Jerusalem's Eastern Wall, which some expect the returned Messiah to open *(Russ Busby photo)*

Soon after it was written the book came to be called "The Apocalypse of John" in order to differentiate it from many other "apocalypses" in circulation. In the fourth century the title was expanded to include the words "the Divine." This designation points to John the Apostle as the human instrument through whom the revelation came. The inspired title, however, is "The Revelation of (Concerning) Jesus Christ."

AUTHOR

External evidence to the Revelation as an authentic work of the Apostle John is substantial and completely adequate. Justin Martyr, Irenaeus, Tertullian, and Hippolytus in the West and Clement of Alexandria and Origen in the East give clear evidence of its genuineness. Victorinus, who wrote the earliest commentary of the Apocalypse that is still in existence, ascribes the book to John the Apostle. The Muratorian Fragment also received the work as apostolic and genuine.

Internal evidence is also ample. Four times the writer calls himself John (1:1, 4, 9; 22:8). As in the case of the fourth Gospel, the humility of the writer of the Apocalypse serves to identify him with the Apostle John. The author does not call himself an apostle but merely a "servant" of Christ (1:1) and a "brother and partaker with you in the tribulation and kingdom and patience which are in Jesus" (1:9).

The author of the Revelation was an exile on the small island of Patmos in the Aegean Sea (1:9). The Fathers declared that it was John the Apostle who was banished there, returning to the mainland after the death of Emperor Domitian. Irenaeus says that the Apostle John thereafter remained at Ephesus until the reign of Trajan.

Objections against apostolic authorship on linguistic grounds have not been successful. Differences in vocabulary, grammar, and general style between the Revelation and other Johannine writings are explainable on the basis of the apocalyptic nature of the subject matter. These differences are more than counterbalanced by a number of significant similarities in vocabulary, such as "the Word," "water of life," "little lamb," etc. The Hebraic style of the Revelation is to be expected in a book steeped in Old Testament imagery.

BACKGROUND AND DATE

John apparently came to Ephesus in the year A.D. 69 or 70 and worked among a number of churches in the province of Asia. The seven churches of Revelation (chaps. 2, 3) appear to have been in his circuit. He received the revelation while an exile on the island of Patmos, later returning to Asia (after the death of Domitian). The Apocalypse was no doubt intended for both the seven churches of Asia and the Christian Church at large.

On the basis of testimony by Irenaeus, Clement of Alexandria, Eusebius, and others that John was banished to Patmos and received his visions in the later part of Domitian's reign A.D. 81-96), the book is to be dated about A.D. 95 or 96.

DESCRIPTION AND INTERPRETATION

The Revelation belongs to the type of literature known as "apocalyptic." In this kind of writing the predictive element looms large and is couched in figures and symbols. These symbols are frequently unexplained and are to be interpreted *strictly on the basis of other biblical information.* The Revelation dovetails particularly well with such Old Testament apocalyptic and prophetic books as Daniel, Ezekiel, and Zechariah. Without a knowledge of these books in particular and Old and New Testament prophecy in general, the Revelation remains a sealed book. Attempts to interpret it on any basis other than the revealed prophetic Word itself have been complete failures.

The apocalyptic nature of the book is indicated in the opening verse. God sent and "signified" the revelation "by his angel to his servant John" (1:1). The word "signified" means "to put in the form of signs or symbols."

Since the time of its writing the Book of the Revelation has been interpreted in a number of different ways. Four of the major methods of interpretation are contrasted in the following table:

METHODS OF INTERPRETING THE BOOK OF REVELATION	
Allegorical ("Spiritualizing") Method	Mystical, allegorical approach. Denies any earthly millennial kingdom following the second advent. Fails to do justice to the prophetic nature of the book (1:3; 10:11; 22:7) and ignores the interpretive key (1:19) as well as the events preceding and succeeding the second advent. Fails to ground the book in Old Testament prophecy. Especially weak on prophecies of Daniel.
Preterist Method	Holds that the Book has already been essentially fulfilled in the Church's conflict with Judaism (Chaps. 4–11) and paganism (Chaps. 12–19). Chapters 20–22 describe the Church's present conflict. Ignores the interpretive key (1:19), attributes arbitrary meanings to the symbols of the book, and rejects indications of the short time-span of Chapters 4–19.
Continuous-Historical Method	Covers entire span of Church history (John's time to the end of time). Fails to correlate with Bible prophecy as a whole and has all the weaknesses of the Allegorical and Preterist Methods.
Futurist Method	This, we believe, is the *correct view* because 1) it uses the key (1:19) as guide, placing the bulk of the book (Chaps. 4–22) still in the future; 2) it grounds interpretation in Old Testament and New Testament prophecy; 3) it interprets the symbols biblically; and 4) it honors the truth of the imminent return of Christ for his own and his glorious advent to set up his kingdom (Acts 1:6).

OUTLINE

Introduction (1:1-11)
A. The Self-Revelation of Christ—the Things Seen (1:12-20)

1. His relation to the churches (1:12-16)
2. His message to the churches (1:17-20)
B. Christ and His Church—the Things Which Are (chapters 2, 3)
   1. Ephesus, Smyrna, Pergamum, Thyatira (chapter 2)
   2. Sardis, Philadelphia, Laodicea (chapter 3)
C. Christ and History's Consummation—the Things Which Shall Be Hereafter (chapters 4—22)
   1. The preparation in heaven (chapters 4, 5)
   2. The Great Tribulation on earth (chapters 6-18)
      a. The seal judgments (6:1—8:1)
      b. The trumpet judgments (8:2—11:19)
      c. The seven personages (chapters 12, 13)
      d. Preview of the end of the Tribulation (chapter 14)
      e. The bowl judgments (chapters 15, 16)
      f. The Judgment of Babylon (chapters 17, 18)
   3. The second advent and Armageddon (chapter 19)
      a. Rejoicing in heaven (19:1-6)
      b. Marriage of the Lamb (19:7-10)
      c. Advent in glory (19:11-16)
      d. Armageddon (19:17-21)
   4. The establishment of the kingdom (20:1-10)
      a. The binding of Satan (20:1-3)
      b. The millennial reign (20:4-6)
      c. The loosing of Satan and his final doom (20:7-10)
   5. The final judgment (20:11-15)
   6. The eternal state (chapters 21, 22)
      a. The sinless eternity (21:1-7)
      b. The isolation of the wicked (21:8)
      c. The New Jerusalem (21:9—22:5)
Conclusion (22:6-21)

PROPHETIC FOREVIEW OF THE EARTHLY CAREER OF THE CHURCH

"The things seen" (1:19) included the vision of Christ (1:12-20). *"The things which are"* embraces the Church age (chaps. 2, 3). The fact that only seven of the churches of Asia are selected indicates that the Holy Spirit is symbolically comprehending the entire Church, since seven is the number of completion and perfection. It is incredible that in a prophecy covering the Church period ("the things that

are") there should be no such foreview. These messages must contain that foreview, for the Church does not appear after chapter 3. It is also evident that the messages to the seven churches reach beyond the immediate churches addressed and comprehend the entire Church of God.

PROPHETIC FOREVIEW OF THE CHURCH ON EARTH

A.D. *33-100   100-316   316-606   606-1520   1520-1750   1750-1900   1900-?*

Ephesus (Rev. 2:1-7). —————————————————————————→
The Church characterized by good works, endurance, and separation from evil, but guilty of losing its initial love for Christ.

Smyrna (Rev. 2:8-11) —————————————————————————→
The Church under persecution by the Roman Emperors Hadrian (117), Septimius Severus (193), Maximin (235), Decius (249), Valerian (254), Aurelian (270), and Diocletian (284). Also harassed by Christ-hating Jews (2:9)

Pergamos (Rev. 2:12-17) ———————————————————→
The Church compromising because of worldly favor. Held doctrine of Balaam— teaching that corrupts God's people with worldliness (Num. 31:15, 16). Also held doctrine of Nicolaitans (possibly antinomian license but more likely incipient laity-dominating clericalism).

Thyatira (Rev. 2:18-29) ———————————————————→
The paganized Church of the Dark Ages and Middle Ages preceding the Protestant Reformation. Jezebel prefigures teachers who taught the errors and perversions that produced the Papal hierarchy and its perversions of biblical truth and Christian living. Plumbed "the depths of Satan" in occultism and heresy (2:24)

Sardis (Rev. 3:1-6) ———————————————————→
The Church of the Reformation. Swept away rubbish of Romanism but failed to regain vibrant life of faith.

Philadelphia ————————→
(Rev. 3:7-13)
The Church of worldwide evangelistic movements that has kept God's Word and has not denied Christ's name.

Laodicea →
(Rev.
3:14-22)
The apostate Church with unregenerate members who have embraced "liberal theology."

The primary importance of these messages is prophetic, since they delineate seven well-defined, successive periods of Church history. Each of these periods begins at a fairly specific time and continues to the end of Church history. Thus near the end of the Church age characteristics of all seven of the periods can be seen concurrently.

THE REVELATION
AND THE RAPTURE QUESTION

Does the Book of Revelation shed light on the controversial question of the time of the rapture? That the book supports a pretribulation rapture is indicated by the following considerations. A prophetic survey of the history of the Church is given in chapters 2 and 3. This constitutes "the things which are" (1:19), already existing in John's day and continuing throughout the entire Church age.

Chapters 4 to 22 constitute "the things which shall be hereafter" (4:1), that is, "after these (Church) things." In these chapters the Church no longer appears on earth but is instead seen glorified and rewarded in heaven (represented by the twenty-four elders in 4:4, 10, 11). This necessitates a pretribulation outtaking, since chapters 4 to 19 concern the tribulation (both the first and the second half). This agrees perfectly with Paul's description of the rapture in First Thessalonians and with his argument for the pretribulation outtaking in Second Thessalonians 2:1-10.

The invitation to John to "come up hither" (4:1), while not an explicit reference to the rapture of the Church, is certainly an implicit and symbolic representation of this event. This is suggested by the symbolic nature of the book and the pivotal change of time and place indicated by this verse, in accordance with the inspired interpretive key (1:19). (At this point in Revelation the Church age is consummated by the rapture and is followed by the Church in heaven).

Although the rapture is referred to in letters to two of the churches (2:25; 3:11) as a *doctrine*, it is not a featured part of the prophetic foreview of the Apocalypse. This is in accord with the primary objective of the book: to portray the events climaxing in the second advent, the prophetic kingdom, and the eternal state.

Whether or not Revelation 4:1 specifically symbolizes the rapture, this event must have occurred before the events of chapter 4, as evidenced by the subsequent chapters of the Revelation. The word "church," so common in chapters 2 and 3, does not occur again until 22:16 (cf. 19:7). The Church is completely absent from the scenes of the tribulation, which constitute the major portion of the book. People who are saved after the rapture of the Church are described as saved Israelites or saved Gentiles — never as members of the Church.

THE TWENTY-FOUR ELDERS AND
THEIR IDENTITY (4:4, 10; 5:8, 14; 11:16; 19:4)

These elders clearly include the redeemed saints of the Church. Whether they also include Old Testament saints is not certain. They cannot represent angels, for the term "elder" is never applied to angels, nor do angels receive crowns or occupy thrones. These are promised only to redeemed men (Matt. 19:28; 2 Tim. 4:8; 1 Pet. 5:4; Rev. 2:10; 20:4). The 24 elders wear victor's crowns *(stephanoi)* won in the Christian career. The thrones they occupy indicate that they have already been judged for their works (1 Cor. 3:11-15; 2 Cor. 5:10). Their "white garments" distinguish them as a redeemed priesthood (1 Pet. 2:9), active in priestly services (Rev. 5:8). They await the awarding of royal and judicial functions at Christ's advent in glory (20:4-6).

The number 24 is apparently representative of the full number of saints comprising the completed, glorified Church. When King David organized the priests into "courses" he established 24 heads of priestly families to represent the entire priesthood (1 Chron. 24:1-19). Thus the 24 elders of Revelation represent the priestly capacity of the entire Church in heaven. In Old Testament typology the Aaronic priests represent New Testament believers while Aaron, the high priest, typifies Christ.

THE SEVEN-SEALED BOOK (5:1-10)

This is the official document which guarantees dispossession of Satan and evil men from the earth prior to Christ's advent and kingdom. "Sealed with seven seals" denotes complete sealing; the document cannot be opened until a qualified personage appears to execute its contents. The distinguished personage who appears turns out to be none less than "the lion of the tribe of Judah . . . the root of David." By virtue of his divine-human nature and his fully efficacious death, Christ is uniquely qualified both to open the book and to administer its contents.

The transmittal of the scroll from God the Father to Christ as Executor (5:7-10) signals the inauguration of the tribulation judgments. Each sealed portion of the scroll specifies a particular judgment to be poured out on the world's wicked inhabitants (6:1 – 8:5).

After the full fury of six of the seven judgments has been poured out on the earth, God temporarily suspends further judgment while he enumerates the Jews and Gentiles who have been saved during the tribulation period (7:1-17). Then Christ breaks the seventh seal. Heaven's hosts react with stunned silence for about a half hour. Then God's wrath bursts forth on earth again with unprecedented fury. Seven trumpet judgments (8:7 — 11:19) and seven bowl judgments (16:2-21) combine to produce the greatest tribulation in the history of the world. A total of 13 chapters (6 — 18) is required to describe the horrors of this period.

THOSE SAVED IN THE TRIBULATION

After the rapture of the Church all who have rejected the clear preaching of the gospel will be delivered into demonic delusion and ultimate destruction (2 Thess. 2:7-12). Nevertheless, God will see fit to save multitudes of both Jews and Gentiles during the tribulation period. The 144,000 Jews of Revelation 7:1-8 represent those who are preserved from destruction and "sealed" for salvation (cf. Eph. 1:13, 14). Though all tribal genealogies have long since been obliterated from human records, God knows who and where the members of the various tribes are (Isa. 11:11-16; Ezek. 48:1-7).

The corresponding elect body of Gentiles saved during the tribulation is described in 7:9-17. They will also be preserved as an unglorified people on the earth to enter the earthly kingdom. They will have undergone unparalleled suffering and will have been brought to salvation by the preaching of the gospel of the kingdom (Matt. 24:13, 14). This is the good news of Christ's death and resurrection as it pertains to salvation in the light of the kingdom soon to be inaugurated. It is called "the everlasting gospel" (14:6), since Christ's death and resurrection pertain to God's eternal plan and purposes.

DEMONIC POWER AND DECEPTION
OF THE END-TIME

The Revelation discloses the awful outburst of demon power which the Apostle Paul predicted in Second Thessalonians 2:7-12. The locust symbolism (9:1-11) portrays the loosing of myriads of demons from the abyss, the prison of the demons (9:1-3; cf. Luke 8:30). These particular demons are imprisoned at present, but will be released during the tribulation period in order to delude and torment wicked earth-dwellers. Gross idolatry energized by demon worship will result in violence, occultism, sexual lawlessness, and immorality on a colossal scale (9:20, 21).

As the result of spiritual warfare in the heavenlies Satan and his demonic hosts will be cast down to the earth to augment the wickedness and diabolic fury of those days (12:7-12). With the rise of the Beast and the False Prophet (13:1-18), Satanic cunning and demonic delusion will reach their zenith (13:4, 14-18). The Battle of Armageddon will be energized and consummated by demon powers, who will delude the rulers of the earth and their armies in an attempt to take over the earth for Satan and to banish the name of God and his Christ (16:13, 14). But at the height of the battle Christ will return in majestic power to smash the Satanic world system. Satan and his demon hordes will be banished to the abyss (20:1-3) and Christ's millennial kingdom will be inaugurated.

After the millennium Satan and his demons will be released temporarily and will again inspire certain men to rebel against God (20:7-9a). This rebellion will consummate in the final downfall of evil, for God will not only destroy all wicked men but will remand Satan (and doubtless his hosts) to Gehenna forever (20:9b, 10). Death, hades, sin, Satan, demons, and wicked men will be isolated in this quarantine ward for all eternity. This will make possible a sinless eternity (chaps. 21, 22). With sin and sinners rigidly confined, never again to mar God's universe, the divine purpose will at last have been achieved.

THE MYSTERY OF GOD AND "THE LITTLE BOOK" (CHAP. 10)

The "mighty angel" who sets his foot on land and sea (10:2) symbolizes Christ in his right to claim the earth as his own (Psa. 2:7, 8). The angel's shout and the rumble of the seven thunders dramatize Christ's authority over the earth, now to be exercised "without delay" (10:6b, 7a). The theme of the little book is "the mystery of God" (10:7). This truth, previously hidden but now revealed, is the grand subject of the rest of the Revelation. It concerns Christ as the incarnate Redeemer and the imminent King of the earth.

The little book is apparently to be identified with the book which the prophet Daniel was told to seal up "until the time of the end" (Dan. 12:4, 9). The scroll was "sweet as honey" when first "eaten" (read and understood—see Ezek. 2:8, 9; 3:1-3), but "bitter" when the glowing promises of deliverance for Daniel's people, the Jews, were seen to be preceded by awful judgments.

THE SEVEN PERSONAGES OF REVELATION 12 AND 13	
The Person	*The Identification*
The Woman (12:1, 2)	Symbolizes Israel clothed in regal and governmental splendor, the 12 stars denoting her 12 tribes (Gen. 37:9). Her travail represents Israel's tribulation agony, during which she gives birth to the godly Jewish remnant (12:17; Mic. 5:2, 3).
The Dragon (12:3, 4)	Symbolizes Satan as the serpent (Gen. 3:1-5, 13-15). "Red" shows his murderous character (John 8:44). His diadem and horns identify him with the final form of Gentile power. He appears in historical perspective (cf. Isa. 14:12-14; Ezek. 28:12-15).
The Male Child (12:5, 6)	Christ prefigured in his *birth,* his *destiny of conquest* (Psa. 2:9), his *ascension,* and his *position on God's throne.*
Michael (12:7-12)	The archangel, special protector of the Jews (Dan. 12:1; cf. Dan. 10:13-21). He and his angels expel Satan and his angels from the heavenlies (Job 1:6; Eph. 2:2; 6:12).
The Remnant (12:17)	Satan turns against these godly Jews. They "keep the commandments of God" and bear witness to Jesus.
The Beast out of the Sea (13:1-10)	Head of revived Roman Empire, who arises out of the unsettled political condition ("the sea"—Isa. 57:20; Dan. 7:24-28). Has demon-inspired career of persecution of the saints (Dan. 7:21, 22).
The Beast out of the Earth (13:11-18)	The Prophet of the Beast (the Antichrist). Directs worship of the first beast through miraculous powers, giving life to the Beast's image. He is the culmination of fallen man's wickedness.

THE TWO WITNESSES (11:3-12)

These two miracle-workers of God are evidently members of the latter-day saved remnant of Israel. They are *Christ's* witnesses, the term "my witnesses" referring to Christ as symbolized by the mighty angel of chapter 10. They are "clothed in sackcloth" to symbolize their mourning over the grievous sin of Israel (cf. Joel 1:13; Jer. 4:8). Their message centers in Christ's imminent kingship over the earth.

The reference to "the two olive trees and the two lampstands" (Zech. 4:2, 3) point to Messiah as King-Priest, since Zechariah's olive trees indicate these two offices. He will soon rule as the light of the world over restored Israel, prefigured by the gold lampstand of Zechariah 4. Like Moses and Elijah, the two witnesses are endowed with the power of God. They effect drought like Elijah (1 Kings 17:1; James 5:17), turn water into blood (Exod. 7:19), and perform other signs like Moses (Exod. 7—10). They are murdered by the Beast, the leader of the revived Roman Empire, but not until after they have finished their testimony (11:7).

God then resurrects and translates the two witnesses in the cloud of the Shekinah glory (Ezek. 10:19; Matt. 17:5) and punishes their persecutors with an earthquake (11:11-13). Although the two witnesses have sometimes been associated with Moses and Elijah or Moses and Enoch, these identifications are hardly possible, since both of the witnesses are killed and resurrected. This could not be true of the actual Old Testament men, since they have already received glorified bodies (see Matt. 17:3).

THE SEVEN BOWL JUDGMENTS	
Bowl 1 (16:2)	Poured out upon those having the mark of the Beast. They are afflicted with a grievous ulcer.
Bowl 2 (16:3)	Poured out upon the sea, which becomes blood. Doubtless symbolic of the complete moral and spiritual death of godless society.
Bowl 3 (16:4-7)	Poured out upon fresh waters, which become blood. Doubtless symbolic of the moral pollution of all the sources of inspiration and refreshment.
Bowl 4 (16:8, 9)	Poured out upon the sun, which scorches men with heat. Men's blasphemy reveals their inveterately wicked character.
Bowl 5 (16:10, 11)	Poured out upon the throne of the Beast. His kingdom is plunged into gross darkness – physical, moral, and spiritual.
Bowl 6 (16:12-16)	Poured out upon the Euphrates River (1780 miles in length), symbolizing the removal of every barrier for the advance of "the kings from the east" to Armageddon.
Bowl 7 (16:17-21)	Poured out "upon the air," Satan's realm (Eph. 2:2). Worldwide earthquake signifies the consummation of God's wrath in judgment upon the Satanic world-system. Only one kingdom escapes. It is the kingdom of Christ, for it cannot be shaken (Dan. 2:44). Huge hailstones, about 100 pounds in weight, bring God's wrath to a close and prelude Messiah's glorious advent.

THE SEVEN BOWLS

The loosing of the seventh seal (8:1-6) completes the opening of the sealed scroll (5:1), so that its full contents (the trumpets and the bowls) may be released on the earth to free it from the grasp of Satan and wicked men. The seven trumpets announce three "woes." The fifth trumpet announces the first woe—the loosing of myriads of demons from the abyss (9:1-11). The sixth trumpet announces the second woe—evidently an infernal spirit army (9:13-21). The seventh trumpet announces the third woe—all the remaining judgments prior to the setting up of the kingdom (11:15—20:3), especially the terrible "bowl judgments" (16:2-21).

Chapter 16 introduces the seven bowls, which symbolize the consummation of God's wrath poured out on wicked men of the earth. This effusion of God's wrath eventuates in the Battle of Armageddon and the advent of Christ in glory as supreme King and absolute Lord (19:11-21).

THE VISION OF ECCLESIASTICAL BABYLON

Babylon symbolizes the world system headed by Satan. It consists of unsaved men led by Satan and his principles. In Revelation 17 the emphasis is on the religious or ecclesiastical aspects of this system, while in chapter 18 the stress is on the commercial aspects of Babylon. Actually the fall of Babylon had been briefly predicted as early as chapter 14: "Fallen, fallen" (14:8) is a Hebraism meaning "completely fallen" in the sense of totally doomed. Babylon's destruction is also foreseen in 16:19.

The doom of ecclesiastical Babylon is presented in detail in chapter 17 under the symbol of a harlot. This evil woman personifies the final form of religious apostasy and revolt against God. Representing corrupt religionism, especially as it will appear in the last days, she denotes a vast religious system that sacrifices truth in order to gain power in the Satanic world system. In Scripture symbolism a woman often portrays something out of place religiously (cf. Matt. 13:33; Rev. 2:20).

This system rises to power by exploiting the peoples ("waters") of the earth (17:1) and by prostituting truth and purity. It uses the state wherever possible, riding into power on political Babylon, the beast's kingdom, and the final form of Gentile world government (17:2, 3; cf. 13:1-10). The "golden cup" filled with "abominations" (idolatries) and "the filthiness of her fornication" portray her gross infidelity to God and his Word (17:4). The harlot represents all false religious movements from their inception in the ancient Babylon of Nimrod (Gen. 10:8-10) to their awful fruition in the apostate religionism of the tribulation period.

Ecclesiastical Babylon is guilty of murdering both Old Testament "saints" and New Testament "martyrs of Jesus" (17:6). In the terrible persecutions of the tribulation period this wicked system will collaborate with the Beast (the political power) in the wholesale murder of the true followers of Jesus (17:6).

THE DESTRUCTION OF ECCLESIASTICAL BABYLON

The Beast, the end-time ruler of the *revived* Roman Empire, will turn against the harlotrous religious system and will destroy both it and its headquarters in the Beast's capital, the city of Rome (17:16-18). The end-time revival of the Roman power is foretold (17:8). It "was" (existed) in John's day, but today it "is not," exactly as foretold. ". . . Yet is" refers to the end-time, when it will return with Satanic powers from the abyss (cf. 2 Thess. 2:8-10; Rev. 9:1-11; 11:7; 13:2). However, its last-day form will be brief. It will go into perdition at Christ's second advent (19:20).

The form of government of the revived Roman Empire is specified (17:10). The seven heads represent the seven hills of Rome on which the harlot sits (17:9), as well as seven kings (17:10). These apparently allude to seven distinct forms of government which characterized the Roman Empire from 32 B.C. to A.D. 476. The "five . . . which had fallen" are kings, consuls, dictators, decemvirs, and tribunes. The "one" that "is" represents the imperial government of John's day. "The other" (the seventh) is still future; it will remain in full power for only three and one-half years (13:5).

The last king (17:11) rules the ten-kingdom federation and wars with the Lamb (16:14; 19:19) in the gigantic struggle for sovereignty over the earth (19:16). The evil system which has dominated and exploited the peoples of the earth (17:15) by riding into power on the Beast will find this deceptive ruler turning against it (17:16). God will fulfill his Word by allowing the Beast to utterly destroy ecclesiastical Babylon (17:17). The doom of this system is the just fate of the wicked harlot. Her lust for power in the Satanic world system invites her destruction (17:18).

THE DESTRUCTION OF COMMERCIAL BABYLON

Her utter ruin is announced: "Babylon the great is fallen, is fallen" (18:2). Her godless commercialism is her undoing (18:2, 3). Elsewhere God's people are warned to separate from her (2 Cor. 6:14-18) because her cup of iniquity is full (cf. Gen. 15:16) and her punishment is overdue (18:6-8). She is bewailed by those who grew wealthy on her evil traffic (18:9-11) and her rich commerce (18:12-19).

Commercial Babylon's downfall is effected by God, who through Christ's redemptive work is the real destroyer of the Satanic world system in both its ecclesiastical and commercial aspects. The "millstone" thrown into the sea graphically represents Babylon's swift and terrible dissolution, for she is guilty of murdering God's people (18:21-24).

The Satanic world system is mentioned in more than 30 New Testament passages. Satan is its leader (John 12:31; 14:30; 16:11; Rev. 2:13). God regards it as thoroughly evil (Gal. 1:4; Col. 1:13; 2 Pet. 2:20; James 4:4). The Apostle John declared it to be limited and temporary (1 John 2:17), as Revelation 17 and 18 amply attest. Christ by virtue of his redemptive work sentenced it for destruction. At Christ's second advent (19:11-16) the wicked are slain and Satan is imprisoned in the abyss (19:11 – 20:3). As a result the greed, pride, and war that characterize this evil system (James 4:1-4) are brought to an end. No longer will Babylon be a snare to God's people in the kingdom age (cf. 1 John 2:16; Rev. 18:4, 5). Heaven thus rejoices at Babylon's fall (19:1-5).

THE MARRIAGE OF THE LAMB

This grand event honors Christ in his redemptive ministry, for it is featured as the marriage not of the Bride but of "the Lamb." The Bride, the wife-to-be, represents the Church (Eph. 5:25-33). The figure of the wife symbolizes the Church's future consummating union with Christ in public glory and dignity. It is the outward expression of the inner spiritual union between Christ and his Church (1 Cor. 12: 12, 13; Rom. 6:3, 4; Gal. 3:27; Eph. 5:25-33; Rev. 21:9).

The Bride is seen preparing herself for the wedding. This presupposes her fitness for this glorious event by virtue of Christ's finished redemptive work (Col. 1:12). It also includes the evaluation of her works at the judgment seat of Christ (1 Cor. 3:11-15; 2 Cor. 5:10). The Bride's robes represent Christ's righteousness imputed to her (Rom. 3: 21, 22) and manifested through her (Phil. 2:13).

The guests at the wedding are Old Testament saints (John 3:29). They are clearly distinguished from the Bride and are specified as "blessed" or "happy." The marriage supper is in sharp contrast to the supper of judgment of the wicked (19:17, 18). The judgment seat of Christ and the marriage of the Lamb are a necessary prelude to Christ's advent and kingdom rule.

CHRIST'S SECOND ADVENT IN GLORY

Christ's coming, described in symbolic vision (19:11-16), portrays the departure of the Redeemer-Conqueror from heaven with his saints and angels to claim his rightful kingship over the earth. His position "on a white horse" signifies his conquest in battle (Rev. 6:2; Psa. 45:4). He appears as both a judge and a warrior. His assured triumph is on the basis of his fidelity to the will of God (Phil. 2:5-11). His omniscient judgment is indicated by his "eyes as a flame of fire" (Rev. 1:14; 2:18). His inscrutable name and his many diadems attest his absolute power and lordship (Rev. 19:12). His garments "dipped in (his enemies') blood" (cf. Isa. 63:1-4) denote his vengeance upon his foes.

He comes as God and Creator (John 1:1, 3), since he is the "Word of God" as well as the Redeemer (John 1:1, 14). He has the right to reign in the dual role of Creator and Redeemer (Rev. 5:1-7). Associated with him in his triumph are "the armies of heaven" (saints and angels). The sharing of his conquest is indicated by the horse riders accompanying Christ on his own steed (19:14).

THE DESTRUCTION
OF THE SATANIC WORLD SYSTEM

Christ's glorious return destroys this evil world system. Satan's hosts are put in the abyss (20:1-3) and Christ's enemies are slain (19: 15-21). Christ's conquest is supernatural. The "sharp sword" is not a material weapon but the omnipotent Word of God that spoke the universe into existence. This is the weapon that slays Christ's enemies (Isa. 11:4; Heb. 11:3). With Satan, his hosts, and wicked men put down, the world system collapses and is replaced by Christ's millennial kingdom.

Christ will rule as a peaceful Shepherd, but rebels will find his shepherd's staff a rod of iron (19:15; cf. 12:5; Psa. 2:9) — a symbol of relentless severity against evildoers. The figure of treading the vintage (19:15) shows that Christ will render unsparing judgment on evil (cf. Isa. 63:3, 6). He alone will have absolute authority as King par excellence and Lord par excellence. (19:16).

THE BATTLE OF ARMAGEDDON

This gigantic contest for the possession of the earth will be engineered and energized by demonic spirits (16:13, 14; cf. 1 Kings 22:20-

28). These demons, symbolized by frogs, will delude the nations into the supreme folly of attempting to oust God and Christ from the earth. Armageddon ("Hill of Megiddo"), in the plain of Esdraelon, is an ancient battlefield (cf. Judg. 6:19; 2 Kings 9:27; 2 Chron. 35:22). It represents the place of the gathering of the nations, even as the Valley of Jehoshaphat (Joel 3:2, 12) symbolizes the place of slaughter. This battle decides the question of who shall govern the earth—Christ or Satan.

Christ will settle the issue of Armageddon with the omnipotent word of his mouth. The colossal destruction of wicked men fighting against God under Satan's control will furnish the flesh for the great supper of God (19:17, 18). This awful supper on earth contrasts vividly with the blissful marriage supper of the Lamb in heaven. Armageddon ends in the total destruction of Christ's foes (19:19-21). The Beast and the False Prophet are both cast alive into Gehenna to be punished (19:20). Satan and his hosts are remanded to the abyss for the duration of Christ's earthly kingdom (20:1-3), to be cast into Gehenna after the final revolt (20:10).

THE MILLENNIUM

Christ's return, the binding of Satan, and the destruction of the Satanic world system open the way for the establishment of Christ's kingdom on the earth. It will supplant the Satanic world system that has operated since man's fall in Eden. The kingdom is both indicated in the Revelation and necessitated by Old Testament prophecy (cf. Isa. 9:1-7; 11:1—12:6; Ezek. 40:1—48:35; Zech. 12:1—14:21; etc.). The reason it is not more fully developed in Revelation is that it has already been thoroughly expounded in Old Testament prophecy.

John the Revelator fills in additional details (20:4-6). He outlines the classes of saints who will reign with Christ in the kingdom. *The first group* consists of all believers from Abel to the rapture of the Church (cf. Dan. 7:9, 10, ASV). *The second group* consists of the souls of the martyrs of the first part of the tribulation period (6:9-11). *The third group* consists of the martyrs of the last period of the tribulation, those who did not worship the Beast (13:15-17).

All of these groups belong to "the first resurrection" and are "blessed and holy"; they share in kingdom glory. They are separate from the unsaved ("the rest of the dead"), who are resurrected to perdition at the second resurrection (20:11-15). "The second death" (Gehenna) has no power over the saved. They will be king-priests of God associated with Christ, the great King-Priest (Zech. 6:9-15). They will reign over Israel with Christ during the thousand years of the earthly kingdom (Acts 1:6).

SATAN'S FINAL DOOM

Satan's earthly history does not end with his imprisonment in the abyss during the kingdom age. After his thousand-year imprisonment he will be temporarily released from the abyss. He will test man's loyalty to God under the ideal conditions of the Millennium, the last of God's ordered ages before the dawn of eternity (20:7). Satan will successfully deceive "the nations." This postmillennial rebellion will be reminiscent of the premillennial revolt (Ezek. 38, 39). Hence it is metaphorically called "Gog and Magog" (see "Ezekiel's Prophecies of Israel's Restoration," Ezekiel 37 – 39).

This consummating Satanic rebellion will be worldwide. It will constitute the final confederation against God, God's people, and the Holy City (20:7-9a). The rebels will be individuals among the king-dom nations who were never truly regenerated, who yielded only out-ward allegiance to Messiah's rigid rule (Psa. 2:9). Israel will remain loyal to her Messiah (Jer. 31:31-34; Rom. 11:26) and will doubtless be preserved as a glorified people in the new earth. The revolt will be completely crushed and will mark the end of God's toleration of evil on the earth (20:9b, 10).

Satan's final doom will then be executed. He will be consigned to his eternal fate in Gehenna, prepared for both him and all created human and angelic beings who have followed him (Matt. 25:41). He will join the Beast and False Prophet, who have been in Gehenna for a thousand years (20:10).

THE FINAL JUDGMENT

This judgment involves all the unsaved dead from Adam to the end of world history. It will include those who have been raised to condemnation in the second resurrection (John 5:29) as well as believ-ers of the kingdom age who have died (since the first resurrection oc-curred before their death). This is why "the book of life" is opened (20:12, 15).

The unsaved face "a great white throne" (20:11). It is the greatest judgment ever held in that it comprises the largest number of persons ever judged at one time. The throne is white because it represents God's infinite holiness. Christ himself is the Judge (John 5:22), and each unsaved person faces him alone. Each is confronted with eternal hell in the lake of fire because he failed to appropriate Christ's salvation. Each is judged on the basis of his works (20:12, 13) and suffers degrees of punishment in Gehenna on the basis of his response to the moral law of God.

This judgment preludes eternity in that it represents God's final dealing with all sin and sinners prior to a sinless universe in the eternal state. Gehenna serves as the quarantine ward for all evil and evildoers. Its existence will make possible an eventual sinless universe (20:14, 15; cf. 21:8).

THE ETERNAL HOME
AND DESTINY OF THE REDEEMED

The eternal abode and the glory of the redeemed of all ages are symbolized by a magnificent city called "the new Jerusalem" (21:9–22:5). God's people have through the ages envisioned such a city (Heb. 11:10, 16; 13:14). It will be inhabited by God the Father (21:11), glorified Old Testament saints (Heb. 11:16), New Testament Church saints, hosts of unfallen angels, and our Lord Jesus Christ himself (Heb. 12:22-24). Both Israel and the Church share the glories of the city (21:12, 14), as well as tribulation and millennial saints.

The great wall of the city signifies the security of its inhabitants as they bask in God's unveiled glory. The city is apparently a solid golden cube 12,000 furlongs (1500 miles) long, wide, and high. This is equal to the colossal volume of 3,375,000,000 cubic miles.

The startling splendor of the city is an index to the glorious destiny and home of the redeemed in eternity. The apocalyptic imagery employs the figure of precious stones in order to convey to unglorified minds something of the indescribable beauty of their blissful future (21:18-21). No visible temple will be seen in the New Jerusalem, for the whole city will be suffused with the divine glory. Worship will be continuous and universal on the part of its inhabitants.

No external source of light will be needed to illuminate the city, for God himself will be manifested in unveiled glory (21:23, 24). Her gates will never be closed, for her enemies will all have been banished to Gehenna; all her citizenry will be sinless and undefiled (21:25-27).

PARADISE RESTORED

The marvelous revelation of an eventual sinless eternity is climaxed by the restoration of the paradise forfeited by man's fall. The complete removal of sin and its curse more than restores the blessings of the Edenic paradise. In paradise regained there will be a new heaven, a new earth, a new city, and a sinless universe.

The new paradise is symbolized and portrayed in terms of the old paradise in Eden. The "pure river of water of life, clear as crystal, proceeding out of the throne of God and the Lamb" (22:1) speaks of fullness of divine life and blessing (cf. Gen. 2:10; Zech. 14:8). The tree of life (22:2; cf. Gen. 2:9; 3:22) prefigures the complete fruition of eternal life. The leaves of the tree are for the health of the nations (22:2). There will be no more sickness, pain, or death in the eternal state (21: 4), for there will be "no more curse" (cf. Gen. 3:16-19). All the toil, futility, and sin which have marred man's history will at last be past.

The glorified redeemed will joyfully submit to their sovereign Lord. They will see his face in ecstatic fellowship. They will be identified with their Lord by his name on their foreheads. They will reign with him in blissful fellowship forever.